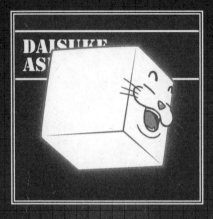

I debated for a long time which character I was going to put on the cover—Suwa, Arafune, Murakami or Nasu. I decided on Suwa, who had been working hard since the invasion. It's not because it would make my author portrait super easy. Here's *World Trigger* volume 11.

—Daisuke Ashihara, 2015

Daisuke Ashihara began his manga career at the age of 27 when his manga *Room 303* won second place in the 75th Tezuka Awards. His first series, *Super Dog Rilienthal*, began serialization in *Weekly Shonen Jump* in 2009. *World Trigger* is his second serialized work in *Weekly Shonen Jump*. He is also the author of several shorter works, including the one-shots *Super Dog Rilienthal*, *Trigger Keeper* and *Elite Agent Jin*.

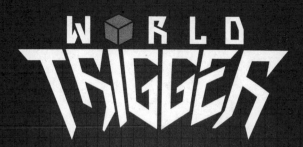

WORLD TRIGGER VOL. 11
SHONEN JUMP Manga Edition

STORY AND ART BY DAISUKE ASHIHARA

Translation/Lillian Olsen
Touch-Up Art & Lettering/Annaliese Christman
Design/Sam Elzway
Weekly Shonen Jump Editors/Hope Donovan, Marlene First
Graphic Novel Editor/Marlene First

Printed in the U.S.A.

Published by VIZ Media, LLC
P.O. Box 77010
San Francisco, CA 94107

10 9 8 7 6 5 4 3 2 1
First printing, July 2016

SHONEN JUMP MANGA EDITION

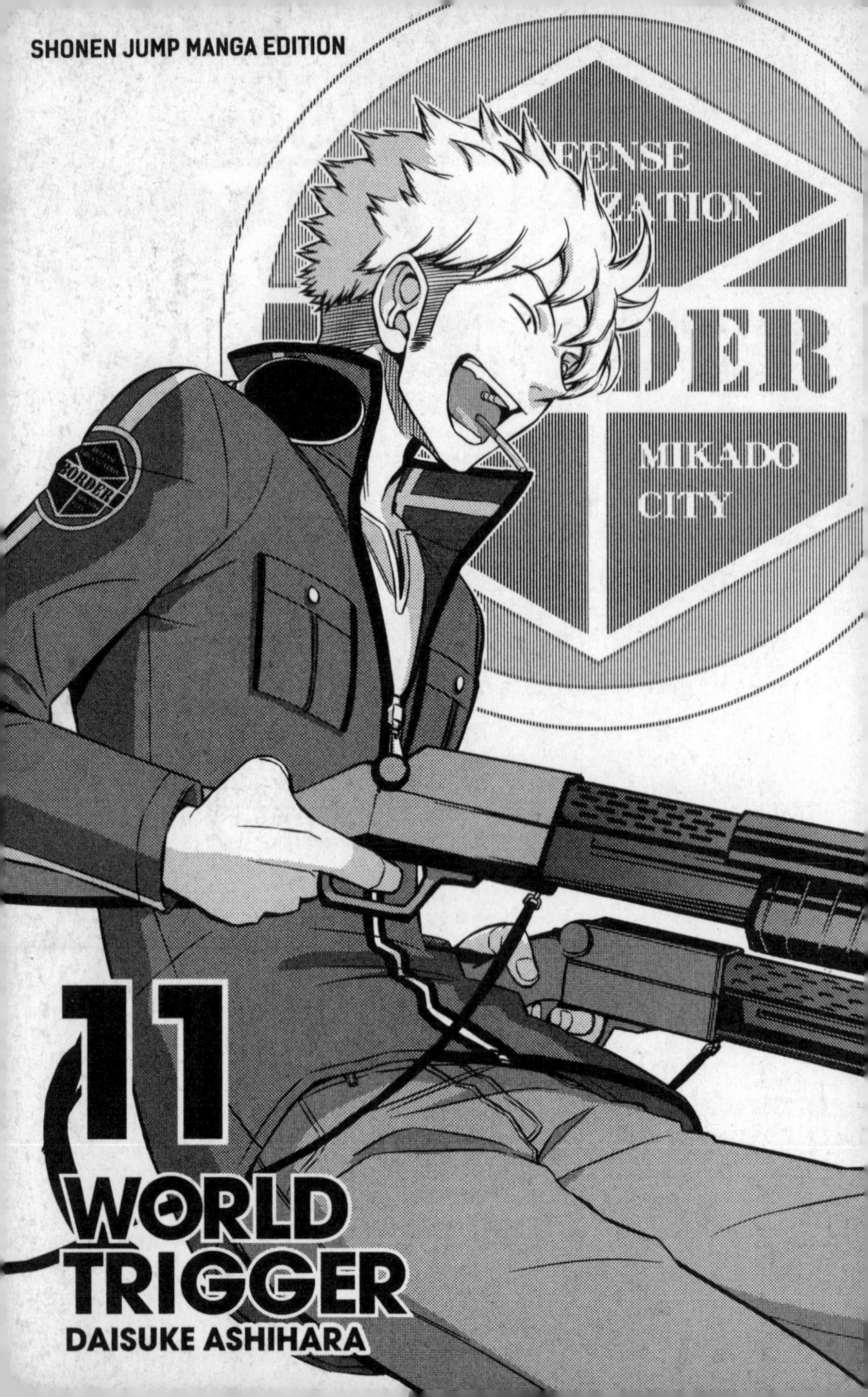

MIKADO
CITY

11

WORLD TRIGGER

DAISUKE ASHIHARA

WORLD TRIGGER DATA BASE

BORDER

An agency founded to protect the city's peace from Neighbors.

S-Rank
Black Trigger Users
(i.e. Tsukihiko Amo)
A-Rank
(Elite)
Away teams selected from here (Arashiyama, Miwa Squads)
Promoted in Rank Wars
B-Rank
(Main force)
Agents on defense duty must be at least B-Rank (Tamakoma-2)
Promoted at 4,000 solo points
C-Rank
(Trainees)
Use trainee Triggers only in emergencies (Izuho Natsume)

ON!!
TRIGGER...

TRIGGER

A technology created by Neighbors to manipulate Trion. Used mainly as weapons, Triggers come in various types.

ARE YOU INSANE?
ANYTHING BIGGER THAN THAT WOULD REQUIRE TOO MUCH TRION TO LAUNCH!
AWW.

◀ Away mission ships also run on Trion.

POSITIONS

Border classifies them into three groups: Attacker, Gunner and Sniper.

Attacker

Close-range attacks. Weapons include: close-range Scorpions that are good for surprise attacks, the balanced Kogetsu sword, and the defense-heavy Raygust.

Gunner

Shoots from mid-range. There are several types of bullets, including multipurpose Asteroids, twisting Vipers, exploding Meteors, and tracking Hounds. People who don't use gun-shaped Triggers are called Shooters.

METEOR.

◀ Osamu and Izumi are Shooters.

Sniper

Fires from a long distance. There are three sniping rifles: the well-balanced Egret, the light and easy Lightning, and the powerful but unwieldy Ibis.

Operator

Supports combatants by relaying information such as enemy positions and abilities.

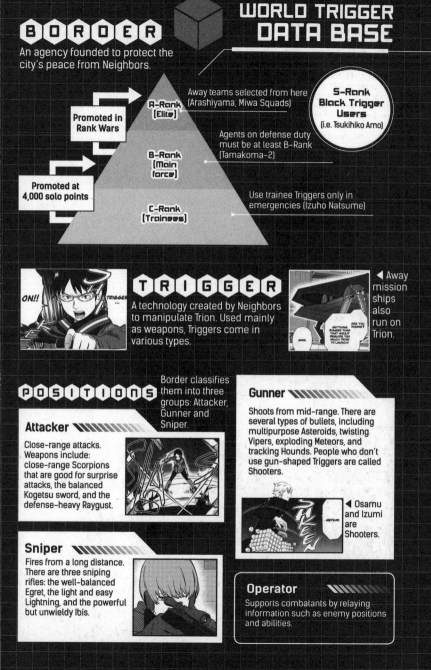

RANK WARS

Practice matches between Border agents. Promotions in Border are based on good results in the Rank Wars and defense duty achievements.

B-Rank agents are split into top, middle, and bottom groups. Three to four teams fight in a melee battle. Defeating an opposing squad member earns you one point and surviving to the end nets two points. Top squads from the previous season get a bonus.

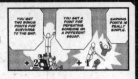

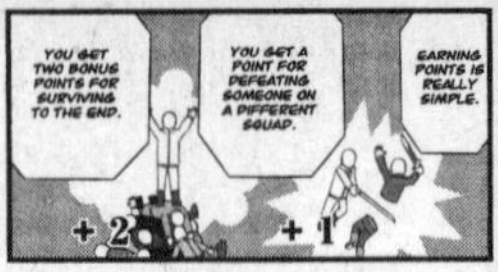
EARNING POINTS IS REALLY SIMPLE.
YOU GET A POINT FOR DEFEATING SOMEONE ON A DIFFERENT SQUAD.
YOU GET TWO BONUS POINTS FOR SURVIVING TO THE END.
+1
+2

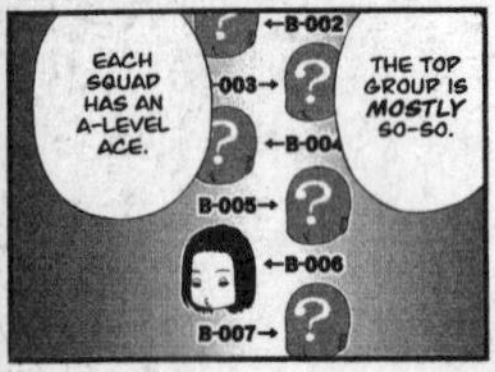
THE TOP GROUP IS *MOSTLY* SO-SO.
EACH SQUAD HAS AN A-LEVEL ACE.
←B-002
003→
←B-004
B-005→
←B-006
B-007→

B-Rank middle groups have set strategies. Top groups all have an A-Rank-level ace.

The lowest-ranked squad in each match gets to pick the stage.

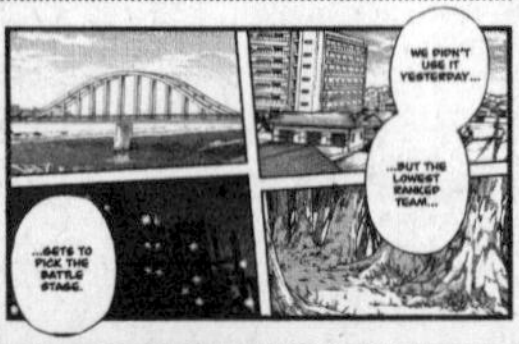
WE DIDN'T USE IT YESTERDAY...
...BUT THE LOWEST RANKED TEAM...
...GETS TO PICK THE BATTLE STAGE.

A-Rank

Top two B-Rank squads get to challenge A-Rank.

B-Rank

Agents ▶ (B-Rank and above) can't fight trainees (C-Rank) for points.

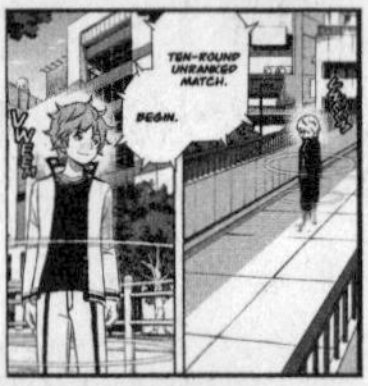
TEN-ROUND UNRANKED MATCH.
BEGIN.
VWEN

C-Rank Wars are fought through solo matches. Beating someone with more points than you gets you a lot of points. On the other hand, beating someone with fewer points doesn't get you as many.

C-Rank

STORY

About four years ago, a Gate connecting to another dimension opened in Mikado City, leading to the appearance of invaders called Neighbors. After the establishment of the Border Defense Agency, people were able to return to their normal lives.

Osamu Mikumo is a junior high student who meets Yuma Kuga, a Neighbor. Yuma is targeted for capture by Border, but Tamakoma branch agent Yuichi Jin steps in to help. He convinces Yuma to join Border instead, then gives his Black Trigger to HQ in exchange for Yuma's enlistment. Now Osamu, Yuma and Osamu's friend Chika work toward making A-Rank together.

Aftokrator, the largest military nation in the Neighborhood, begins another large-scale invasion! Border succeeds in driving them back, but over thirty C-Rank trainees are kidnapped in the process. Border implements more plans for away missions to retrieve the missing Agents.

Tamakoma-2 enters the Rank Wars to be chosen for the away team. They pass the first match with flying colors, and the second match, against the middle B-Rank Suwa and Arafune Squads, is about to begin!

WORLD TRIGGER CHARACTERS

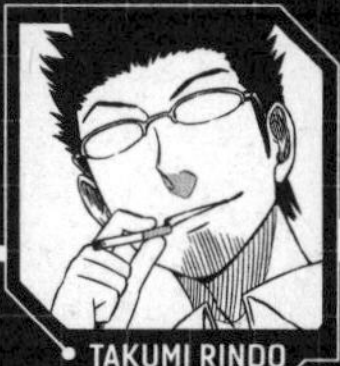

TAKUMI RINDO

Tamakoma Branch Director.

TAMAKOMA BRANCH

Understanding toward Neighbors. Considered divergent from Border's main philosophy.

TAMAKOMA-2

Tamakoma's B-Rank Squad, aiming to get promoted to A-Rank.

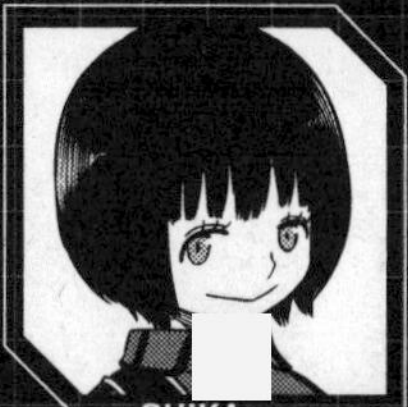

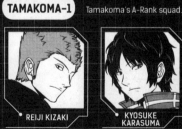

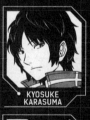

CHIKA AMATORI

Osamu's childhood friend. She has high Trion levels.

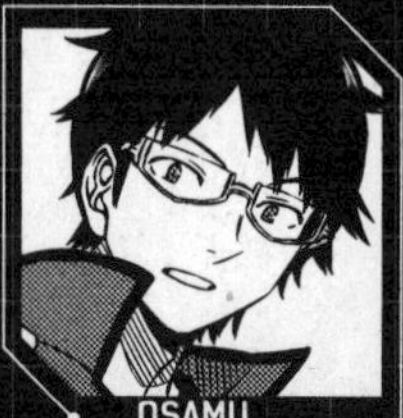

OSAMU MIKUMO

Ninth-grader who's compelled to help those in trouble. Captain of Tamakoma-2 (Mikumo Squad).

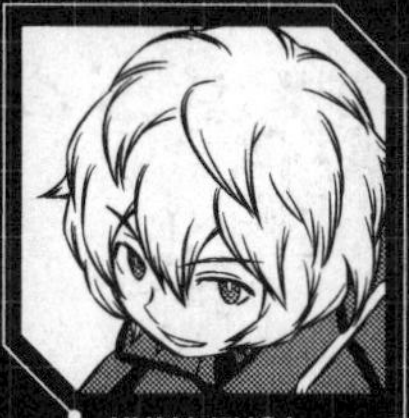

YUMA KUGA

A Neighbor who carries a Black Trigger.

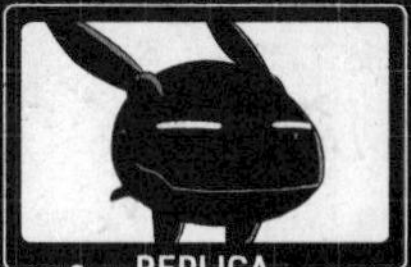

REPLICA

Yuma's chaperone. Missing after recent invasion.

TAMAKOMA-1

Tamakoma's A-Rank squad.

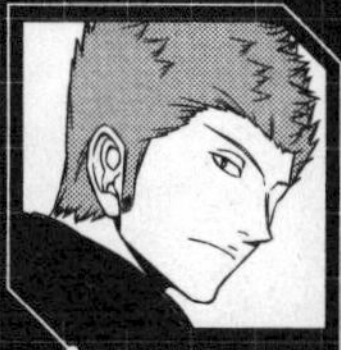

REIJI KIZAKI

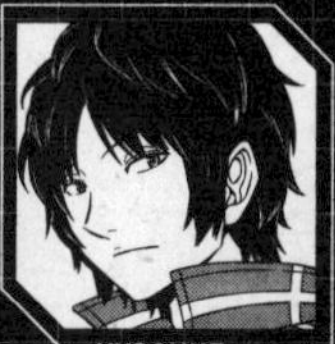

KYOSUKE KARASUMA

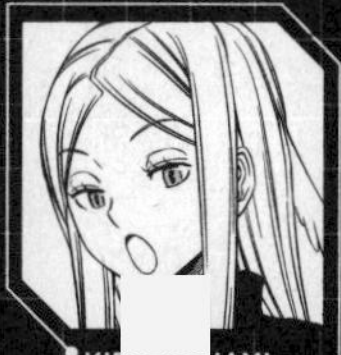

KIRIE KONAMI

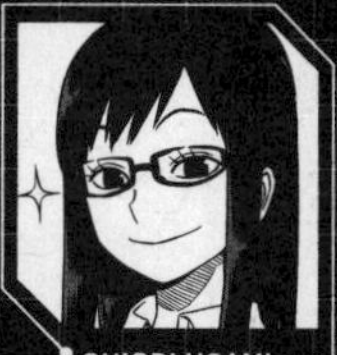

SHIORI USAMI

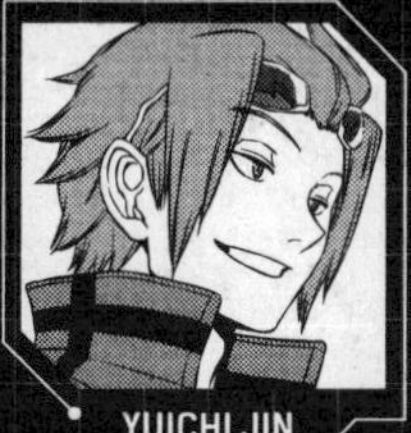

YUICHI JIN

Former S-Rank Black Trigger user. His Side Effect lets him see the future.

A-RANK AGENTS

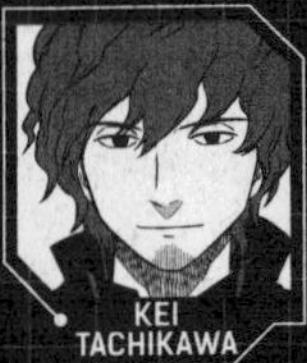
KEI TACHIKAWA
A-Rank #1 Squad captain.

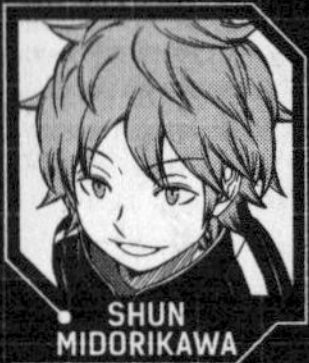
SHUN MIDORIKAWA
A-Rank #4 Kusakabe Squad Attacker.

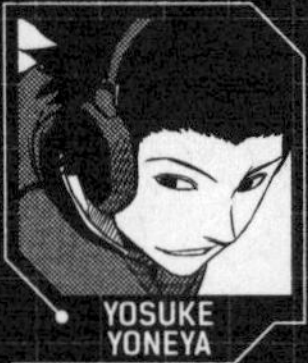
YOSUKE YONEYA
A-Rank #7 Miwa Squad Attacker.

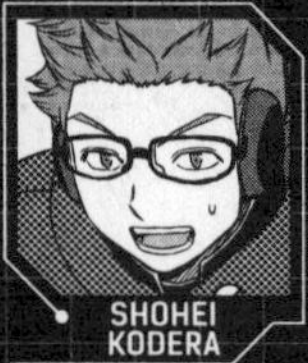
SHOHEI KODERA
A-Rank #7 Miwa Squad Sniper.

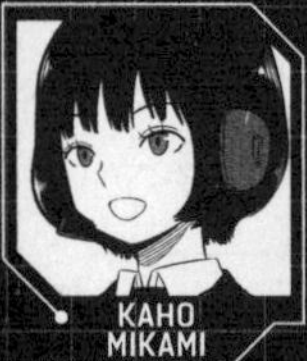
KAHO MIKAMI
A-Rank #3 Kazama Squad Operator.

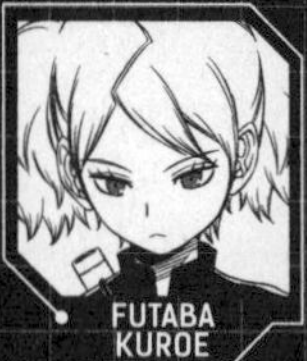
FUTABA KUROE
A-Rank #6 Kako Squad Attacker.

B-RANK AGENTS

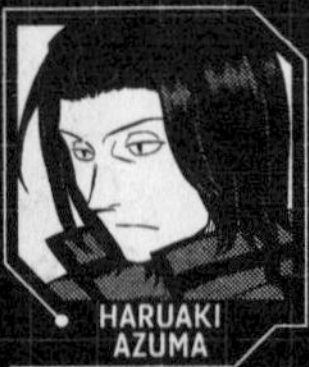
HARUAKI AZUMA
B-Rank #6 Squad captain and sniper.

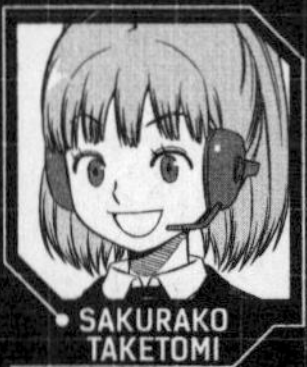
SAKURAKO TAKETOMI
B-Rank #18 Ebina Squad Operator.

SUWA SQUAD

HQ B-Rank #8 Squad.

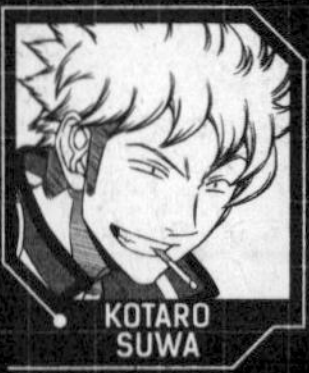
KOTARO SUWA

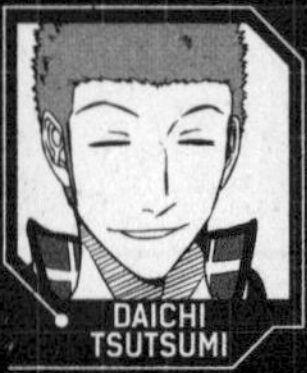
DAICHI TSUTSUMI

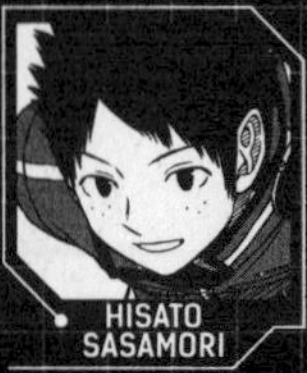
HISATO SASAMORI

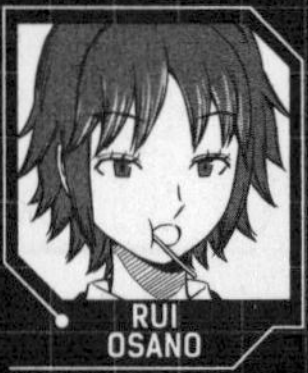
RUI OSANO

ARAFUNE SQUAD

HQ B-Rank #10 all-Sniper Squad.

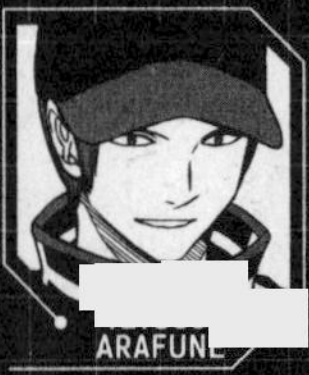
[redacted] ARAFUNE[redacted]

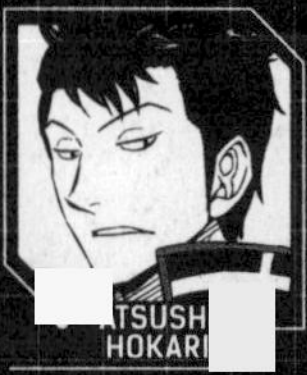
[redacted]ATSUSH[redacted] HOKARI[redacted]

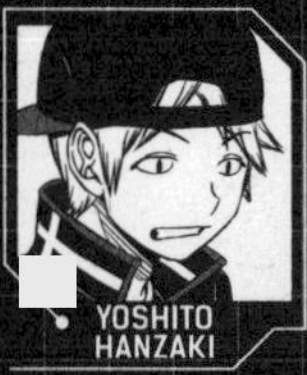
YOSHITO HANZAKI

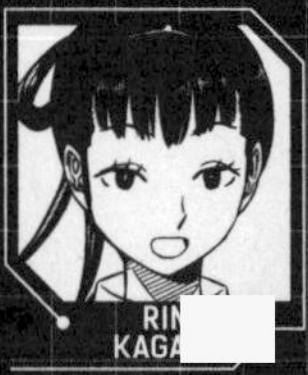
RI[redacted] KAGA[redacted]

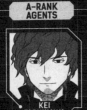

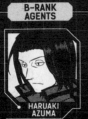

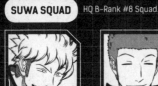

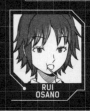

WORLD TRIGGER
CONTENTS

11

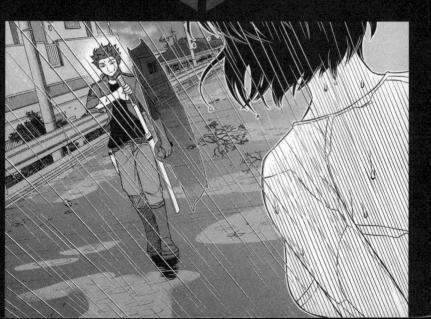

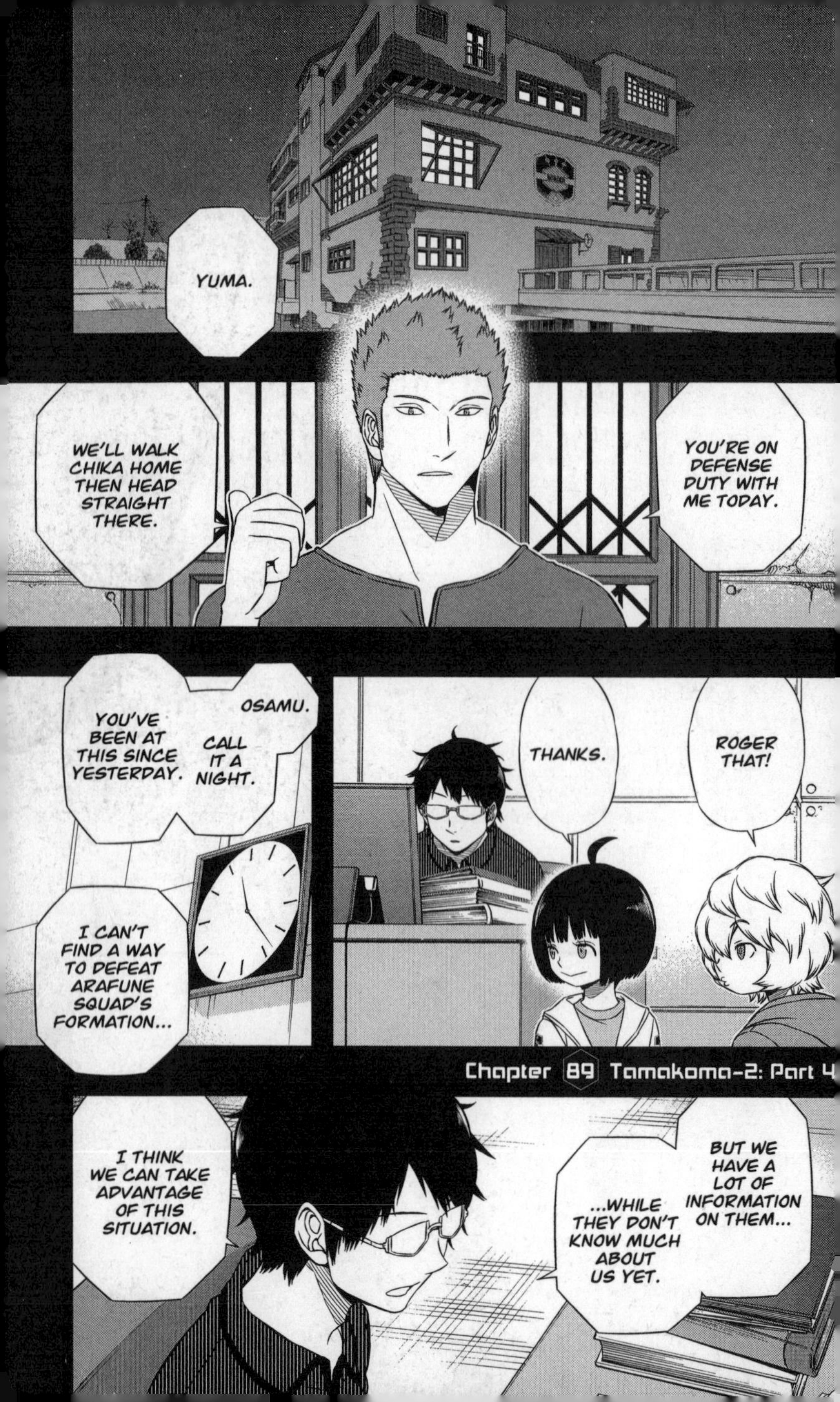
YUMA.
YOU'RE ON DEFENSE DUTY WITH ME TODAY.
WE'LL WALK CHIKA HOME THEN HEAD STRAIGHT THERE.
ROGER THAT!
THANKS.
OSAMU.
CALL IT A NIGHT.
YOU'VE BEEN AT THIS SINCE YESTERDAY.
I CAN'T FIND A WAY TO DEFEAT ARAFUNE SQUAD'S FORMATION...
Chapter 89 Tamakoma-2: Part 4
BUT WE HAVE A LOT OF INFORMATION ON THEM...
...WHILE THEY DON'T KNOW MUCH ABOUT US YET.
I THINK WE CAN TAKE ADVANTAGE OF THIS SITUATION.

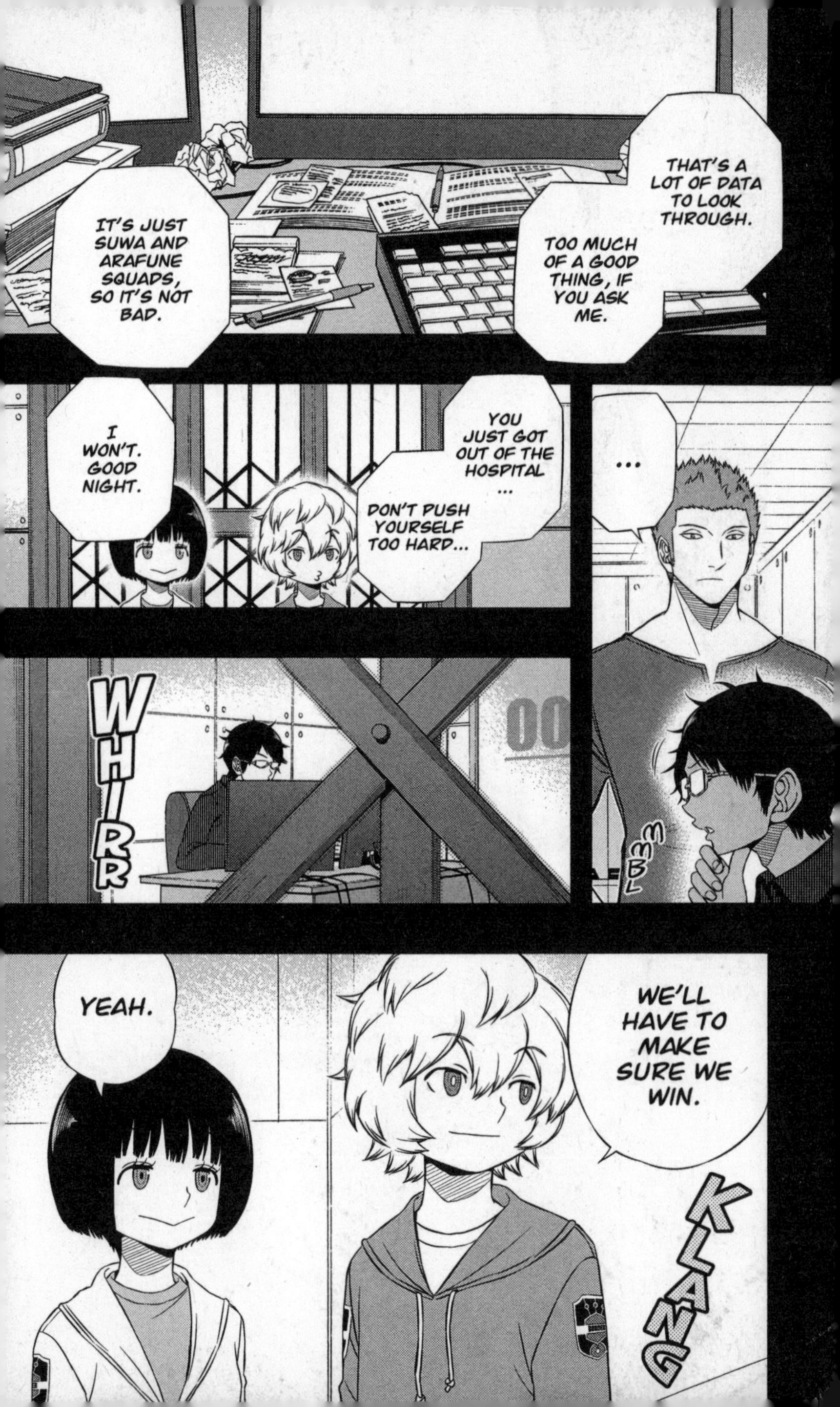
THAT'S A LOT OF DATA TO LOOK THROUGH.
TOO MUCH OF A GOOD THING, IF YOU ASK ME.
IT'S JUST SUWA AND ARAFUNE SQUADS, SO IT'S NOT BAD.
...
MMBL
YOU JUST GOT OUT OF THE HOSPITAL ...
DON'T PUSH YOURSELF TOO HARD...
I WON'T. GOOD NIGHT.
WHIRR
WE'LL HAVE TO MAKE SURE WE WIN.
KLANG
YEAH.

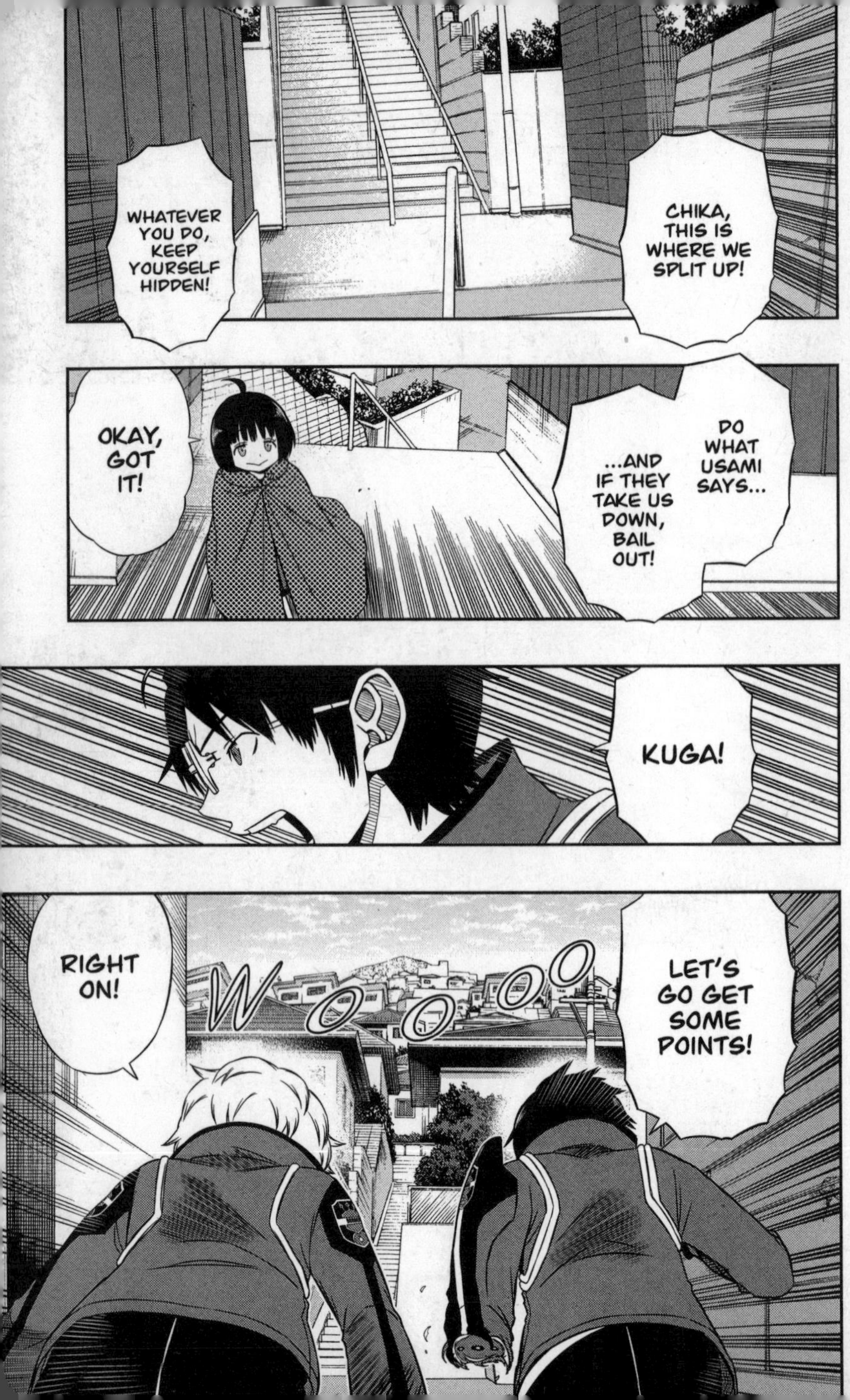
CHIKA, THIS IS WHERE WE SPLIT UP!
WHATEVER YOU DO, KEEP YOURSELF HIDDEN!
DO WHAT USAMI SAYS...
...AND IF THEY TAKE US DOWN, BAIL OUT!
OKAY, GOT IT!
KUGA!
LET'S GO GET SOME POINTS!
WOOOO
RIGHT ON!

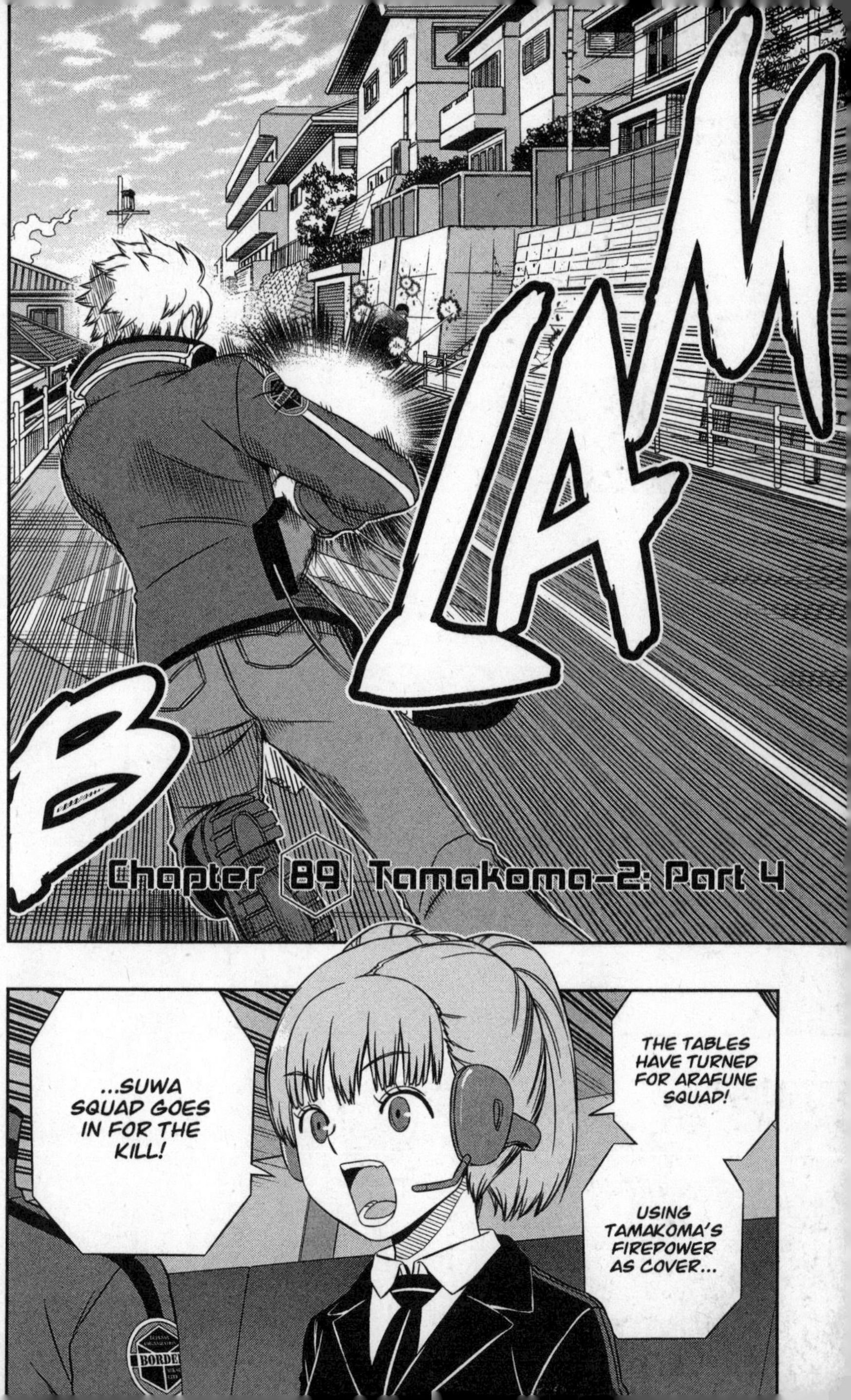
BLAM
Chapter 89 Tamakoma-2: Part 4
THE TABLES HAVE TURNED FOR ARAFUNE SQUAD!
USING TAMAKOMA'S FIREPOWER AS COVER...
...SUWA SQUAD GOES IN FOR THE KILL!

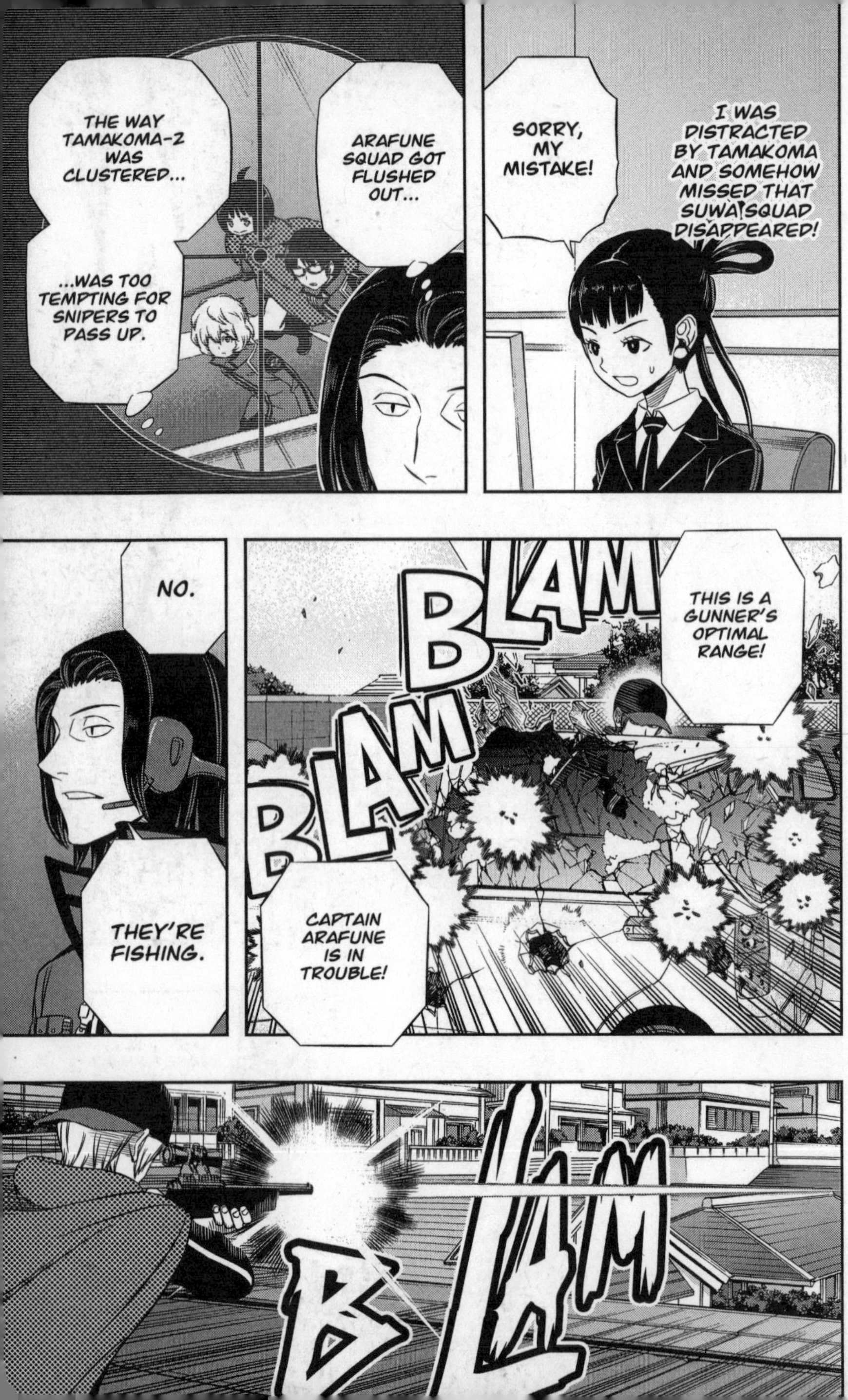
SORRY, MY MISTAKE!
I WAS DISTRACTED BY TAMAKOMA AND SOMEHOW MISSED THAT SUWA SQUAD DISAPPEARED!
ARAFUNE SQUAD GOT FLUSHED OUT...
THE WAY TAMAKOMA-2 WAS CLUSTERED...
...WAS TOO TEMPTING FOR SNIPERS TO PASS UP.
THIS IS A GUNNER'S OPTIMAL RANGE!
BLAM
BLAM
CAPTAIN ARAFUNE IS IN TROUBLE!
NO.
THEY'RE FISHING.
BLAM

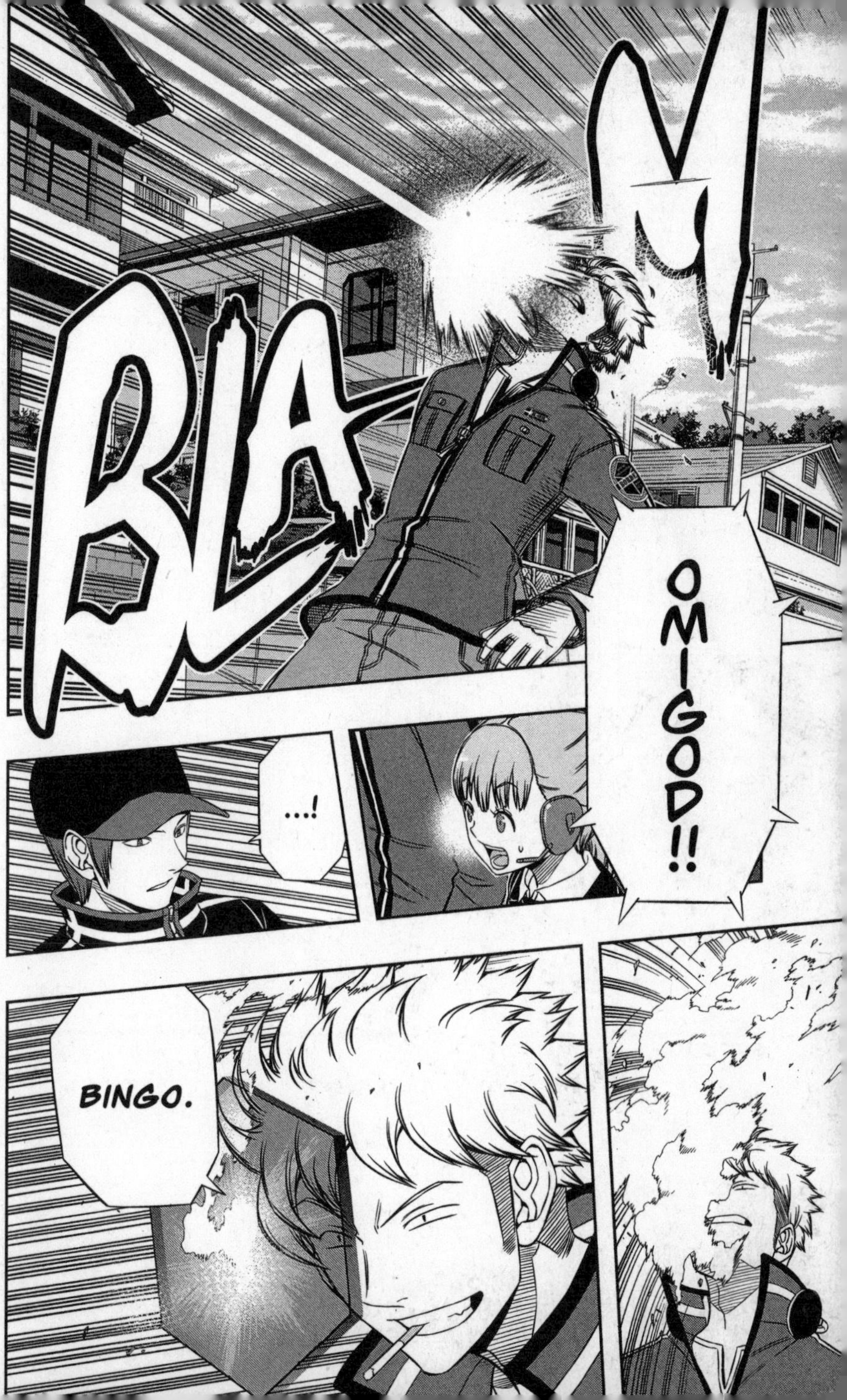
BLAM
OMIGOD!!
...!
BINGO.

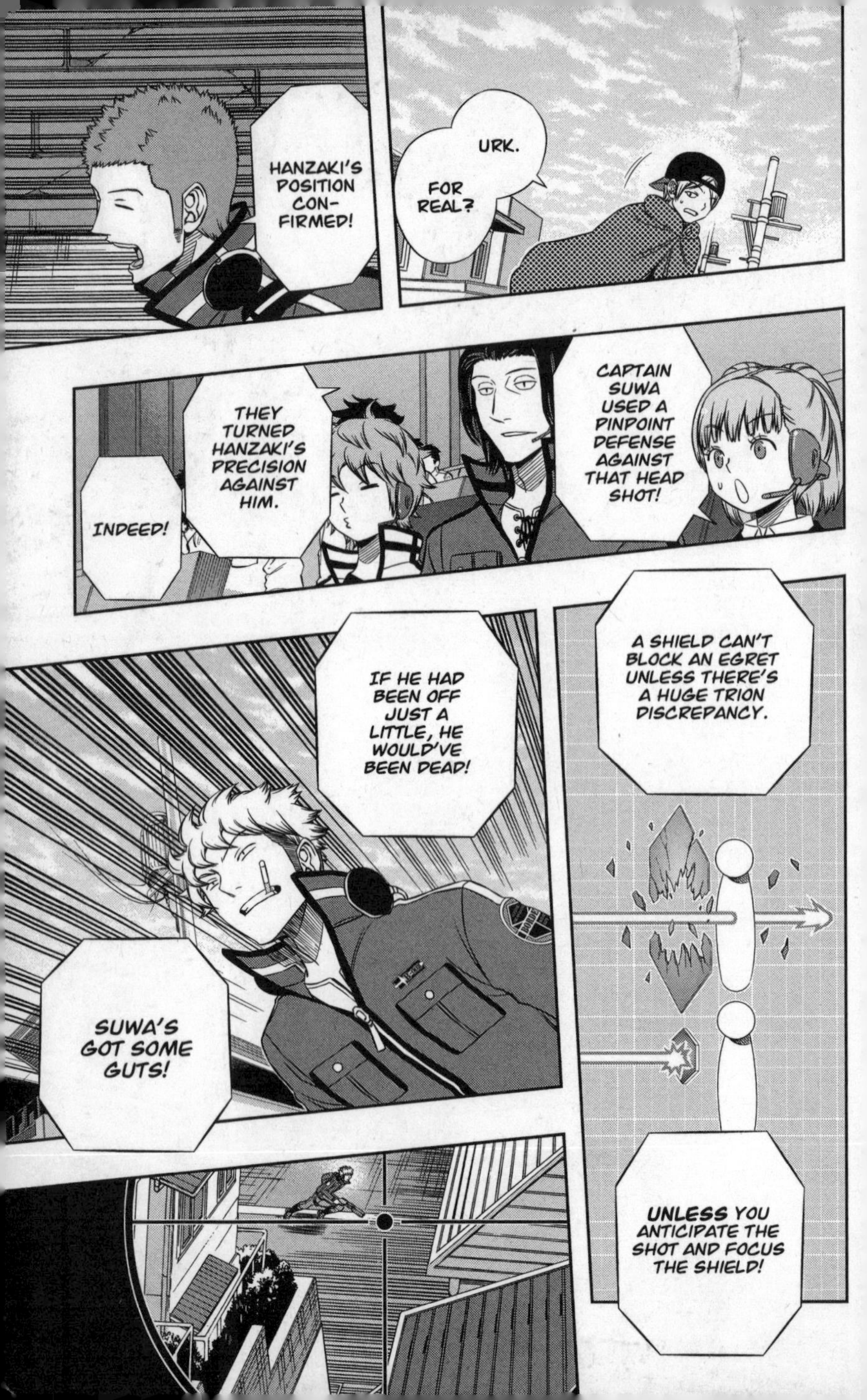
URK.
FOR REAL?
HANZAKI'S POSITION CON-FIRMED!
CAPTAIN SUWA USED A PINPOINT DEFENSE AGAINST THAT HEAD SHOT!
THEY TURNED HANZAKI'S PRECISION AGAINST HIM.
INDEED!
A SHIELD CAN'T BLOCK AN EGRET UNLESS THERE'S A HUGE TRION DISCREPANCY.
UNLESS YOU ANTICIPATE THE SHOT AND FOCUS THE SHIELD!
IF HE HAD BEEN OFF JUST A LITTLE, HE WOULD'VE BEEN DEAD!
SUWA'S GOT SOME GUTS!

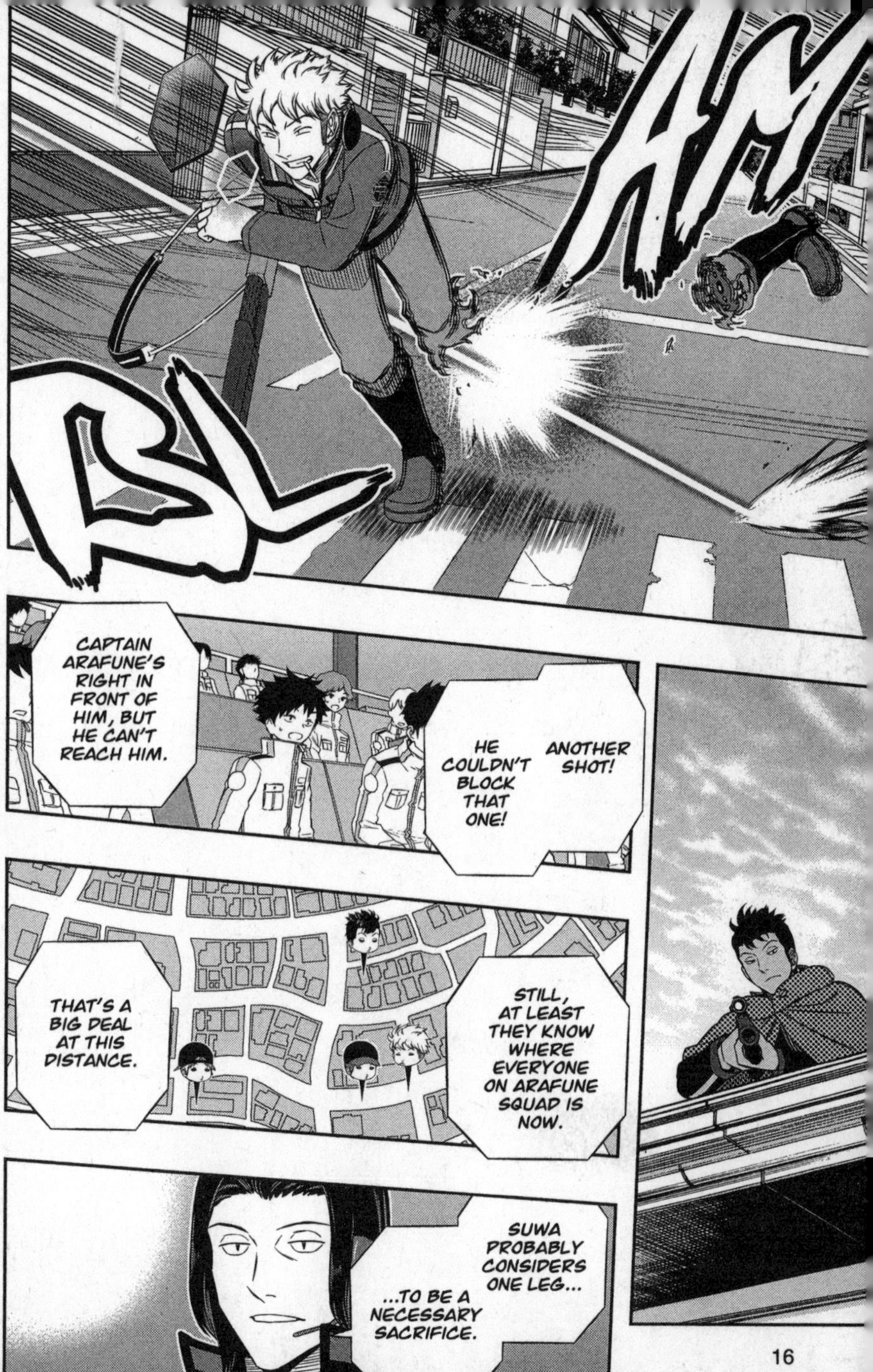
ANOTHER SHOT!
HE COULDN'T BLOCK THAT ONE!
CAPTAIN ARAFUNE'S RIGHT IN FRONT OF HIM, BUT HE CAN'T REACH HIM.
STILL, AT LEAST THEY KNOW WHERE EVERYONE ON ARAFUNE SQUAD IS NOW.
THAT'S A BIG DEAL AT THIS DISTANCE.
SUWA PROBABLY CONSIDERS ONE LEG...
...TO BE A NECESSARY SACRIFICE.

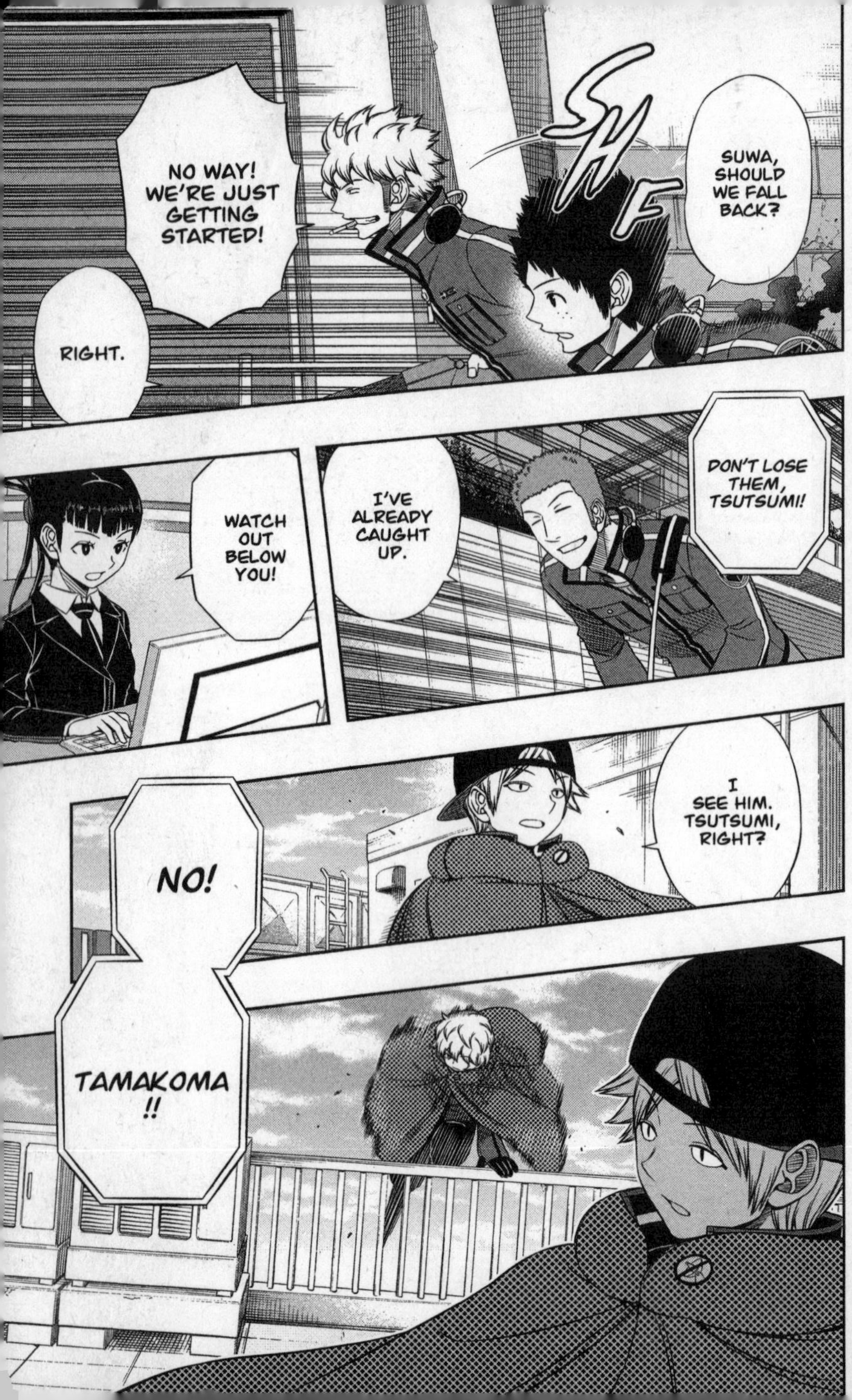
SUWA, SHOULD WE FALL BACK?
SHF
NO WAY! WE'RE JUST GETTING STARTED!
RIGHT.
DON'T LOSE THEM, TSUTSUMI!
I'VE ALREADY CAUGHT UP.
WATCH OUT BELOW YOU!
I SEE HIM. TSUTSUMI, RIGHT?
NO!
TAMAKOMA !!

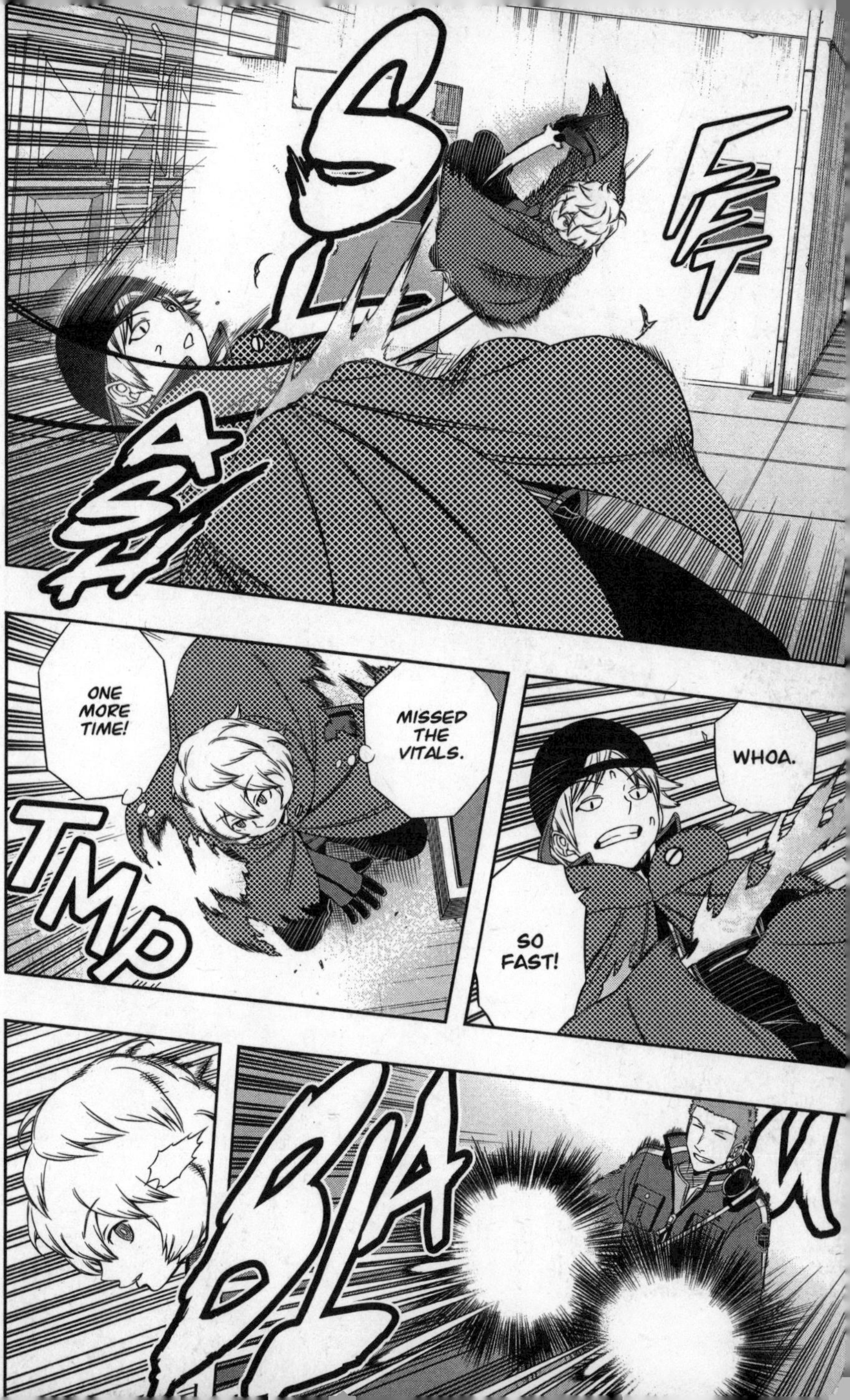
FFT
SLASH
WHOA.
SO FAST!
MISSED THE VITALS.
ONE MORE TIME!
TMP

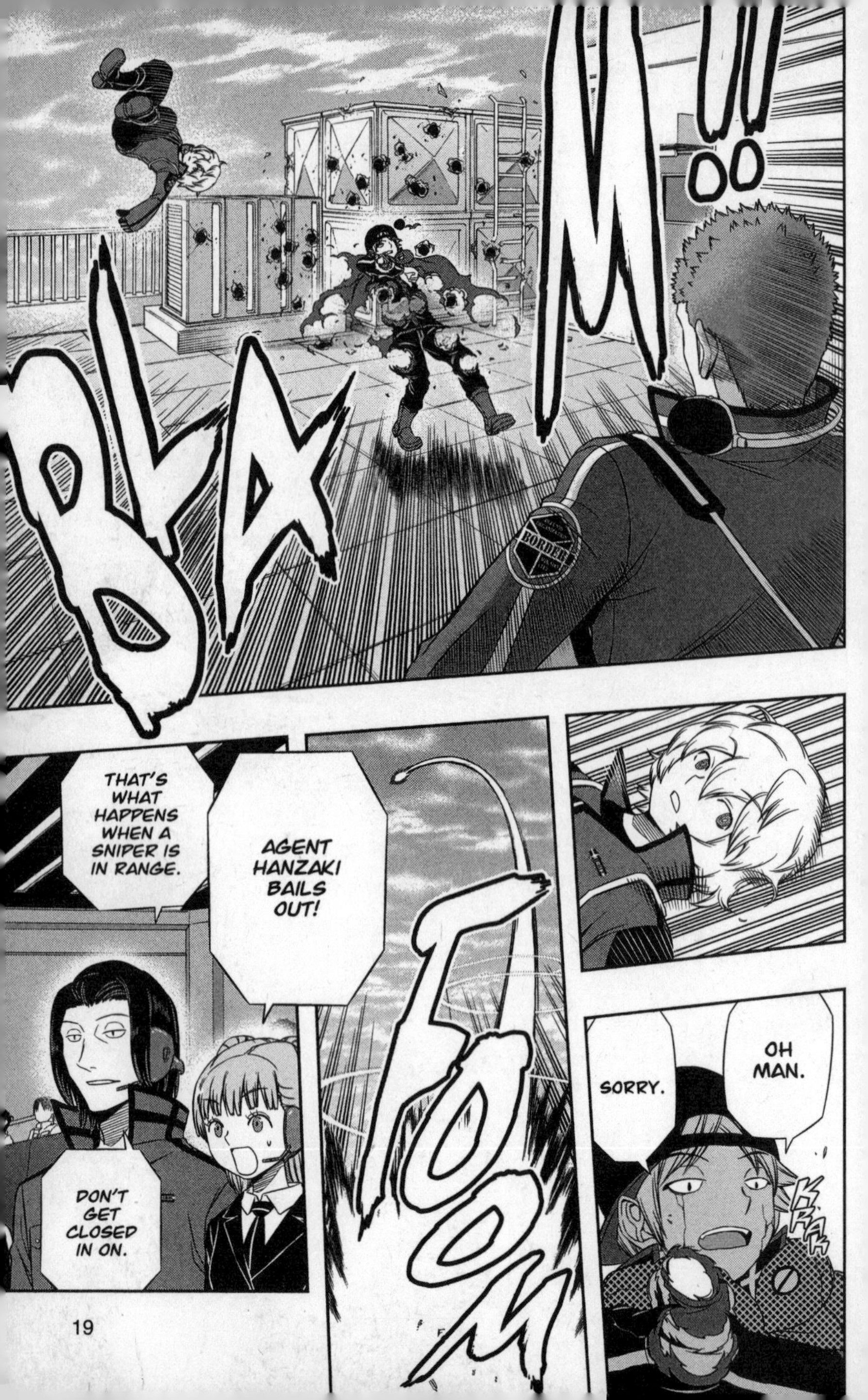
BLAMOO!!
OH MAN.
SORRY.
KRAK
FOOM
AGENT HANZAKI BAILS OUT!
THAT'S WHAT HAPPENS WHEN A SNIPER IS IN RANGE.
DON'T GET CLOSED IN ON.

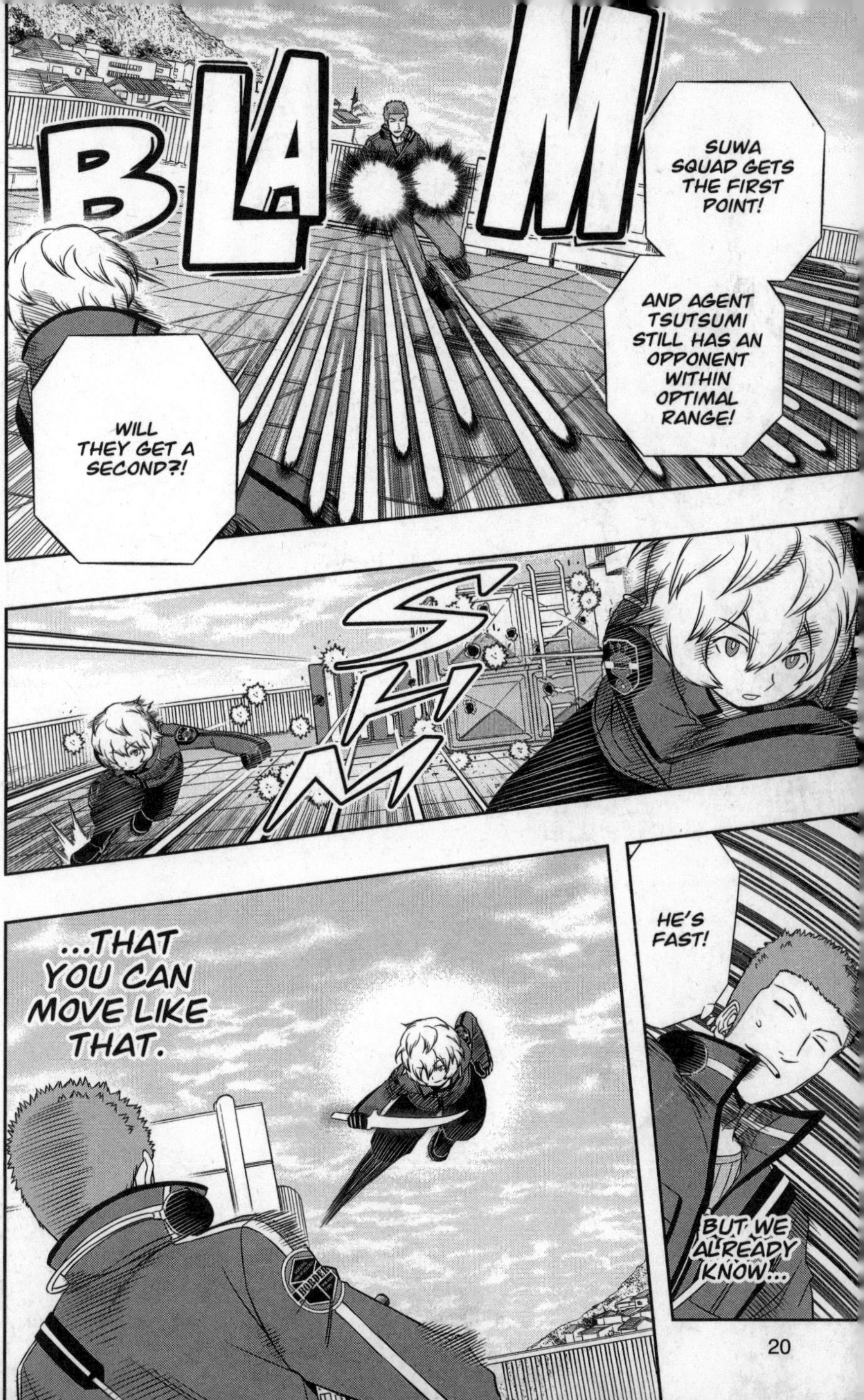
SUWA SQUAD GETS THE FIRST POINT!
BLAM
AND AGENT TSUTSUMI STILL HAS AN OPPONENT WITHIN OPTIMAL RANGE!
WILL THEY GET A SECOND?!
SHM
HE'S FAST!
BUT WE ALREADY KNOW...
...THAT YOU CAN MOVE LIKE THAT.

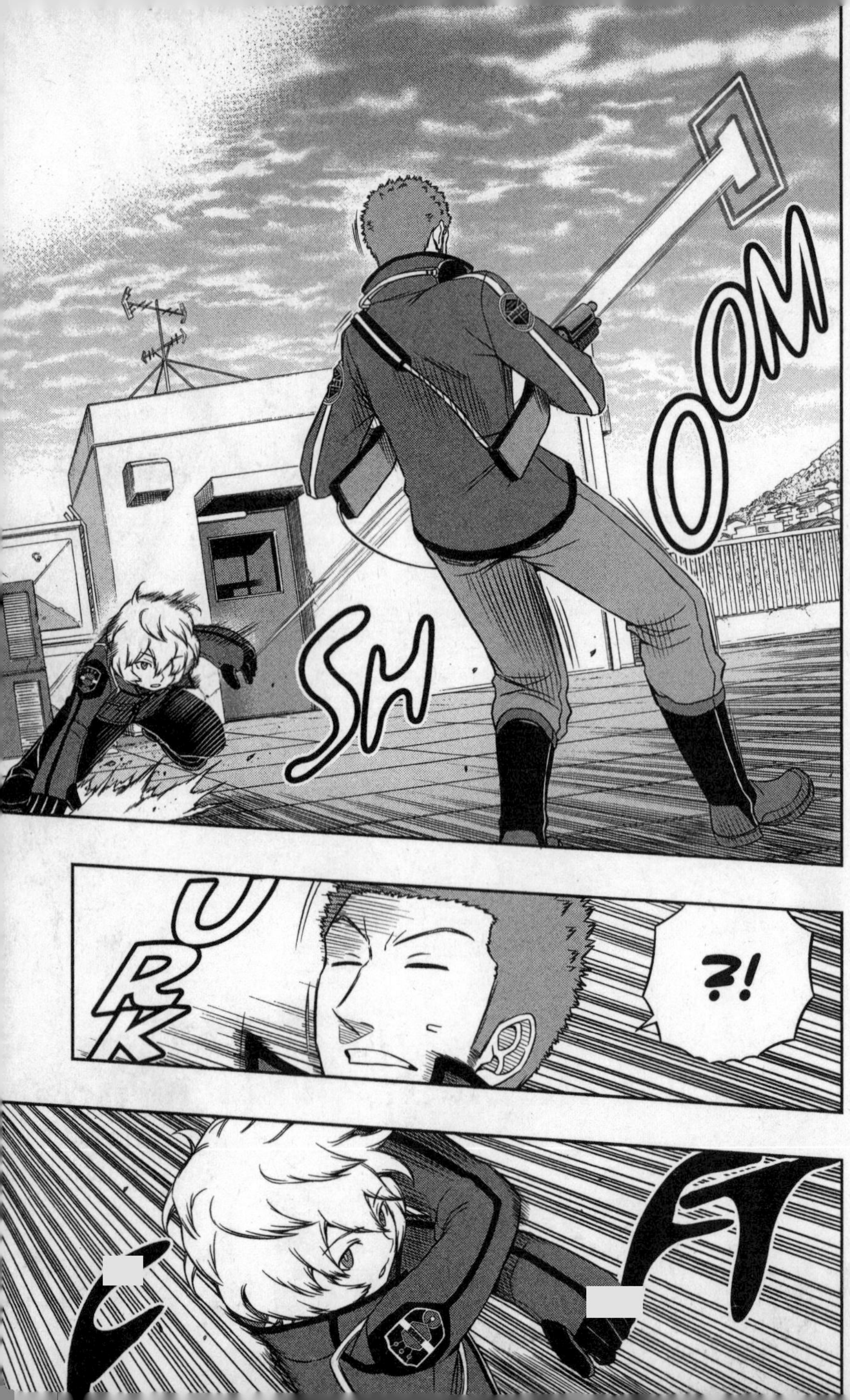
SH
OOM
?!
URK
FT

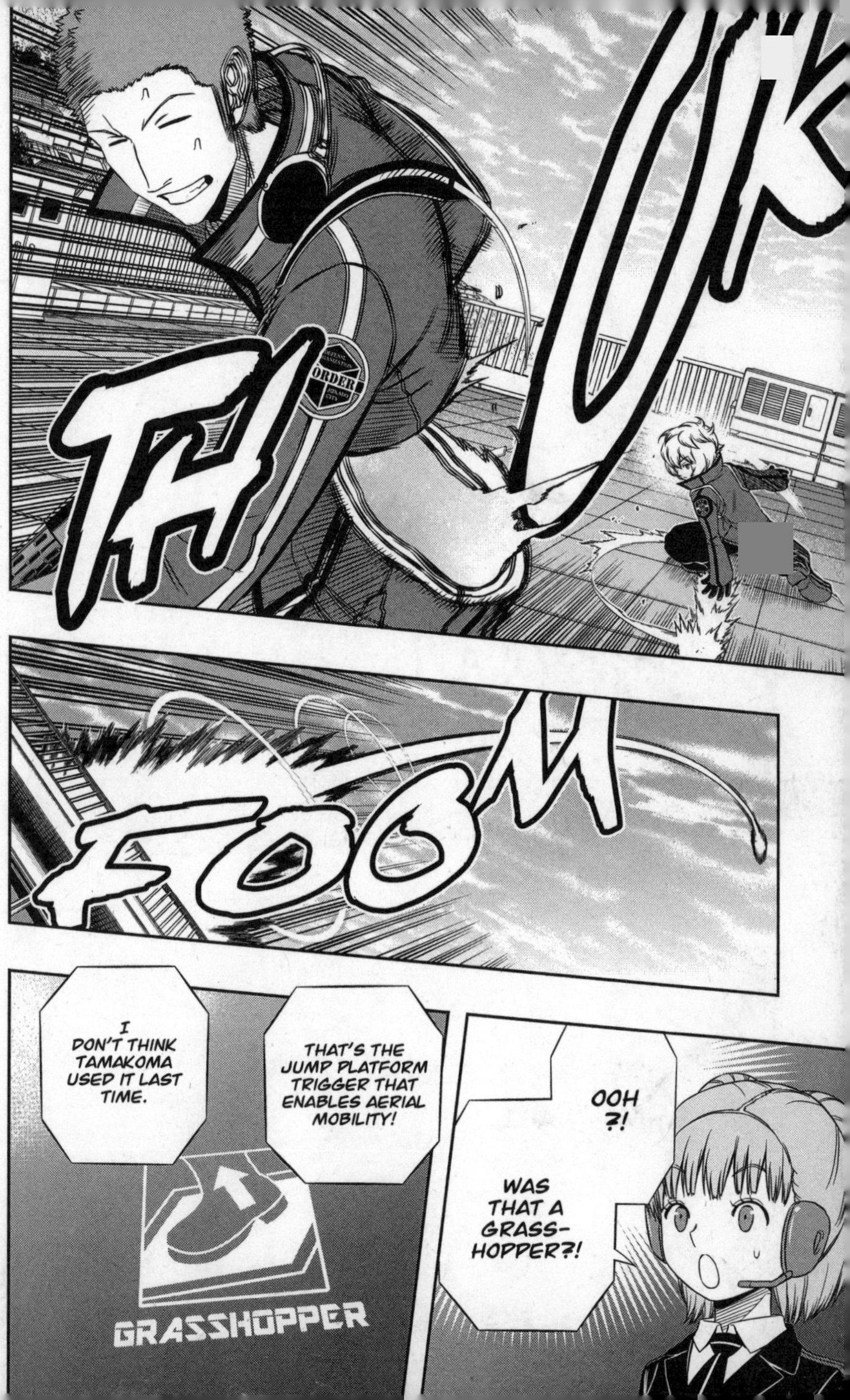
THUNK
FOOM
OOH ?!
WAS THAT A GRASS-HOPPER?!
THAT'S THE JUMP PLATFORM TRIGGER THAT ENABLES AERIAL MOBILITY!
I DON'T THINK TAMAKOMA USED IT LAST TIME.
GRASSHOPPER

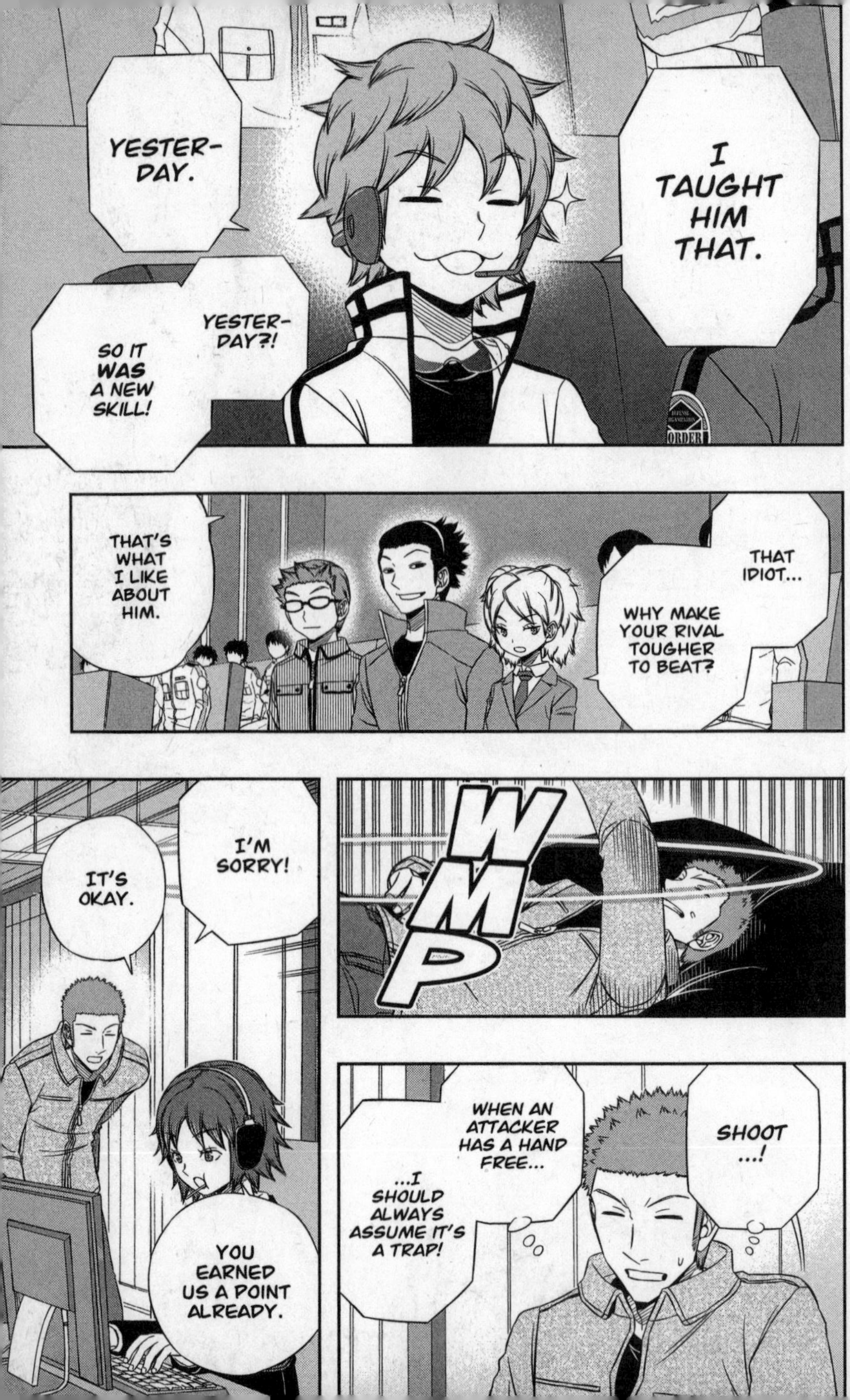
I TAUGHT HIM THAT.
YESTER-DAY.
YESTER-DAY?!
SO IT WAS A NEW SKILL!
THAT IDIOT...
WHY MAKE YOUR RIVAL TOUGHER TO BEAT?
THAT'S WHAT I LIKE ABOUT HIM.
WMP
SHOOT...!
WHEN AN ATTACKER HAS A HAND FREE...
...I SHOULD ALWAYS ASSUME IT'S A TRAP!
I'M SORRY!
IT'S OKAY.
YOU EARNED US A POINT ALREADY.

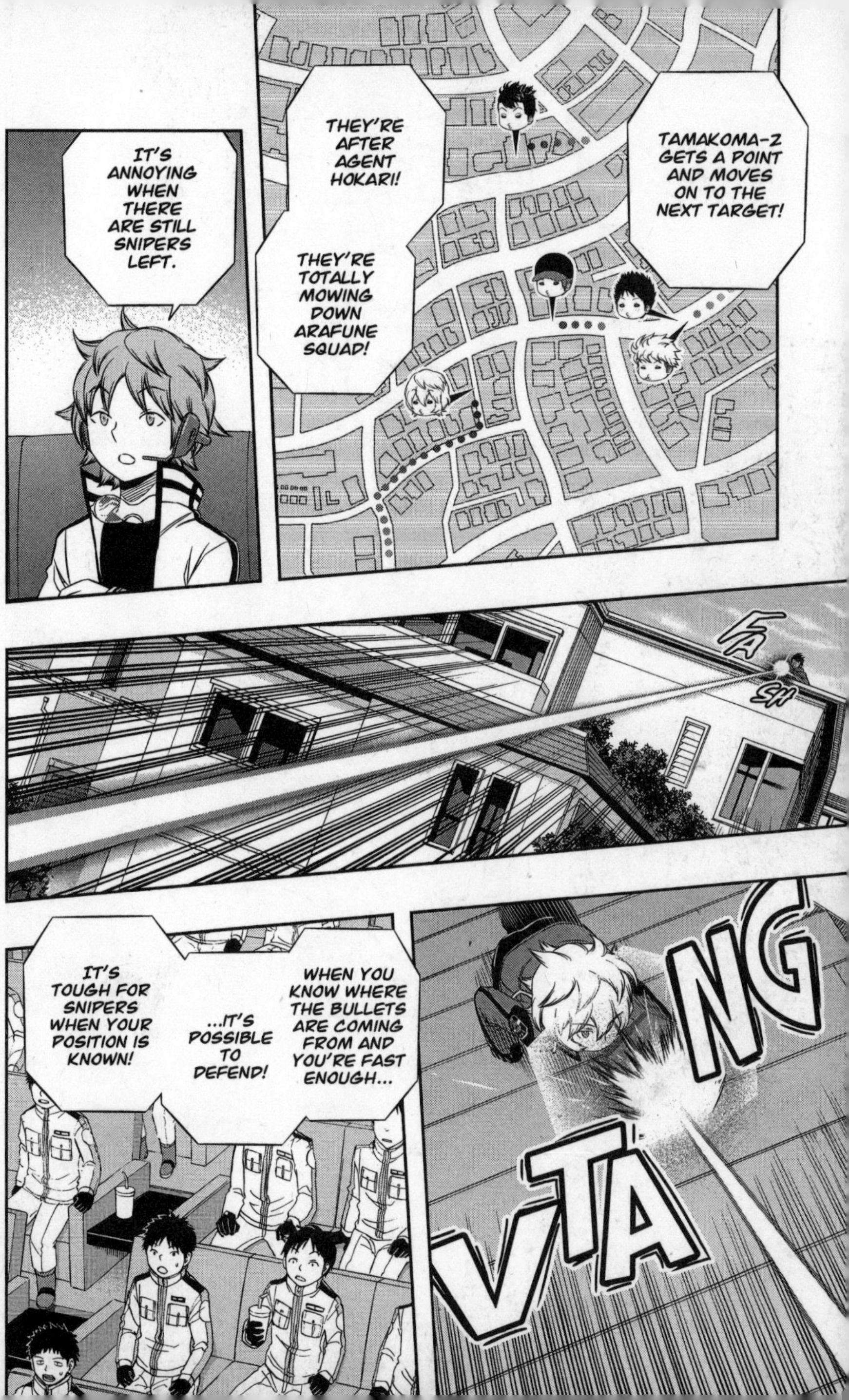
TAMAKOMA-2 GETS A POINT AND MOVES ON TO THE NEXT TARGET!
THEY'RE AFTER AGENT HOKARI!
THEY'RE TOTALLY MOWING DOWN ARAFUNE SQUAD!
IT'S ANNOYING WHEN THERE ARE STILL SNIPERS LEFT.
FASH
TANG
WHEN YOU KNOW WHERE THE BULLETS ARE COMING FROM AND YOU'RE FAST ENOUGH...
...IT'S POSSIBLE TO DEFEND!
IT'S TOUGH FOR SNIPERS WHEN YOUR POSITION IS KNOWN!

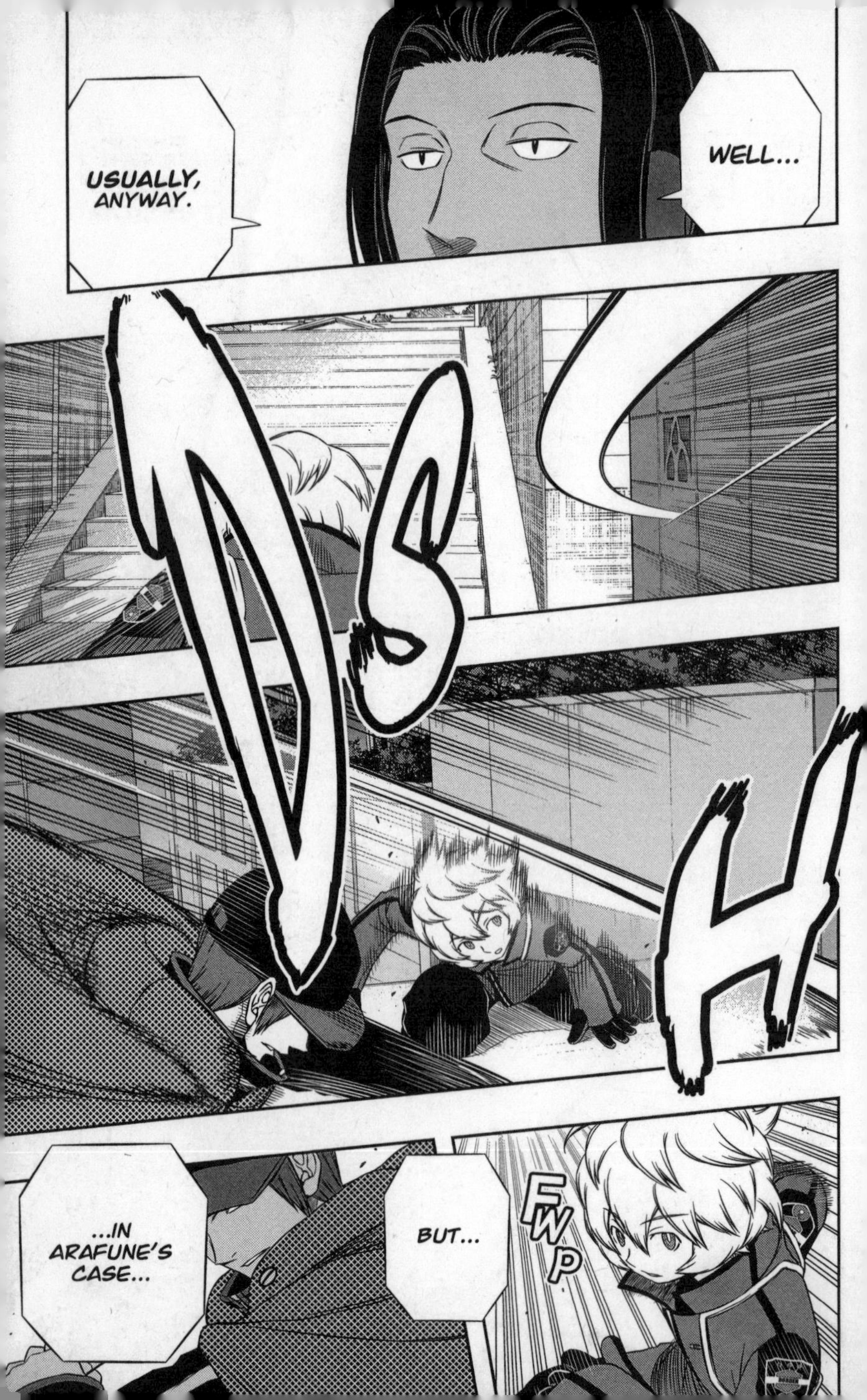
WELL...
USUALLY, ANYWAY.
FWP
BUT...
...IN ARAFUNE'S CASE...

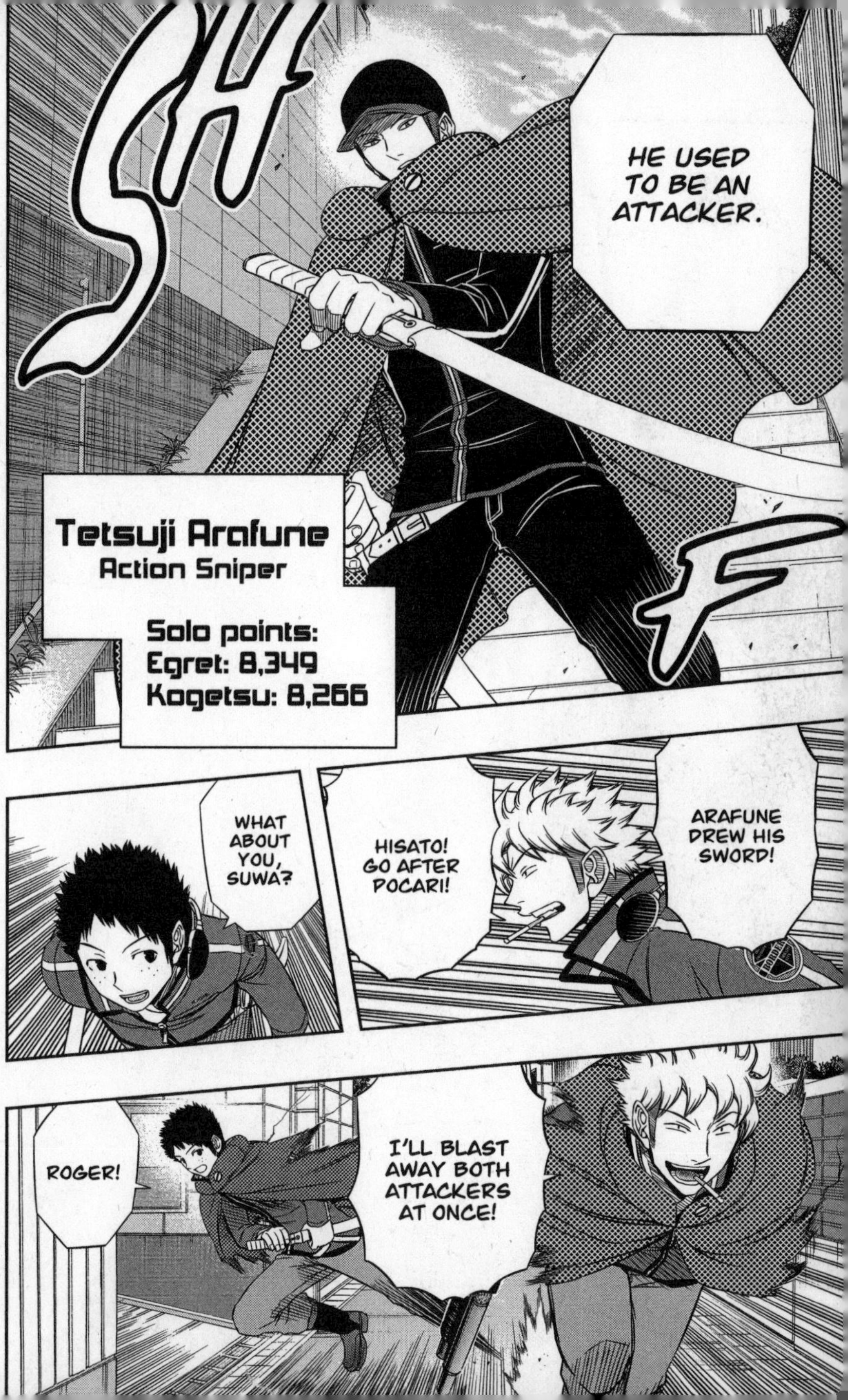
HE USED TO BE AN ATTACKER.
SHF
Tetsuji Arafune
Action Sniper
Solo points:
Egret: 8,349
Kogetsu: 8,266
ARAFUNE DREW HIS SWORD!
HISATO! GO AFTER POCARI!
WHAT ABOUT YOU, SUWA?
I'LL BLAST AWAY BOTH ATTACKERS AT ONCE!
ROGER!

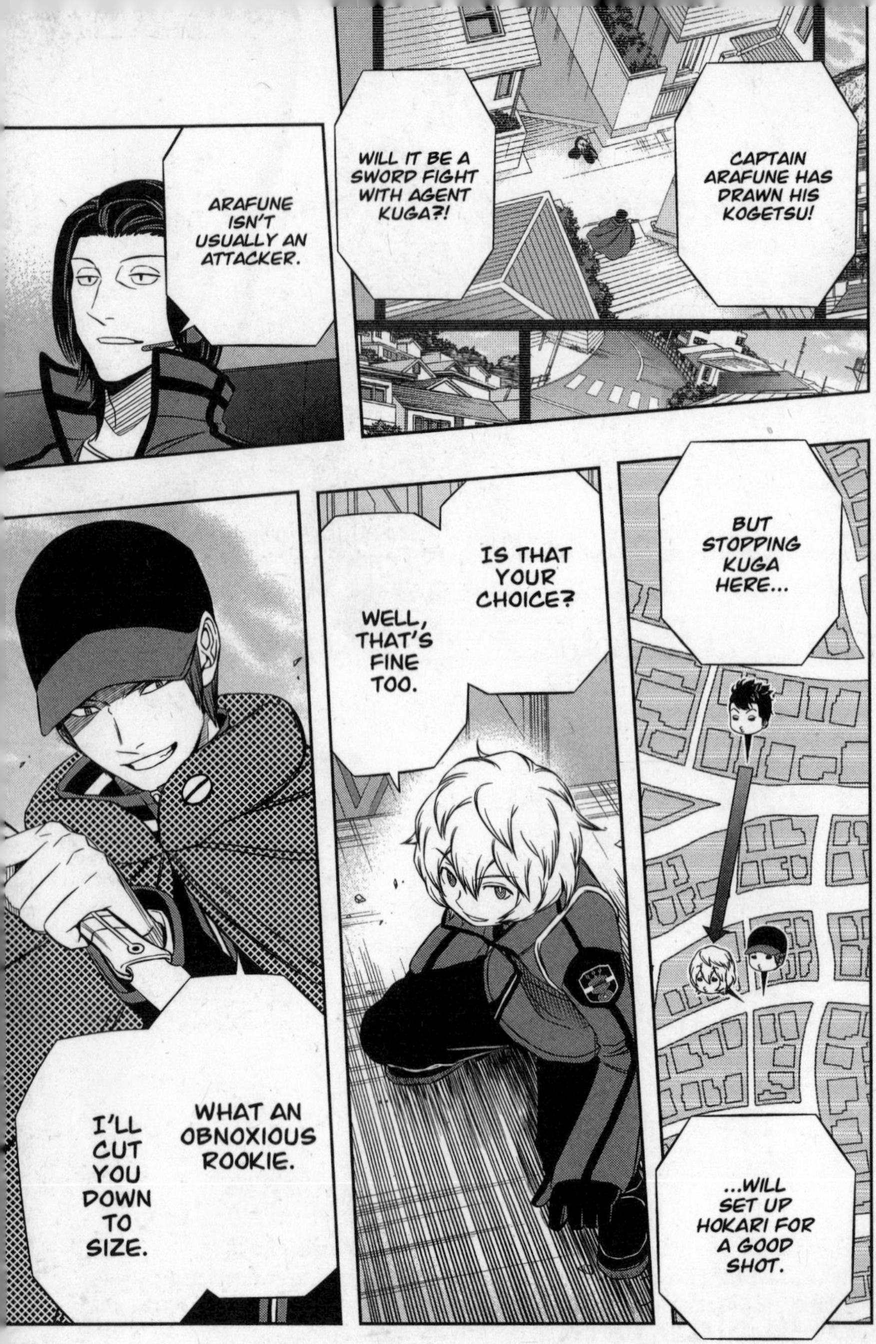
CAPTAIN ARAFUNE HAS DRAWN HIS KOGETSU!
WILL IT BE A SWORD FIGHT WITH AGENT KUGA?!
ARAFUNE ISN'T USUALLY AN ATTACKER.
BUT STOPPING KUGA HERE...
...WILL SET UP HOKARI FOR A GOOD SHOT.
IS THAT YOUR CHOICE?
WELL, THAT'S FINE TOO.
WHAT AN OBNOXIOUS ROOKIE.
I'LL CUT YOU DOWN TO SIZE.

Hokkaido

Osamu getting close to a brown bear for some reason.

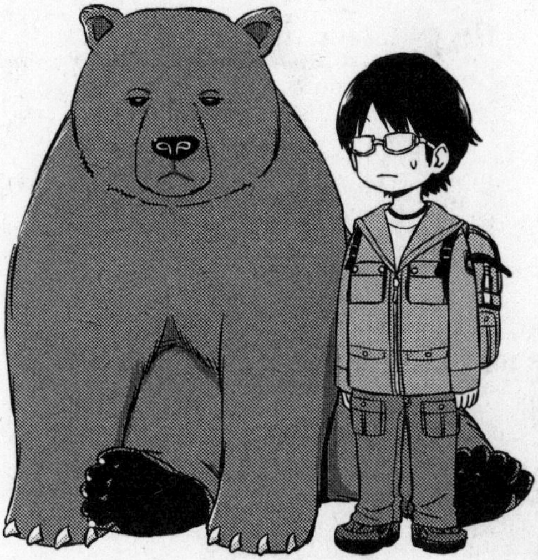

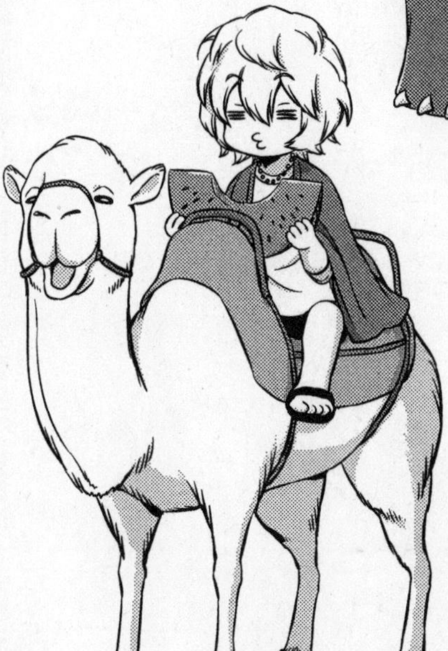

Tottori Prefecture

Yuma the camel rider (with watermelon).

■ 2015 *Weekly Shonen Jump* 22–23 Issue special

This was a part of a map of Japan with characters showcasing the local specialties of each of the 47 prefectures. I was so busy that I had my manager do the coloring...but I treated him to BBQ the other day. So we're even now, right?

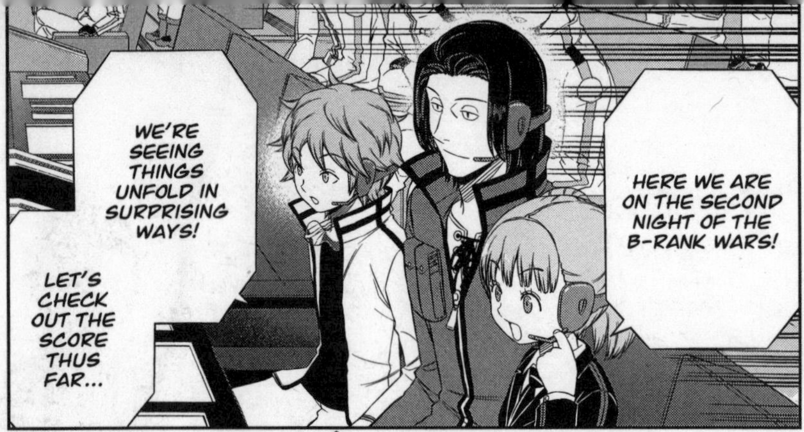
HERE WE ARE ON THE SECOND NIGHT OF THE B-RANK WARS!
WE'RE SEEING THINGS UNFOLD IN SURPRISING WAYS!
LET'S CHECK OUT THE SCORE THUS FAR...

Chapter 90 Tamakoma-2: Part 5

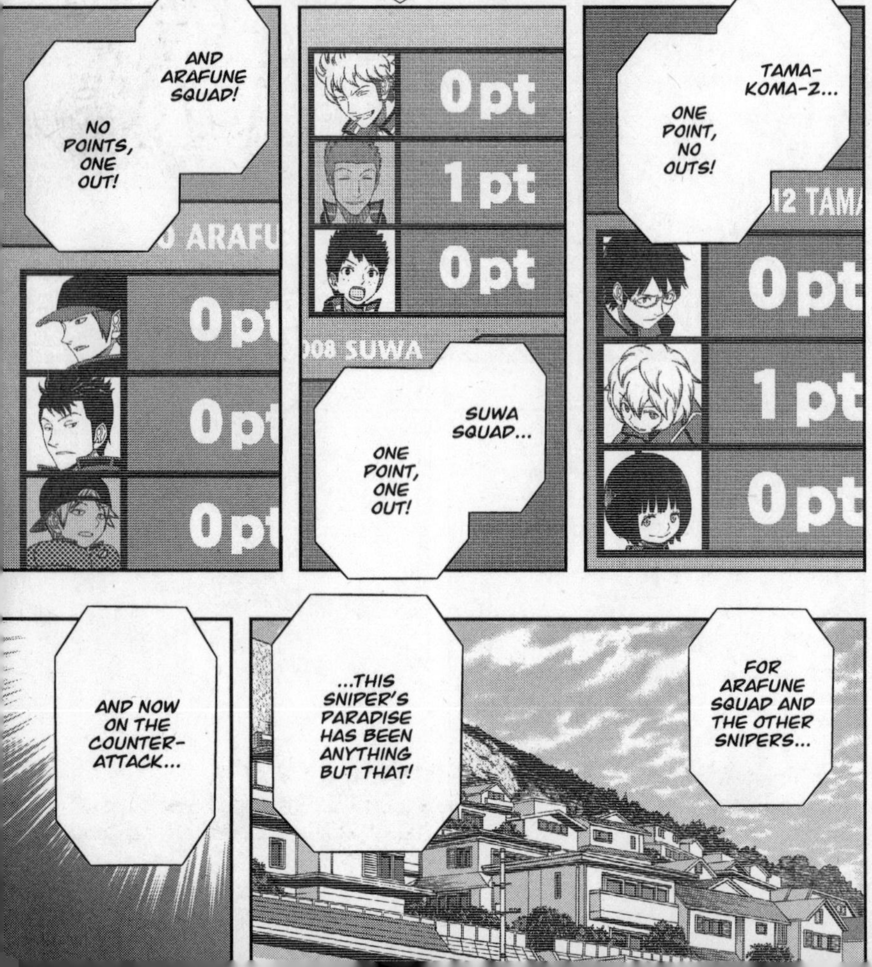
TAMA-KOMA-2...
ONE POINT, NO OUTS!
0pt
1pt
0pt
0pt
1pt
0pt
008 SUWA
SUWA SQUAD...
ONE POINT, ONE OUT!
AND ARAFUNE SQUAD!
NO POINTS, ONE OUT!
0pt
0pt
0pt
FOR ARAFUNE SQUAD AND THE OTHER SNIPERS...
...THIS SNIPER'S PARADISE HAS BEEN ANYTHING BUT THAT!
AND NOW ON THE COUNTER-ATTACK...

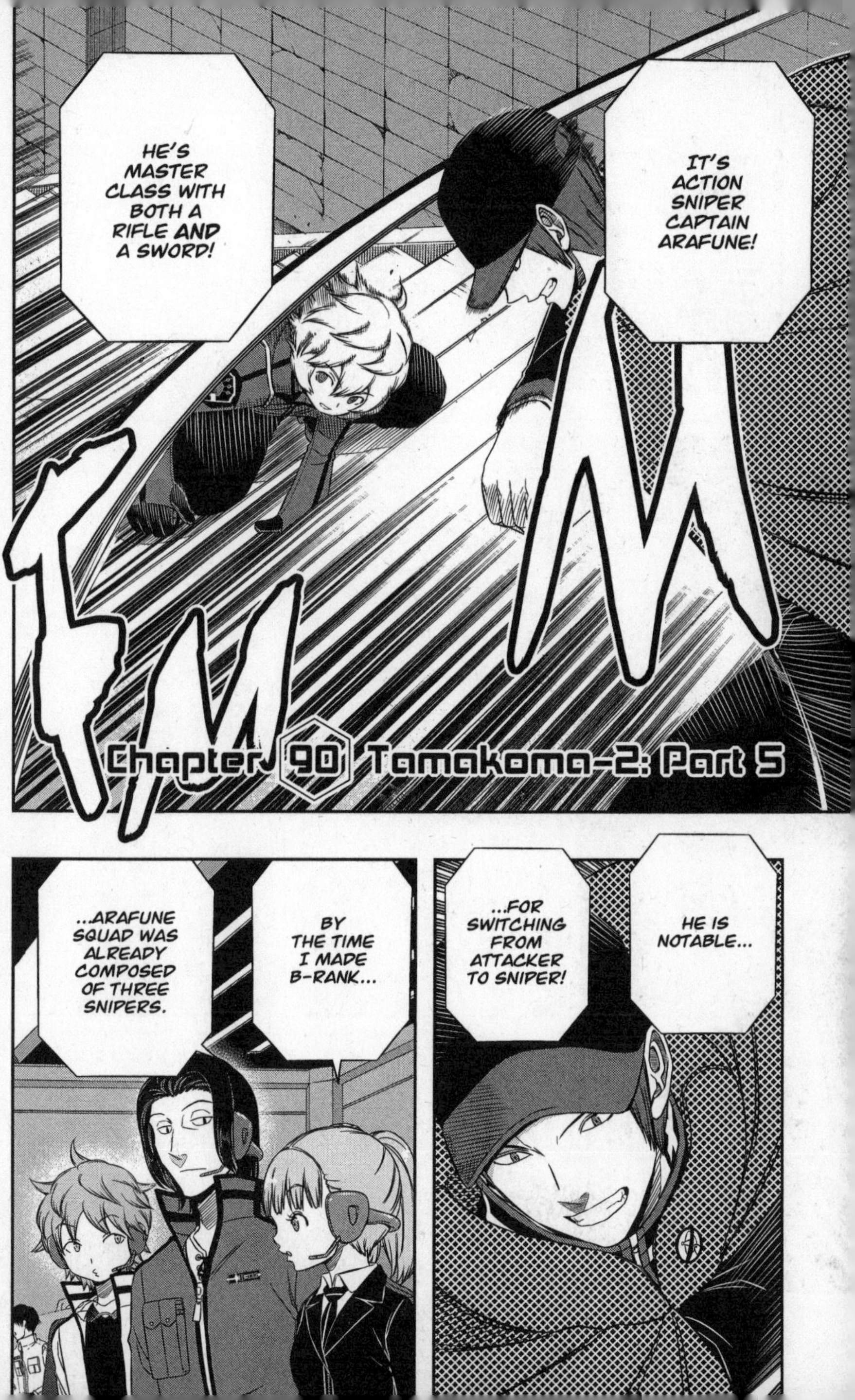
IT'S ACTION SNIPER CAPTAIN ARAFUNE!
HE'S MASTER CLASS WITH BOTH A RIFLE AND A SWORD!
Chapter 90 Tamakoma-2: Part 5
HE IS NOTABLE...
...FOR SWITCHING FROM ATTACKER TO SNIPER!
BY THE TIME I MADE B-RANK...
...ARAFUNE SQUAD WAS ALREADY COMPOSED OF THREE SNIPERS.

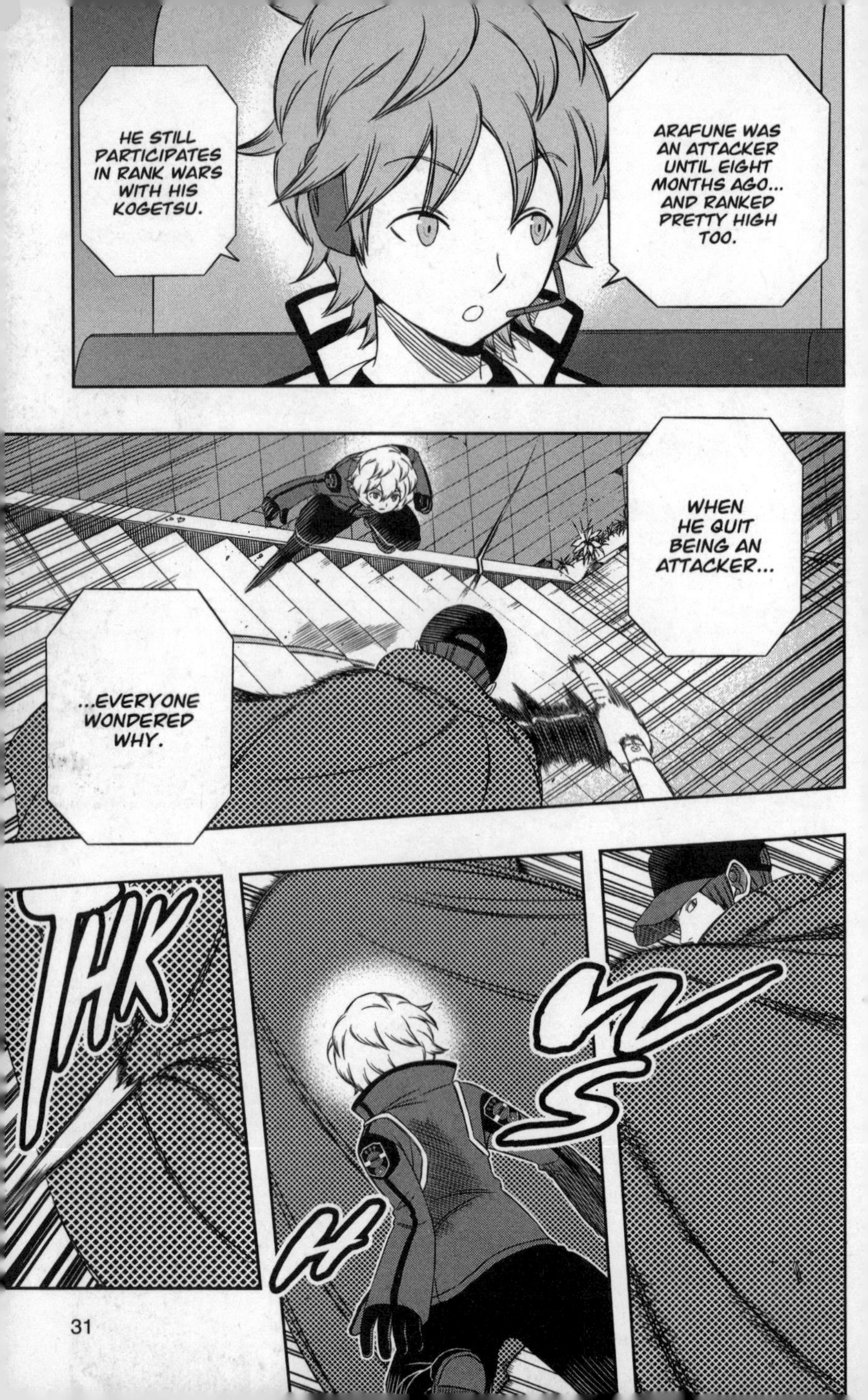
ARAFUNE WAS AN ATTACKER UNTIL EIGHT MONTHS AGO... AND RANKED PRETTY HIGH TOO.
HE STILL PARTICIPATES IN RANK WARS WITH HIS KOGETSU.
WHEN HE QUIT BEING AN ATTACKER...
...EVERYONE WONDERED WHY.
WSH
THK

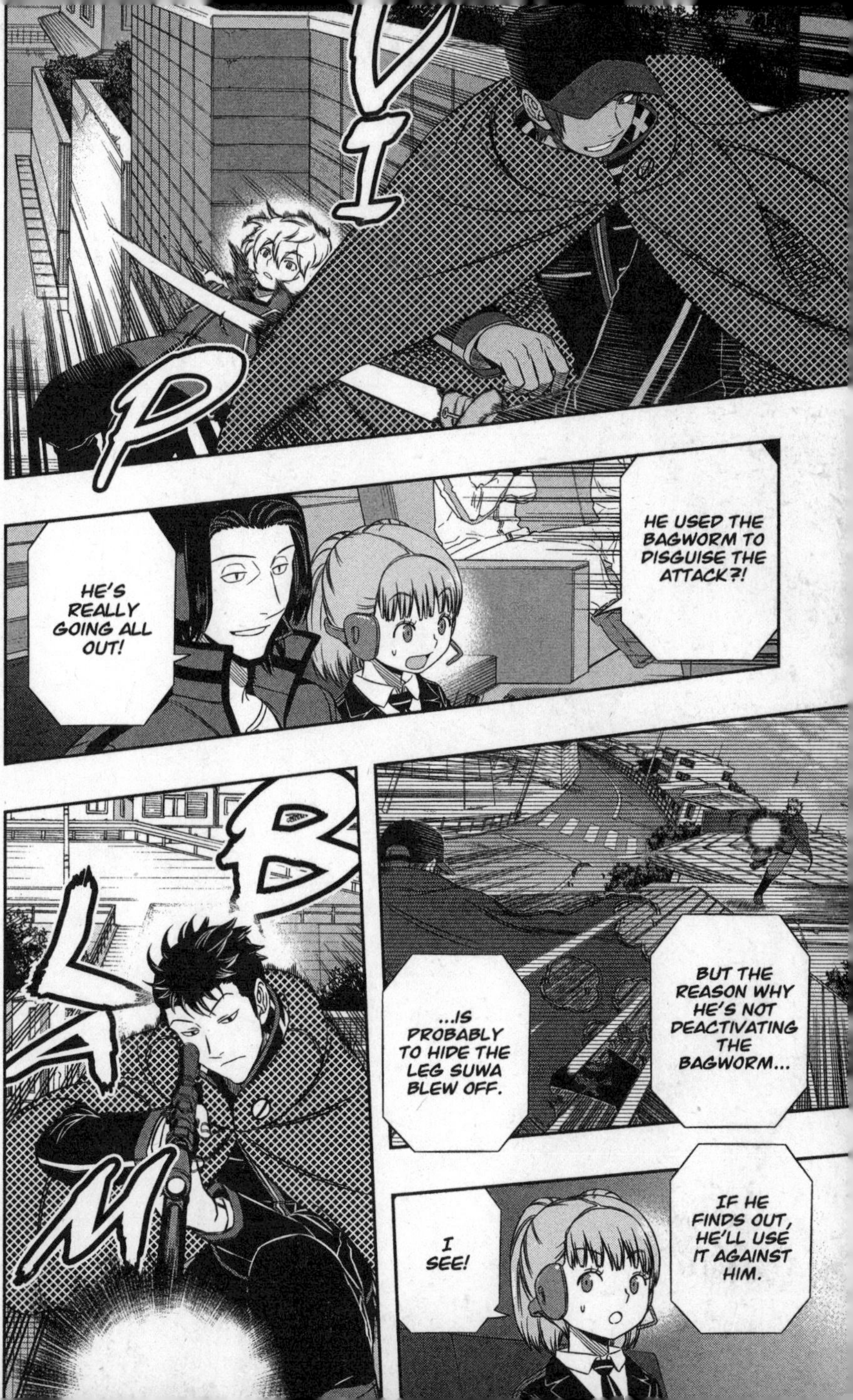
HE USED THE BAGWORM TO DISGUISE THE ATTACK?!
HE'S REALLY GOING ALL OUT!
BUT THE REASON WHY HE'S NOT DEACTIVATING THE BAGWORM...
...IS PROBABLY TO HIDE THE LEG SUWA BLEW OFF.
IF HE FINDS OUT, HE'LL USE IT AGAINST HIM.
I SEE!

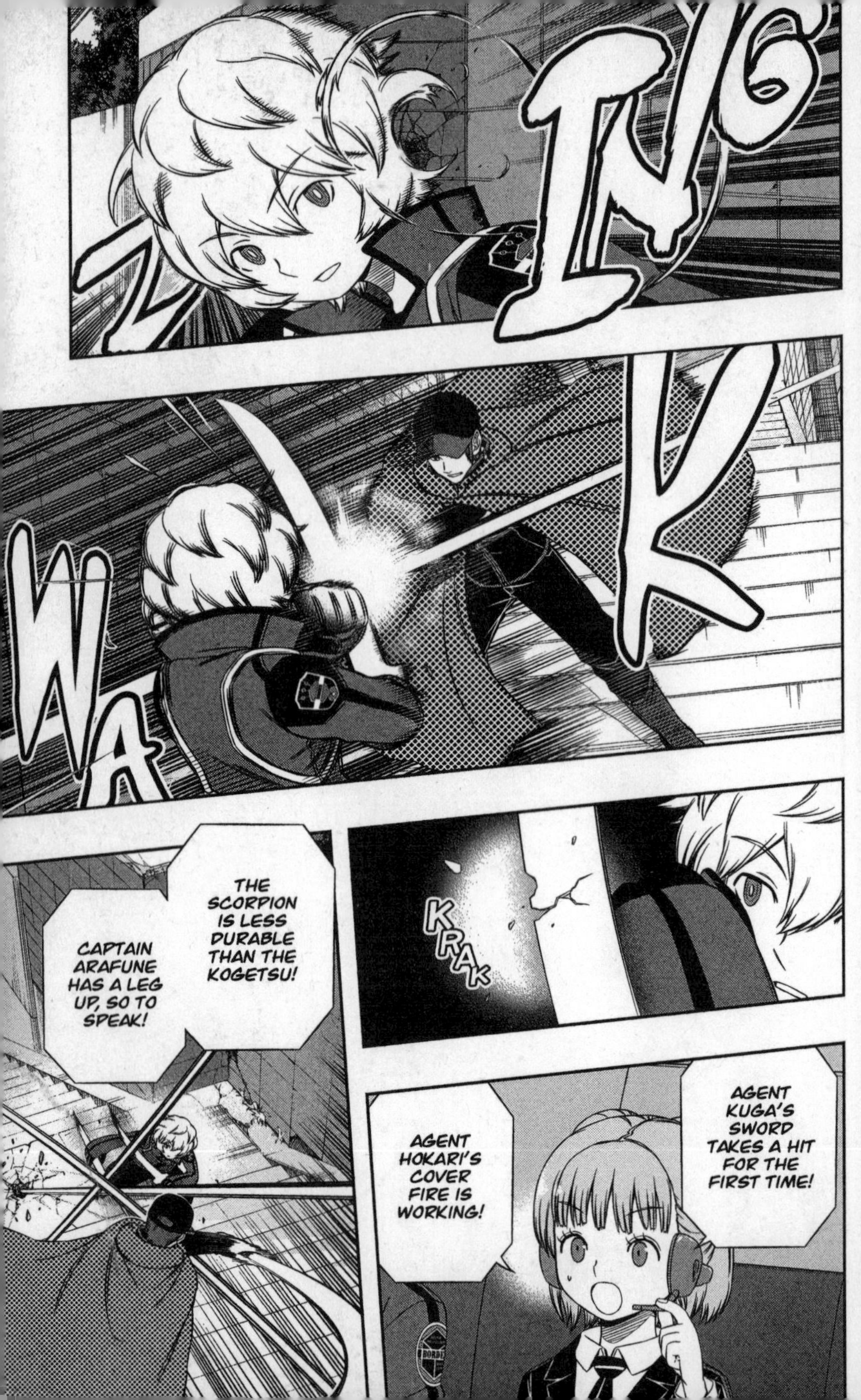
ZING
WAK
KRAK
THE SCORPION IS LESS DURABLE THAN THE KOGETSU!
CAPTAIN ARAFUNE HAS A LEG UP, SO TO SPEAK!
AGENT KUGA'S SWORD TAKES A HIT FOR THE FIRST TIME!
AGENT HOKARI'S COVER FIRE IS WORKING!

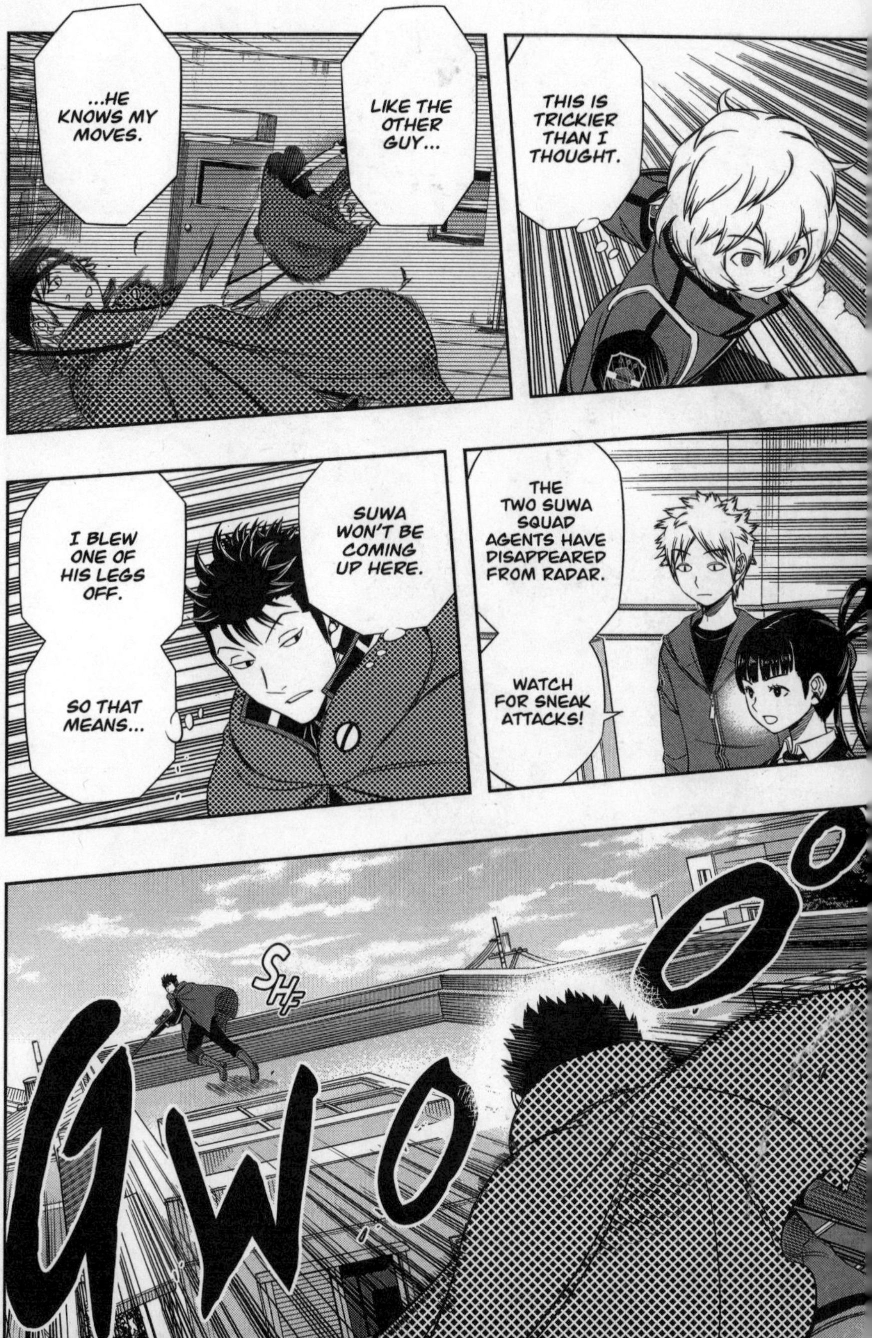
THIS IS TRICKIER THAN I THOUGHT.
LIKE THE OTHER GUY...
...HE KNOWS MY MOVES.
THE TWO SUWA SQUAD AGENTS HAVE DISAPPEARED FROM RADAR.
WATCH FOR SNEAK ATTACKS!
SUWA WON'T BE COMING UP HERE.
I BLEW ONE OF HIS LEGS OFF.
SO THAT MEANS...
SHF
GWOOOO

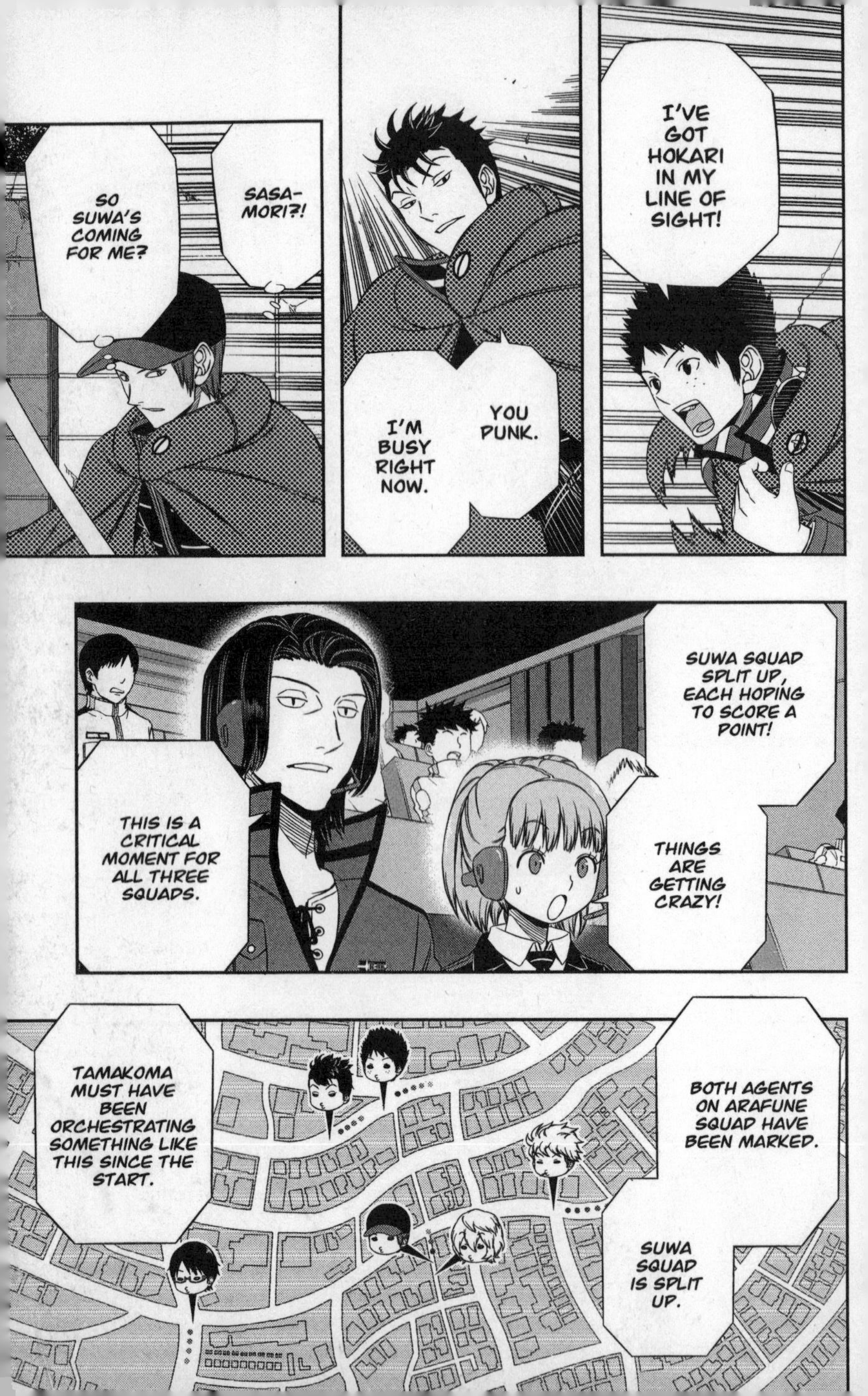
I'VE GOT HOKARI IN MY LINE OF SIGHT!
YOU PUNK.
I'M BUSY RIGHT NOW.
SASAMORI?!
SO SUWA'S COMING FOR ME?
SUWA SQUAD SPLIT UP, EACH HOPING TO SCORE A POINT!
THINGS ARE GETTING CRAZY!
THIS IS A CRITICAL MOMENT FOR ALL THREE SQUADS.
BOTH AGENTS ON ARAFUNE SQUAD HAVE BEEN MARKED.
SUWA SQUAD IS SPLIT UP.
TAMAKOMA MUST HAVE BEEN ORCHESTRATING SOMETHING LIKE THIS SINCE THE START.

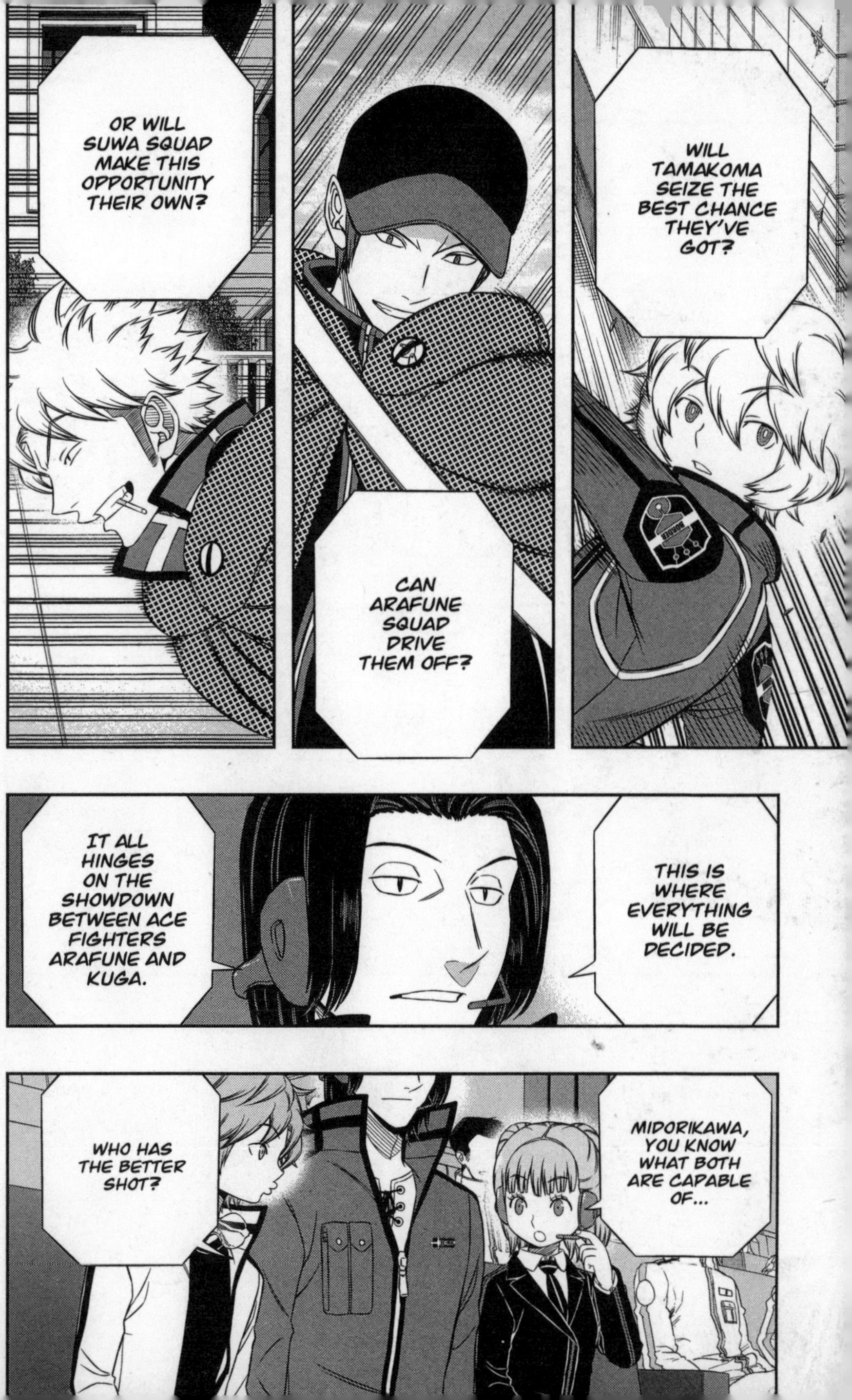

WILL TAMAKOMA SEIZE THE BEST CHANCE THEY'VE GOT?
CAN ARAFUNE SQUAD DRIVE THEM OFF?
OR WILL SUWA SQUAD MAKE THIS OPPORTUNITY THEIR OWN?
THIS IS WHERE EVERYTHING WILL BE DECIDED.
IT ALL HINGES ON THE SHOWDOWN BETWEEN ACE FIGHTERS ARAFUNE AND KUGA.
MIDORIKAWA, YOU KNOW WHAT BOTH ARE CAPABLE OF...
WHO HAS THE BETTER SHOT?

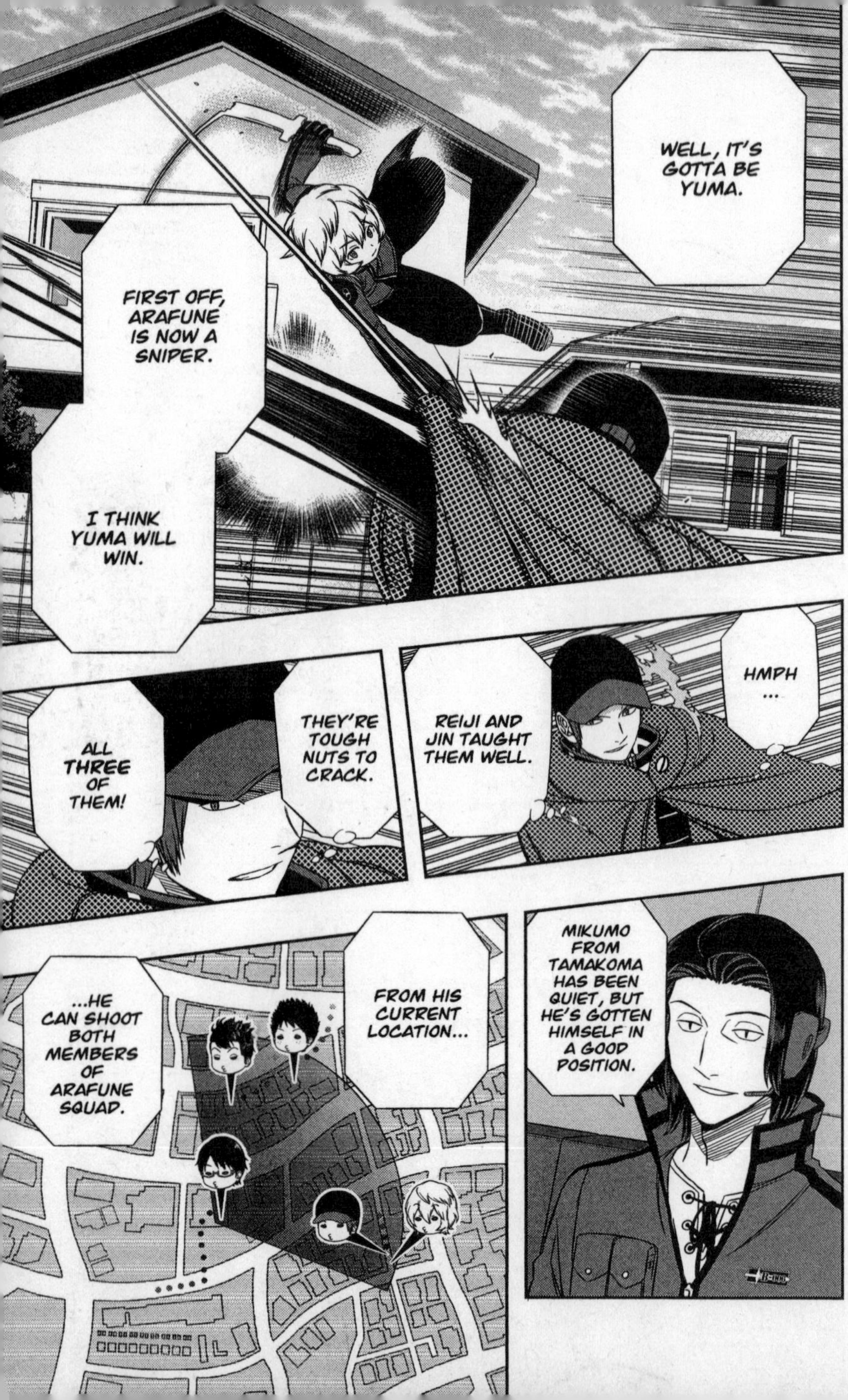
WELL, IT'S GOTTA BE YUMA.
FIRST OFF, ARAFUNE IS NOW A SNIPER.
I THINK YUMA WILL WIN.
HMPH ...
REIJI AND JIN TAUGHT THEM WELL.
THEY'RE TOUGH NUTS TO CRACK.
ALL THREE OF THEM!
MIKUMO FROM TAMAKOMA HAS BEEN QUIET, BUT HE'S GOTTEN HIMSELF IN A GOOD POSITION.
FROM HIS CURRENT LOCATION...
...HE CAN SHOOT BOTH MEMBERS OF ARAFUNE SQUAD.

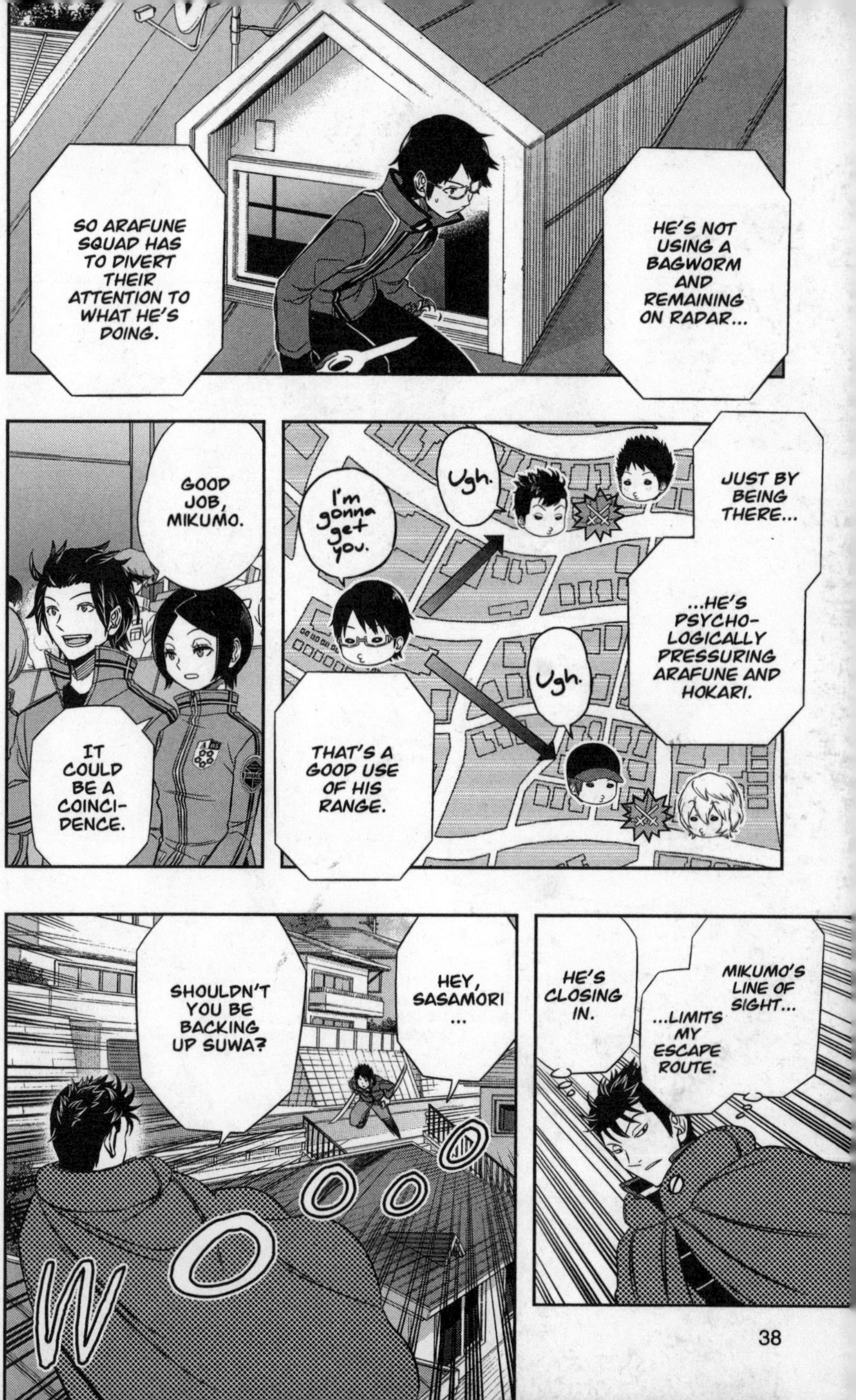
HE'S NOT USING A BAGWORM AND REMAINING ON RADAR...
SO ARAFUNE SQUAD HAS TO DIVERT THEIR ATTENTION TO WHAT HE'S DOING.
JUST BY BEING THERE...
Ugh.
I'm gonna get you.
...HE'S PSYCHOLOGICALLY PRESSURING ARAFUNE AND HOKARI.
Ugh.
THAT'S A GOOD USE OF HIS RANGE.
GOOD JOB, MIKUMO.
IT COULD BE A COINCIDENCE.
MIKUMO'S LINE OF SIGHT...
...LIMITS MY ESCAPE ROUTE.
HE'S CLOSING IN.
HEY, SASAMORI...
SHOULDN'T YOU BE BACKING UP SUWA?
WOOOO

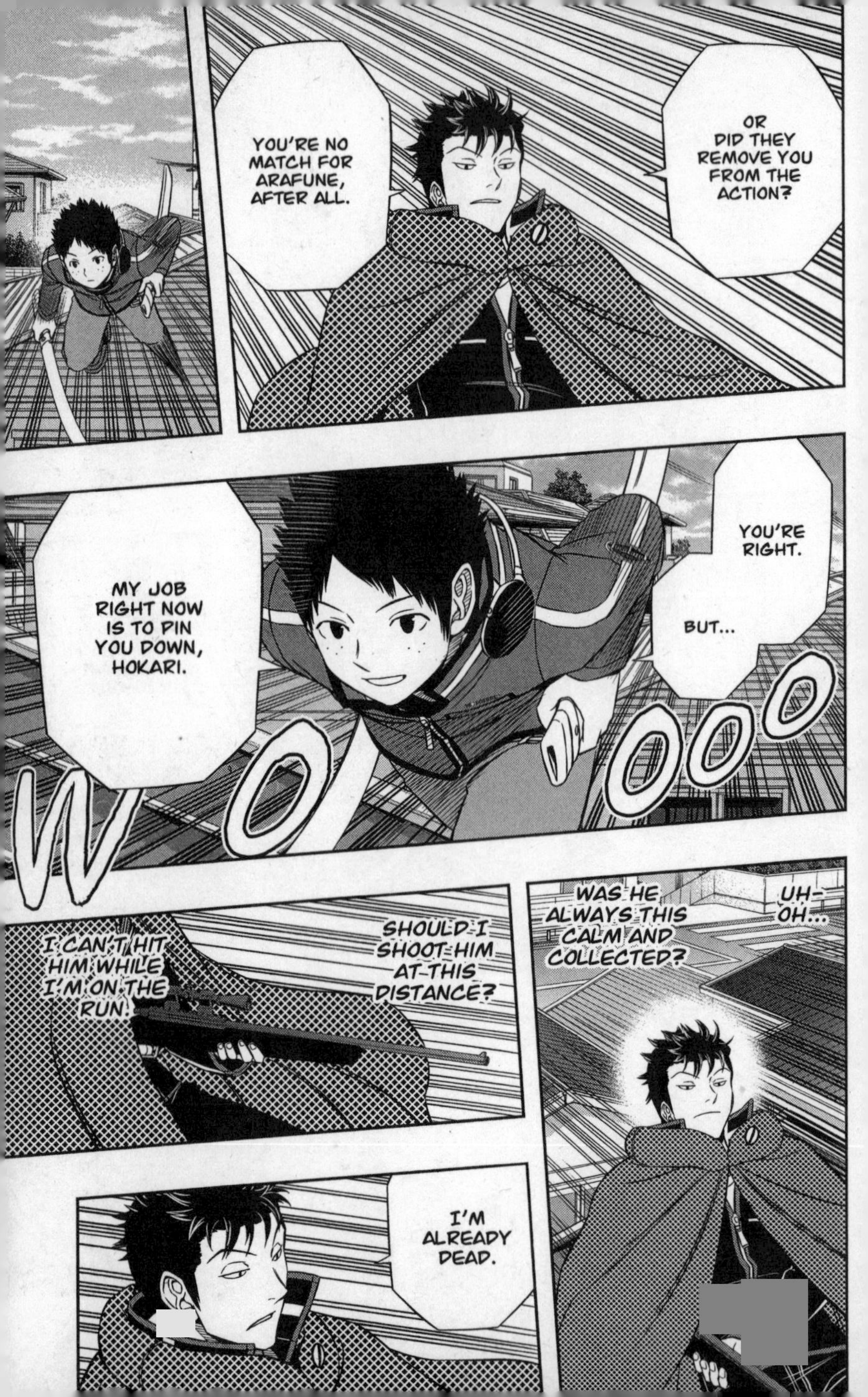
YOU'RE NO MATCH FOR ARAFUNE, AFTER ALL.
OR DID THEY REMOVE YOU FROM THE ACTION?
YOU'RE RIGHT.
BUT...
MY JOB RIGHT NOW IS TO PIN YOU DOWN, HOKARI.
WOOOOO
UH-OH...
WAS HE ALWAYS THIS CALM AND COLLECTED?
SHOULD I SHOOT HIM AT THIS DISTANCE?
I CAN'T HIT HIM WHILE I'M ON THE RUN.
I'M ALREADY DEAD.

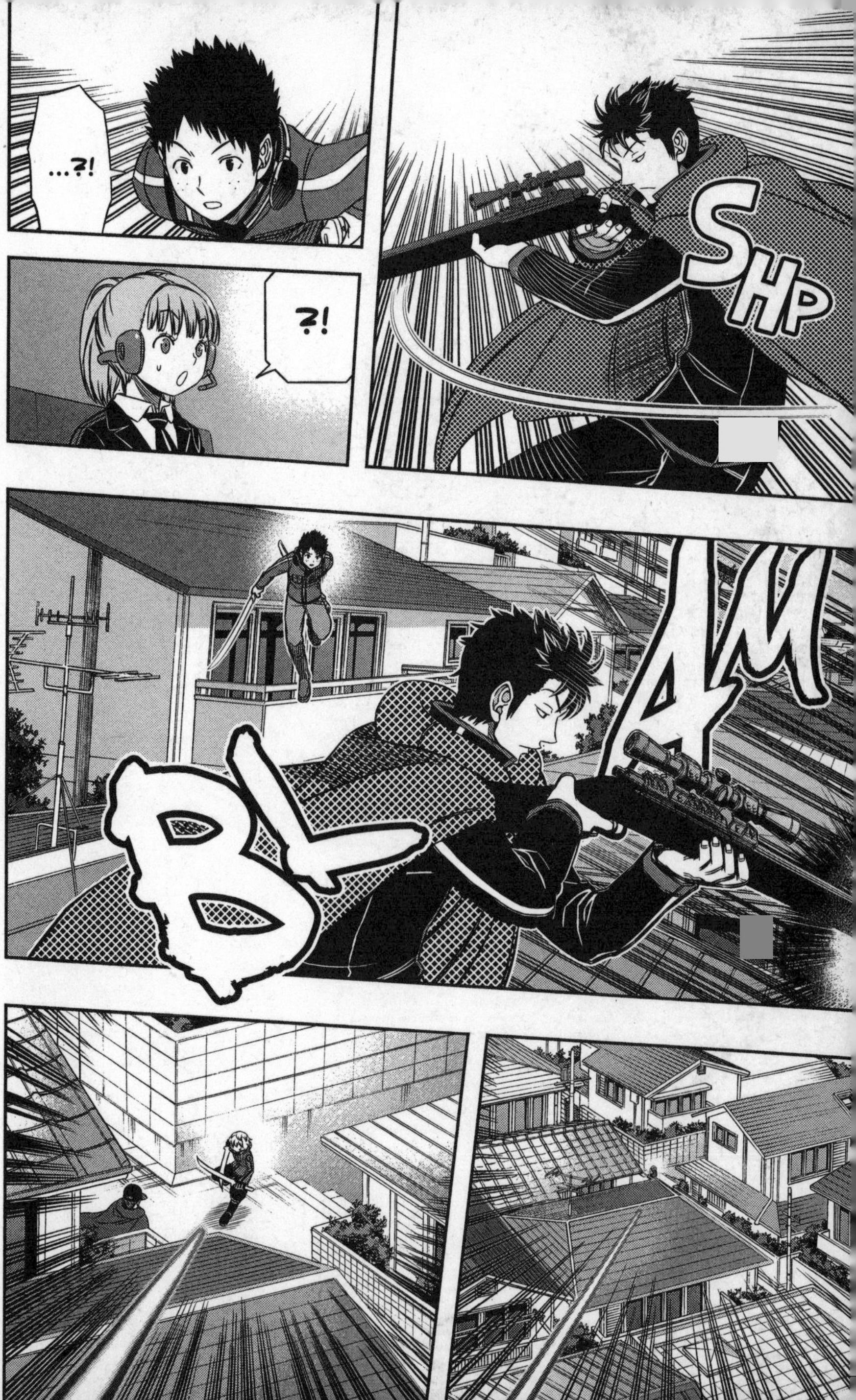
SHP
...?!
?!
BLAM

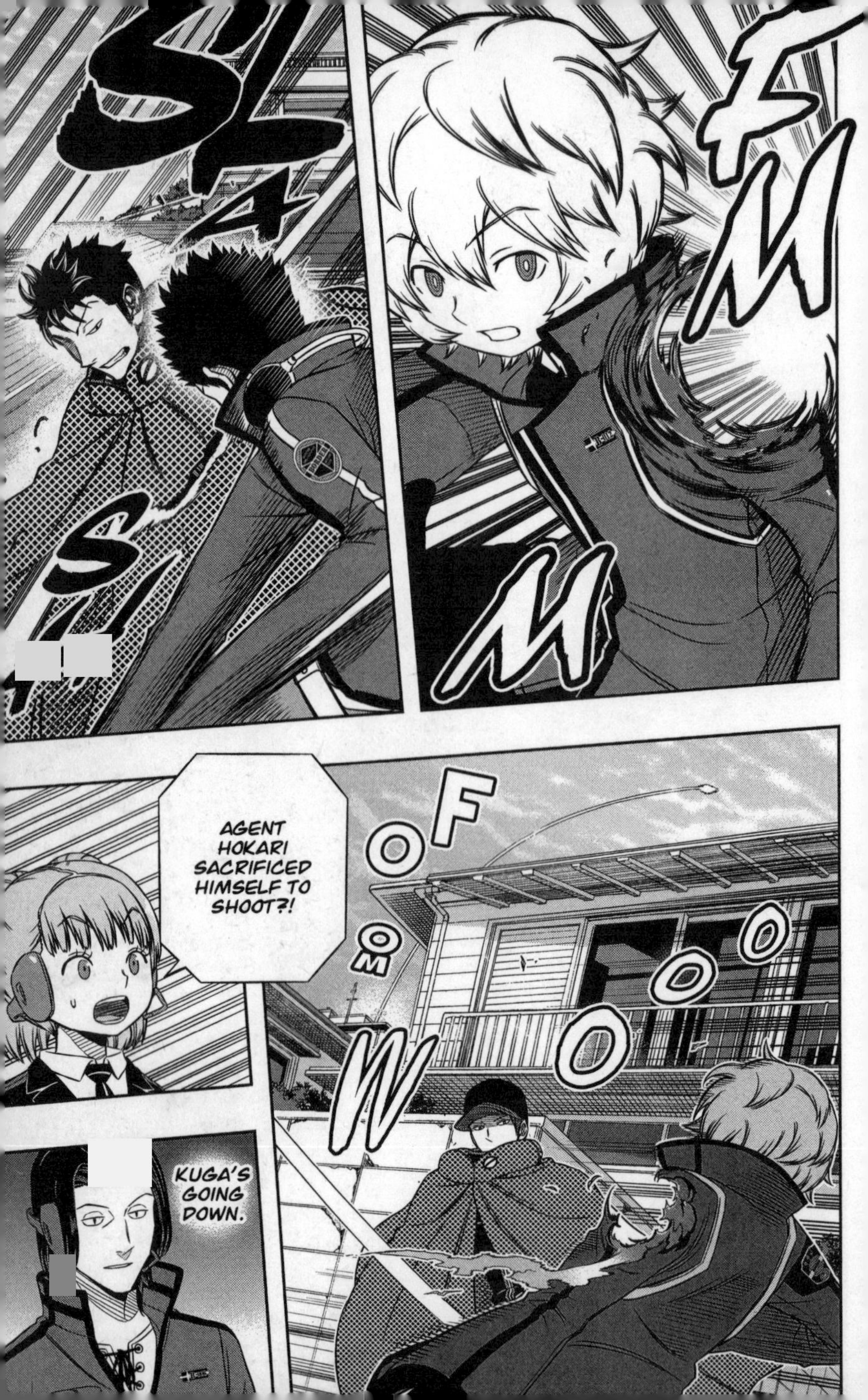
AGENT HOKARI SACRIFICED HIMSELF TO SHOOT?!
KUGA'S GOING DOWN.

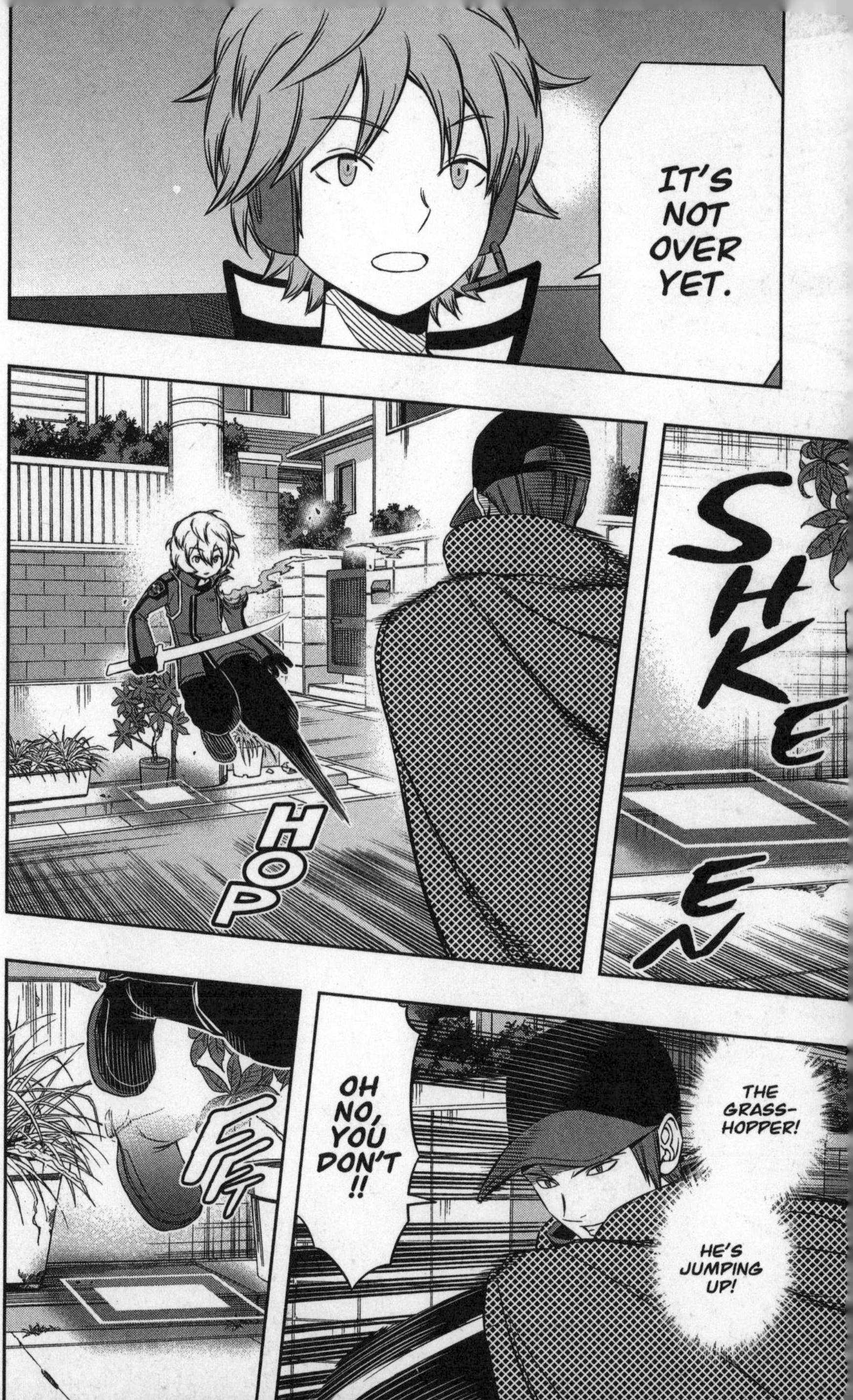
IT'S NOT OVER YET.
SHKEEN
HOP
THE GRASS-HOPPER!
HE'S JUMPING UP!
OH NO, YOU DON'T!!

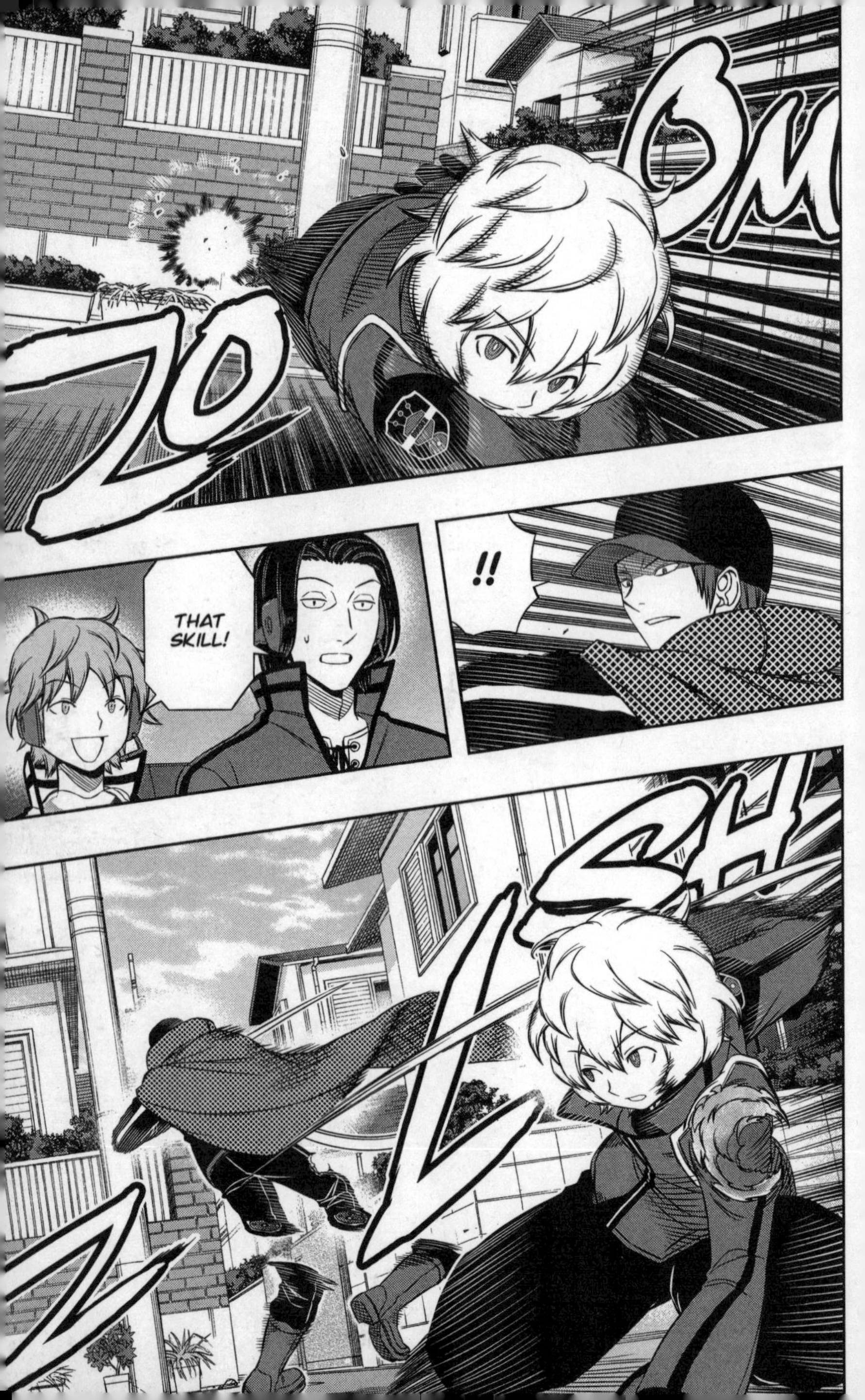
ZOOM
!!
THAT SKILL!

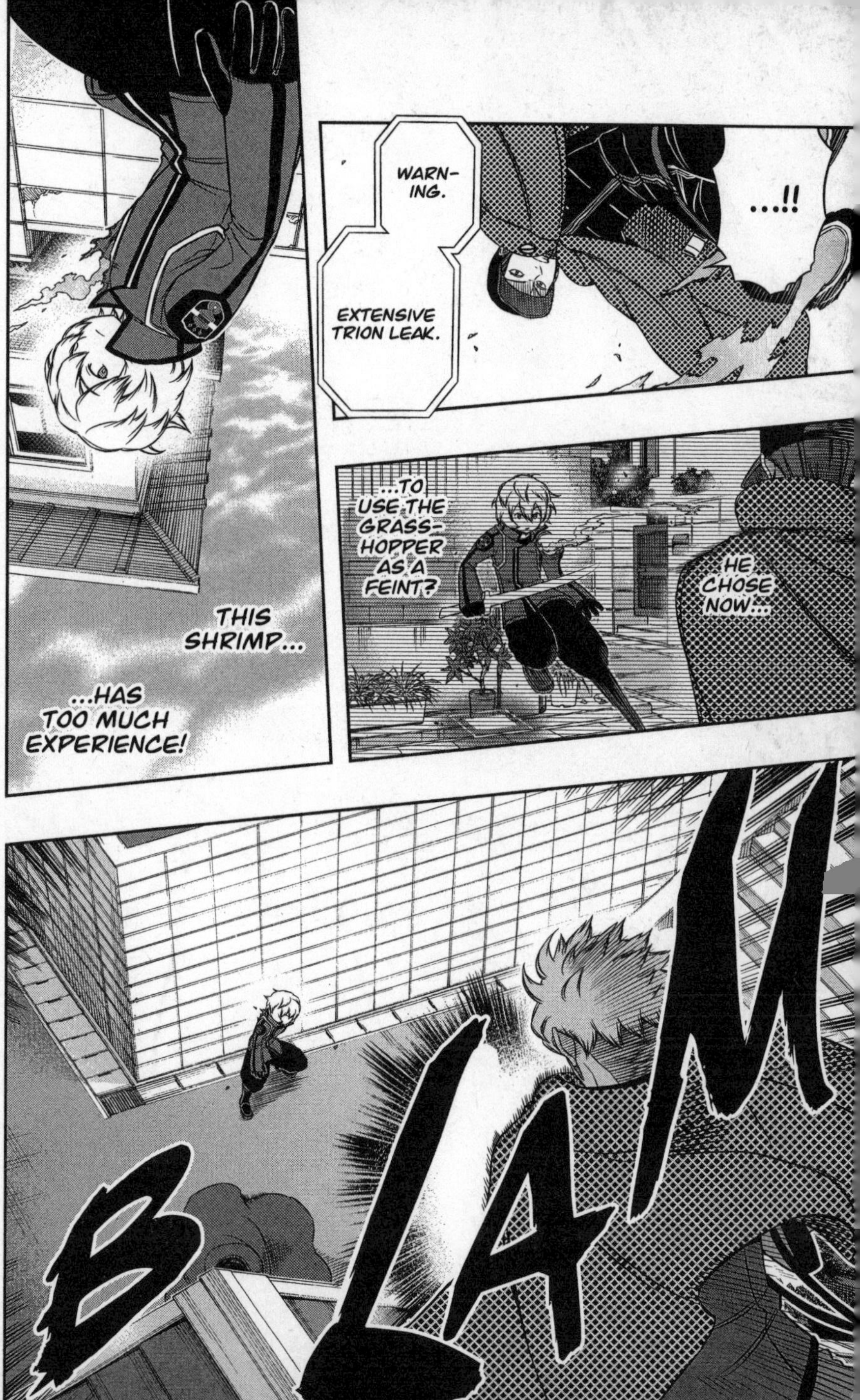
...!!
WARNING.
EXTENSIVE TRION LEAK.
HE CHOSE NOW...
...TO USE THE GRASSHOPPER AS A FEINT?
THIS SHRIMP...
...HAS TOO MUCH EXPERIENCE!
BLAM

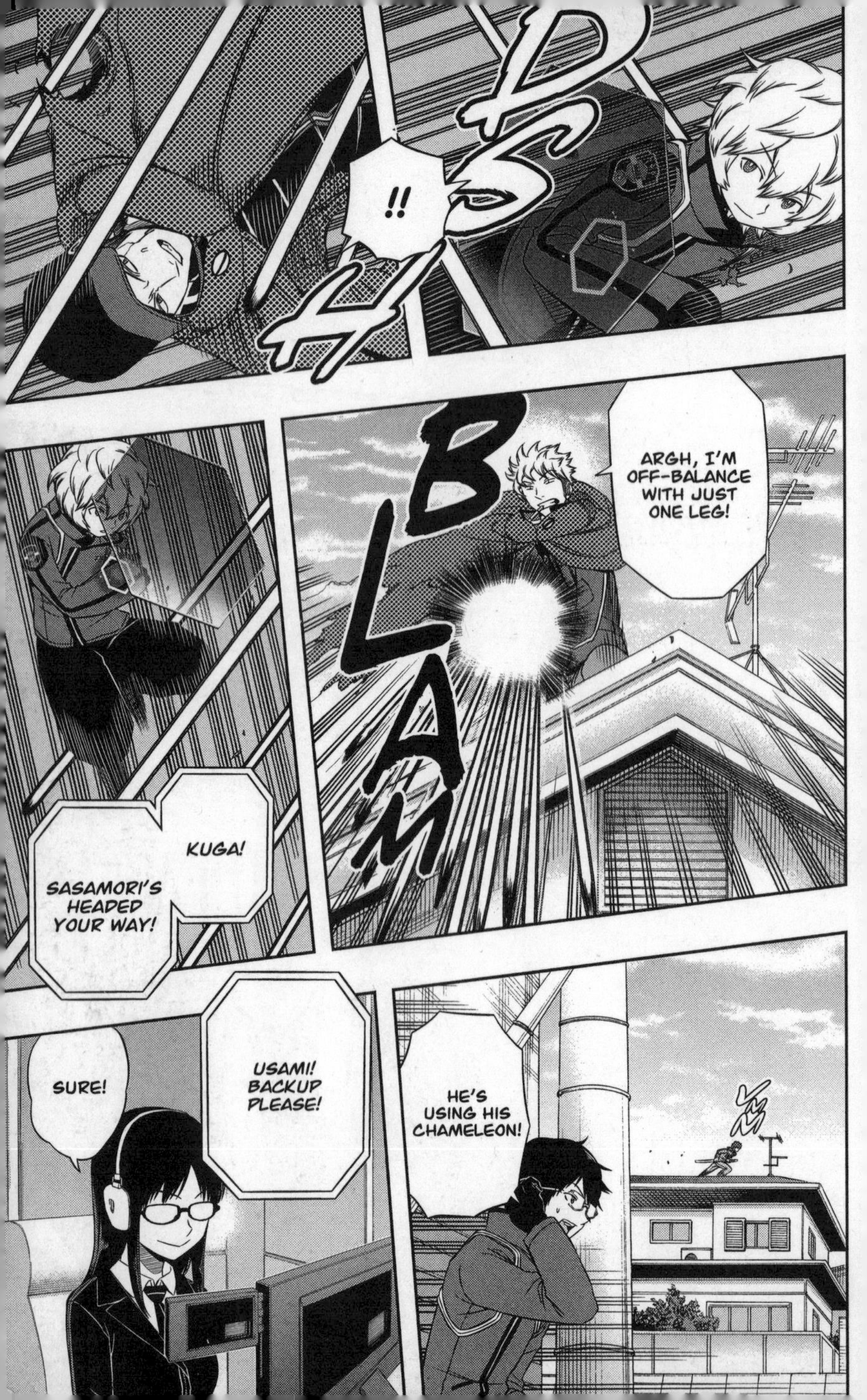
DASH
!!
BLAM
ARGH, I'M OFF-BALANCE WITH JUST ONE LEG!
KUGA!
SASAMORI'S HEADED YOUR WAY!
HE'S USING HIS CHAMELEON!
USAMI! BACKUP PLEASE!
SURE!

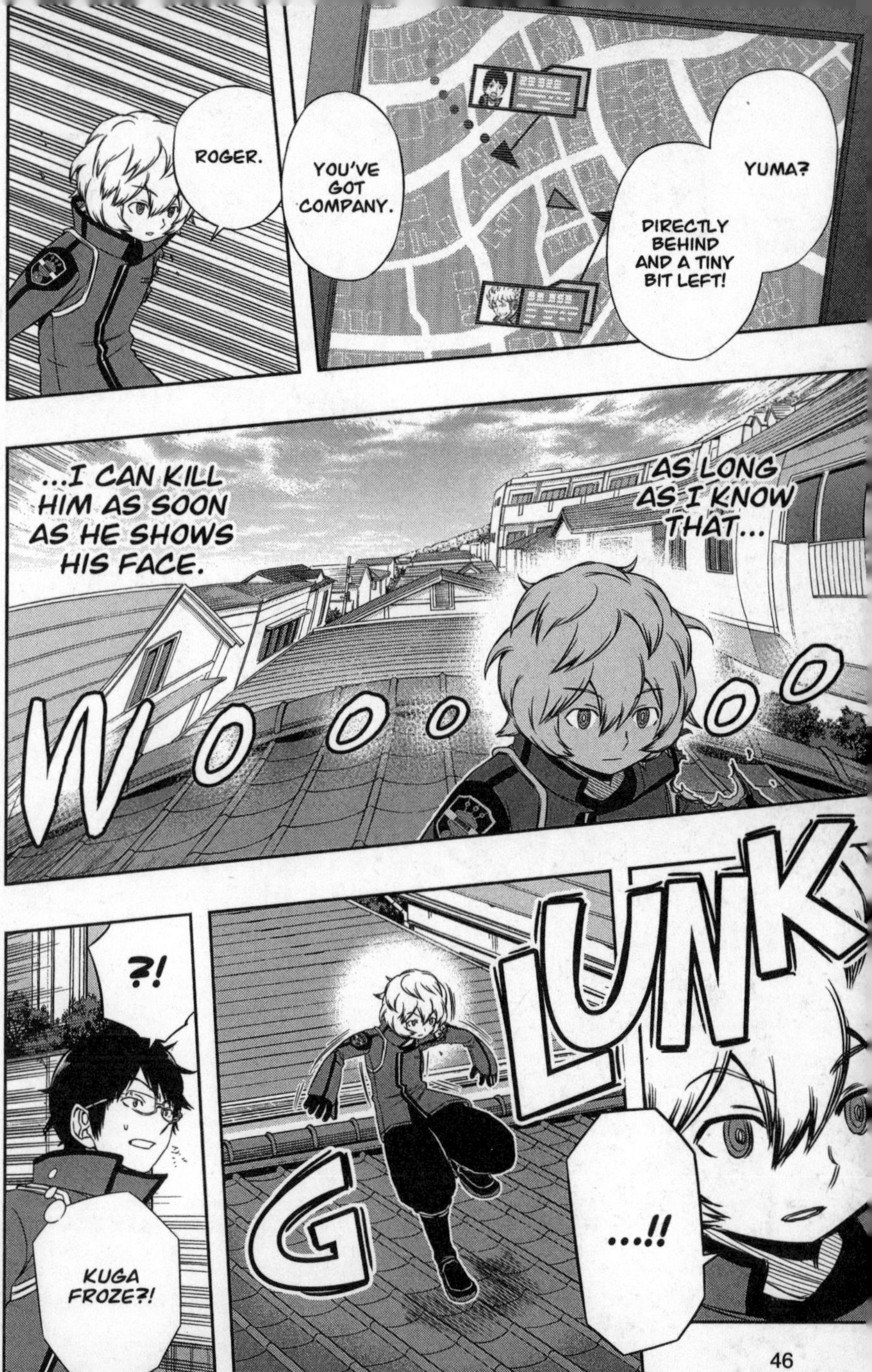
YUMA?
DIRECTLY BEHIND AND A TINY BIT LEFT!
YOU'VE GOT COMPANY.
ROGER.
AS LONG AS I KNOW THAT...
...I CAN KILL HIM AS SOON AS HE SHOWS HIS FACE.
WOOOOO
...!!
GLUNK
?!
KUGA FROZE?!

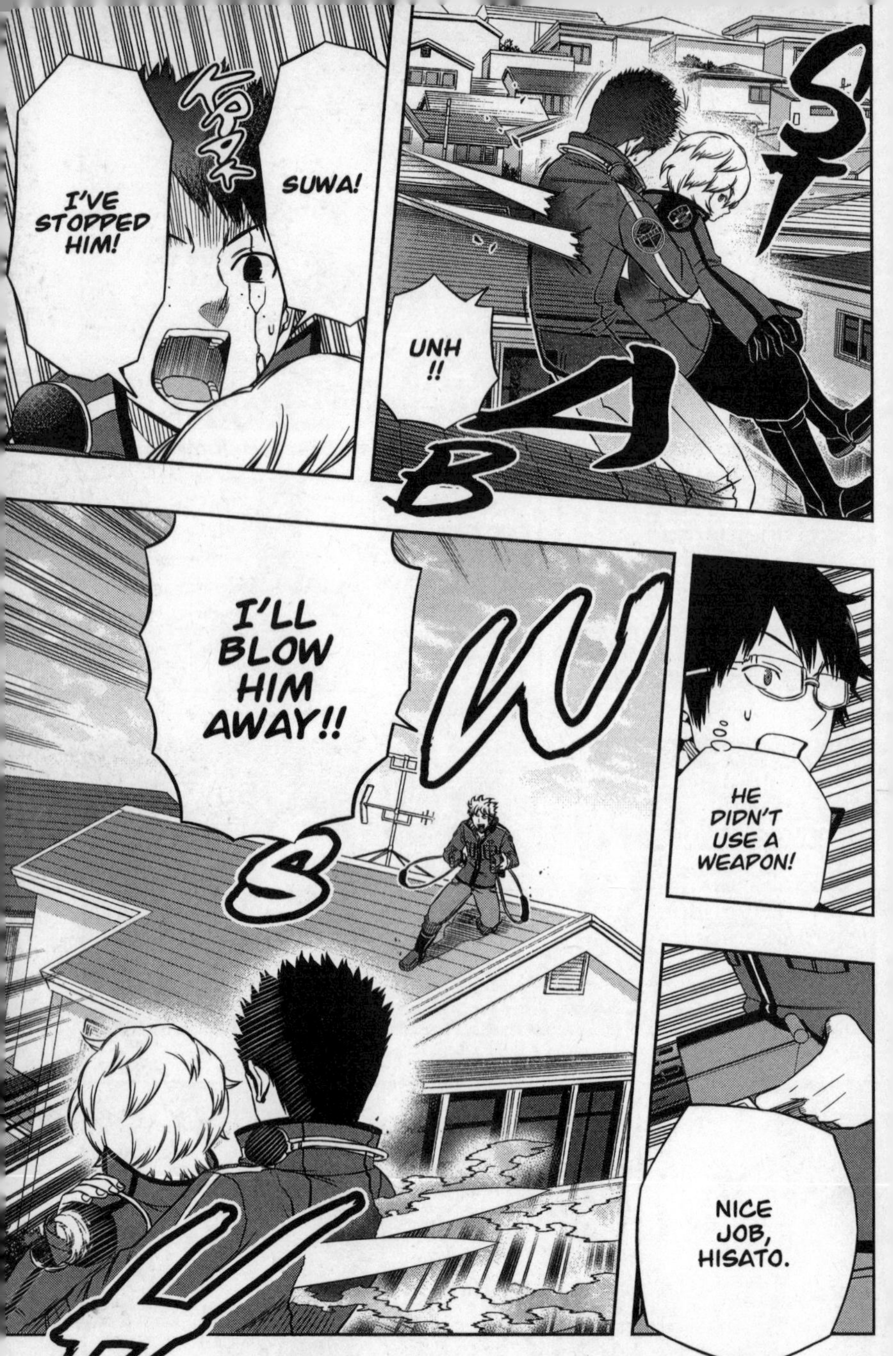
S
UNH!!
B
KRAK
SUWA!
I'VE STOPPED HIM!
HE DIDN'T USE A WEAPON!
NICE JOB, HISATO.
W
I'LL BLOW HIM AWAY!!
S
H

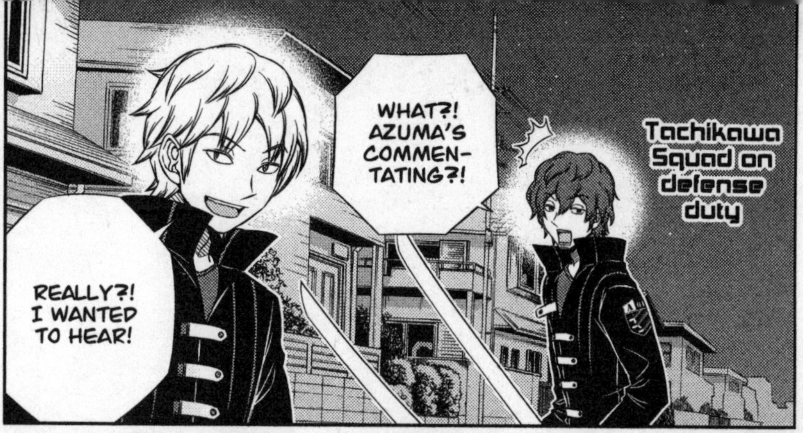
Tachikawa Squad on defense duty
WHAT?! AZUMA'S COMMENTATING?!
REALLY?! I WANTED TO HEAR!

Bonus page that ran in Issue 8 of *Shonen Jump* in 2015.

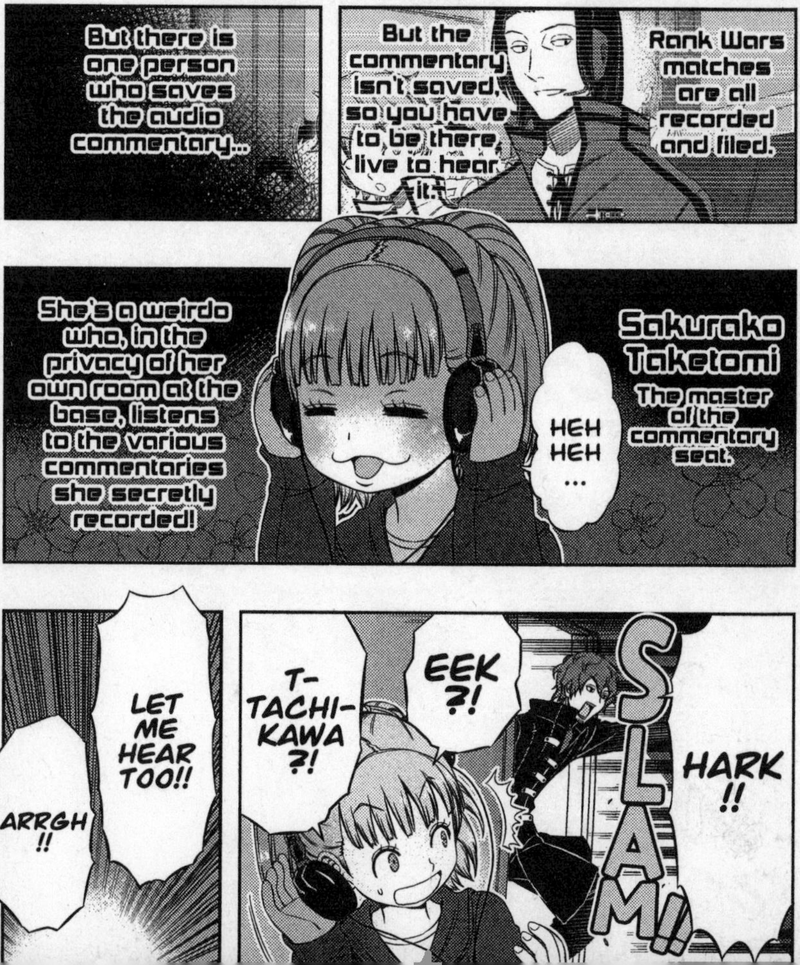
Rank Wars matches are all recorded and filed.
But the commentary isn't saved, so you have to be there live to hear it.
But there is one person who saves the audio commentary...
Sakurako Taketomi
The master of the commentary seat.
HEH HEH ...
She's a weirdo who, in the privacy of her own room at the base, listens to the various commentaries she secretly recorded!
SLAM!!
HARK !!
EEK ?!
T-TACHIKAWA ?!
LET ME HEAR TOO!!
ARRGH !!

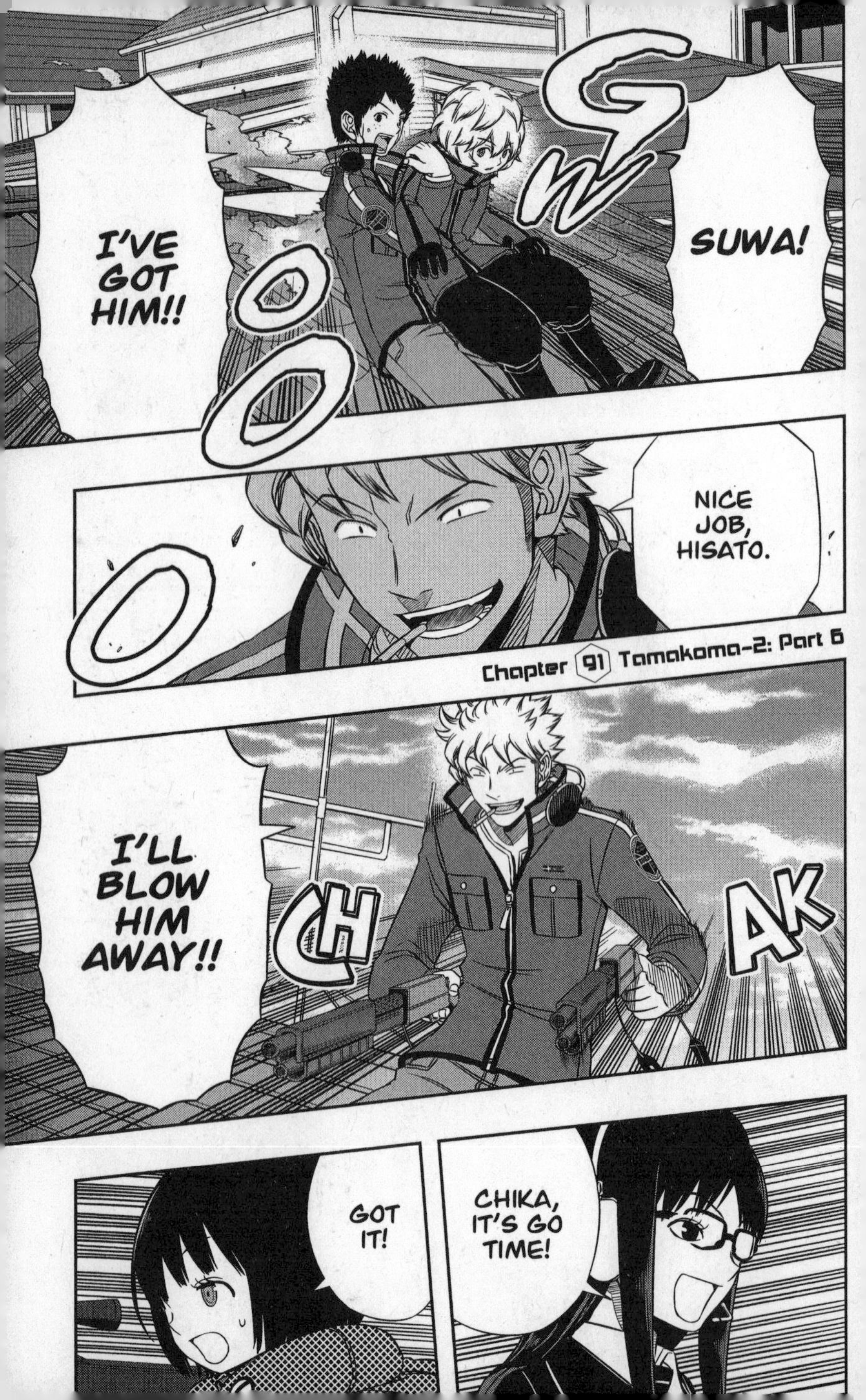
SUWA!
I'VE GOT HIM!!
NICE JOB, HISATO.
Chapter 91 Tamakoma-2: Part 6
CH
AK
I'LL BLOW HIM AWAY!!
CHIKA, IT'S GO TIME!
GOT IT!

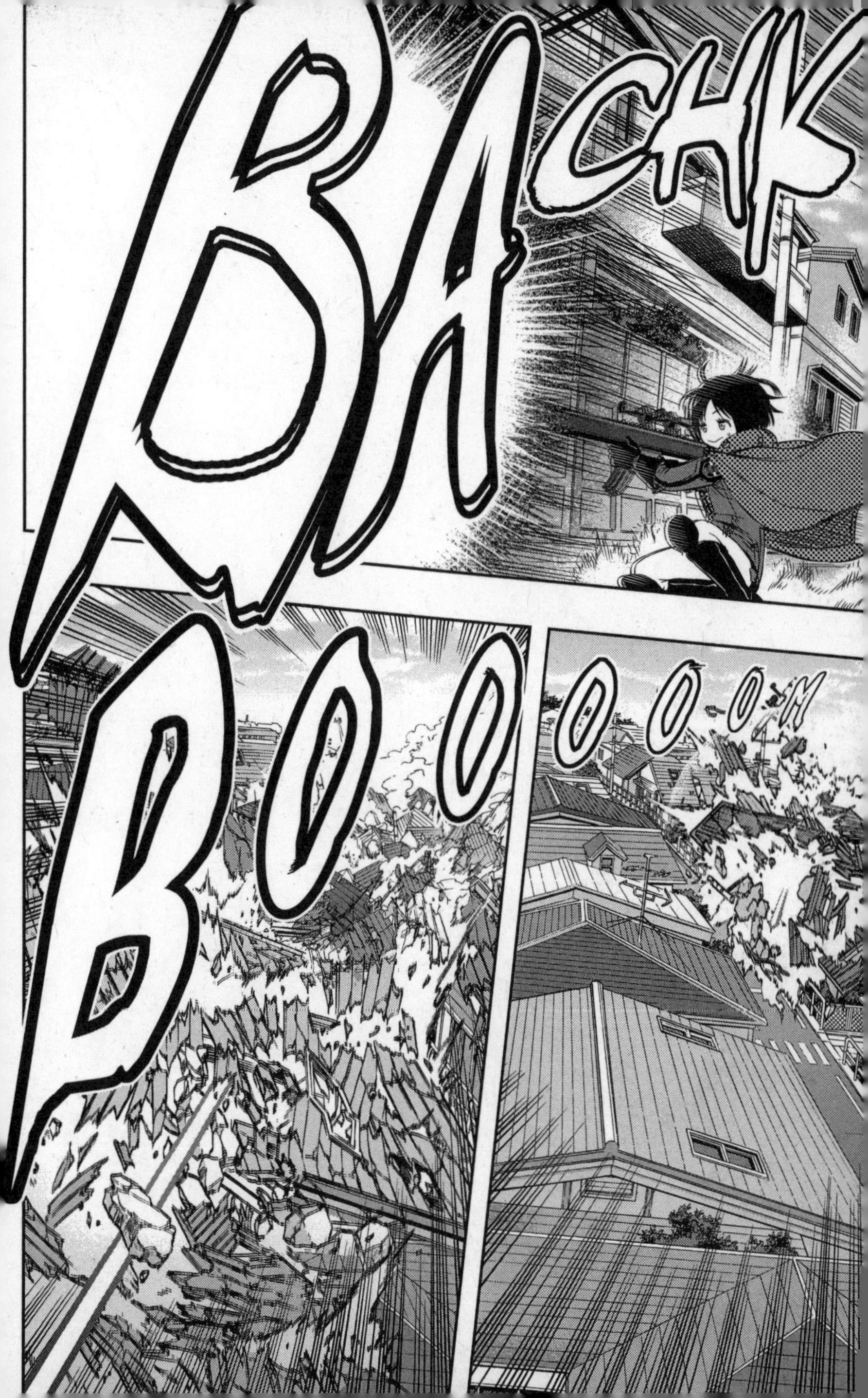
BRACHK
BOOOOO-OOM

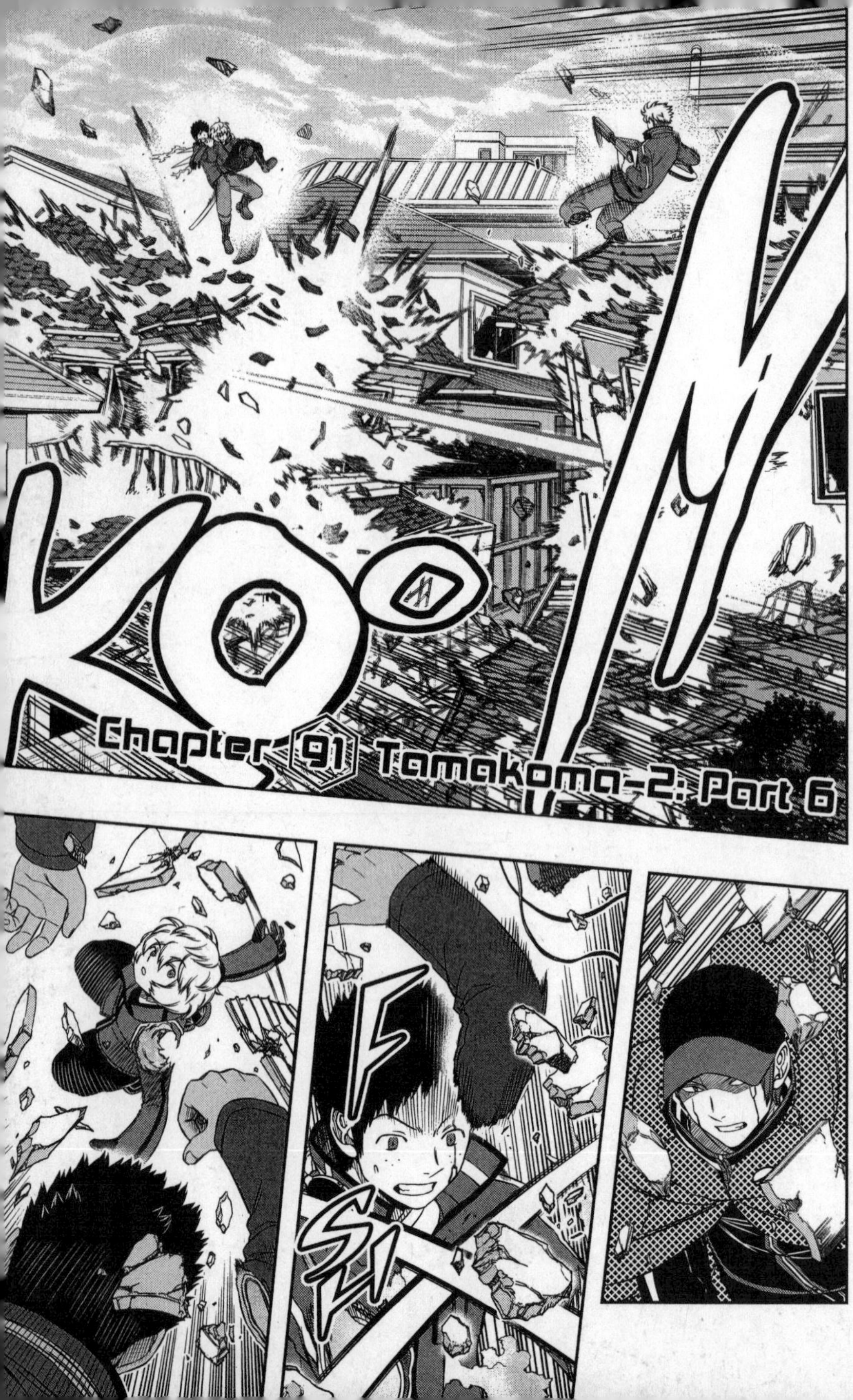
Chapter 91 Tamakoma-2: Part 6

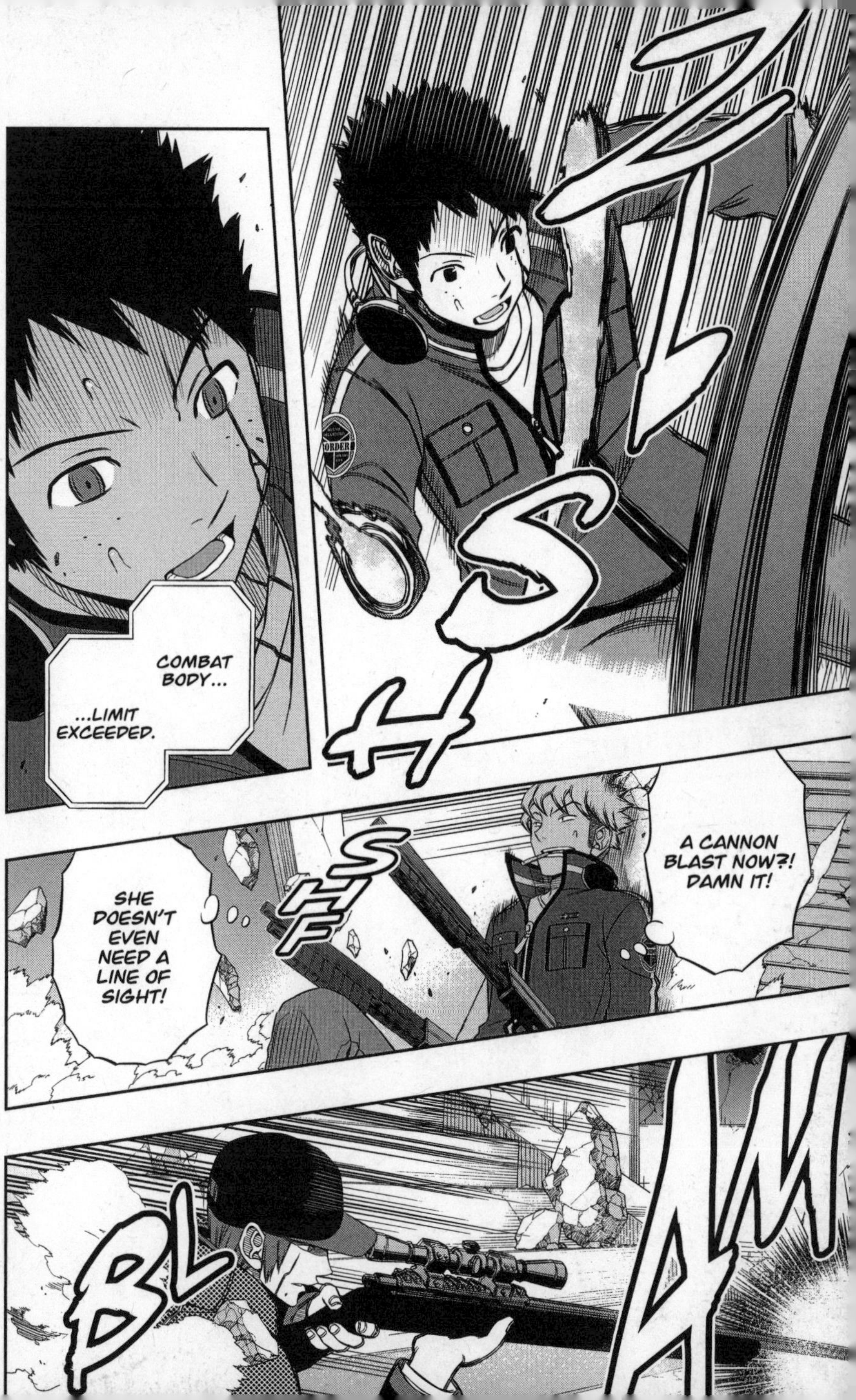

ZZSH
COMBAT BODY...
...LIMIT EXCEEDED.
A CANNON BLAST NOW?! DAMN IT!
SHF
SHE DOESN'T EVEN NEED A LINE OF SIGHT!
BLAM

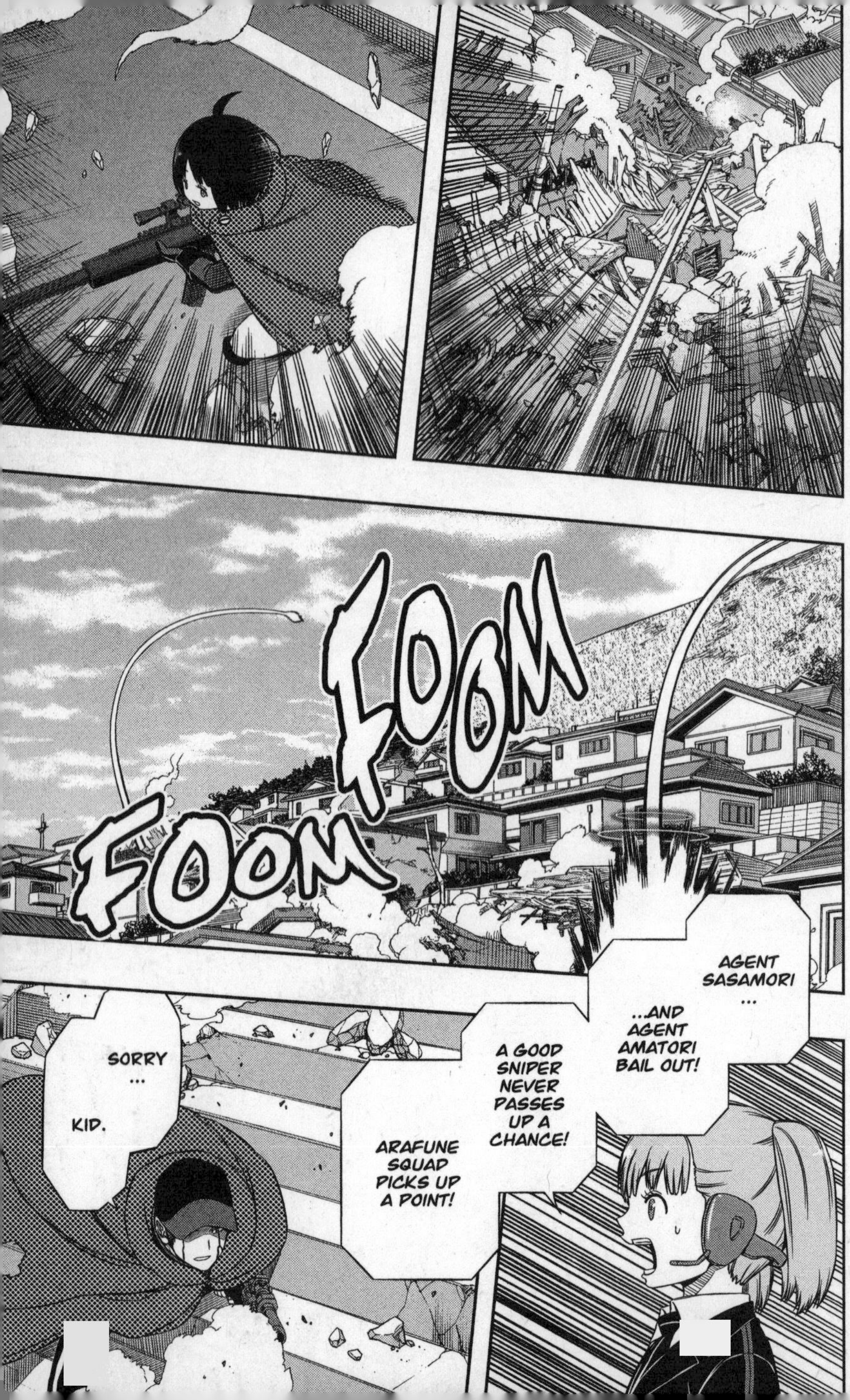
FOOM
FOOM
AGENT SASAMORI ...
...AND AGENT AMATORI BAIL OUT!
A GOOD SNIPER NEVER PASSES UP A CHANCE!
ARAFUNE SQUAD PICKS UP A POINT!
SORRY ...
KID.

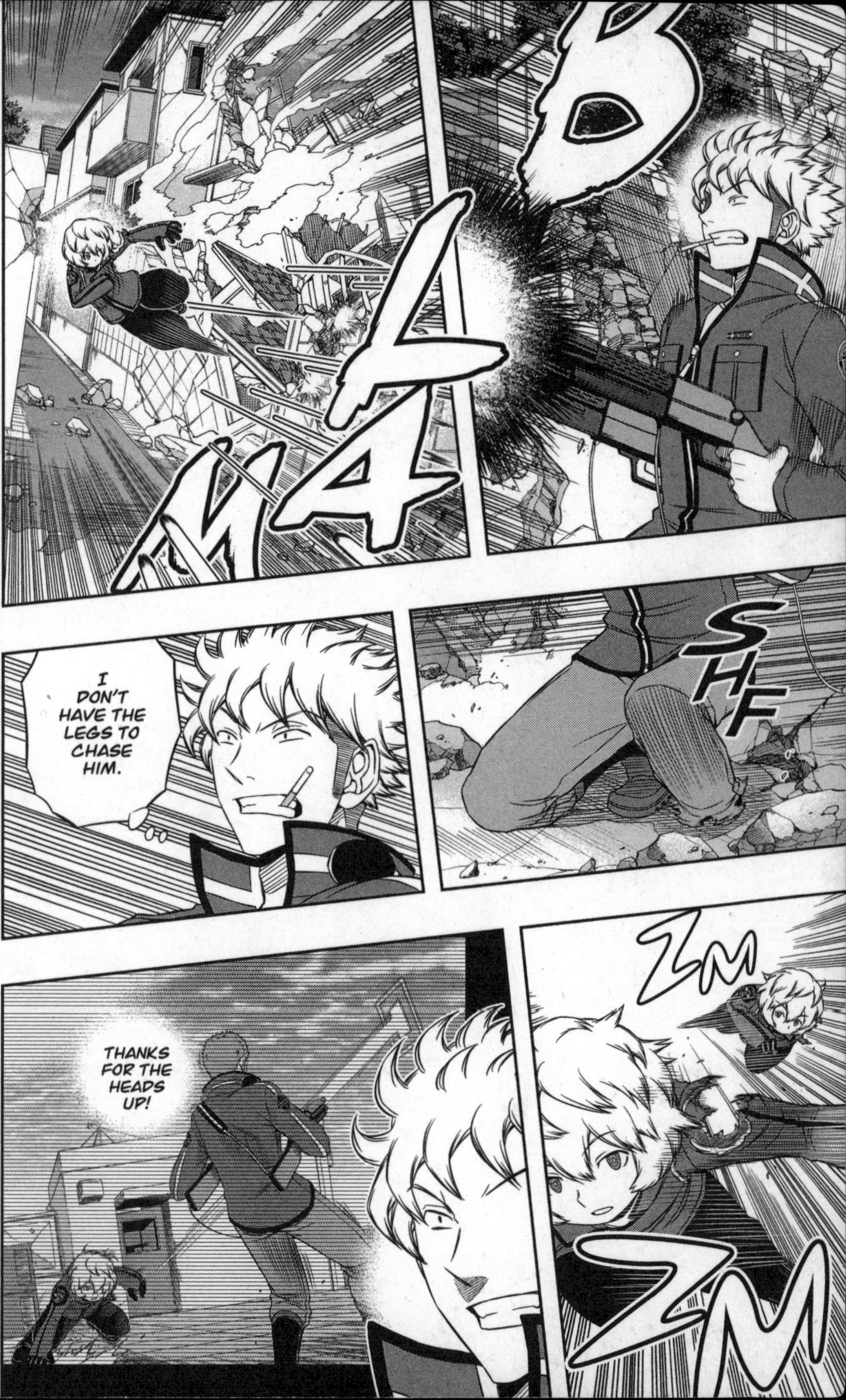
SHF
I DON'T HAVE THE LEGS TO CHASE HIM.
ZM
ZM
THANKS FOR THE HEADS UP!

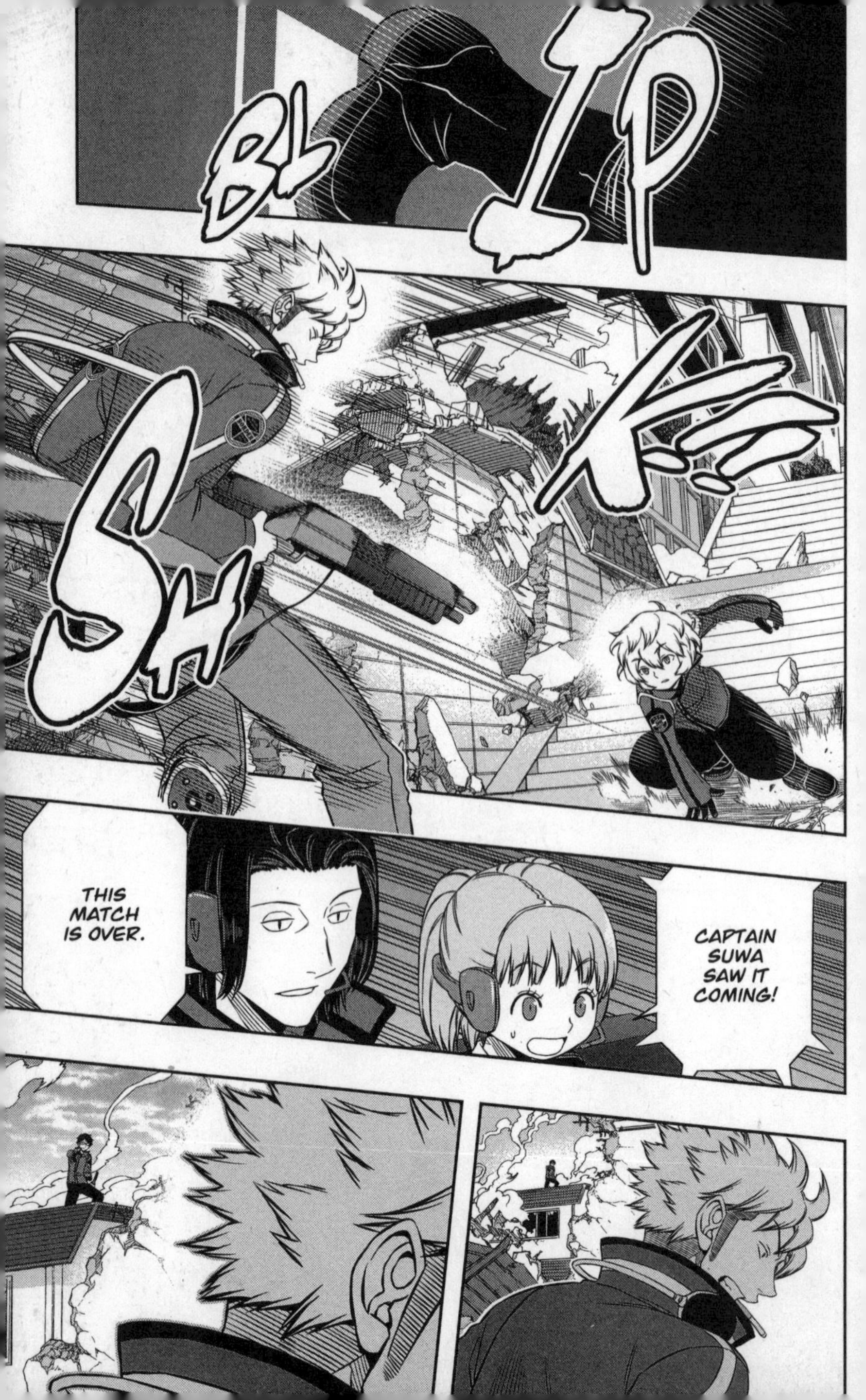
BLIP
SHK
CAPTAIN SUWA SAW IT COMING!
THIS MATCH IS OVER.

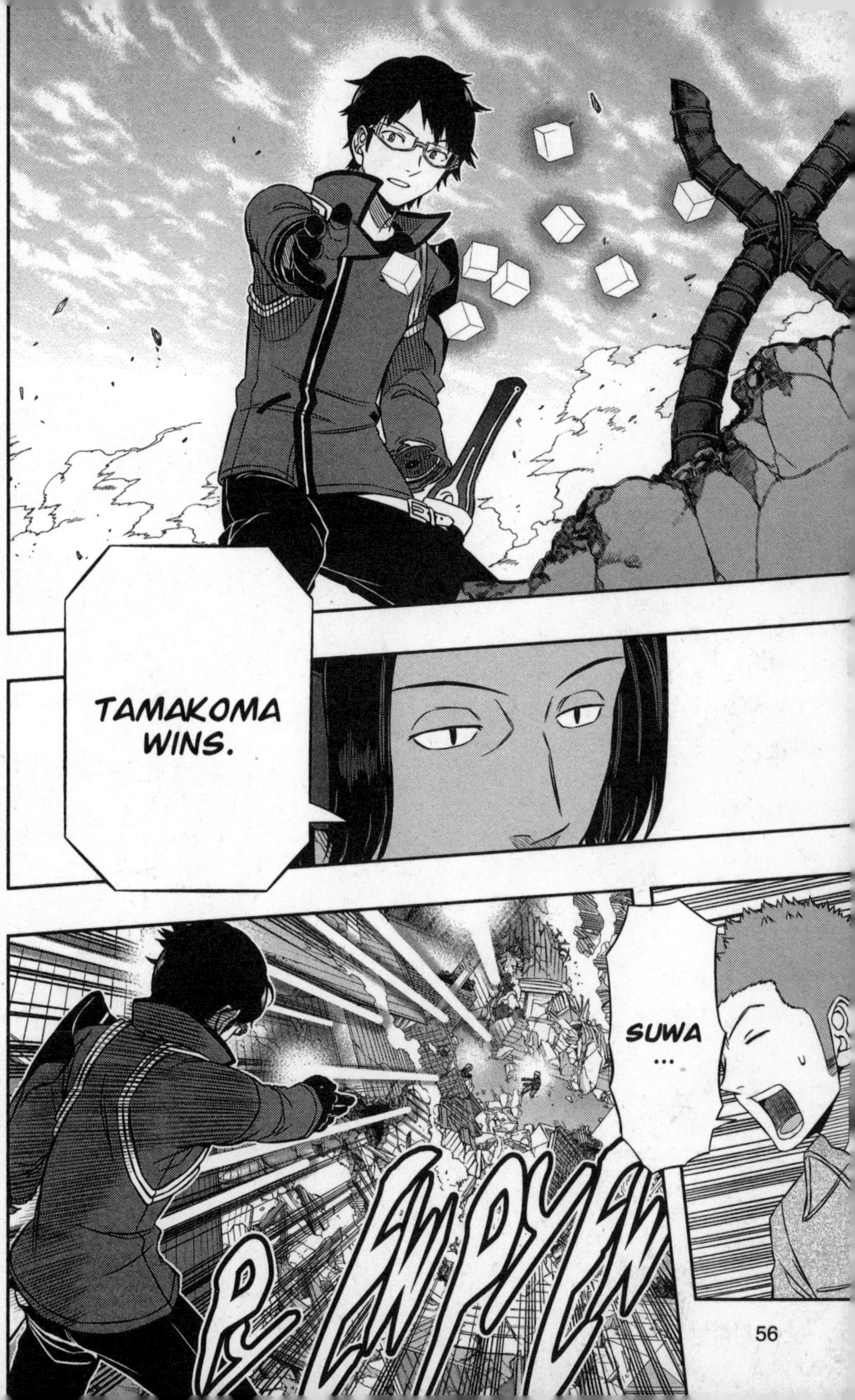
TAMAKOMA WINS.
SUWA ...

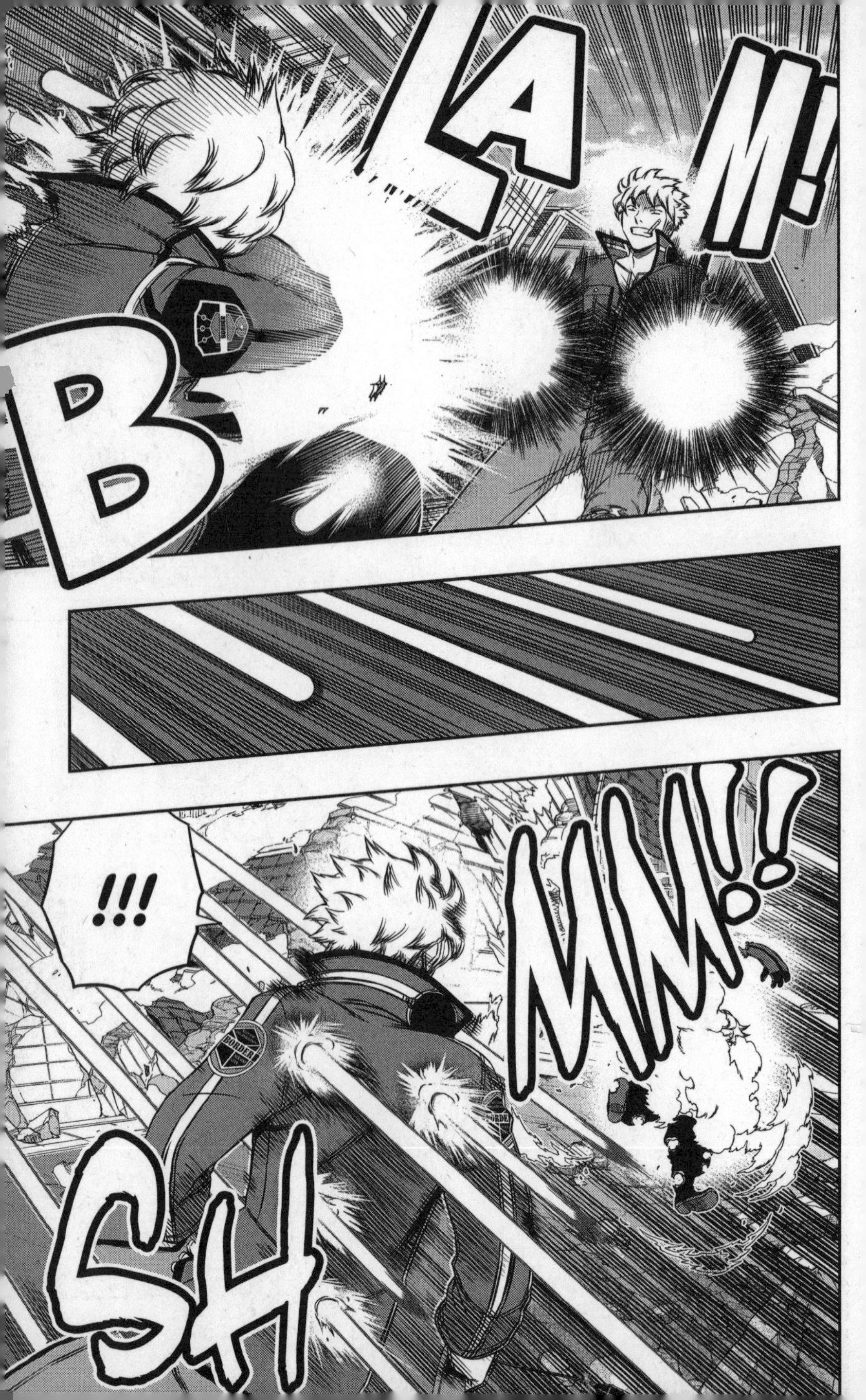
BAM!
!!!
SH MM!

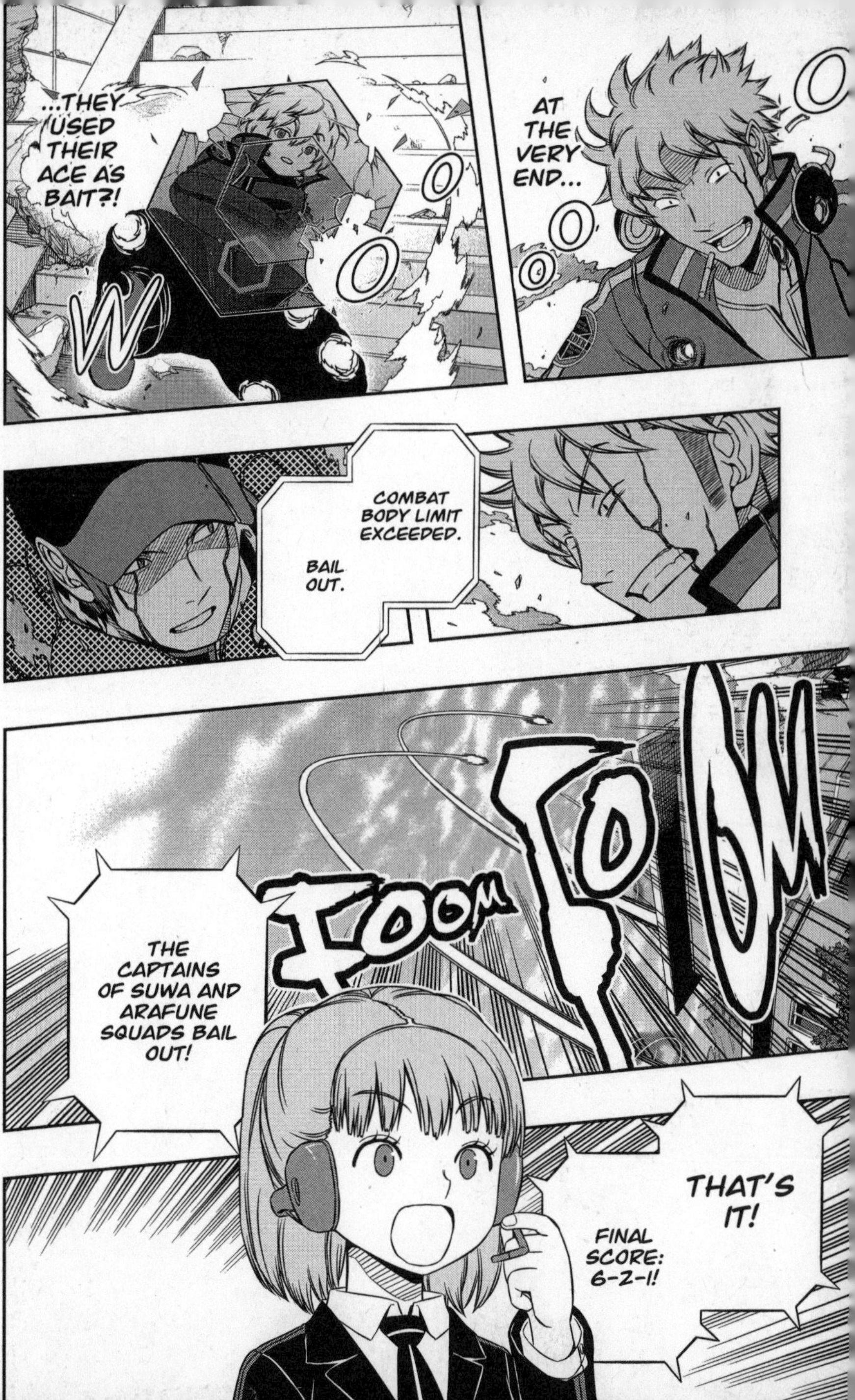

AT THE VERY END...
...THEY USED THEIR ACE AS BAIT?!
COMBAT BODY LIMIT EXCEEDED.
BAIL OUT.
FOOM
FOOM
THE CAPTAINS OF SUWA AND ARAFUNE SQUADS BAIL OUT!
THAT'S IT!
FINAL SCORE: 6-2-1!

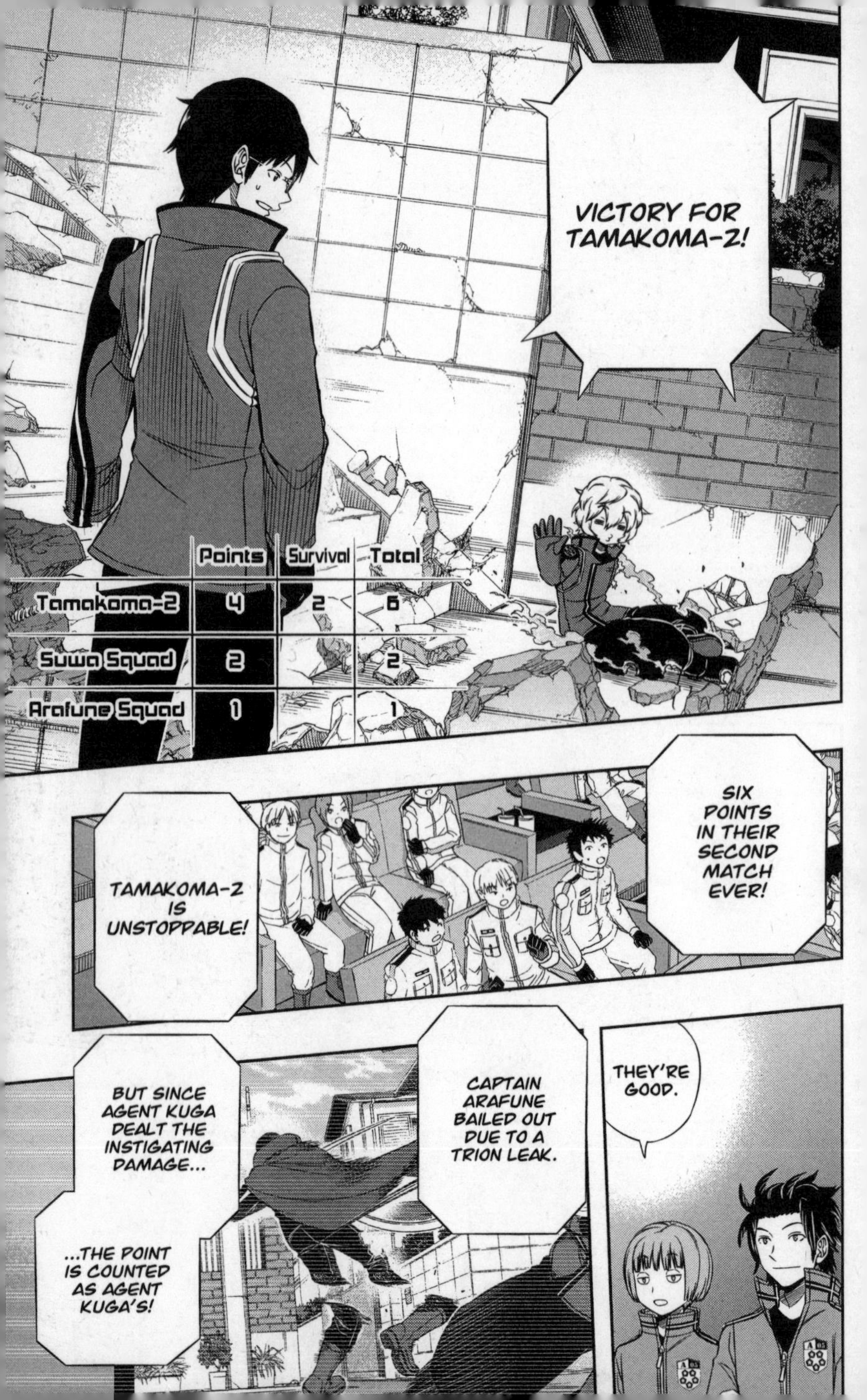
VICTORY FOR TAMAKOMA-2!
SIX POINTS IN THEIR SECOND MATCH EVER!
TAMAKOMA-2 IS UNSTOPPABLE!
THEY'RE GOOD.
CAPTAIN ARAFUNE BAILED OUT DUE TO A TRION LEAK.
BUT SINCE AGENT KUGA DEALT THE INSTIGATING DAMAGE...
...THE POINT IS COUNTED AS AGENT KUGA'S!

	Points	Survival	Total
Tamakoma-2	4	2	6
Suwa Squad	2		2
Arafune Squad	1		1

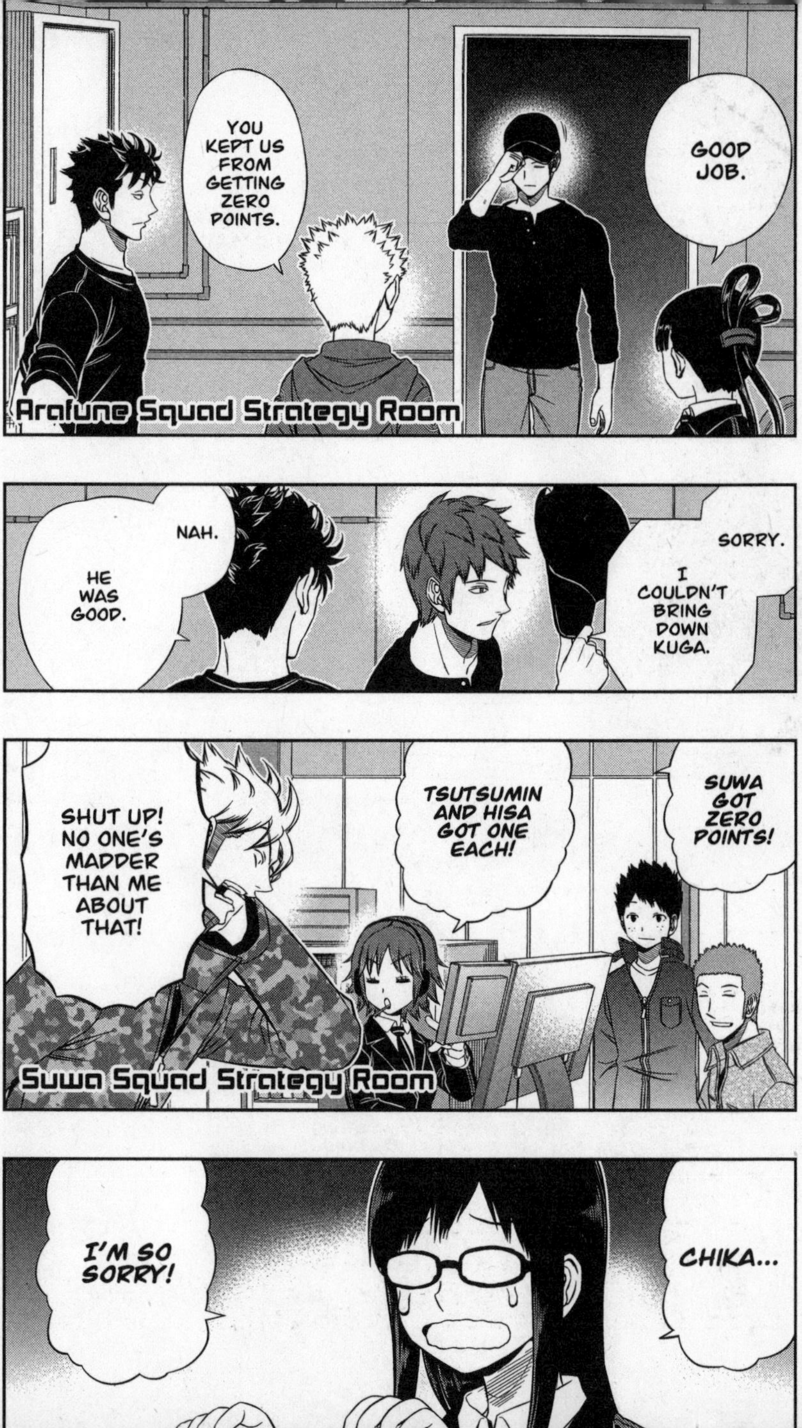
GOOD JOB.
YOU KEPT US FROM GETTING ZERO POINTS.
Arafune Squad Strategy Room
SORRY.
I COULDN'T BRING DOWN KUGA.
NAH.
HE WAS GOOD.
SUWA GOT ZERO POINTS!
TSUTSUMIN AND HISA GOT ONE EACH!
SHUT UP! NO ONE'S MADDER THAN ME ABOUT THAT!
Suwa Squad Strategy Room
CHIKA...
I'M SO SORRY!

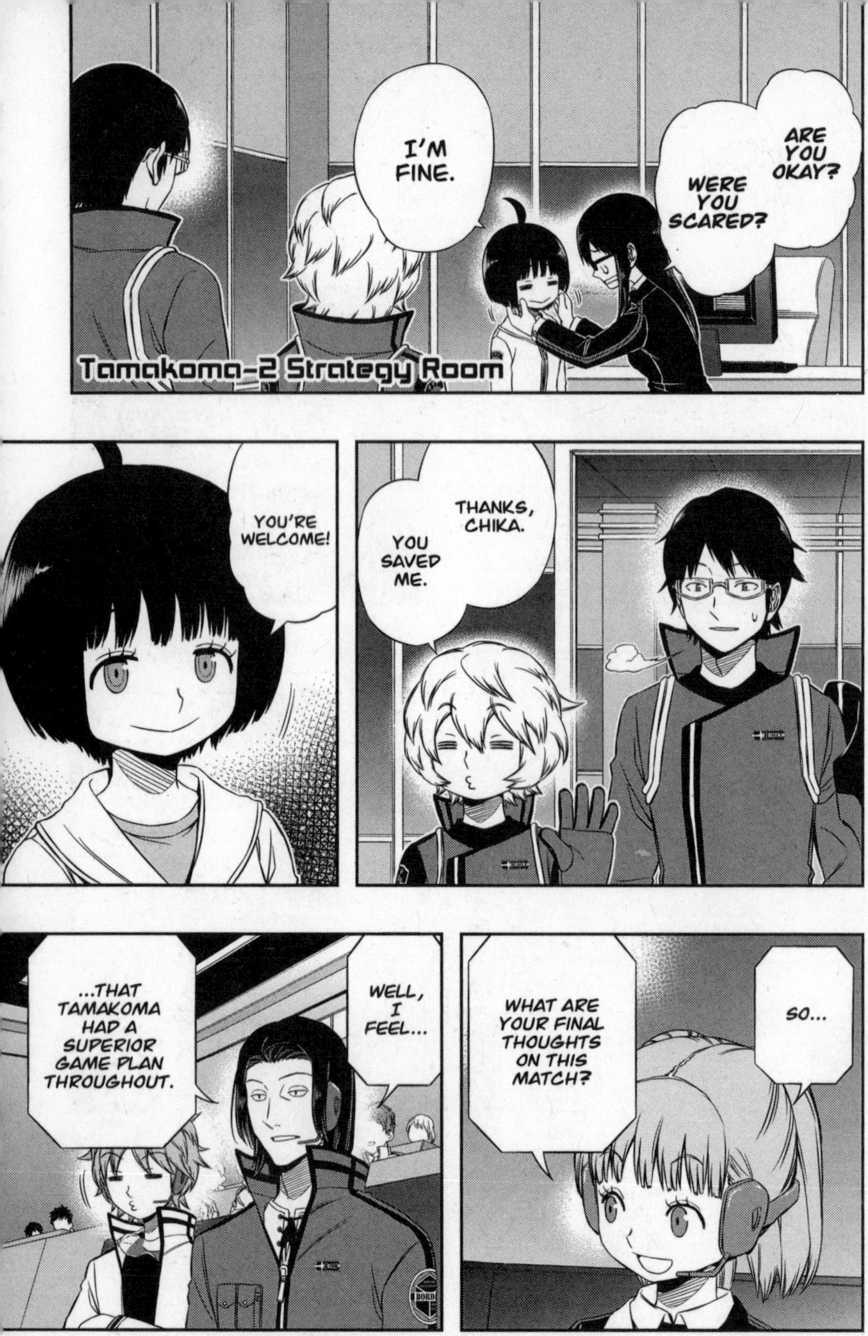
ARE YOU OKAY?
WERE YOU SCARED?
I'M FINE.
Tamakoma-2 Strategy Room
THANKS, CHIKA.
YOU SAVED ME.
YOU'RE WELCOME!
SO...
WHAT ARE YOUR FINAL THOUGHTS ON THIS MATCH?
WELL, I FEEL...
...THAT TAMAKOMA HAD A SUPERIOR GAME PLAN THROUGHOUT.

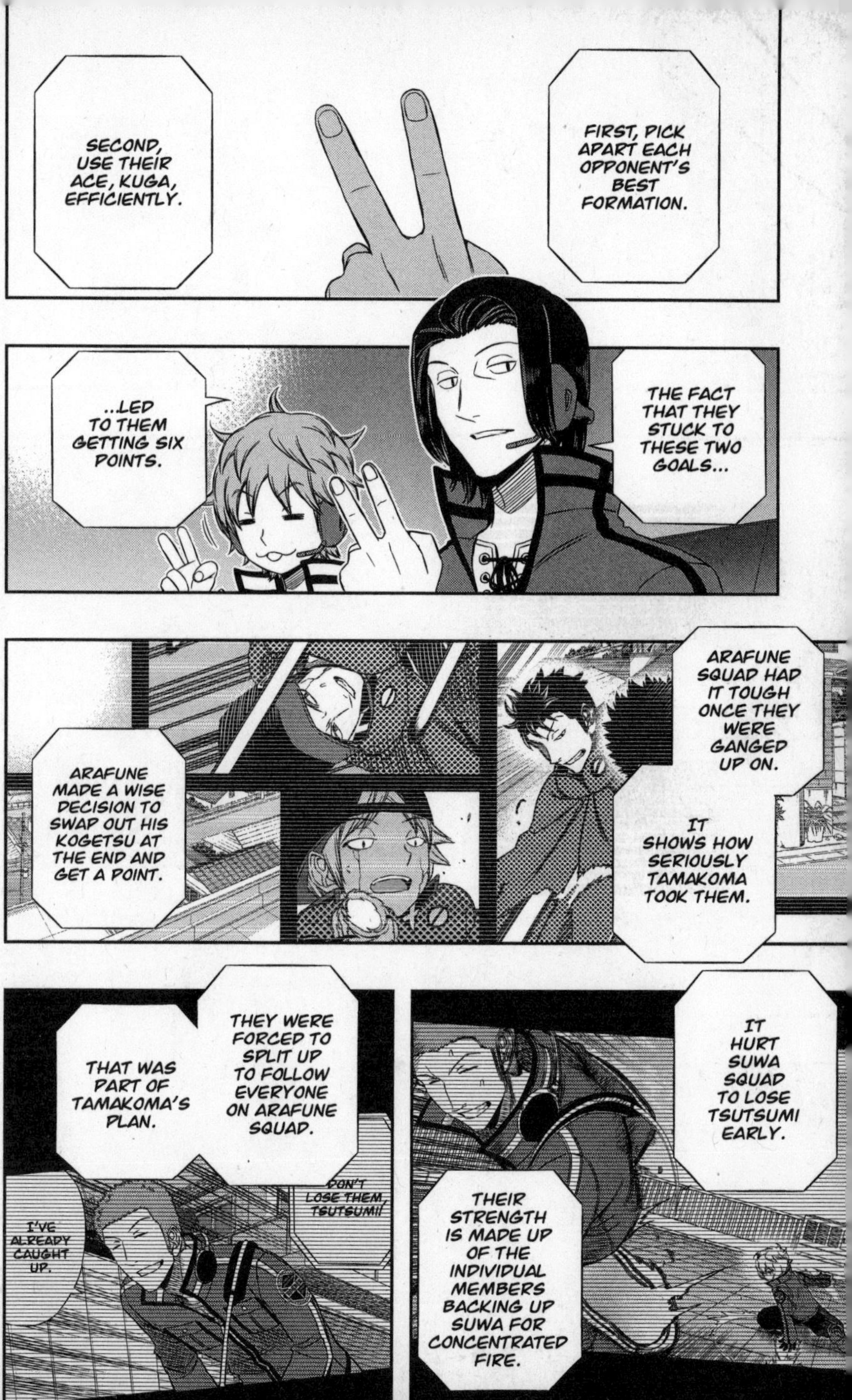
FIRST, PICK APART EACH OPPONENT'S BEST FORMATION.
SECOND, USE THEIR ACE, KUGA, EFFICIENTLY.
THE FACT THAT THEY STUCK TO THESE TWO GOALS...
...LED TO THEM GETTING SIX POINTS.
ARAFUNE SQUAD HAD IT TOUGH ONCE THEY WERE GANGED UP ON.
IT SHOWS HOW SERIOUSLY TAMAKOMA TOOK THEM.
ARAFUNE MADE A WISE DECISION TO SWAP OUT HIS KOGETSU AT THE END AND GET A POINT.
IT HURT SUWA SQUAD TO LOSE TSUTSUMI EARLY.
THEIR STRENGTH IS MADE UP OF THE INDIVIDUAL MEMBERS BACKING UP SUWA FOR CONCENTRATED FIRE.
THEY WERE FORCED TO SPLIT UP TO FOLLOW EVERYONE ON ARAFUNE SQUAD.
THAT WAS PART OF TAMAKOMA'S PLAN.
DON'T LOSE THEM, TSUTSUMI!
I'VE ALREADY CAUGHT UP.

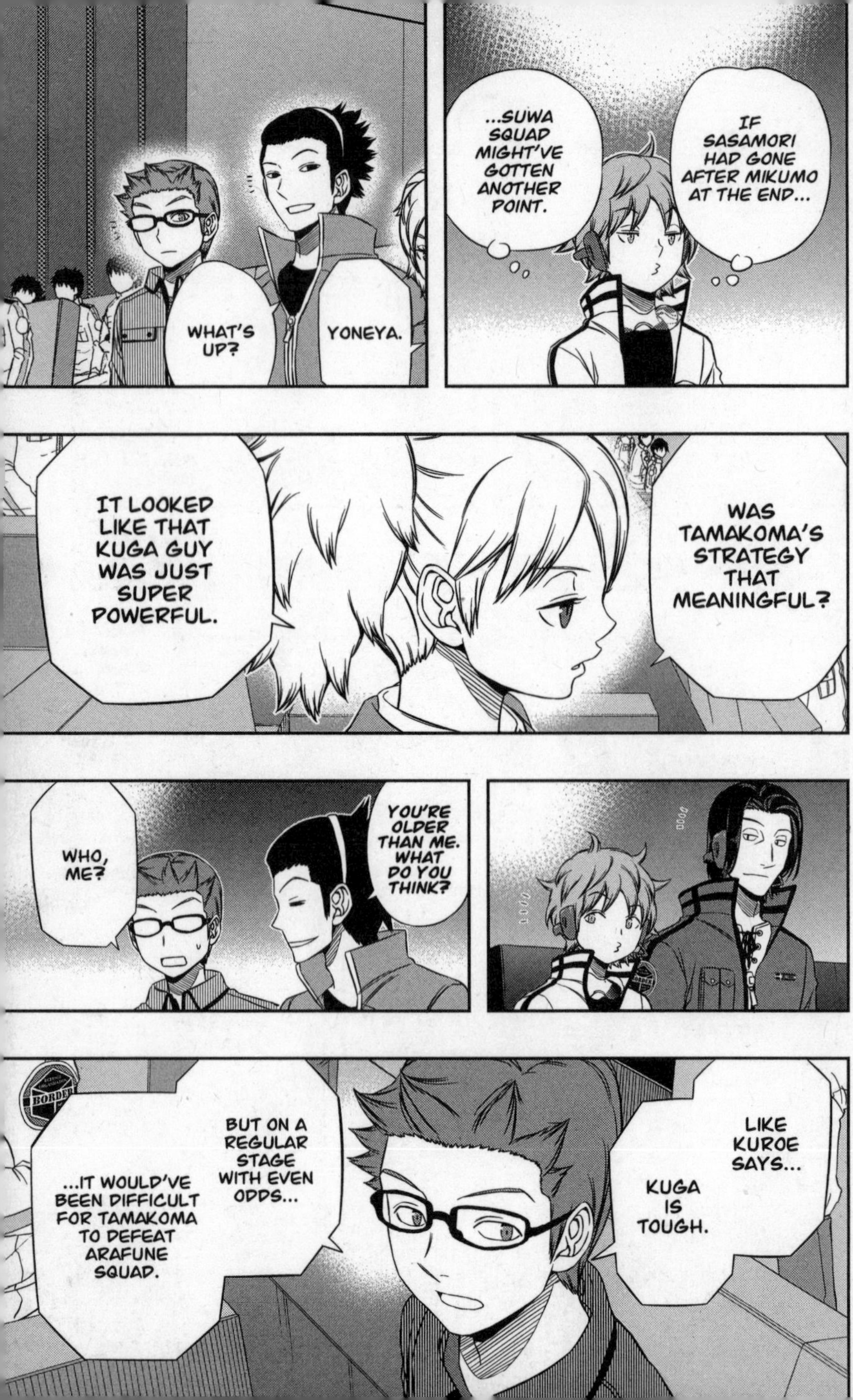
IF SASAMORI HAD GONE AFTER MIKUMO AT THE END...
...SUWA SQUAD MIGHT'VE GOTTEN ANOTHER POINT.
YONEYA.
WHAT'S UP?
WAS TAMAKOMA'S STRATEGY THAT MEANINGFUL?
IT LOOKED LIKE THAT KUGA GUY WAS JUST SUPER POWERFUL.
YOU'RE OLDER THAN ME. WHAT DO YOU THINK?
WHO, ME?
LIKE KUROE SAYS...
KUGA IS TOUGH.
BUT ON A REGULAR STAGE WITH EVEN ODDS...
...IT WOULD'VE BEEN DIFFICULT FOR TAMAKOMA TO DEFEAT ARAFUNE SQUAD.

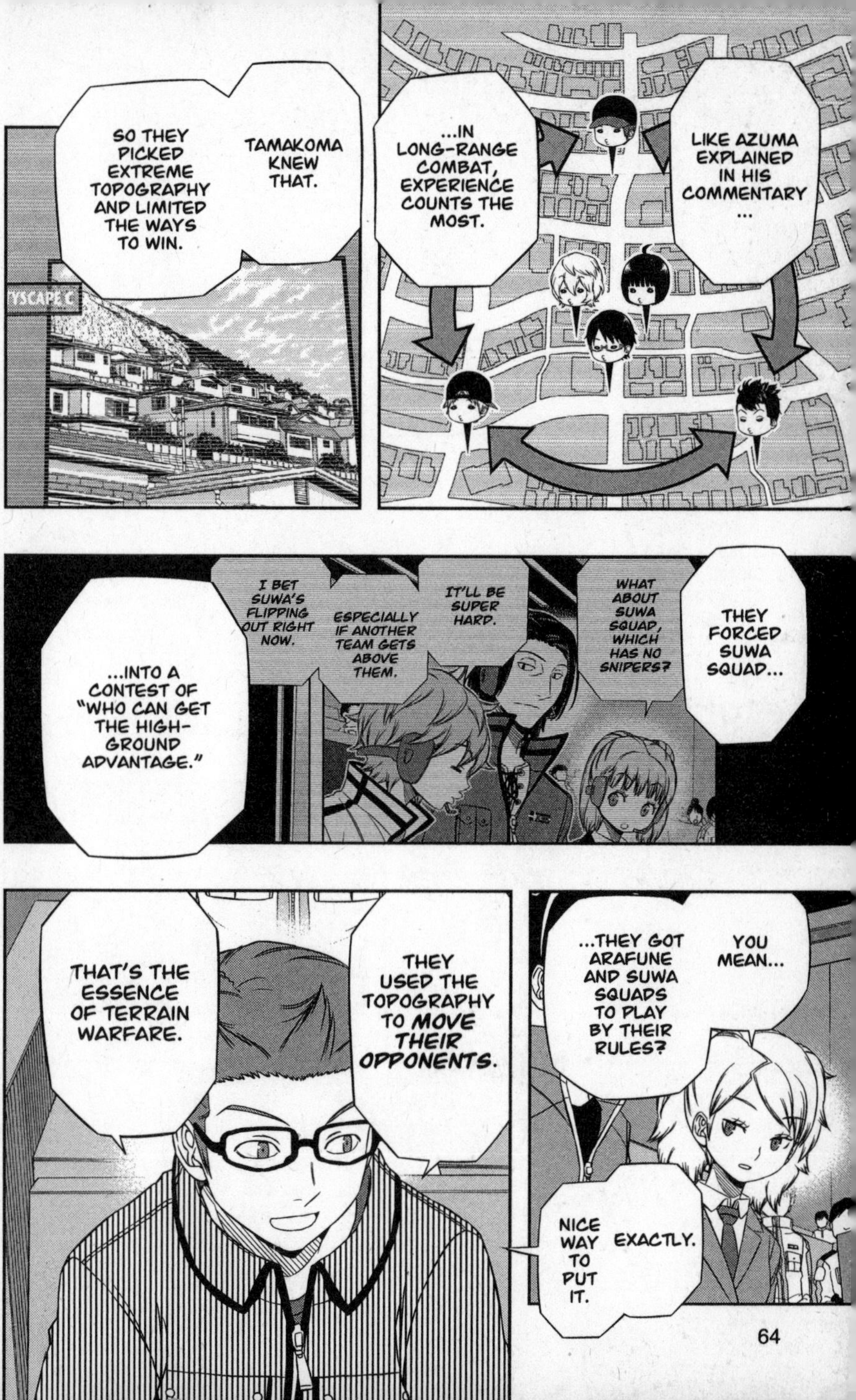
LIKE AZUMA EXPLAINED IN HIS COMMENTARY...
...IN LONG-RANGE COMBAT, EXPERIENCE COUNTS THE MOST.
TAMAKOMA KNEW THAT.
SO THEY PICKED EXTREME TOPOGRAPHY AND LIMITED THE WAYS TO WIN.
YSCAPE C
THEY FORCED SUWA SQUAD...
WHAT ABOUT SUWA SQUAD, WHICH HAS NO SNIPERS?
IT'LL BE SUPER HARD.
ESPECIALLY IF ANOTHER TEAM GETS ABOVE THEM.
I BET SUWA'S FLIPPING OUT RIGHT NOW.
...INTO A CONTEST OF "WHO CAN GET THE HIGH-GROUND ADVANTAGE."
YOU MEAN...
...THEY GOT ARAFUNE AND SUWA SQUADS TO PLAY BY THEIR RULES?
EXACTLY.
NICE WAY TO PUT IT.
THEY USED THE TOPOGRAPHY TO *MOVE THEIR OPPONENTS*.
THAT'S THE ESSENCE OF TERRAIN WARFARE.

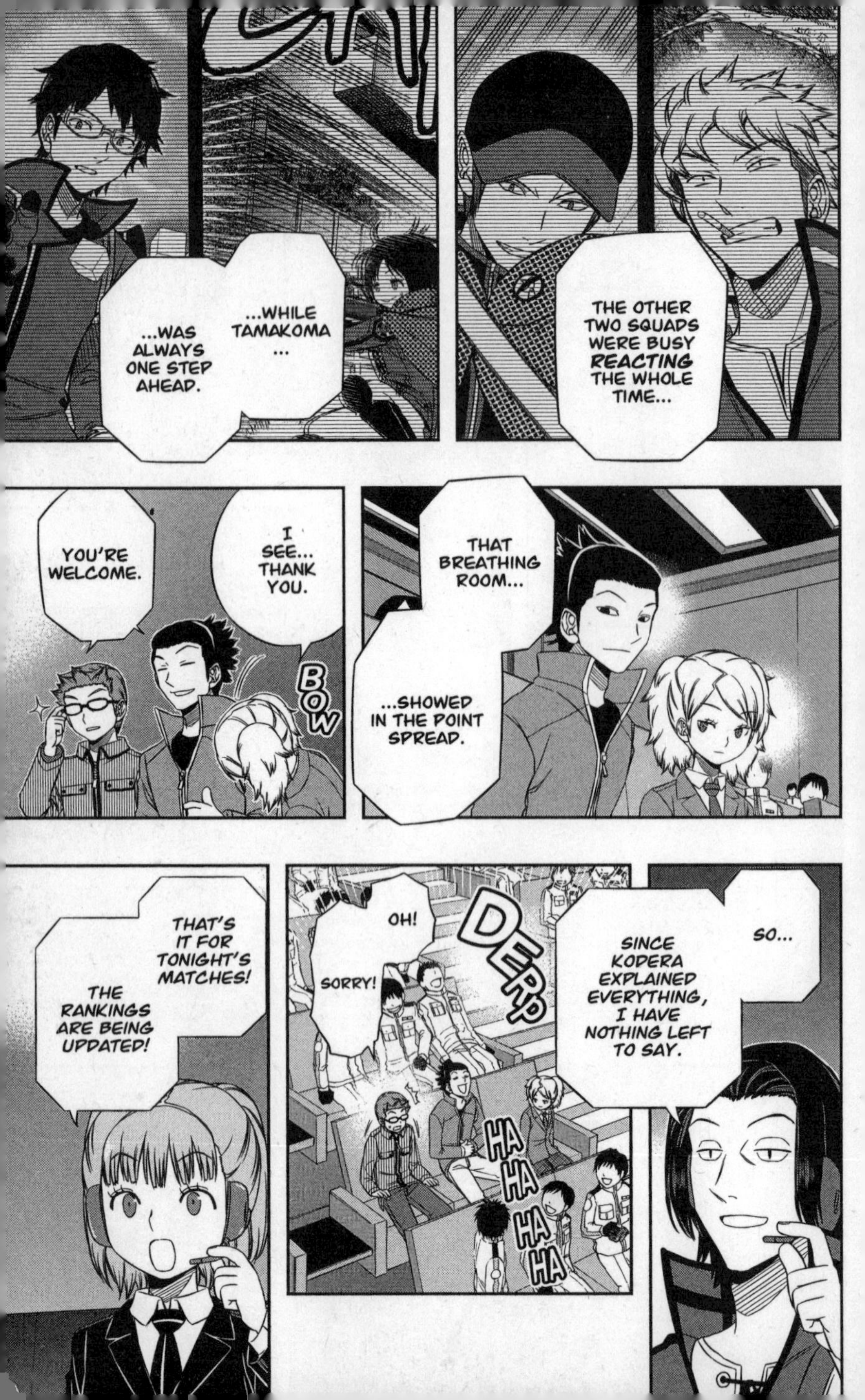
THE OTHER TWO SQUADS WERE BUSY REACTING THE WHOLE TIME...
...WHILE TAMAKOMA ...
...WAS ALWAYS ONE STEP AHEAD.
THAT BREATHING ROOM...
...SHOWED IN THE POINT SPREAD.
I SEE... THANK YOU.
YOU'RE WELCOME.
BOW
SO...
SINCE KODERA EXPLAINED EVERYTHING, I HAVE NOTHING LEFT TO SAY.
DERP
OH!
SORRY!
HA HA HA HA
THAT'S IT FOR TONIGHT'S MATCHES!
THE RANKINGS ARE BEING UPDATED!

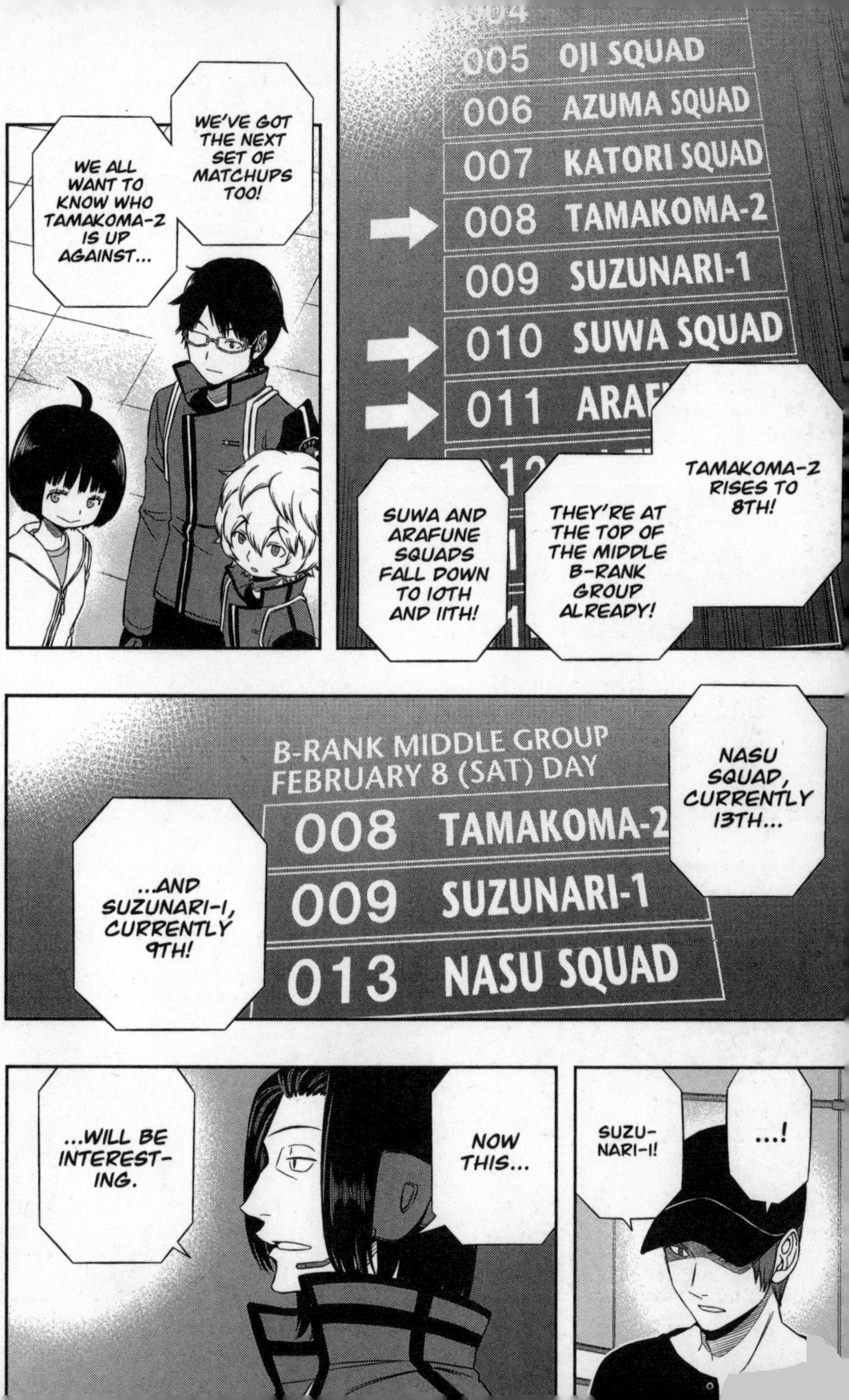
005 OJI SQUAD
006 AZUMA SQUAD
007 KATORI SQUAD
008 TAMAKOMA-2
009 SUZUNARI-1
010 SUWA SQUAD
011
TAMAKOMA-2 RISES TO 8TH!
THEY'RE AT THE TOP OF THE MIDDLE B-RANK GROUP ALREADY!
SUWA AND ARAFUNE SQUADS FALL DOWN TO 10TH AND 11TH!
WE'VE GOT THE NEXT SET OF MATCHUPS TOO!
WE ALL WANT TO KNOW WHO TAMAKOMA-2 IS UP AGAINST...
B-RANK MIDDLE GROUP
FEBRUARY 8 (SAT) DAY
008 TAMAKOMA-2
009 SUZUNARI-1
013 NASU SQUAD
NASU SQUAD, CURRENTLY 13TH...
...AND SUZUNARI-1, CURRENTLY 9TH!
...!
SUZU-NARI-1!
NOW THIS...
...WILL BE INTEREST-ING.

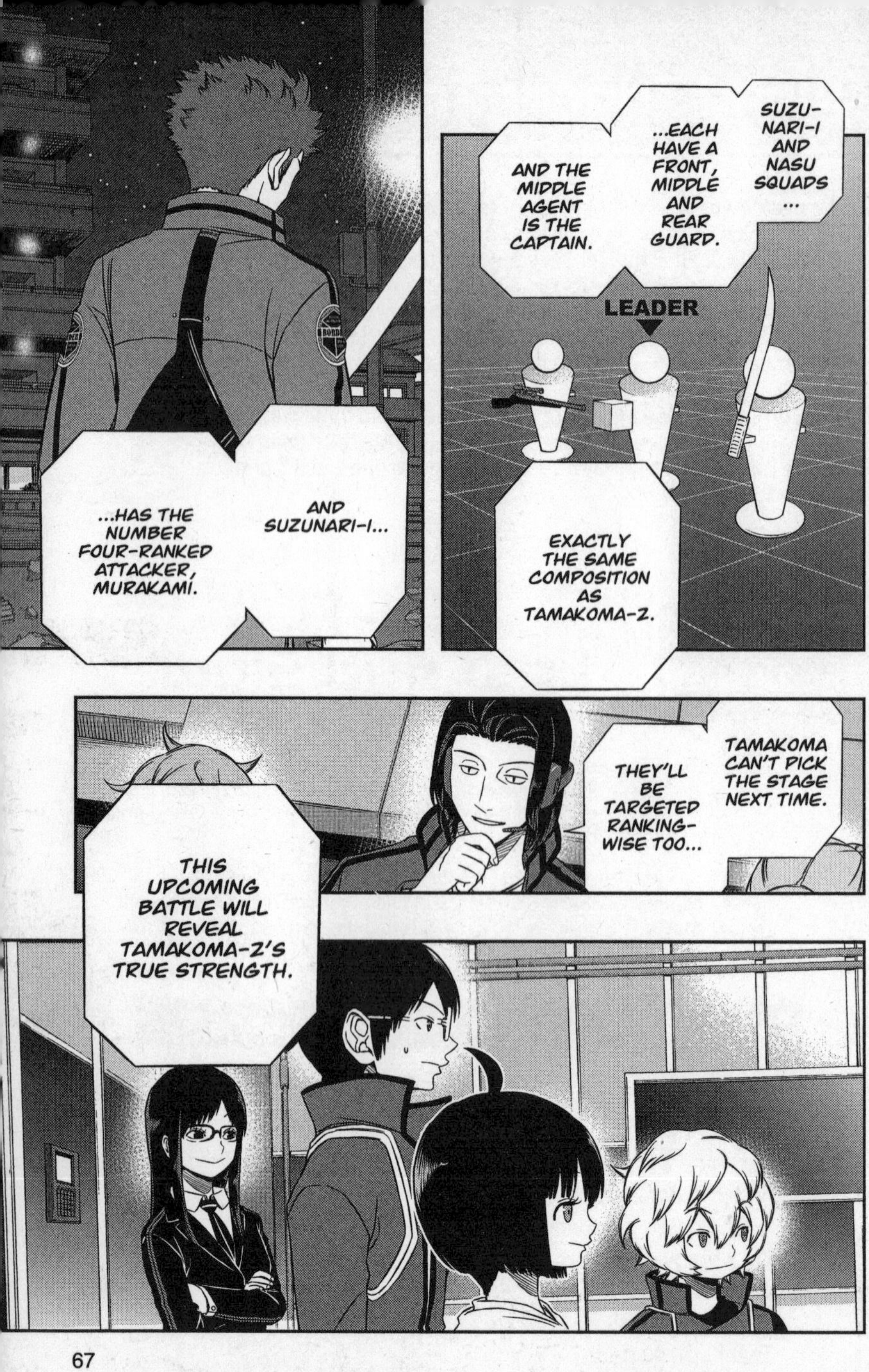
SUZUNARI-1 AND NASU SQUADS ...
...EACH HAVE A FRONT, MIDDLE AND REAR GUARD.
AND THE MIDDLE AGENT IS THE CAPTAIN.
LEADER
EXACTLY THE SAME COMPOSITION AS TAMAKOMA-2.
AND SUZUNARI-1...
...HAS THE NUMBER FOUR-RANKED ATTACKER, MURAKAMI.
TAMAKOMA CAN'T PICK THE STAGE NEXT TIME.
THEY'LL BE TARGETED RANKING-WISE TOO...
THIS UPCOMING BATTLE WILL REVEAL TAMAKOMA-2'S TRUE STRENGTH.

World Trigger Tagline Awards

We decided to do something to commemorate the release of volume 10, so we held a tagline contest in *Shonen Jump* (mostly run by the ad agency and Jean-Baptiste). We wanted to do it over Twitter too. I said, "I'd like to make it look really fun, like maybe you can see the tagline you submit instantly turn into the paper band over the graphic novel!" Then they actually set up a special website to do just that. Ad agencies are amazing. It was worth it to make that suggestion.

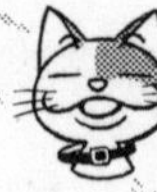

The Jump magazine announced the winners, and there was a huge wall ad in Shibuya. These taglines will actually be used for future print runs. There were some really good ones, so I'll print the best ones here.

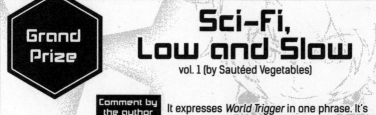

Grand Prize

Sci-Fi, Low and Slow

vol. 1 (by Sautéed Vegetables)

Comment by the author at printing

It expresses *World Trigger* in one phrase. It's creative and works for any volume. Grand prize.

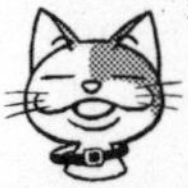

This won, hands down. In only a few words it embodies a condensed, easy to understand characteristic of the manga that makes it so unique. We'll use it for posters and paper bands for all the volumes in Japan. The rest of the winners and honorable mentions will be in the other bonus pages.

Comment by author in the magazine

There were many entries with similar ideas, so we picked the ones with the best wording. If there were entries with the same wording, we picked the ones that were submitted first. There were many entries with lines and phrases taken directly from the manga, so those were rejected. Sorry.
We were pleasantly surprised that we got over 18,000 submissions online and over 300 by mail. I looked over each and every one. It was hard to judge so many, but it was fun. Thank you so much.

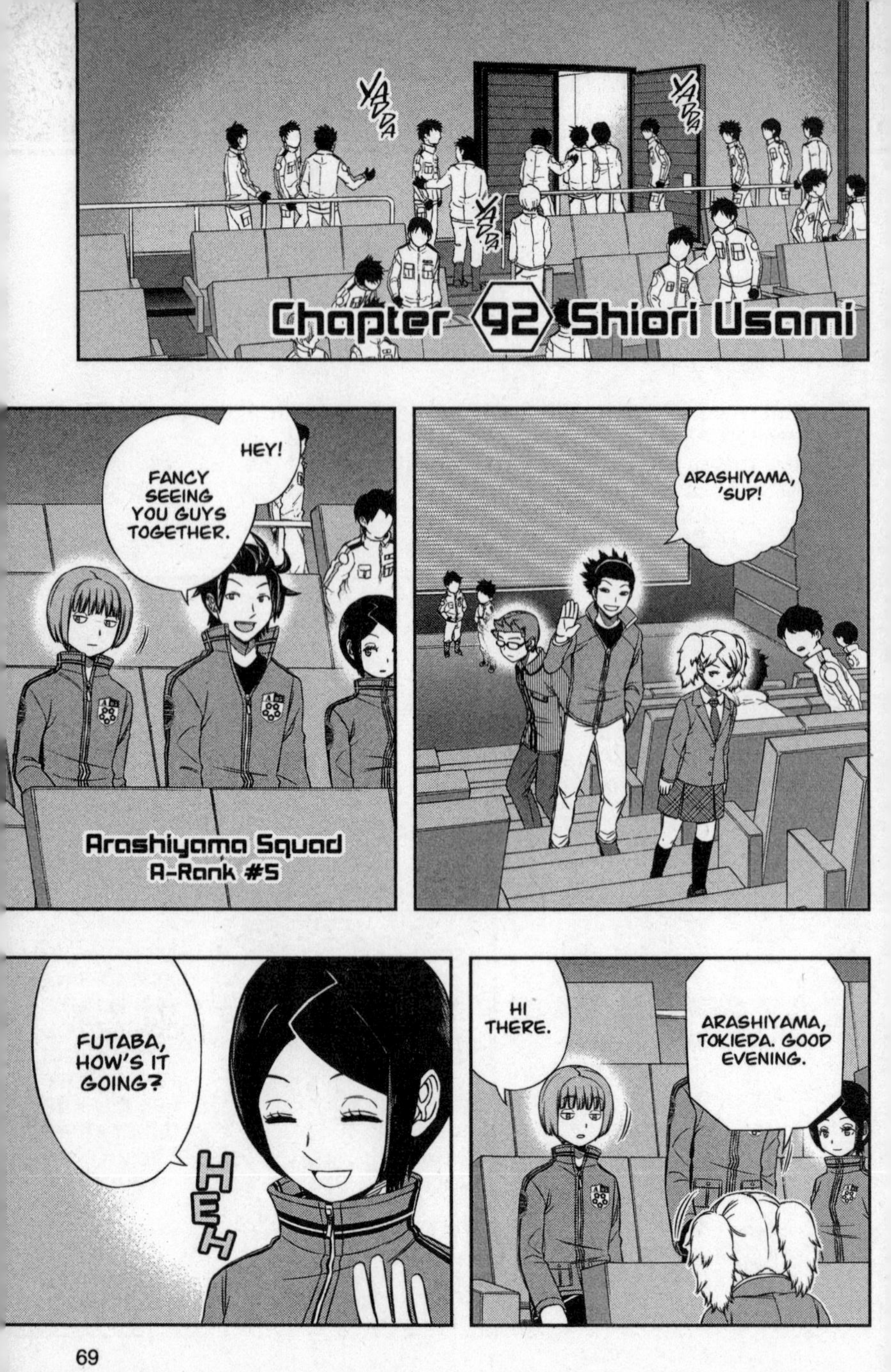
YADDA
YADDA
YADDA
Chapter 92 Shiori Usami
ARASHIYAMA, 'SUP!
HEY!
FANCY SEEING YOU GUYS TOGETHER.
Arashiyama Squad
A-Rank #5
ARASHIYAMA, TOKIEDA. GOOD EVENING.
HI THERE.
FUTABA, HOW'S IT GOING?
HEH

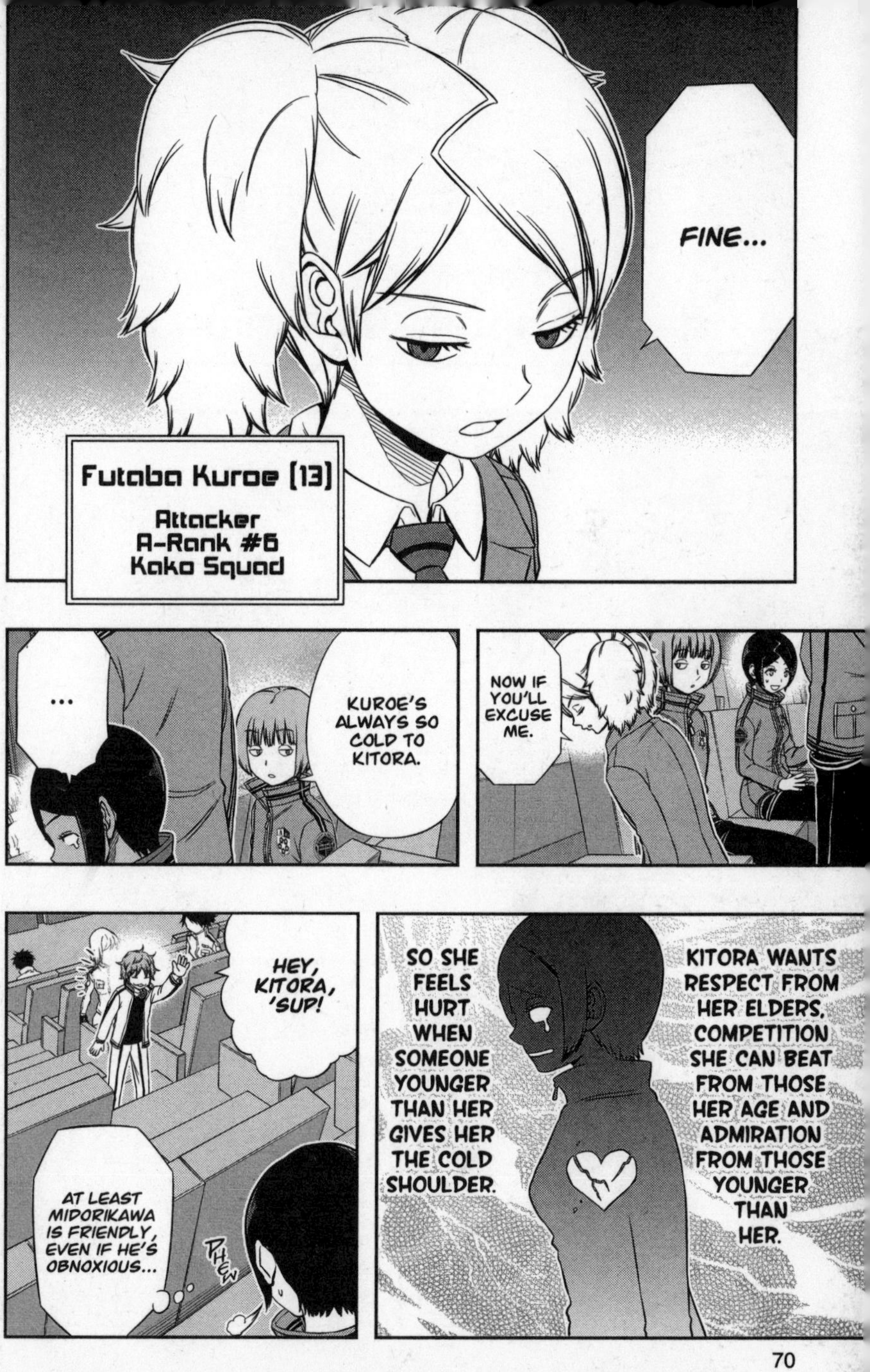
FINE...
Futaba Kuroe (13)
Attacker
A-Rank #6
Kako Squad
NOW IF YOU'LL EXCUSE ME.
KUROE'S ALWAYS SO COLD TO KITORA.
...
KITORA WANTS RESPECT FROM HER ELDERS, COMPETITION SHE CAN BEAT FROM THOSE HER AGE AND ADMIRATION FROM THOSE YOUNGER THAN HER.
SO SHE FEELS HURT WHEN SOMEONE YOUNGER THAN HER GIVES HER THE COLD SHOULDER.
HEY, KITORA, 'SUP!
AT LEAST MIDORIKAWA IS FRIENDLY, EVEN IF HE'S OBNOXIOUS...
PHEW

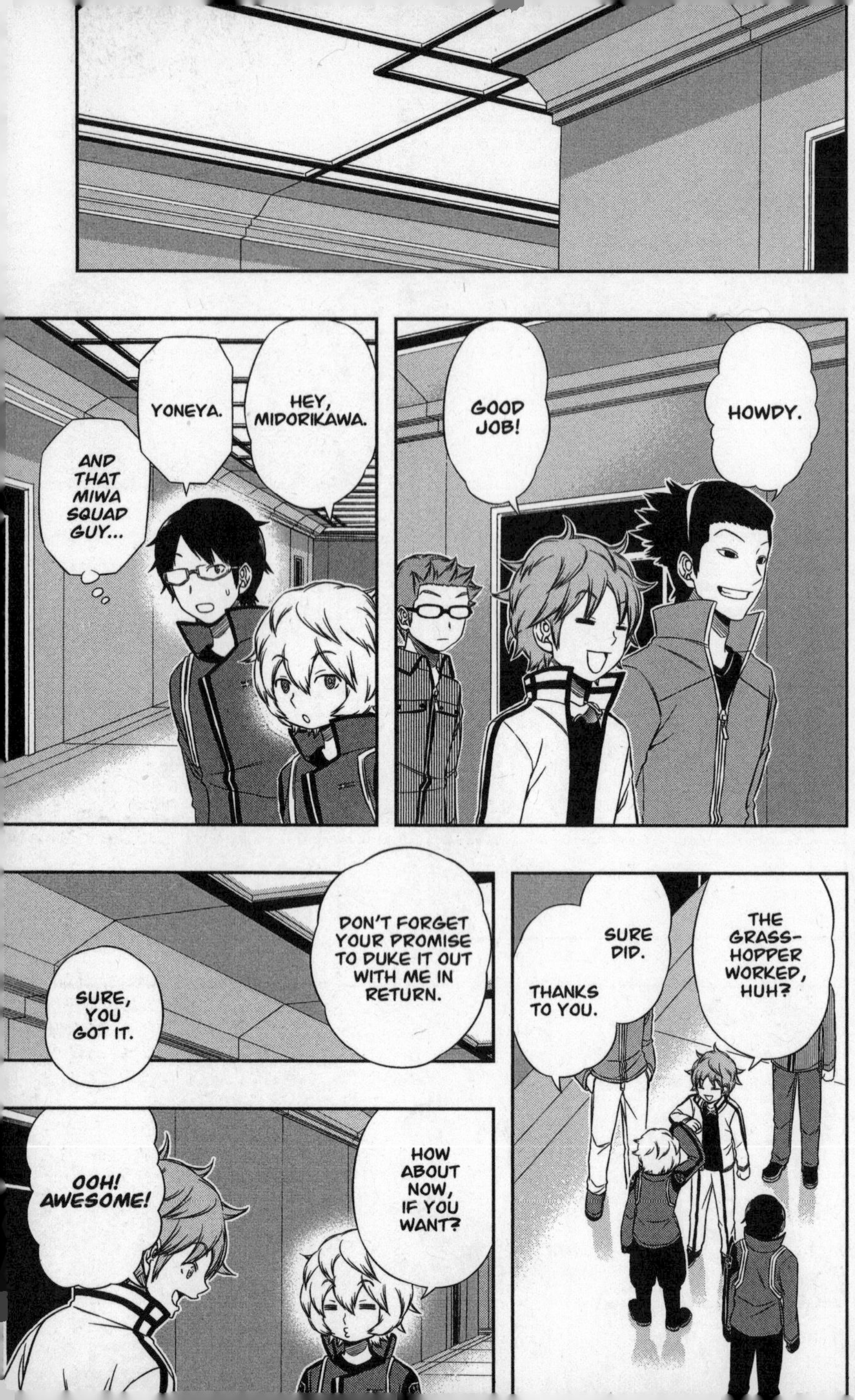
HOWDY.
GOOD JOB!
HEY, MIDORIKAWA.
YONEYA.
AND THAT MIWA SQUAD GUY...
THE GRASS-HOPPER WORKED, HUH?
SURE DID.
THANKS TO YOU.
DON'T FORGET YOUR PROMISE TO DUKE IT OUT WITH ME IN RETURN.
SURE, YOU GOT IT.
HOW ABOUT NOW, IF YOU WANT?
OOH! AWESOME!

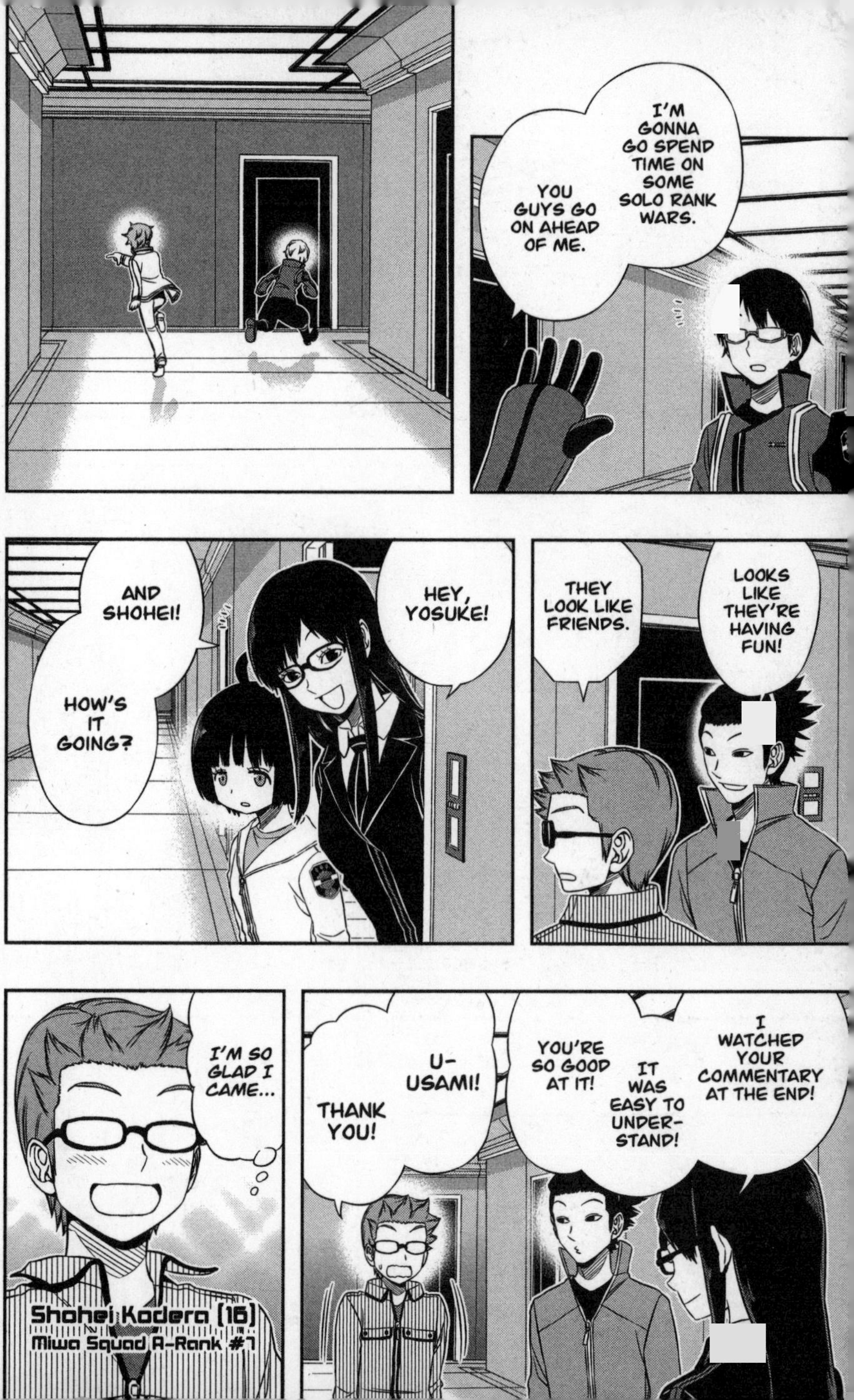
I'M GONNA GO SPEND TIME ON SOME SOLO RANK WARS.
YOU GUYS GO ON AHEAD OF ME.
LOOKS LIKE THEY'RE HAVING FUN!
THEY LOOK LIKE FRIENDS.
HEY, YOSUKE!
AND SHOHEI!
HOW'S IT GOING?
I WATCHED YOUR COMMENTARY AT THE END!
IT WAS EASY TO UNDER-STAND!
YOU'RE SO GOOD AT IT!
U-USAMI!
THANK YOU!
I'M SO GLAD I CAME...
Shohei Kodera (16)
Miwa Squad A-Rank #7

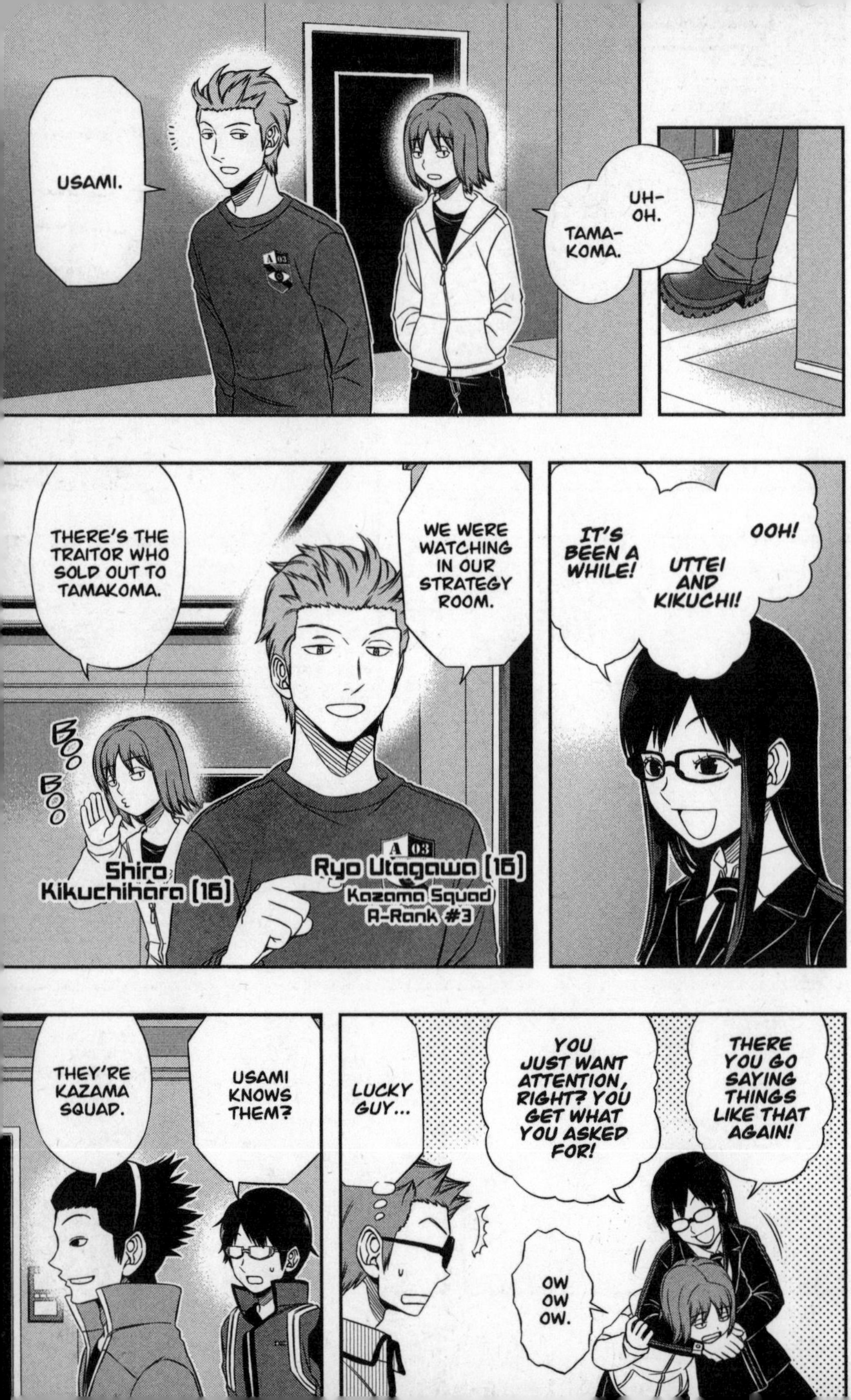

UH-OH.
TAMAKOMA.
USAMI.
OOH!
UTTEI AND KIKUCHI!
IT'S BEEN A WHILE!
WE WERE WATCHING IN OUR STRATEGY ROOM.
Ryo Utagawa (16)
Kazama Squad A-Rank #3
THERE'S THE TRAITOR WHO SOLD OUT TO TAMAKOMA.
BOO BOO
Shiro Kikuchihara (16)
THERE YOU GO SAYING THINGS LIKE THAT AGAIN!
YOU JUST WANT ATTENTION, RIGHT? YOU GET WHAT YOU ASKED FOR!
LUCKY GUY...
OW OW OW.
USAMI KNOWS THEM?
THEY'RE KAZAMA SQUAD.

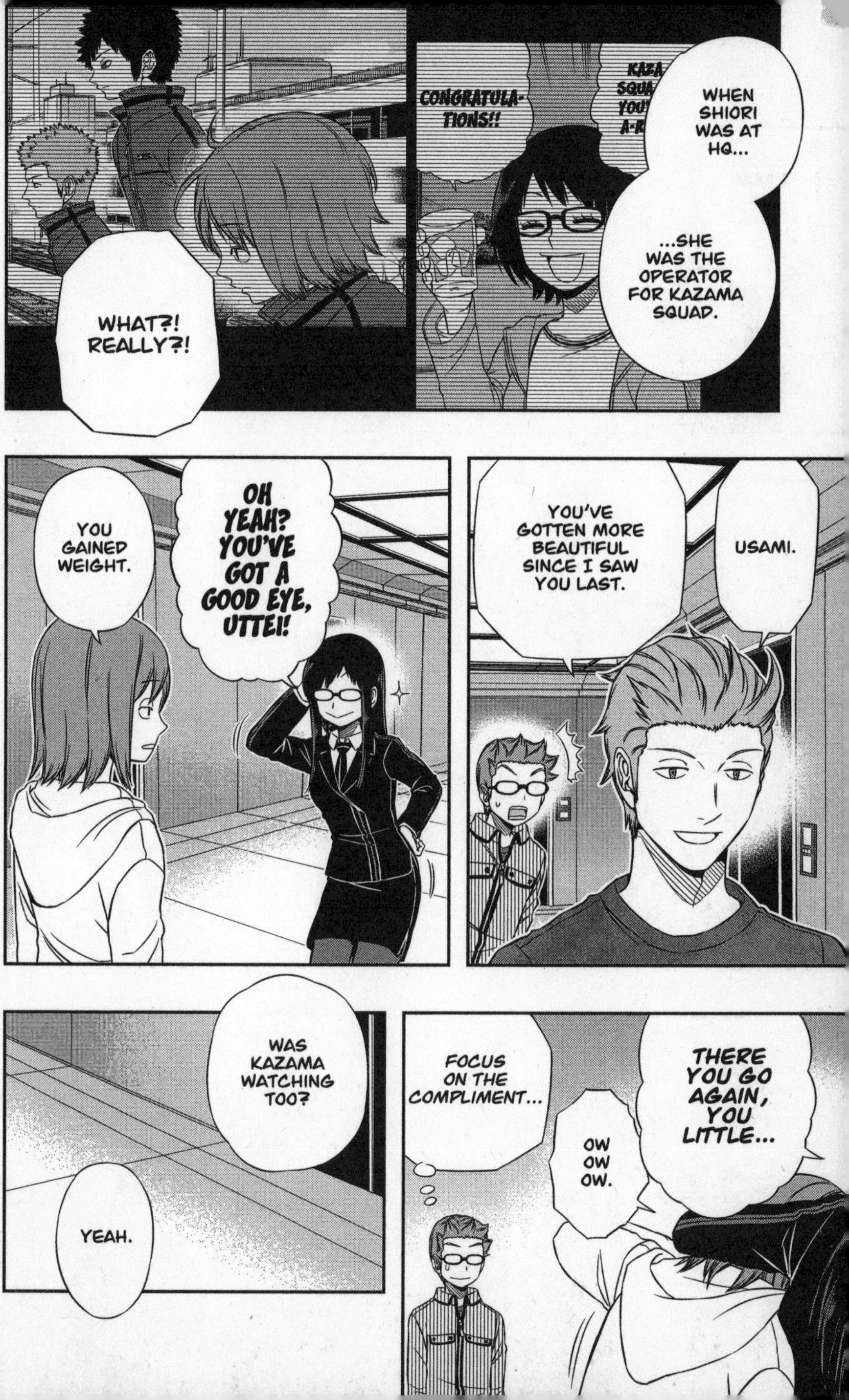
CONGRATULATIONS!!
WHEN SHIORI WAS AT HQ...
...SHE WAS THE OPERATOR FOR KAZAMA SQUAD.
WHAT?! REALLY?!
USAMI.
YOU'VE GOTTEN MORE BEAUTIFUL SINCE I SAW YOU LAST.
YOU GAINED WEIGHT.
OH YEAH? YOU'VE GOT A GOOD EYE, UTTEI!
THERE YOU GO AGAIN, YOU LITTLE...
OW OW OW.
FOCUS ON THE COMPLIMENT...
WAS KAZAMA WATCHING TOO?
YEAH.

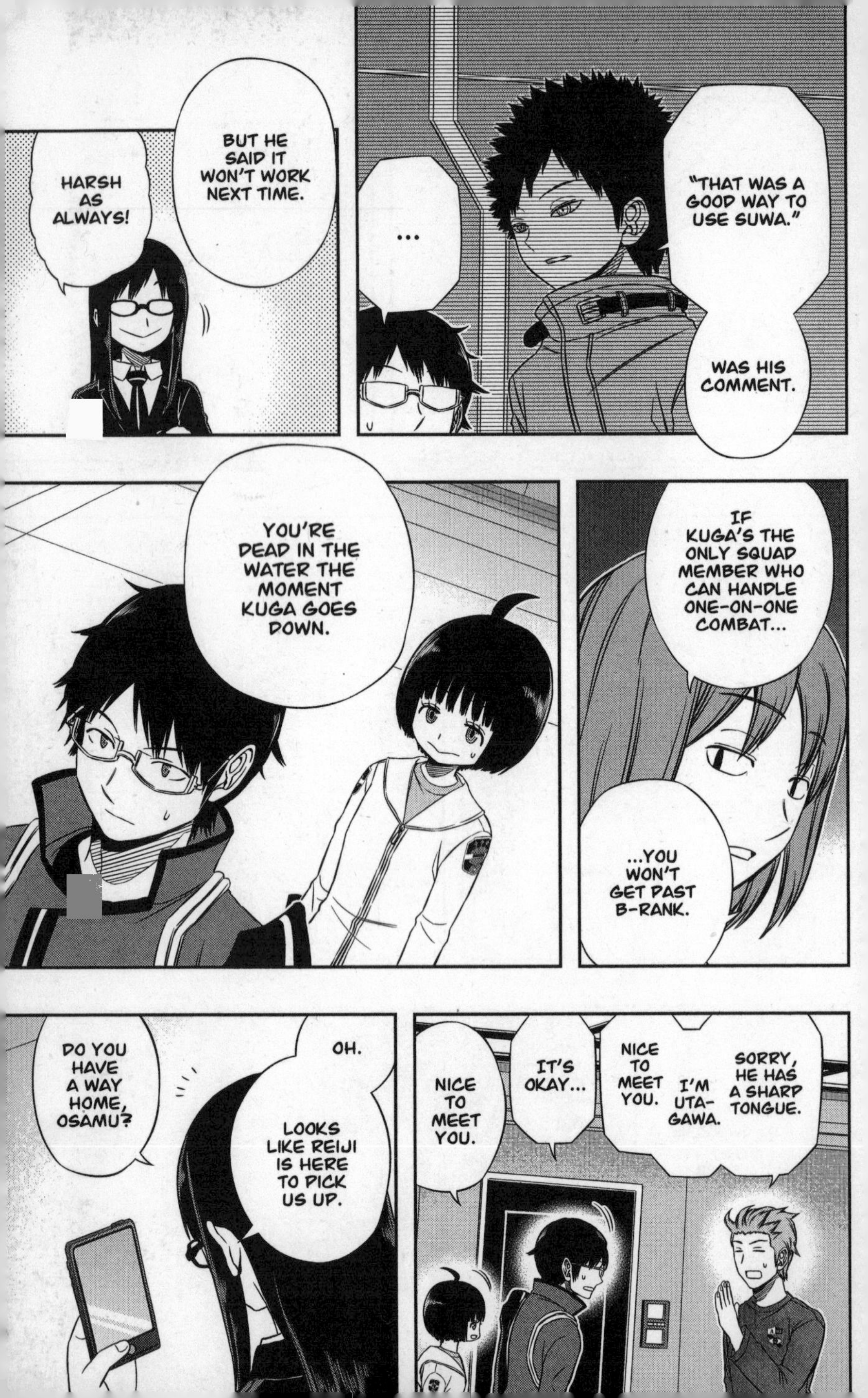
"THAT WAS A GOOD WAY TO USE SUWA."
WAS HIS COMMENT.
...
BUT HE SAID IT WON'T WORK NEXT TIME.
HARSH AS ALWAYS!
IF KUGA'S THE ONLY SQUAD MEMBER WHO CAN HANDLE ONE-ON-ONE COMBAT...
...YOU WON'T GET PAST B-RANK.
YOU'RE DEAD IN THE WATER THE MOMENT KUGA GOES DOWN.
SORRY, HE HAS A SHARP TONGUE.
NICE TO MEET YOU. I'M UTA-GAWA.
IT'S OKAY...
NICE TO MEET YOU.
OH.
LOOKS LIKE REIJI IS HERE TO PICK US UP.
DO YOU HAVE A WAY HOME, OSAMU?

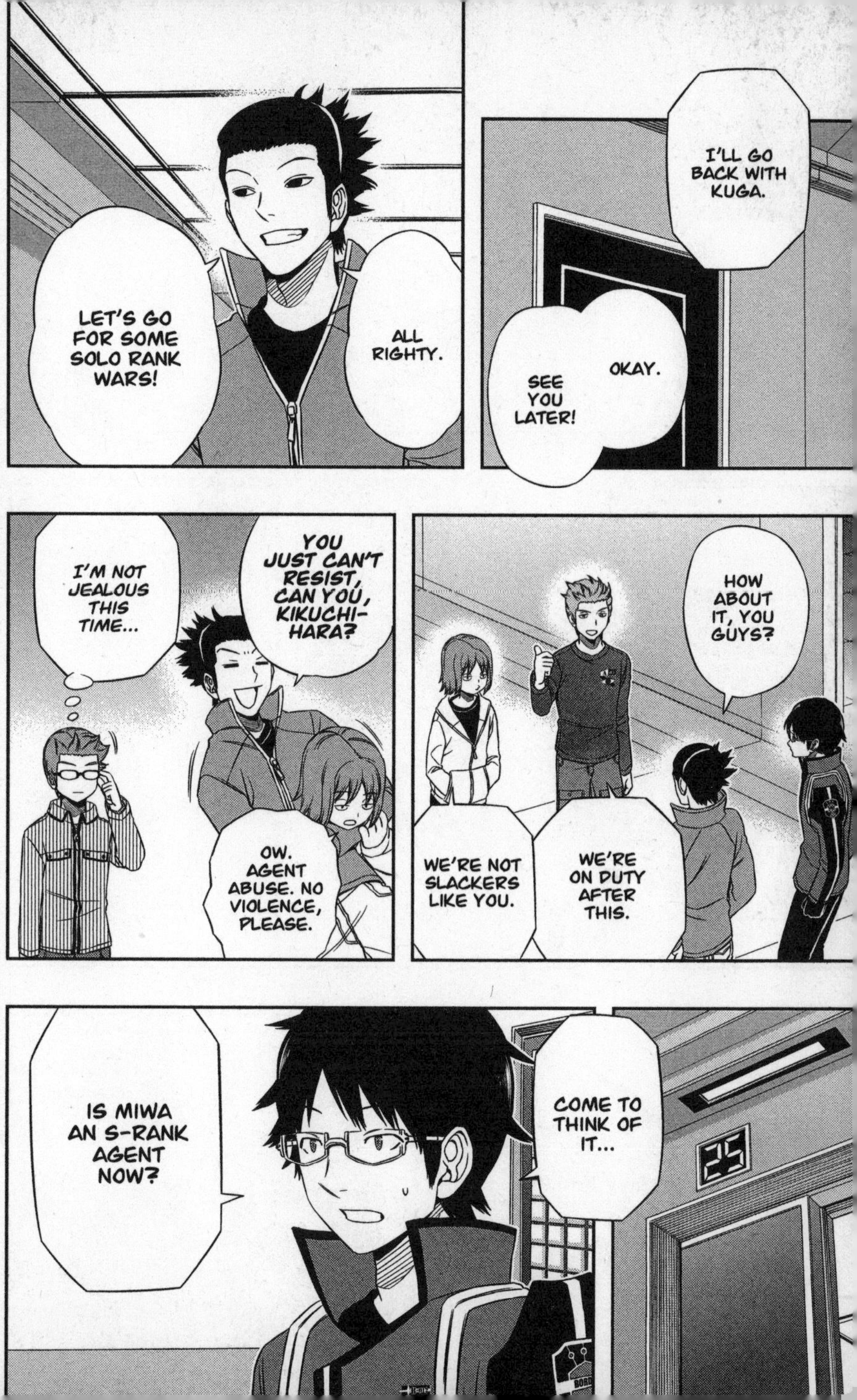
I'LL GO BACK WITH KUGA.
OKAY.
SEE YOU LATER!
ALL RIGHTY.
LET'S GO FOR SOME SOLO RANK WARS!
HOW ABOUT IT, YOU GUYS?
WE'RE ON DUTY AFTER THIS.
WE'RE NOT SLACKERS LIKE YOU.
YOU JUST CAN'T RESIST, CAN YOU, KIKUCHI-HARA?
I'M NOT JEALOUS THIS TIME...
OW. AGENT ABUSE. NO VIOLENCE, PLEASE.
COME TO THINK OF IT...
IS MIWA AN S-RANK AGENT NOW?

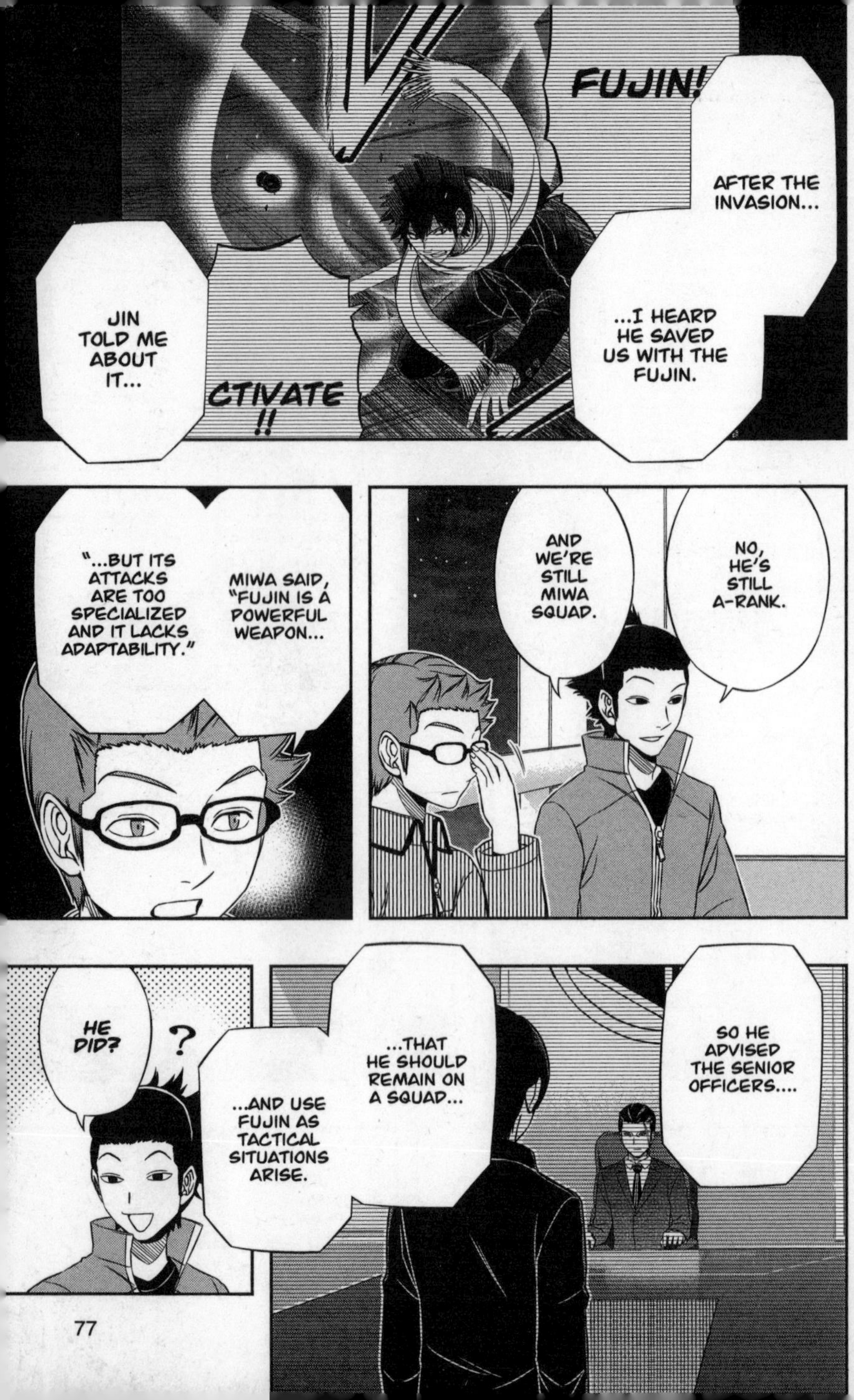
FUJIN!
AFTER THE INVASION...
...I HEARD HE SAVED US WITH THE FUJIN.
CTIVATE!!
JIN TOLD ME ABOUT IT...
NO, HE'S STILL A-RANK.
AND WE'RE STILL MIWA SQUAD.
MIWA SAID, "FUJIN IS A POWERFUL WEAPON...
"...BUT ITS ATTACKS ARE TOO SPECIALIZED AND IT LACKS ADAPTABILITY."
SO HE ADVISED THE SENIOR OFFICERS....
...THAT HE SHOULD REMAIN ON A SQUAD...
...AND USE FUJIN AS TACTICAL SITUATIONS ARISE.
HE DID?
?

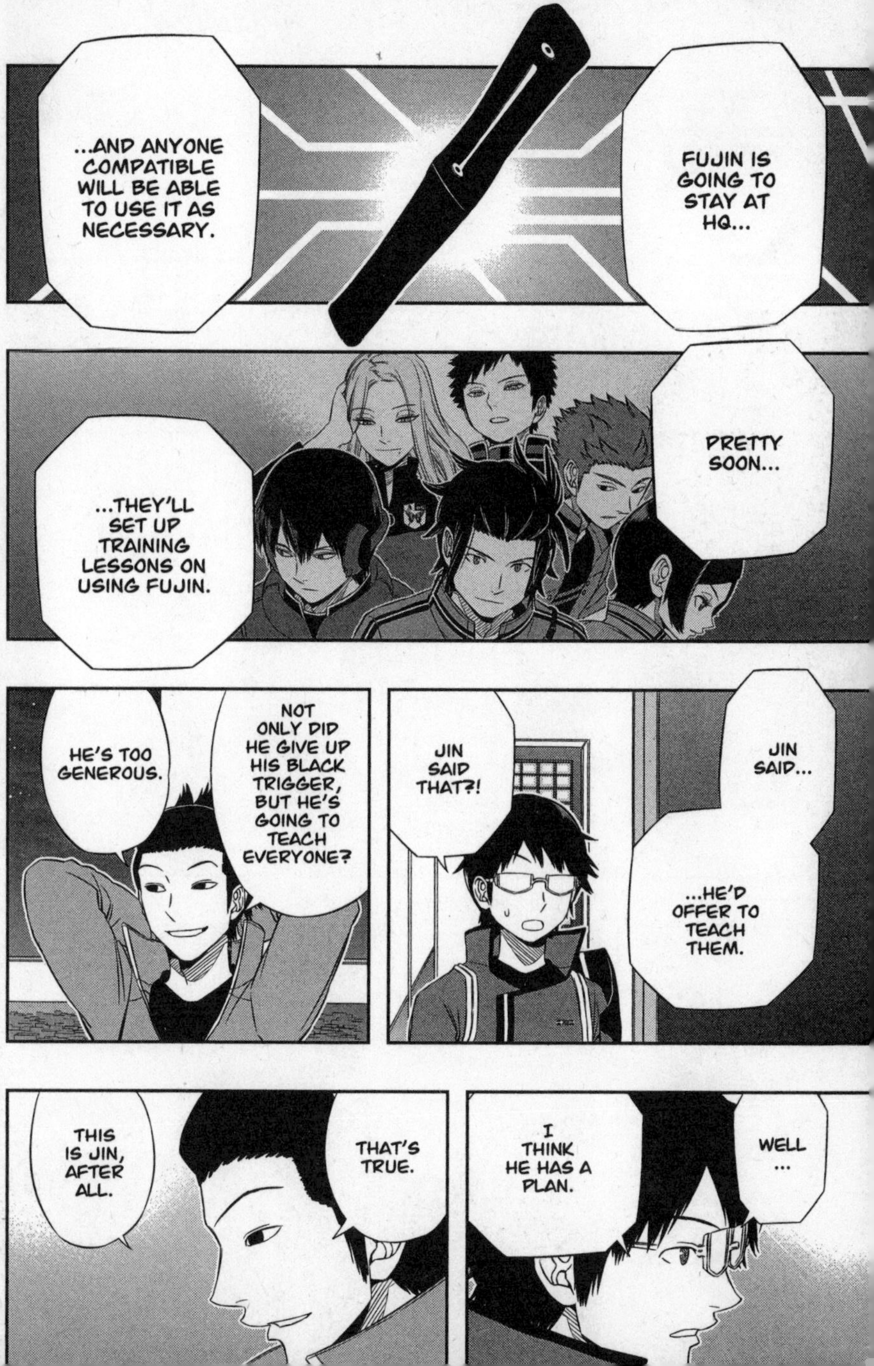
FUJIN IS GOING TO STAY AT HQ...
...AND ANYONE COMPATIBLE WILL BE ABLE TO USE IT AS NECESSARY.
PRETTY SOON...
...THEY'LL SET UP TRAINING LESSONS ON USING FUJIN.
JIN SAID...
...HE'D OFFER TO TEACH THEM.
JIN SAID THAT?!
NOT ONLY DID HE GIVE UP HIS BLACK TRIGGER, BUT HE'S GOING TO TEACH EVERYONE?
HE'S TOO GENEROUS.
WELL ...
I THINK HE HAS A PLAN.
THAT'S TRUE.
THIS IS JIN, AFTER ALL.

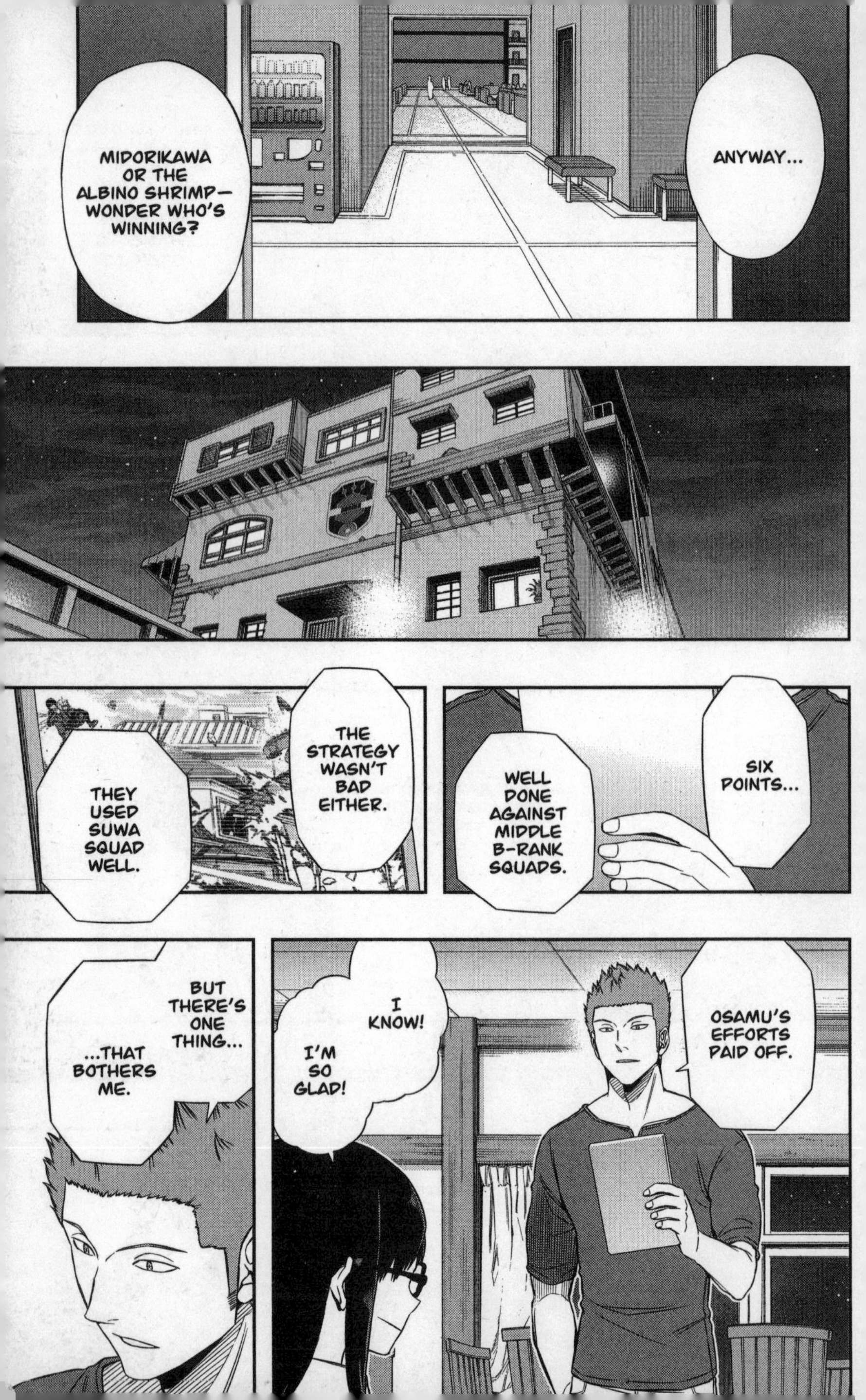
ANYWAY...
MIDORIKAWA OR THE ALBINO SHRIMP—WONDER WHO'S WINNING?
SIX POINTS...
WELL DONE AGAINST MIDDLE B-RANK SQUADS.
THE STRATEGY WASN'T BAD EITHER.
THEY USED SUWA SQUAD WELL.
OSAMU'S EFFORTS PAID OFF.
I KNOW!
I'M SO GLAD!
BUT THERE'S ONE THING...
...THAT BOTHERS ME.

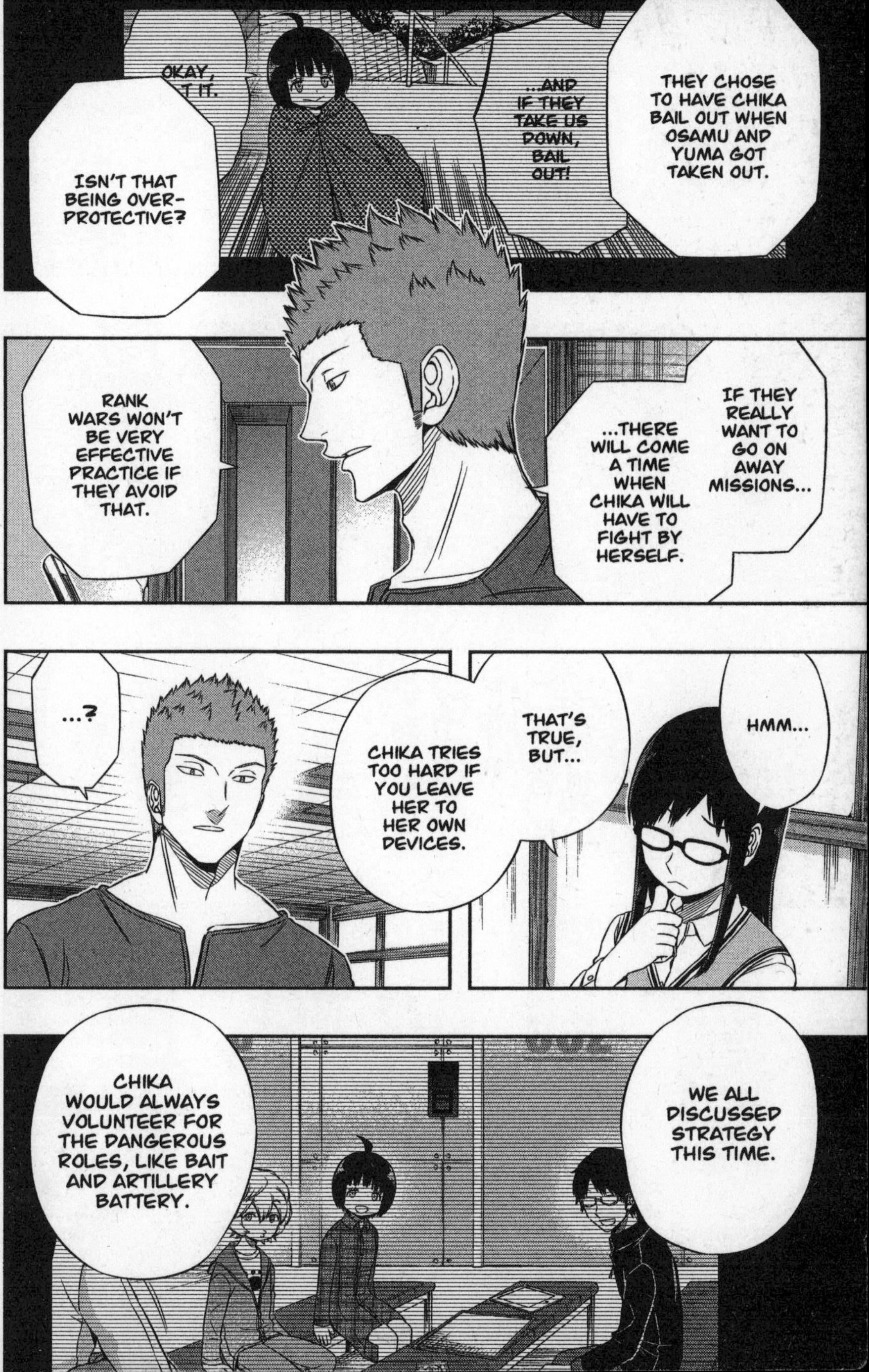
THEY CHOSE TO HAVE CHIKA BAIL OUT WHEN OSAMU AND YUMA GOT TAKEN OUT.
...AND IF THEY TAKE US DOWN, BAIL OUT!
OKAY,
ISN'T THAT BEING OVER-PROTECTIVE?
IF THEY REALLY WANT TO GO ON AWAY MISSIONS...
...THERE WILL COME A TIME WHEN CHIKA WILL HAVE TO FIGHT BY HERSELF.
RANK WARS WON'T BE VERY EFFECTIVE PRACTICE IF THEY AVOID THAT.
HMM...
THAT'S TRUE, BUT...
CHIKA TRIES TOO HARD IF YOU LEAVE HER TO HER OWN DEVICES.
...?
WE ALL DISCUSSED STRATEGY THIS TIME.
CHIKA WOULD ALWAYS VOLUNTEER FOR THE DANGEROUS ROLES, LIKE BAIT AND ARTILLERY BATTERY.

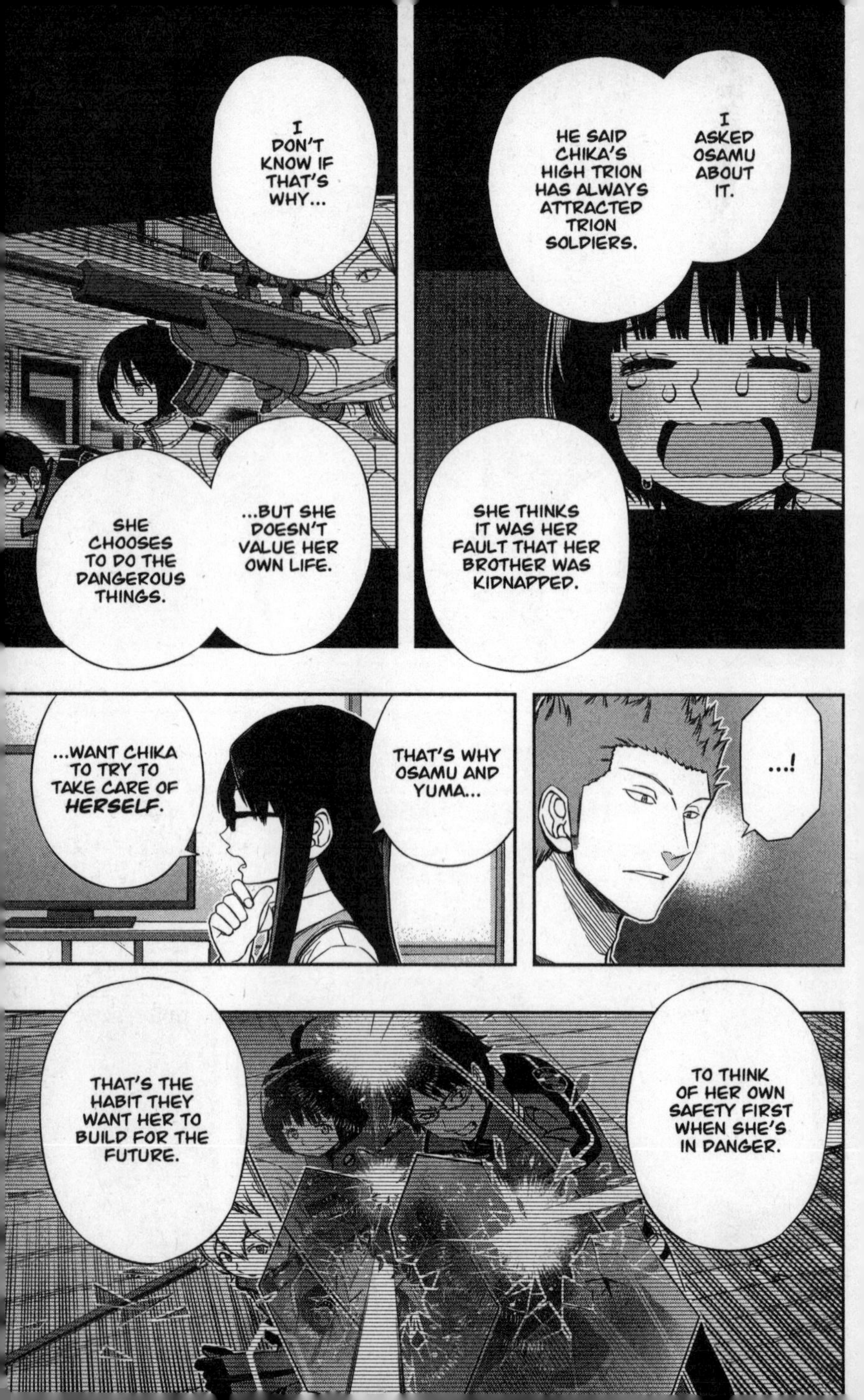
I ASKED OSAMU ABOUT IT.
HE SAID CHIKA'S HIGH TRION HAS ALWAYS ATTRACTED TRION SOLDIERS.
SHE THINKS IT WAS HER FAULT THAT HER BROTHER WAS KIDNAPPED.
I DON'T KNOW IF THAT'S WHY...
...BUT SHE DOESN'T VALUE HER OWN LIFE.
SHE CHOOSES TO DO THE DANGEROUS THINGS.
...!
THAT'S WHY OSAMU AND YUMA...
...WANT CHIKA TO TRY TO TAKE CARE OF **HERSELF**.
TO THINK OF HER OWN SAFETY FIRST WHEN SHE'S IN DANGER.
THAT'S THE HABIT THEY WANT HER TO BUILD FOR THE FUTURE.

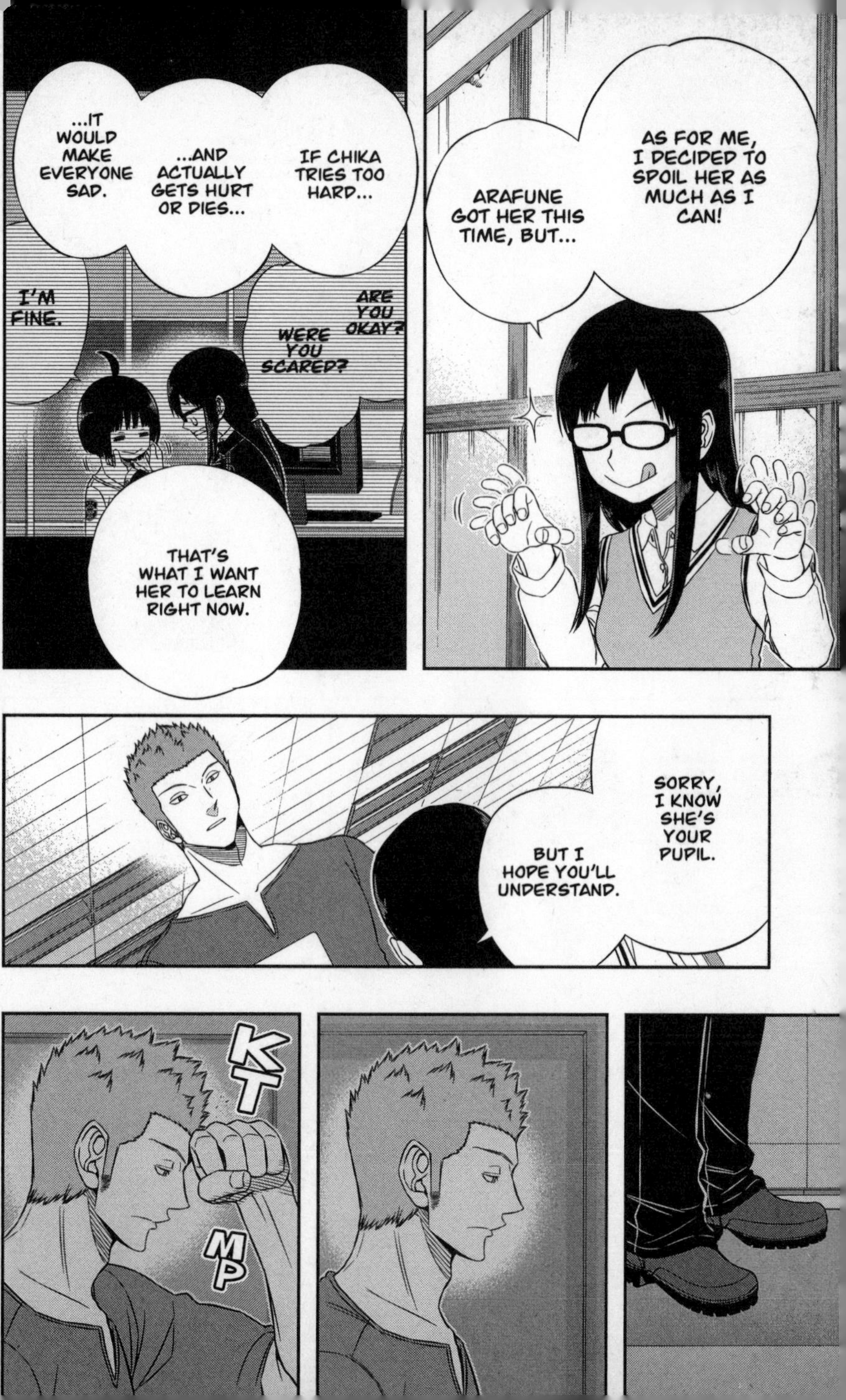
AS FOR ME, I DECIDED TO SPOIL HER AS MUCH AS I CAN!
ARAFUNE GOT HER THIS TIME, BUT...
IF CHIKA TRIES TOO HARD...
...AND ACTUALLY GETS HURT OR DIES...
...IT WOULD MAKE EVERYONE SAD.
ARE YOU OKAY?
WERE YOU SCARED?
I'M FINE.
THAT'S WHAT I WANT HER TO LEARN RIGHT NOW.
SORRY, I KNOW SHE'S YOUR PUPIL.
BUT I HOPE YOU'LL UNDERSTAND.
KT
MP

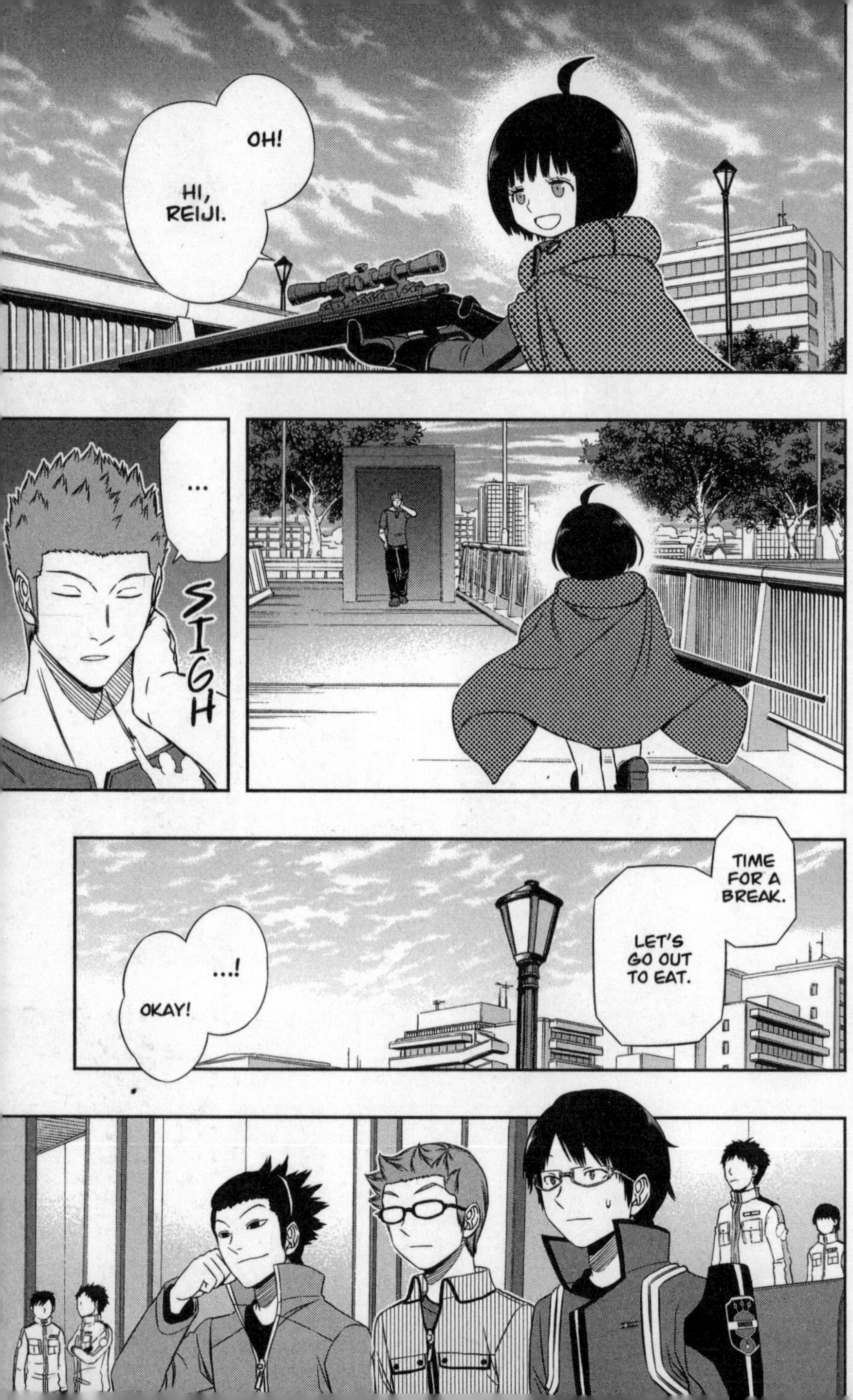
OH!
HI, REIJI.
...
SIGH
TIME FOR A BREAK.
LET'S GO OUT TO EAT.
...!
OKAY!

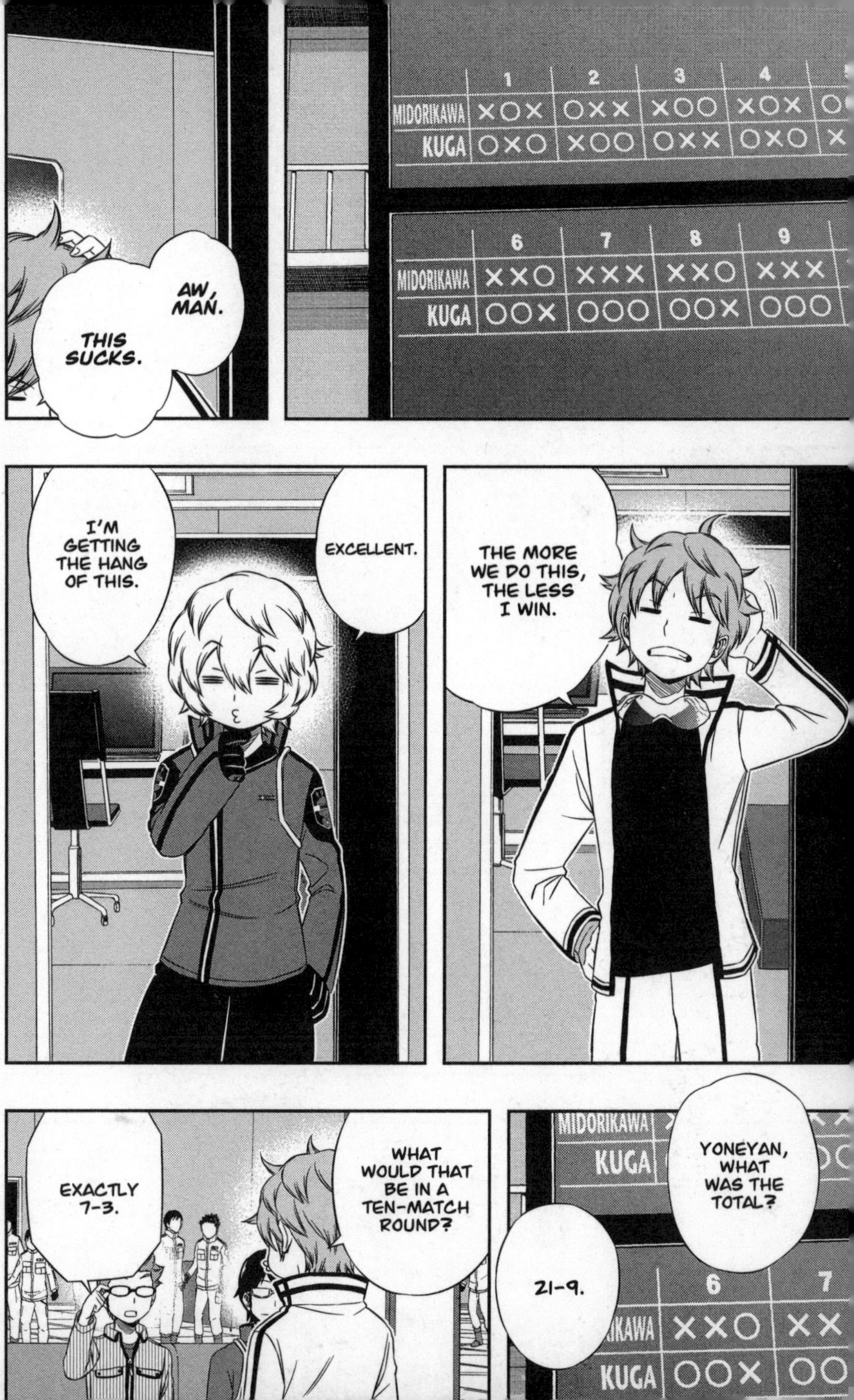

1 2 3 4
MIDORIKAWA ×○× ○×× ×○○ ×○×
KUGA ○×○ ×○○ ○×× ○×○
6 7 8 9
MIDORIKAWA ××○ ××× ××○ ×××
KUGA ○○× ○○○ ○○× ○○○
AW, MAN.
THIS SUCKS.
THE MORE WE DO THIS, THE LESS I WIN.
EXCELLENT.
I'M GETTING THE HANG OF THIS.
YONEYAN, WHAT WAS THE TOTAL?
21-9.
WHAT WOULD THAT BE IN A TEN-MATCH ROUND?
EXACTLY 7-3.

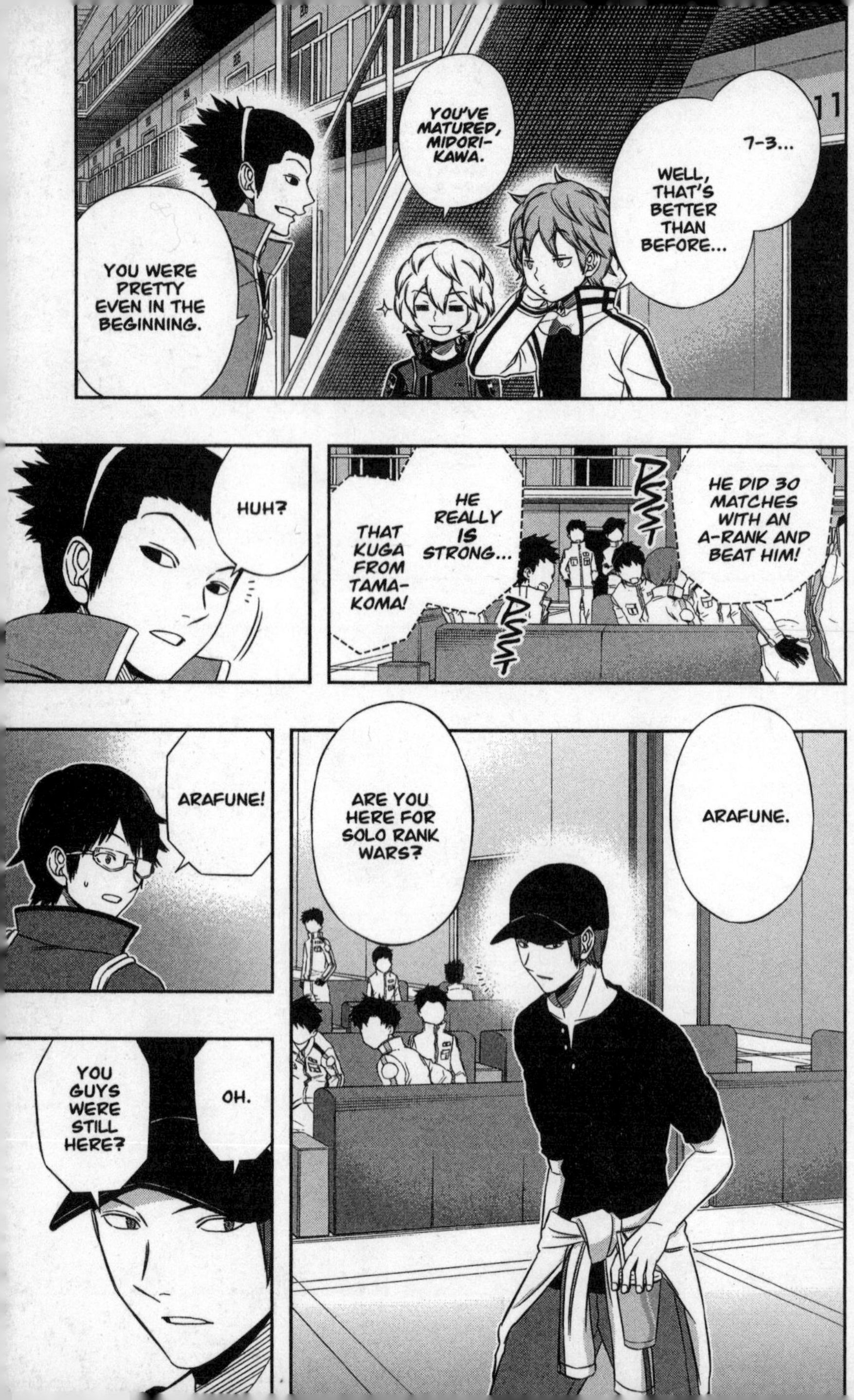
7-3...
WELL, THAT'S BETTER THAN BEFORE...
YOU'VE MATURED, MIDORIKAWA.
YOU WERE PRETTY EVEN IN THE BEGINNING.
HE DID 30 MATCHES WITH AN A-RANK AND BEAT HIM!
PSST
HE REALLY IS STRONG...
THAT KUGA FROM TAMAKOMA!
PSST
HUH?
ARAFUNE.
ARE YOU HERE FOR SOLO RANK WARS?
ARAFUNE!
OH.
YOU GUYS WERE STILL HERE?

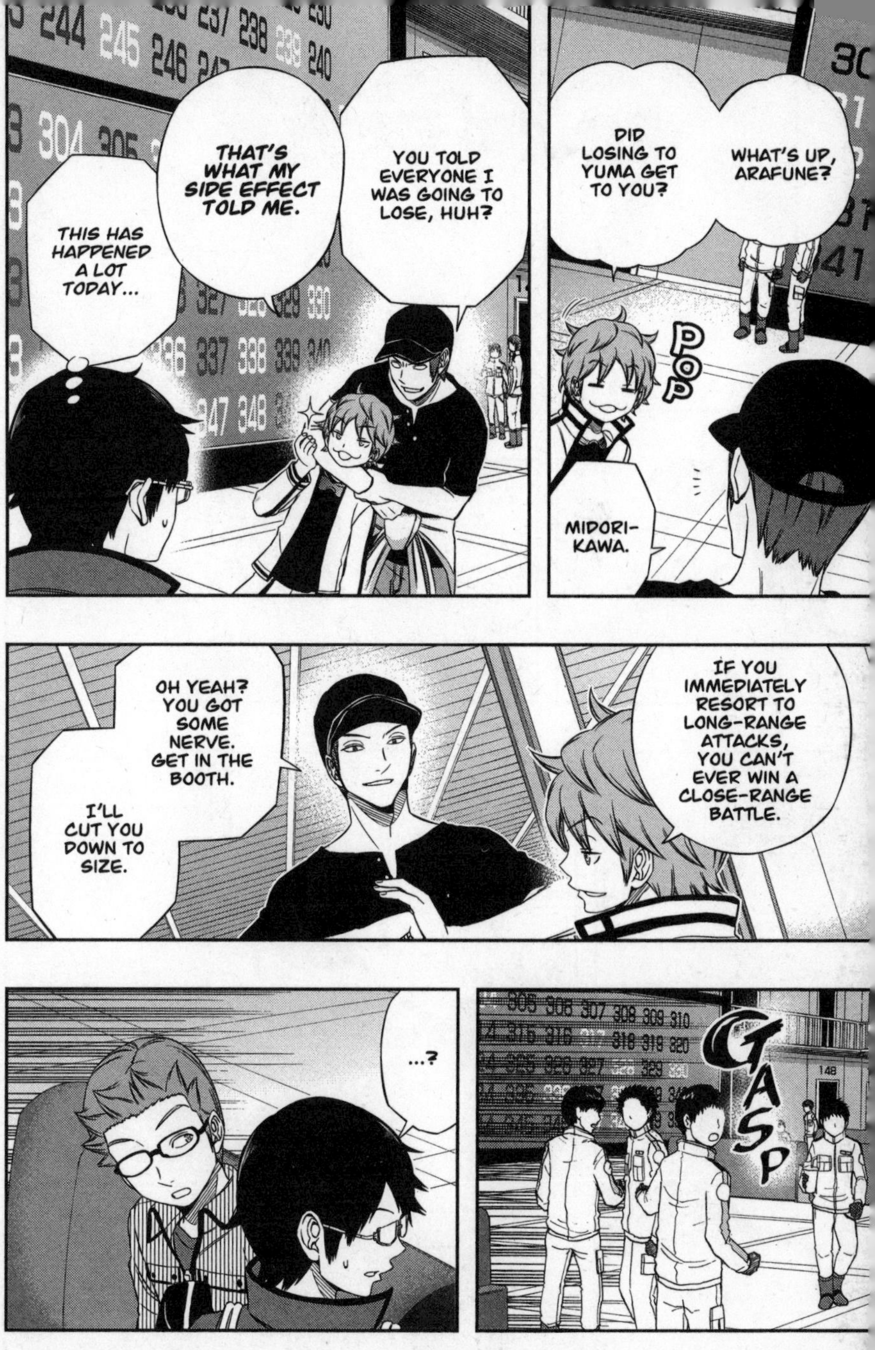
WHAT'S UP, ARAFUNE?
DID LOSING TO YUMA GET TO YOU?
POP
MIDORI-KAWA.
YOU TOLD EVERYONE I WAS GOING TO LOSE, HUH?
THAT'S WHAT MY SIDE EFFECT TOLD ME.
THIS HAS HAPPENED A LOT TODAY...
IF YOU IMMEDIATELY RESORT TO LONG-RANGE ATTACKS, YOU CAN'T EVER WIN A CLOSE-RANGE BATTLE.
OH YEAH? YOU GOT SOME NERVE. GET IN THE BOOTH.
I'LL CUT YOU DOWN TO SIZE.
GASP
...?

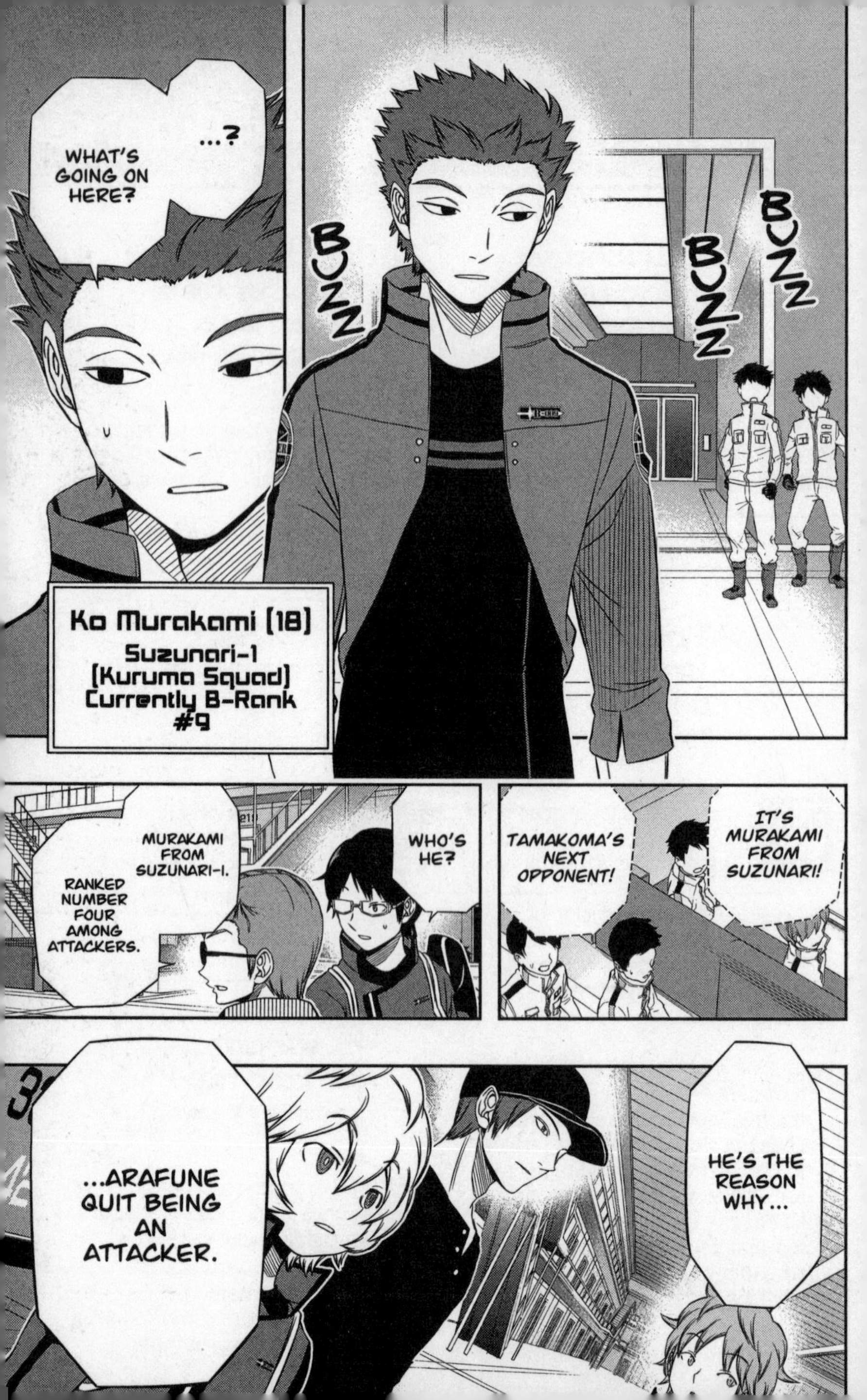
BUZZ
BUZZ
...?
BUZZ
WHAT'S GOING ON HERE?
Ko Murakami (18)
Suzunari-1 (Kuruma Squad) Currently B-Rank #9
IT'S MURAKAMI FROM SUZUNARI!
TAMAKOMA'S NEXT OPPONENT!
WHO'S HE?
MURAKAMI FROM SUZUNARI-1.
RANKED NUMBER FOUR AMONG ATTACKERS.
HE'S THE REASON WHY...
...ARAFUNE QUIT BEING AN ATTACKER.

World Trigger Tagline Awards

A story whose meaning you'll soon realize.
Vol. 1 (by Nakayan)

COM-MENT: I'm happy that this expresses rereadability so well. That's exactly what I want.

I felt my efforts since vol. 1 have all been worthwhile.

Only he doesn't realize he's a hero.
Vol. 2 (by Hyuganatsu)

COM-MENT: It's very Osamu without using a negative phrase that expresses weakness.

I don't think there's a tagline for Osamu that surpasses this. Wow.

Friends become comrades.
Vol. 3 (by Pigeon Manju)

COM-MENT: There were a lot of good ones for vol. 3, but I like this one best. It marks a turning point.

A simple expression of forming a team put simply and passionately without being overly dramatic.

The resistance begins.
Vol. 6 (by Hinaharu)

COM-MENT: There were a lot of "the battle begins." "Resistance" was unique, straightforward and cool.

It seems like a natural expression, yet it was unique and polished.

It hasn't stopped raining.
Vol. 9 (by Arisawa)

COM-MENT: This was the best one among the lines about Miwa's past. I like how it omits everything else.

It doesn't mention Miwa, but it makes a strong impression. It gave me goosebumps.

All of the winning taglines will be used in posters and paper bands for the reprints. These are all written from a point of view that I couldn't come up with on my own and are full of love for the manga. This was a great experience discovering something new about my own manga. There were many honorable mentions, so they'll be at the end of the volume.

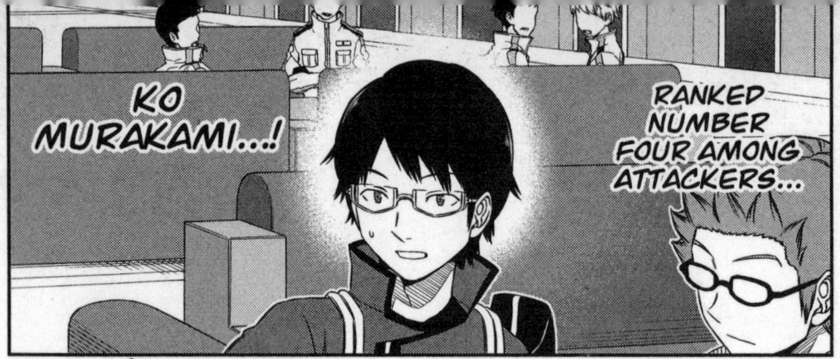
RANKED NUMBER FOUR AMONG ATTACKERS...
KO MURAKAMI...!

Chapter 93 Ko Murakami

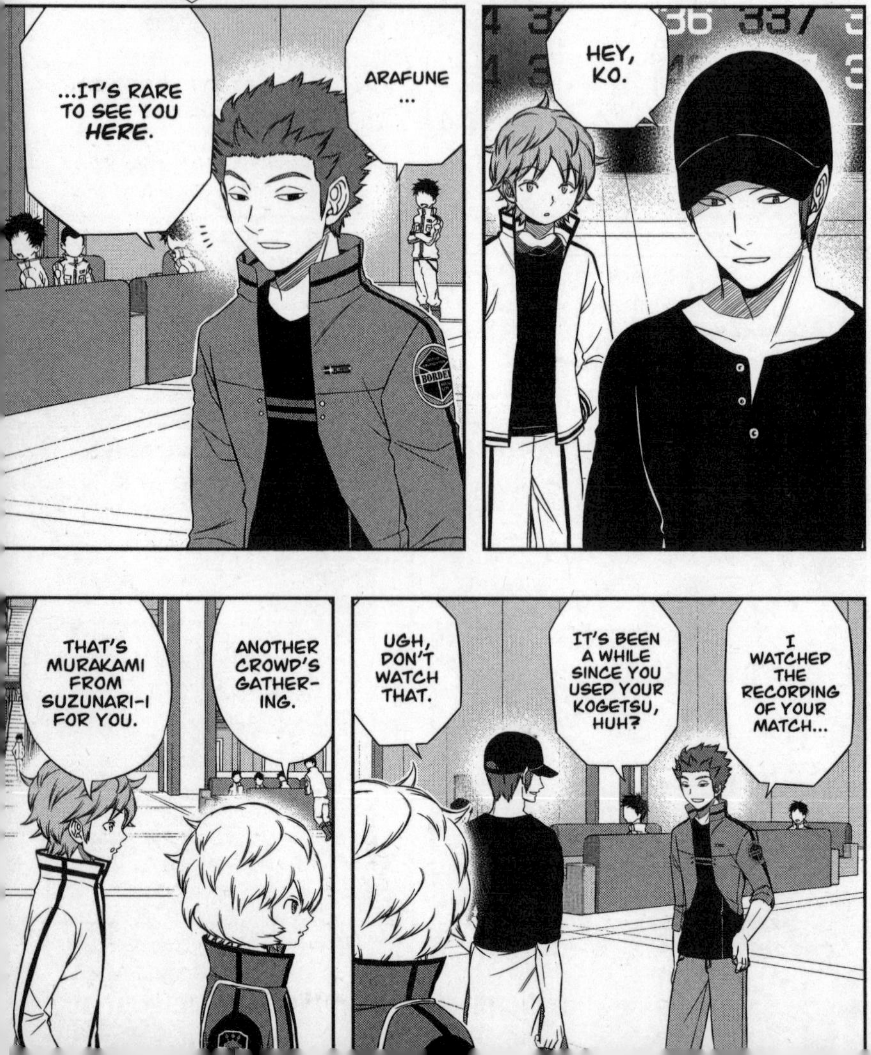
HEY, KO.
ARAFUNE...
...IT'S RARE TO SEE YOU HERE.
I WATCHED THE RECORDING OF YOUR MATCH...
IT'S BEEN A WHILE SINCE YOU USED YOUR KOGETSU, HUH?
UGH, DON'T WATCH THAT.
ANOTHER CROWD'S GATHERING.
THAT'S MURAKAMI FROM SUZUNARI-I FOR YOU.

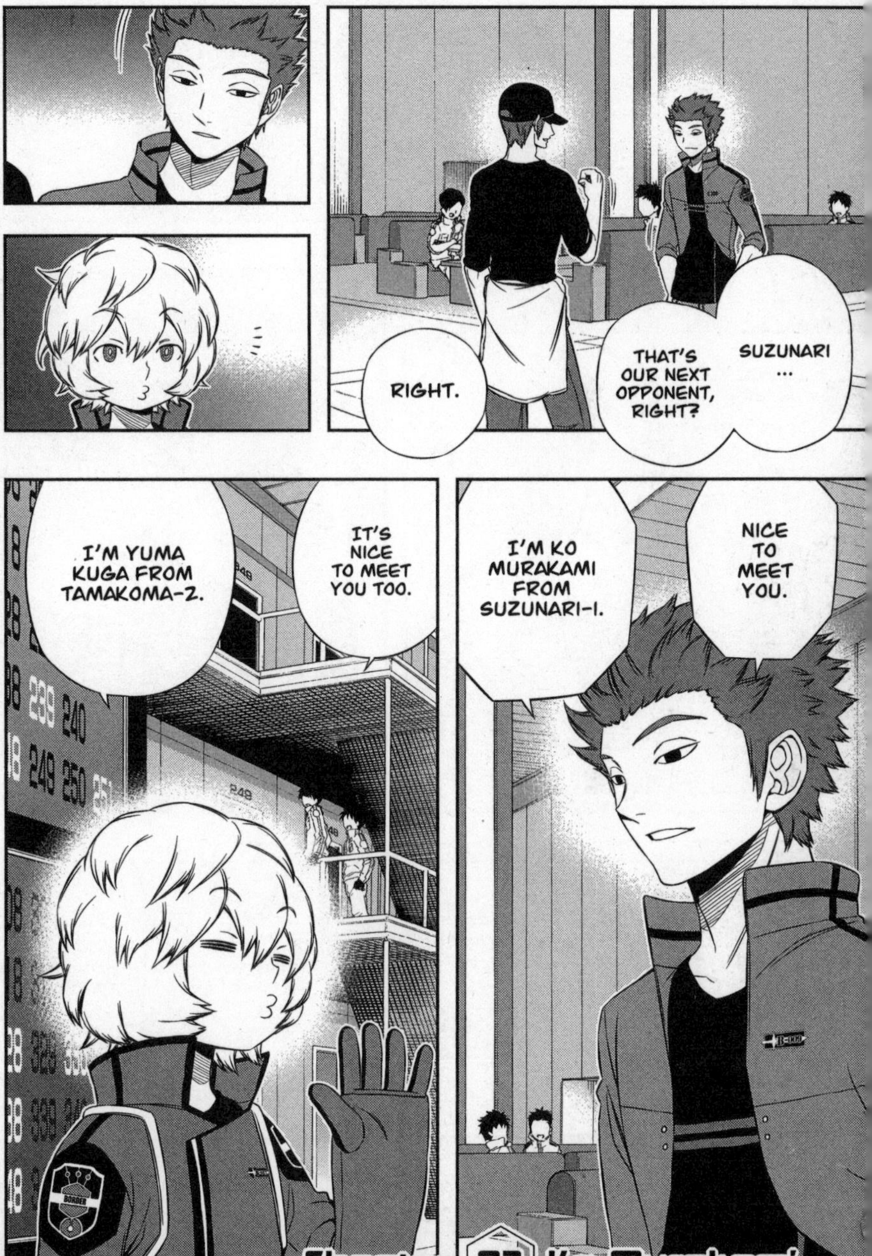
SUZUNARI ...
THAT'S OUR NEXT OPPONENT, RIGHT?
RIGHT.
NICE TO MEET YOU.
I'M KO MURAKAMI FROM SUZUNARI-1.
IT'S NICE TO MEET YOU TOO.
I'M YUMA KUGA FROM TAMAKOMA-2.
Chapter 93 Ko Murakami

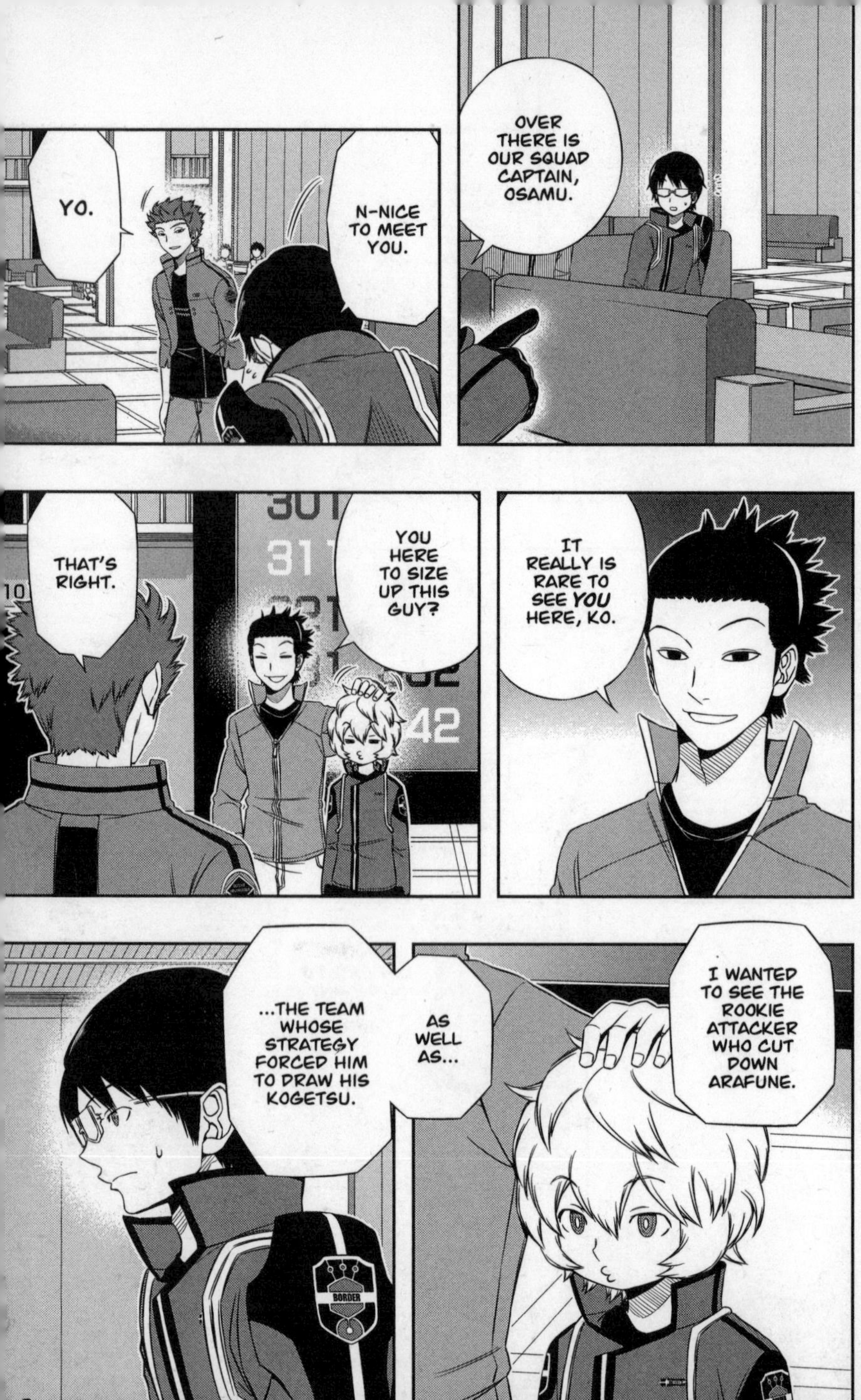
OVER THERE IS OUR SQUAD CAPTAIN, OSAMU.
N-NICE TO MEET YOU.
YO.
IT REALLY IS RARE TO SEE *YOU* HERE, KO.
YOU HERE TO SIZE UP THIS GUY?
THAT'S RIGHT.
I WANTED TO SEE THE ROOKIE ATTACKER WHO CUT DOWN ARAFUNE.
AS WELL AS...
...THE TEAM WHOSE STRATEGY FORCED HIM TO DRAW HIS KOGETSU.

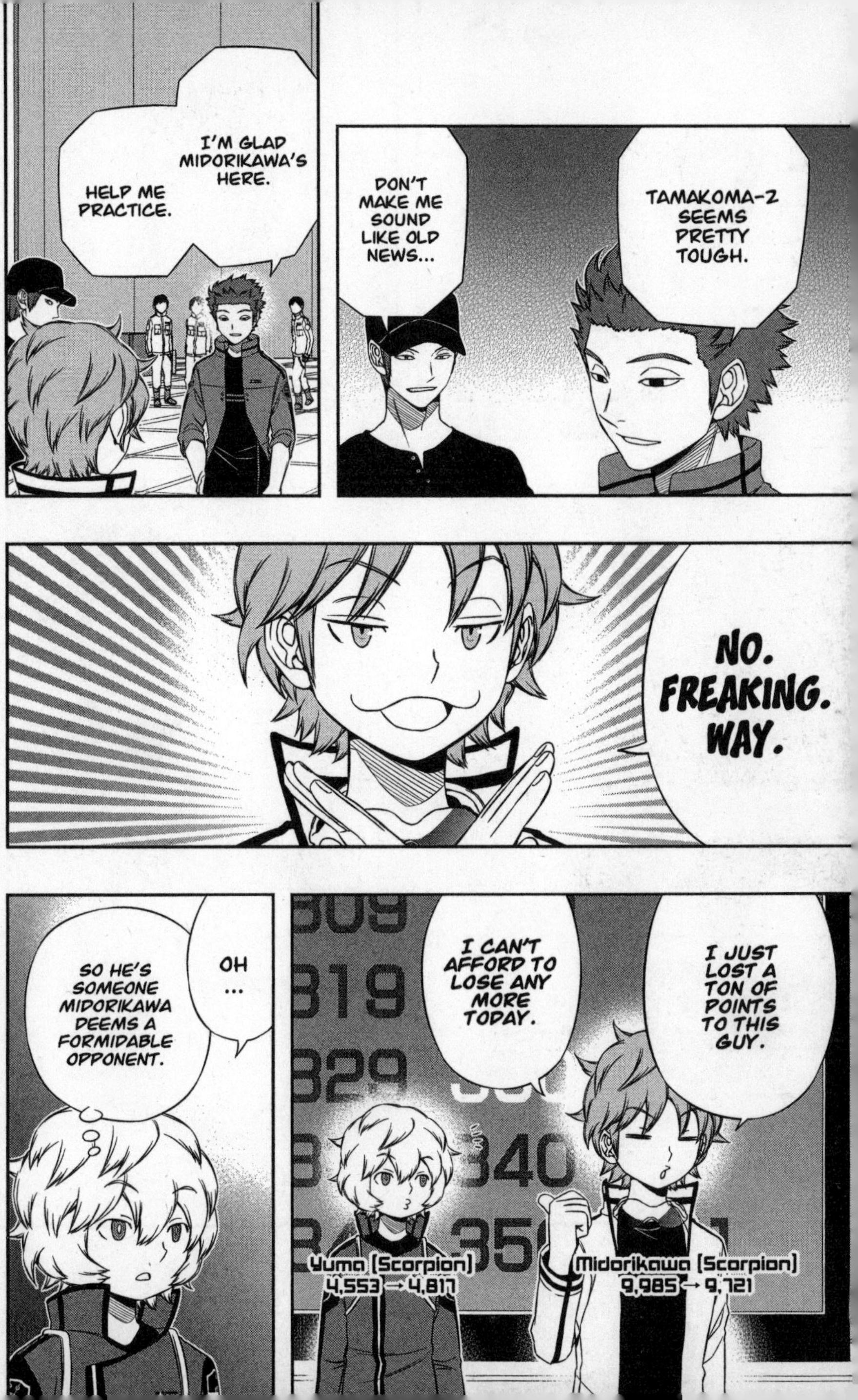
TAMAKOMA-2 SEEMS PRETTY TOUGH.
DON'T MAKE ME SOUND LIKE OLD NEWS...
I'M GLAD MIDORIKAWA'S HERE.
HELP ME PRACTICE.
NO. FREAKING. WAY.
I JUST LOST A TON OF POINTS TO THIS GUY.
I CAN'T AFFORD TO LOSE ANY MORE TODAY.
Midorikawa [Scorpion]
9,985 → 9,721
Yuma [Scorpion]
4,553 → 4,817
OH ...
SO HE'S SOMEONE MIDORIKAWA DEEMS A FORMIDABLE OPPONENT.

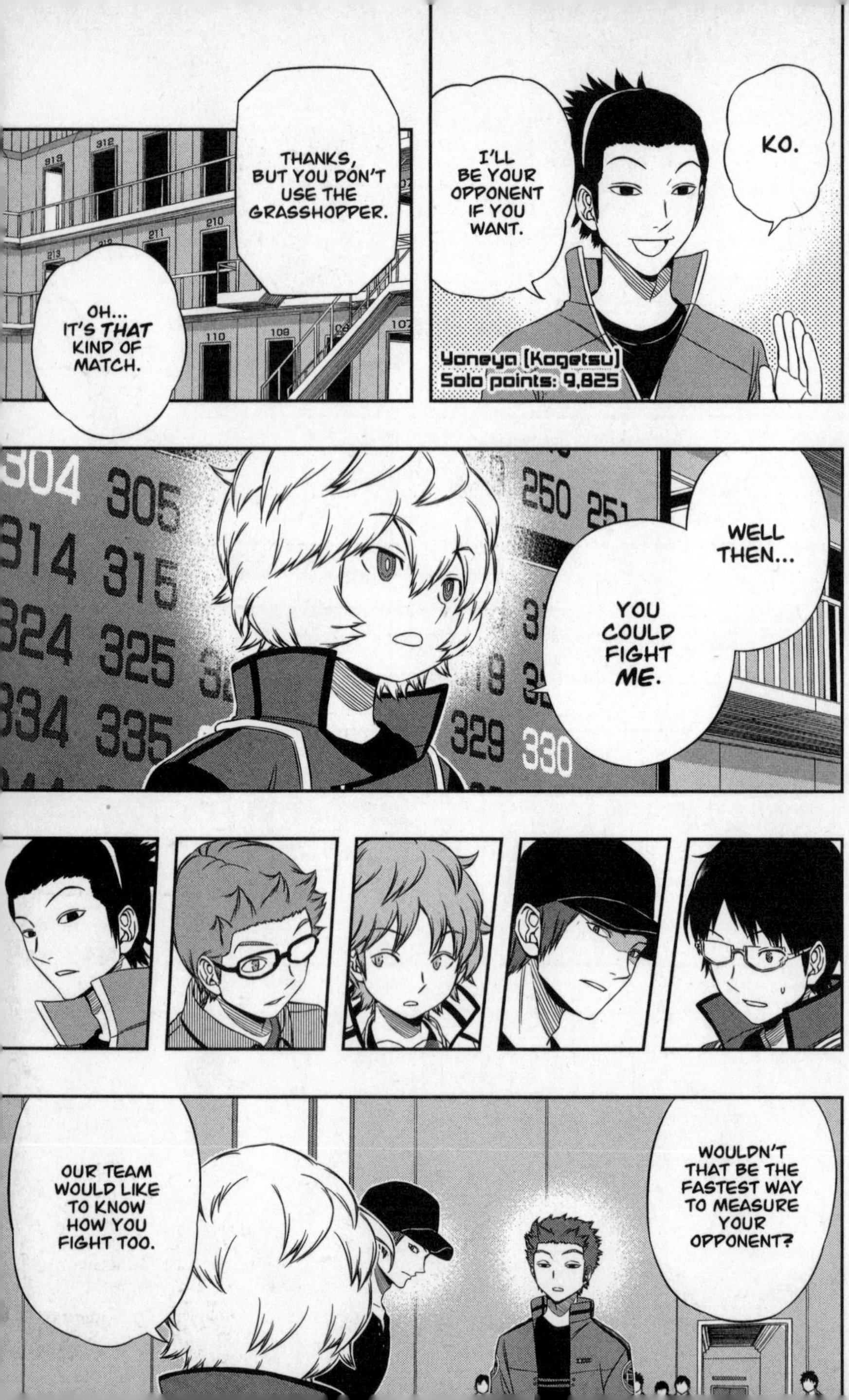
KO.
I'LL BE YOUR OPPONENT IF YOU WANT.
Yoneya [Kogetsu] Solo points: 9,825
THANKS, BUT YOU DON'T USE THE GRASSHOPPER.
OH... IT'S THAT KIND OF MATCH.
WELL THEN...
YOU COULD FIGHT ME.
WOULDN'T THAT BE THE FASTEST WAY TO MEASURE YOUR OPPONENT?
OUR TEAM WOULD LIKE TO KNOW HOW YOU FIGHT TOO.

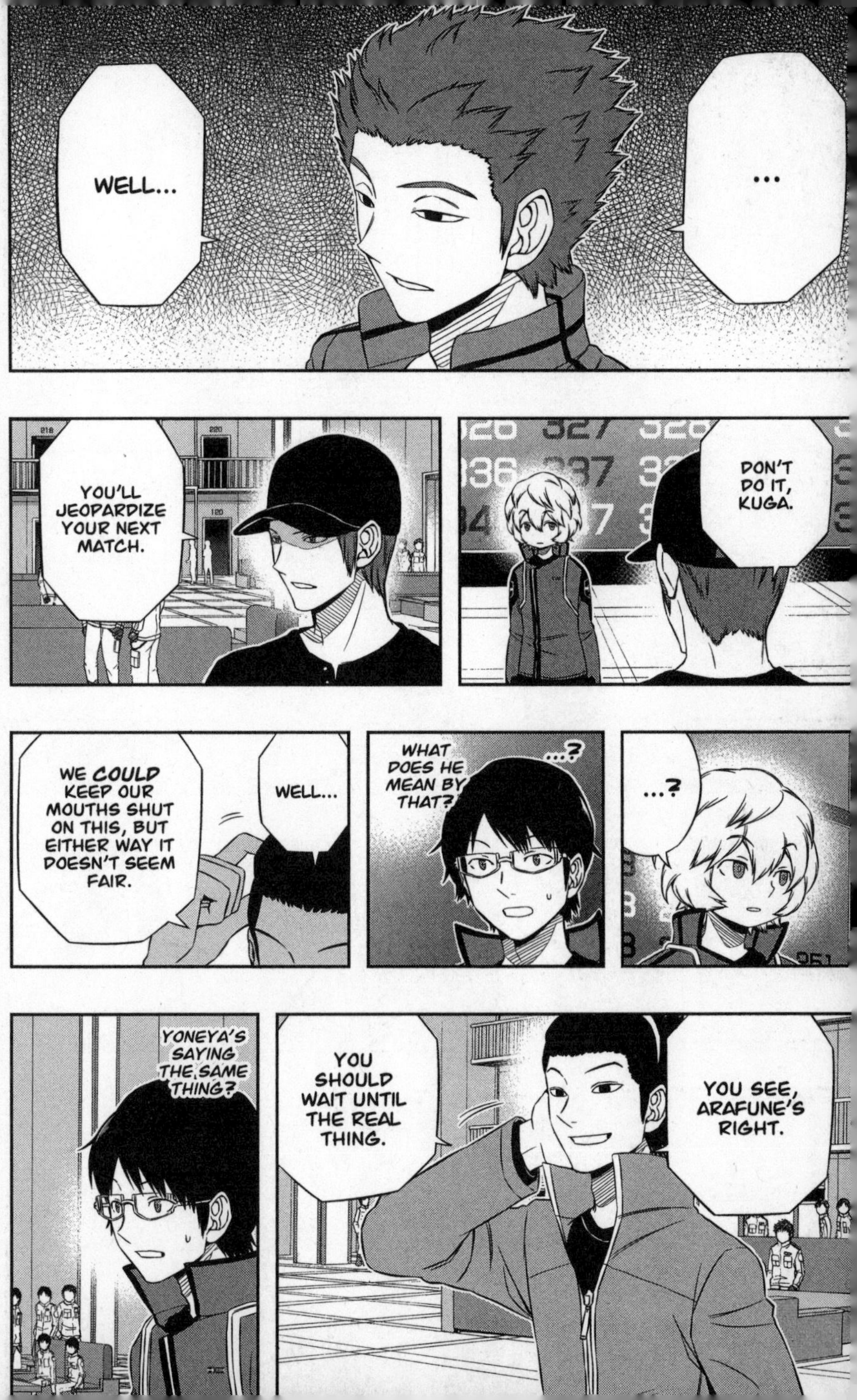
...
WELL...
DON'T DO IT, KUGA.
YOU'LL JEOPARDIZE YOUR NEXT MATCH.
...?
WHAT DOES HE MEAN BY THAT?
...?
WELL...
WE COULD KEEP OUR MOUTHS SHUT ON THIS, BUT EITHER WAY IT DOESN'T SEEM FAIR.
YOU SEE, ARAFUNE'S RIGHT.
YOU SHOULD WAIT UNTIL THE REAL THING.
YONEYA'S SAYING THE SAME THING?

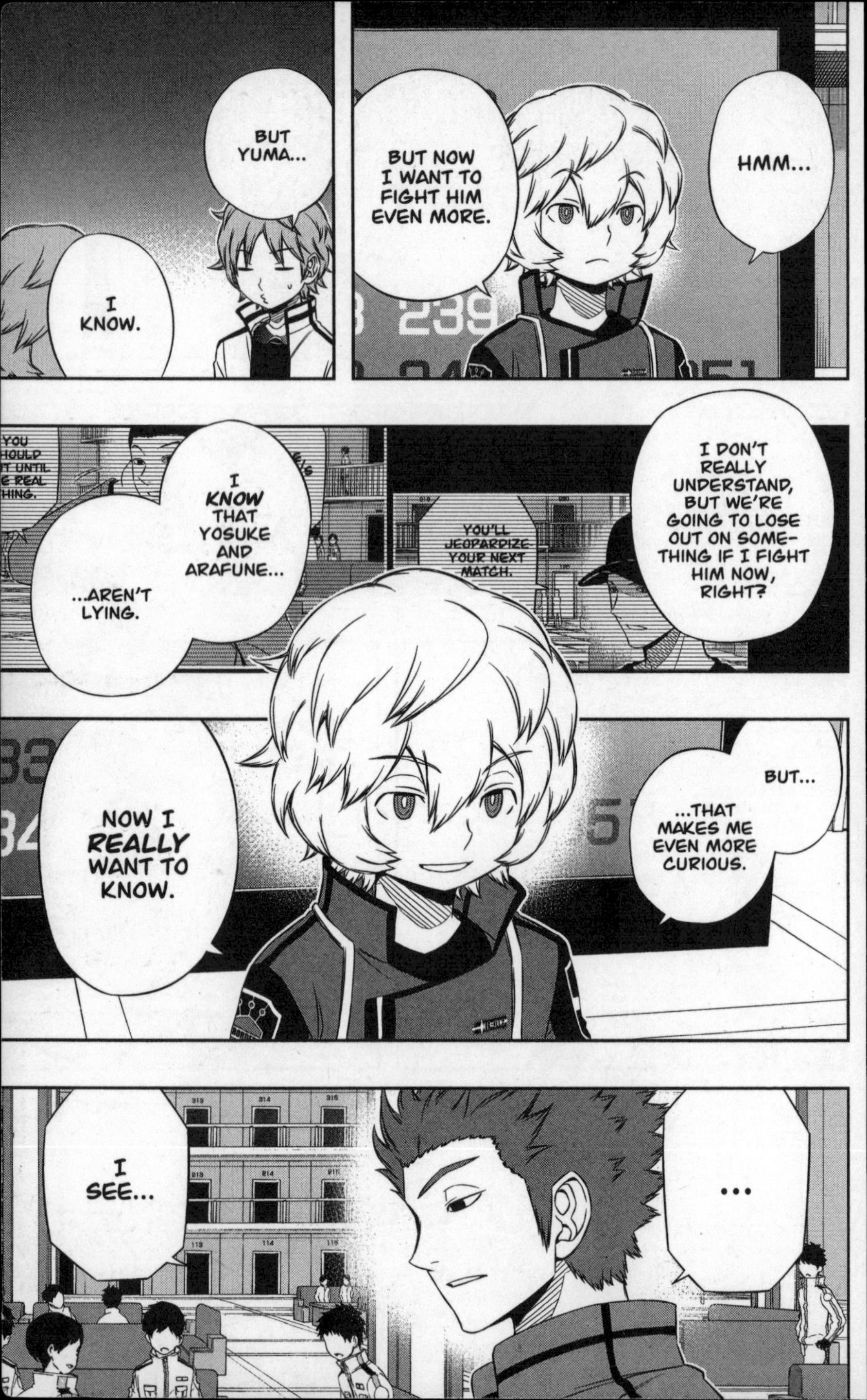
HMM...
BUT NOW I WANT TO FIGHT HIM EVEN MORE.
BUT YUMA...
I KNOW.
I DON'T REALLY UNDERSTAND, BUT WE'RE GOING TO LOSE OUT ON SOME-THING IF I FIGHT HIM NOW, RIGHT?
YOU'LL JEOPARDIZE YOUR NEXT MATCH.
I KNOW THAT YOSUKE AND ARAFUNE...
...AREN'T LYING.
BUT...
...THAT MAKES ME EVEN MORE CURIOUS.
NOW I REALLY WANT TO KNOW.
...
I SEE...

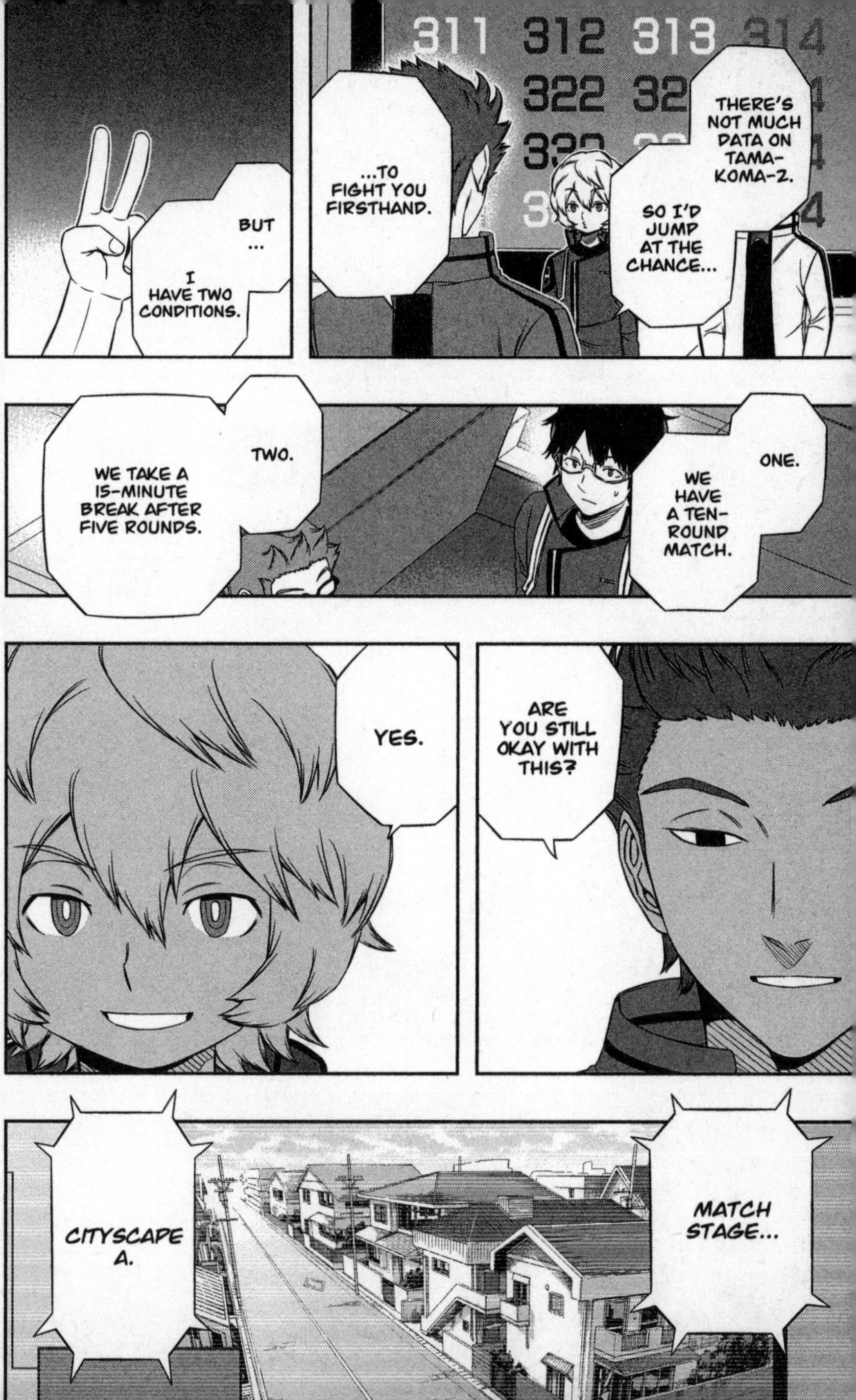
THERE'S NOT MUCH DATA ON TAMA-KOMA-2.
SO I'D JUMP AT THE CHANCE...
...TO FIGHT YOU FIRSTHAND.
BUT...
I HAVE TWO CONDITIONS.
ONE.
WE HAVE A TEN-ROUND MATCH.
TWO.
WE TAKE A 15-MINUTE BREAK AFTER FIVE ROUNDS.
ARE YOU STILL OKAY WITH THIS?
YES.
MATCH STAGE...
CITYSCAPE A.

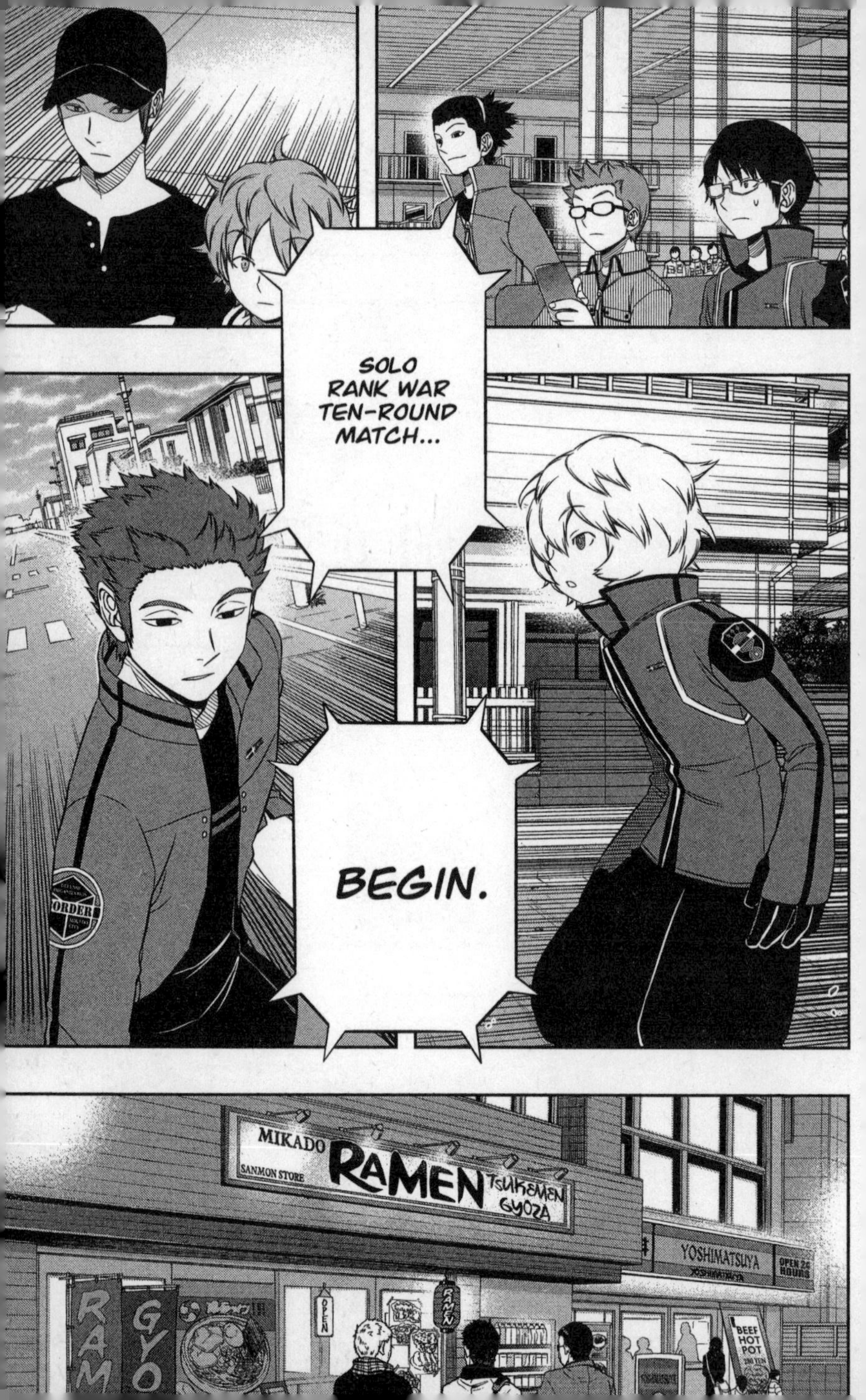
SOLO RANK WAR TEN-ROUND MATCH...
BEGIN.
ORDER
MIKADO
SANMON STORE
RAMEN
TSUKEMEN GYOZA
YOSHIMATSUYA
OPEN 24 HOURS
BEEF HOT POT
OPEN
RAMEN
RAM
GYO

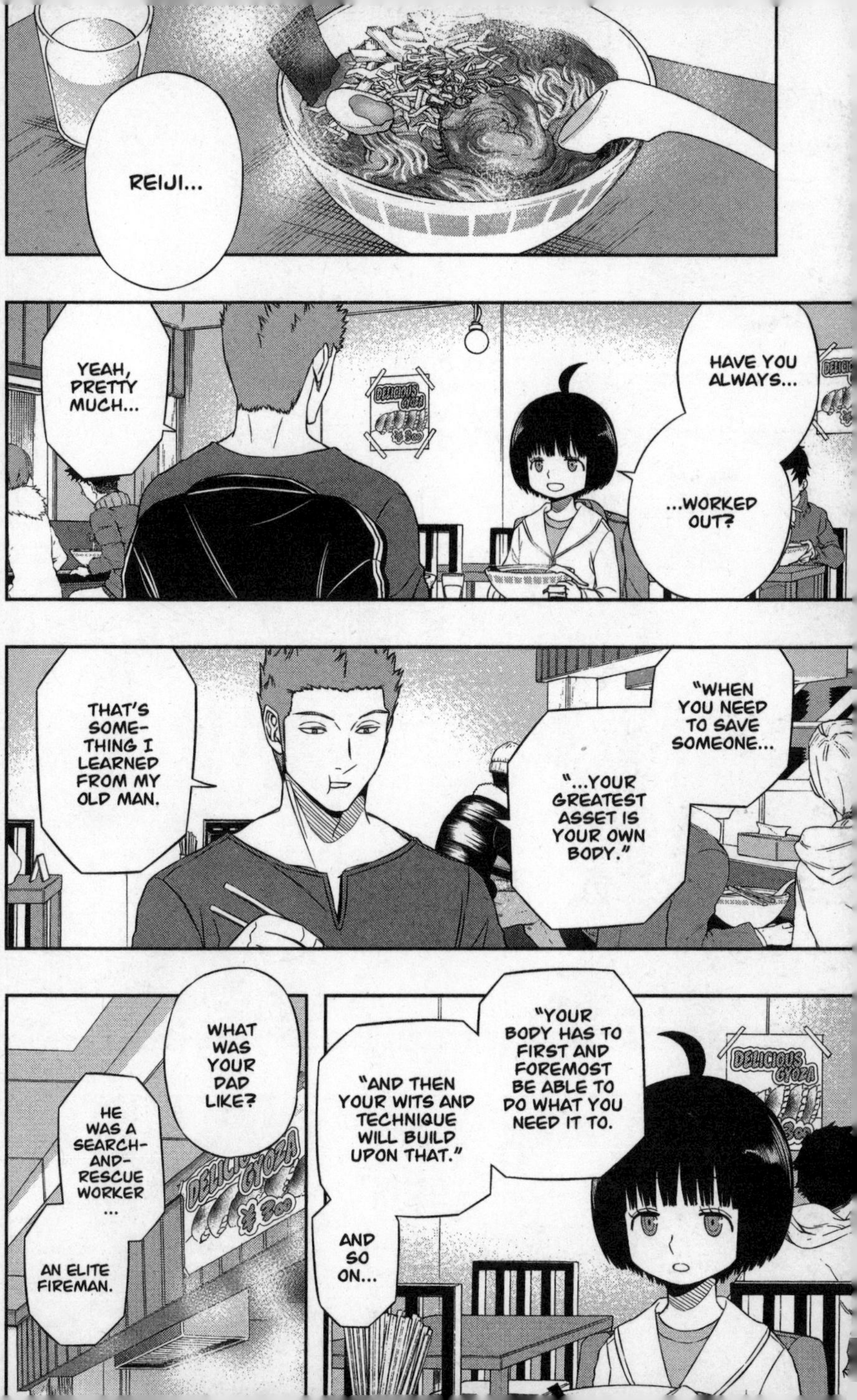
REIJI...
HAVE YOU ALWAYS...
...WORKED OUT?
YEAH, PRETTY MUCH...
"WHEN YOU NEED TO SAVE SOMEONE...
"...YOUR GREATEST ASSET IS YOUR OWN BODY."
THAT'S SOME-THING I LEARNED FROM MY OLD MAN.
"YOUR BODY HAS TO FIRST AND FOREMOST BE ABLE TO DO WHAT YOU NEED IT TO.
"AND THEN YOUR WITS AND TECHNIQUE WILL BUILD UPON THAT."
AND SO ON...
DELICIOUS GYOZA
WHAT WAS YOUR DAD LIKE?
HE WAS A SEARCH-AND-RESCUE WORKER...
AN ELITE FIREMAN.

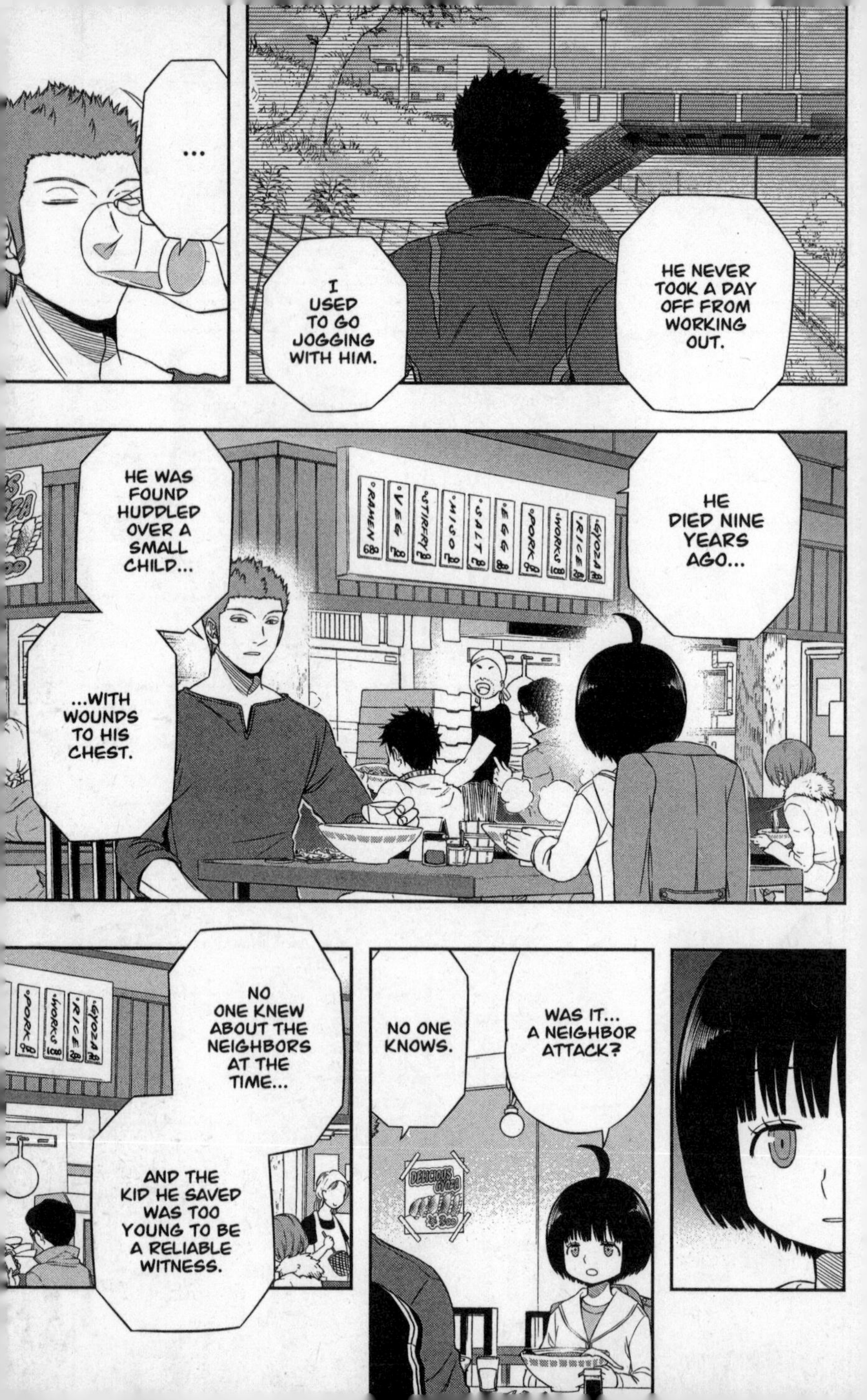
HE NEVER TOOK A DAY OFF FROM WORKING OUT.
I USED TO GO JOGGING WITH HIM.
...
HE DIED NINE YEARS AGO...
HE WAS FOUND HUDDLED OVER A SMALL CHILD...
...WITH WOUNDS TO HIS CHEST.
WAS IT... A NEIGHBOR ATTACK?
NO ONE KNOWS.
DELICIOUS GYOZA
NO ONE KNEW ABOUT THE NEIGHBORS AT THE TIME...
AND THE KID HE SAVED WAS TOO YOUNG TO BE A RELIABLE WITNESS.

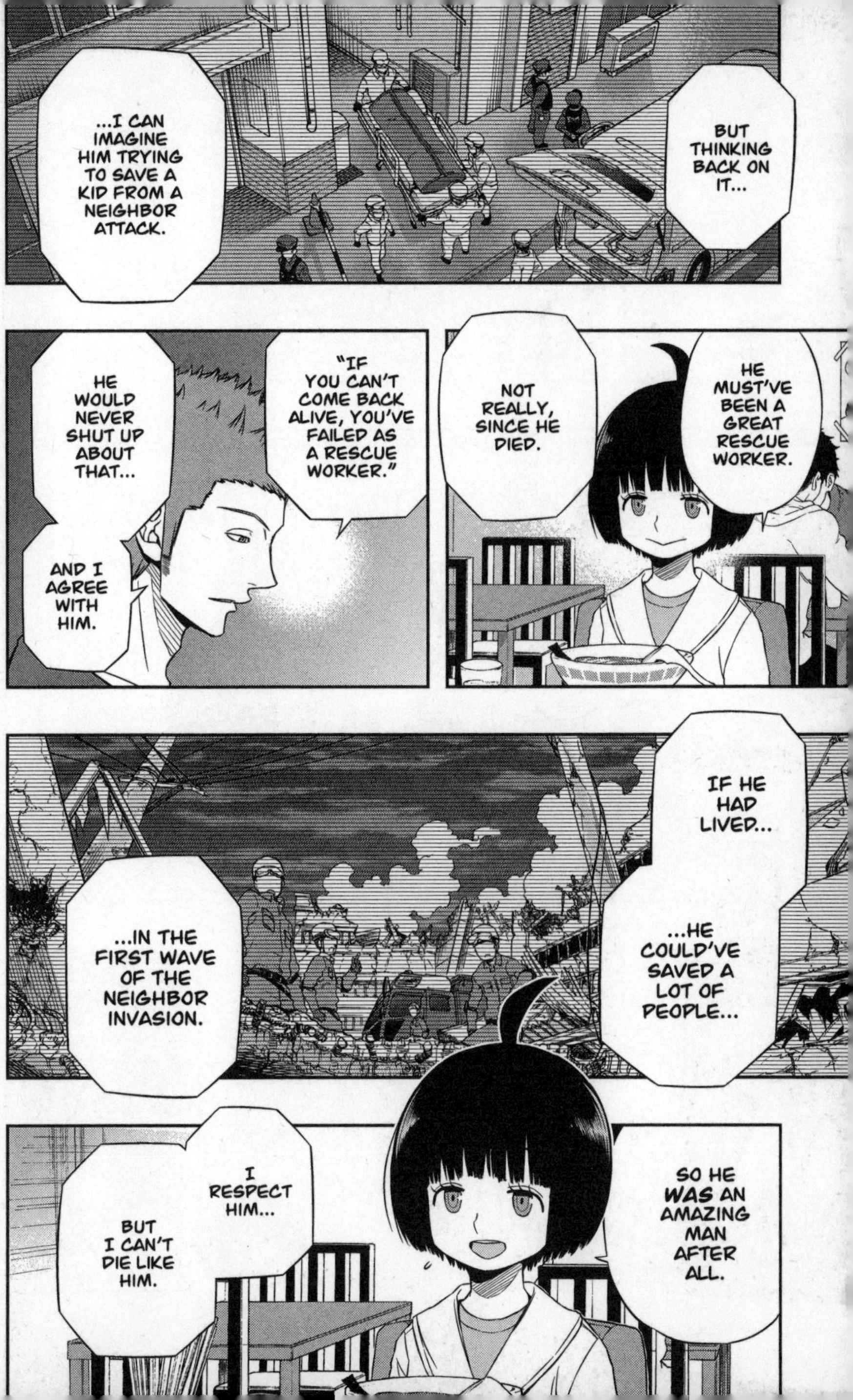
BUT THINKING BACK ON IT...
...I CAN IMAGINE HIM TRYING TO SAVE A KID FROM A NEIGHBOR ATTACK.
HE MUST'VE BEEN A GREAT RESCUE WORKER.
NOT REALLY, SINCE HE DIED.
"IF YOU CAN'T COME BACK ALIVE, YOU'VE FAILED AS A RESCUE WORKER."
HE WOULD NEVER SHUT UP ABOUT THAT...
AND I AGREE WITH HIM.
IF HE HAD LIVED...
...HE COULD'VE SAVED A LOT OF PEOPLE...
...IN THE FIRST WAVE OF THE NEIGHBOR INVASION.
SO HE **WAS** AN AMAZING MAN AFTER ALL.
I RESPECT HIM...
BUT I CAN'T DIE LIKE HIM.

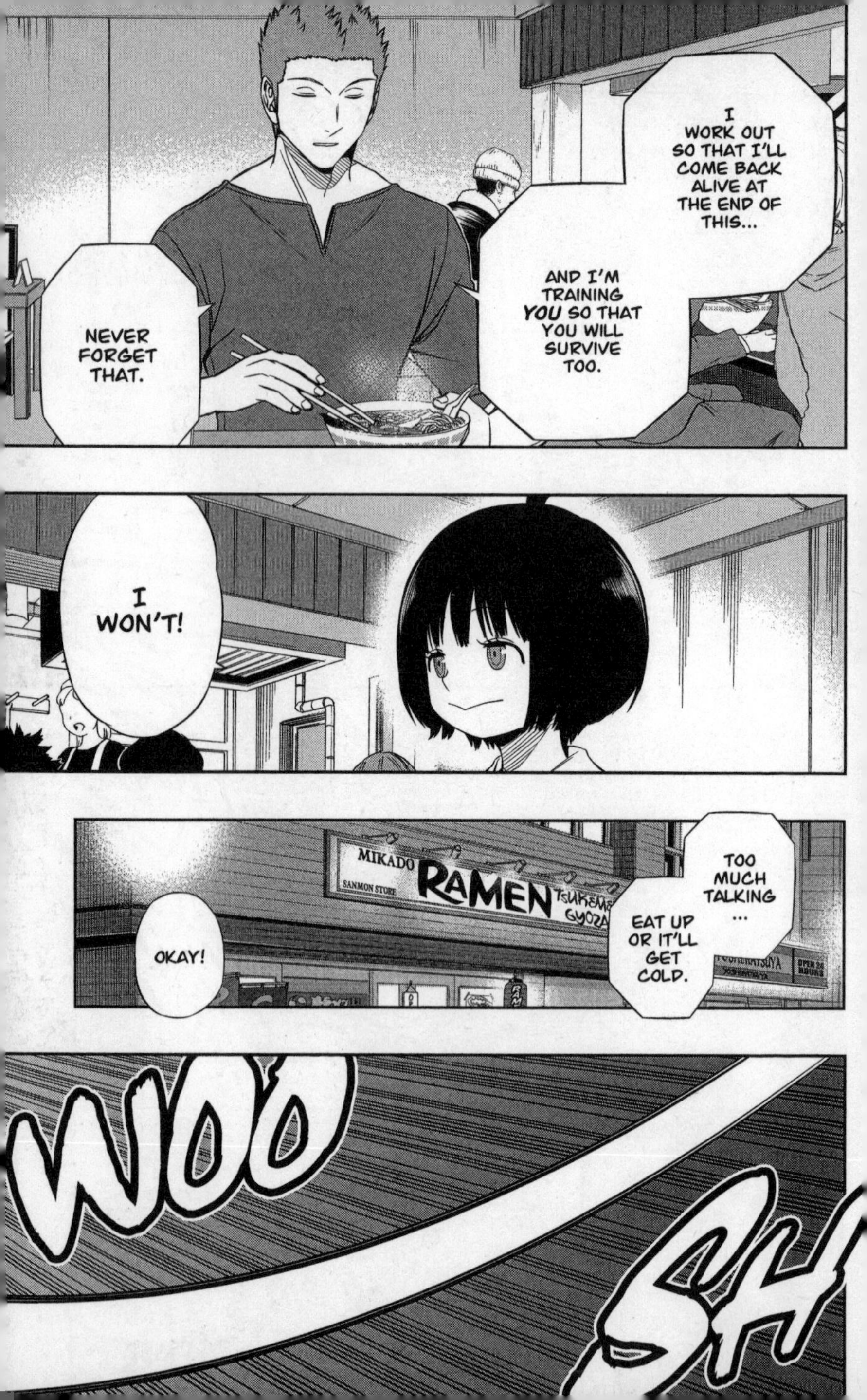
I WORK OUT SO THAT I'LL COME BACK ALIVE AT THE END OF THIS...
AND I'M TRAINING *YOU* SO THAT YOU WILL SURVIVE TOO.
NEVER FORGET THAT.
I WON'T!
MIKADO
SANMON STORE
RAMEN
GYOZA
TOO MUCH TALKING...
EAT UP OR IT'LL GET COLD.
OKAY!
WOO
SH

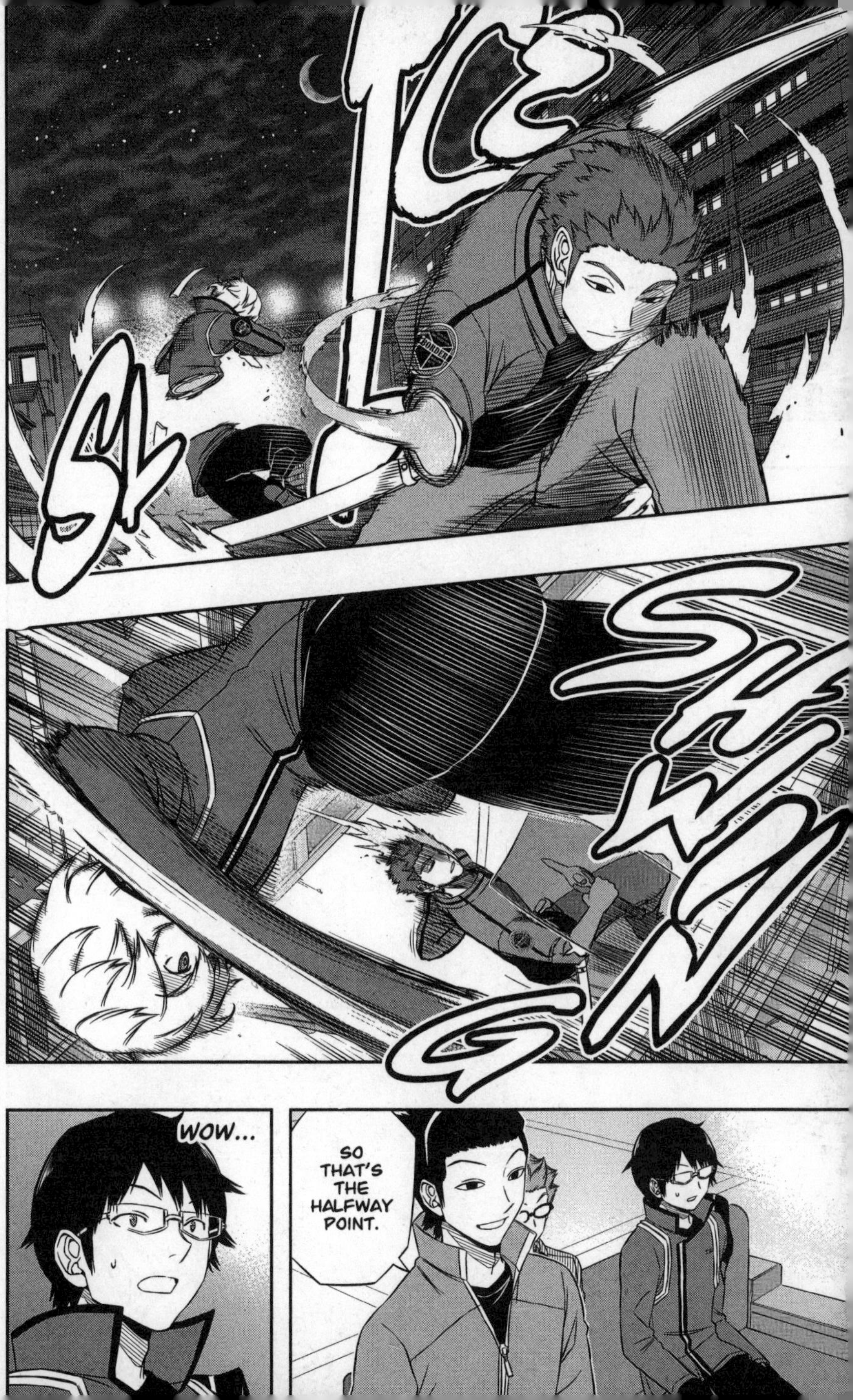
SHING
SO THAT'S THE HALFWAY POINT.
WOW...

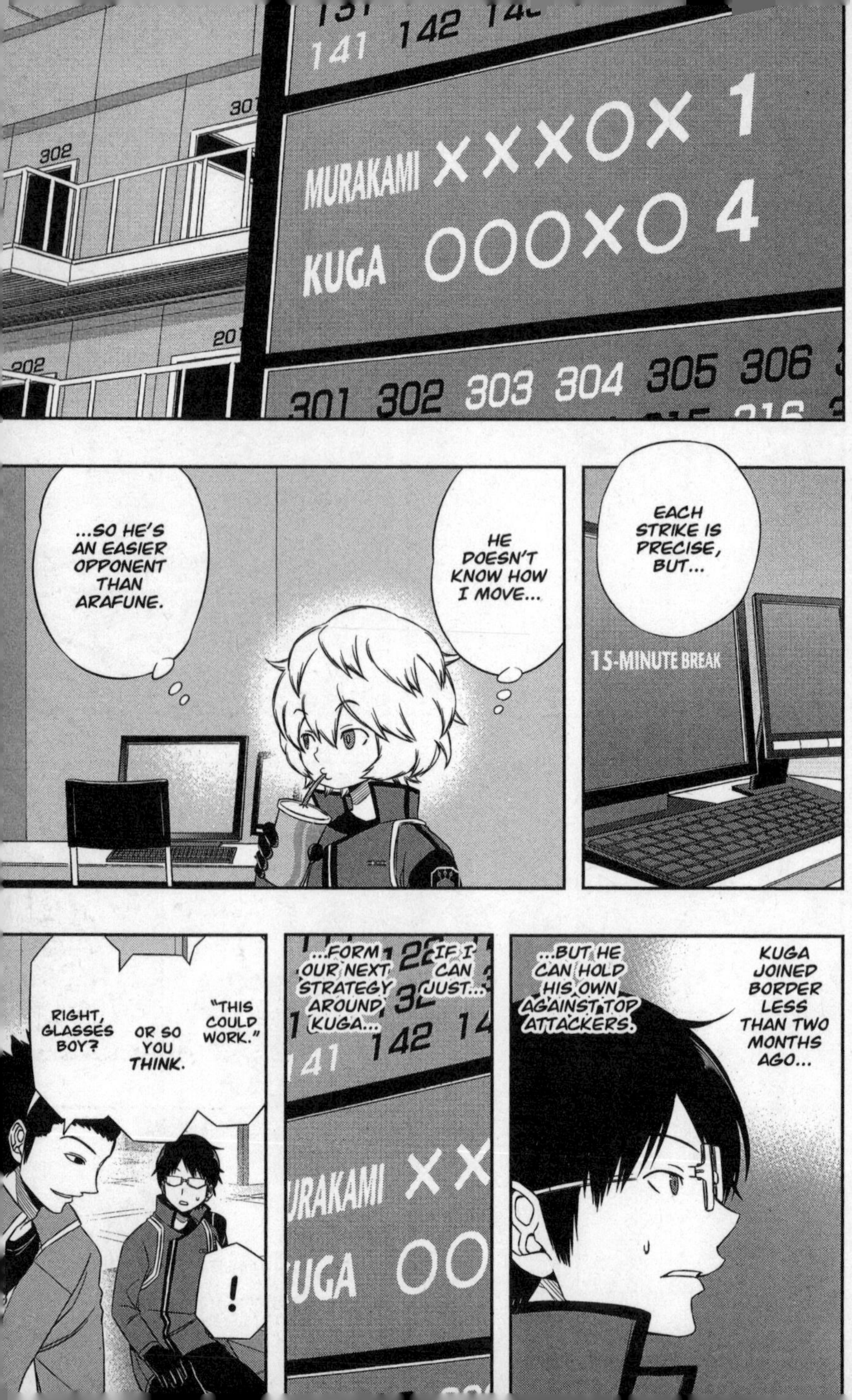141 142
MURAKAMI ×××○× 1
KUGA ○○○×○ 4
301 302 303 304 305 306
EACH STRIKE IS PRECISE, BUT...
15-MINUTE BREAK
HE DOESN'T KNOW HOW I MOVE...
...SO HE'S AN EASIER OPPONENT THAN ARAFUNE.
KUGA JOINED BORDER LESS THAN TWO MONTHS AGO...
...BUT HE CAN HOLD HIS OWN AGAINST TOP ATTACKERS.
IF I CAN JUST...
...FORM OUR NEXT STRATEGY AROUND KUGA...
"THIS COULD WORK."
OR SO YOU THINK.
RIGHT, GLASSES BOY?
!

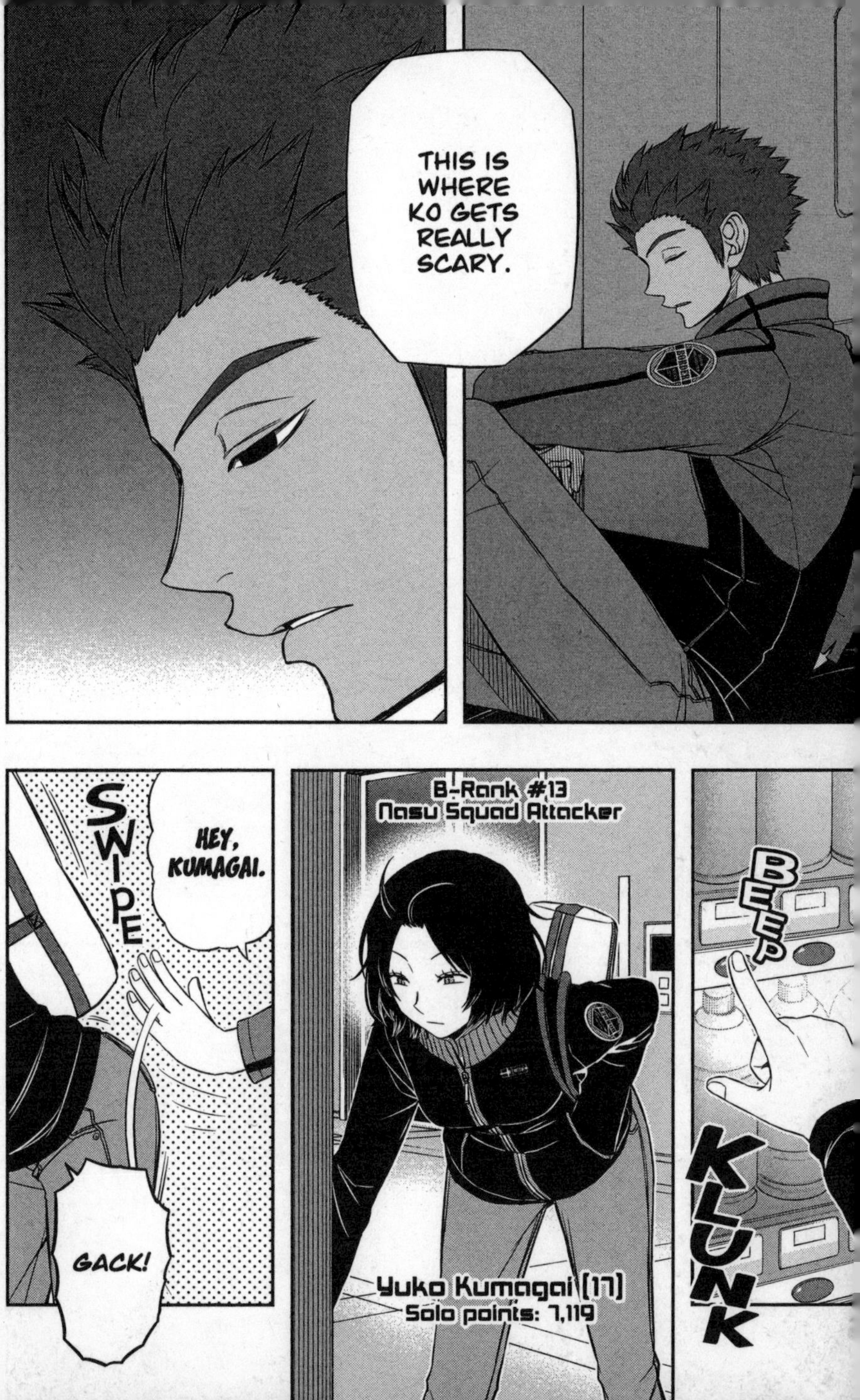
THIS IS WHERE KO GETS REALLY SCARY.
BEEP
KLUNK
B-Rank #13
Nasu Squad Attacker
Yuko Kumagai (17)
Solo points: 7,119
SWIPE
HEY, KUMAGAI.
GACK!

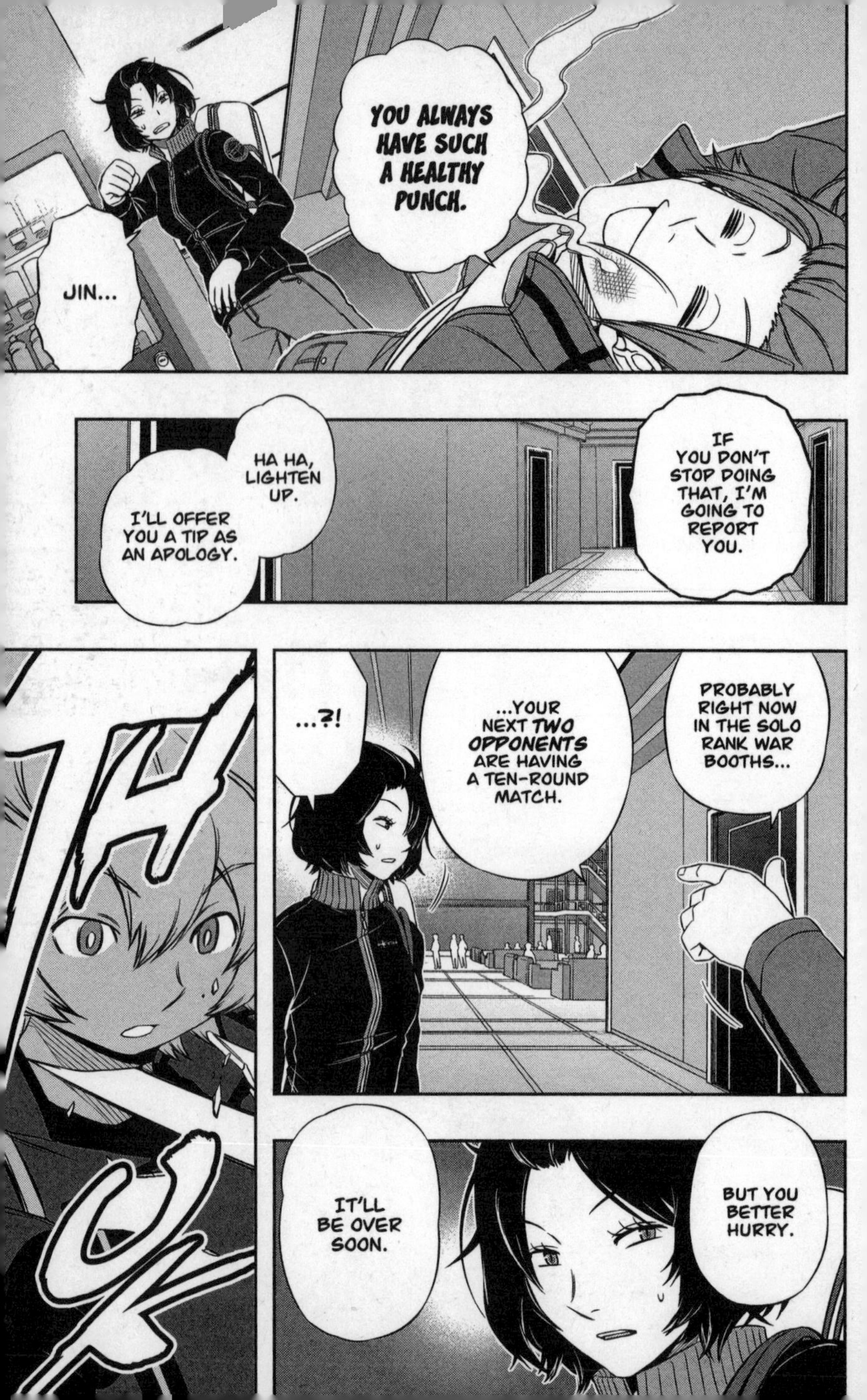
YOU ALWAYS HAVE SUCH A HEALTHY PUNCH.
JIN...
IF YOU DON'T STOP DOING THAT, I'M GOING TO REPORT YOU.
HA HA, LIGHTEN UP.
I'LL OFFER YOU A TIP AS AN APOLOGY.
PROBABLY RIGHT NOW IN THE SOLO RANK WAR BOOTHS...
...YOUR NEXT TWO OPPONENTS ARE HAVING A TEN-ROUND MATCH.
...?!
BUT YOU BETTER HURRY.
IT'LL BE OVER SOON.

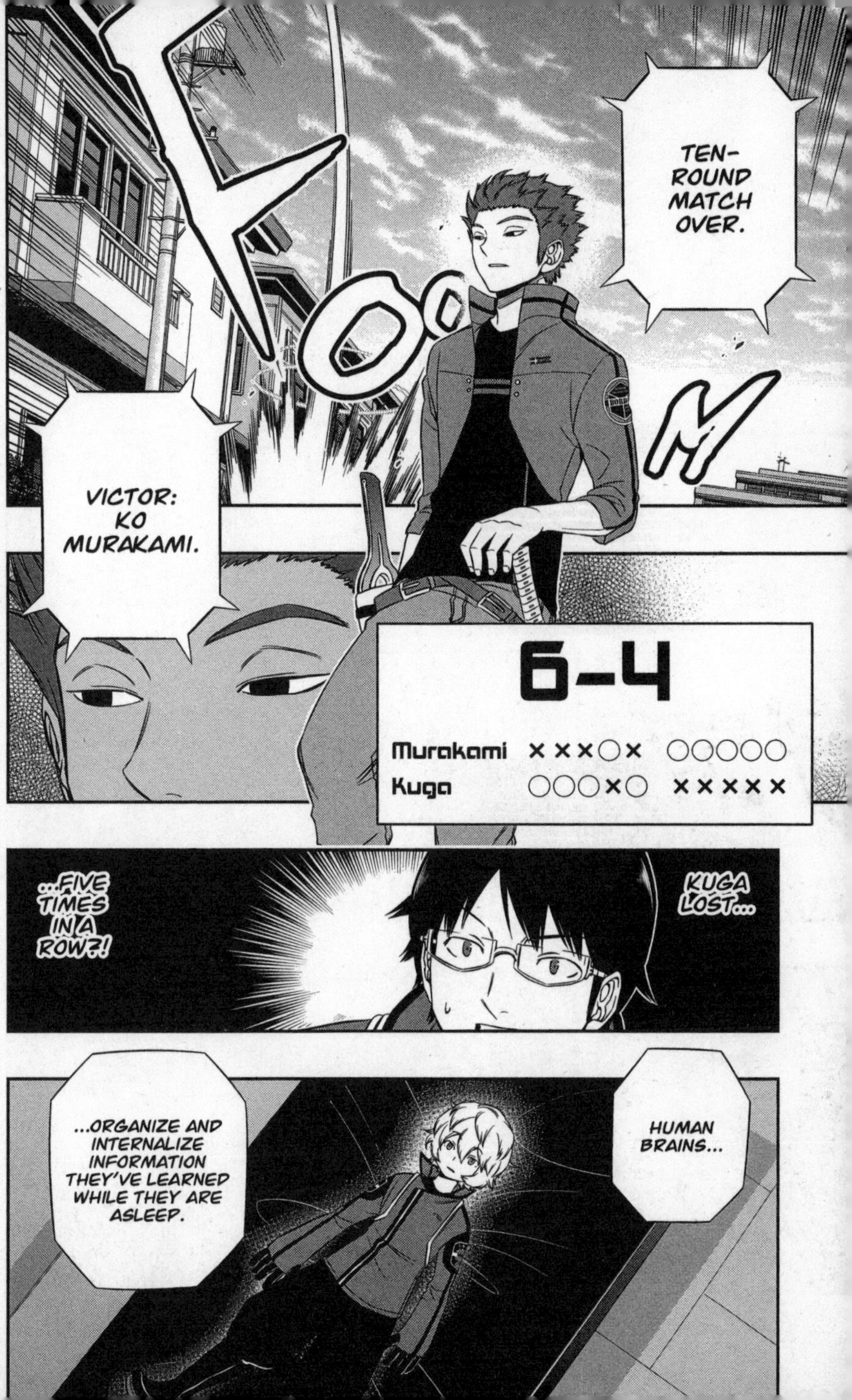
TEN-ROUND MATCH OVER.
VOOM
VICTOR: KO MURAKAMI.
6-4
Murakami ×××○× ○○○○○
Kuga ○○○×○ ×××××
KUGA LOST...
...FIVE TIMES IN A ROW?!
HUMAN BRAINS...
...ORGANIZE AND INTERNALIZE INFORMATION THEY'VE LEARNED WHILE THEY ARE ASLEEP.

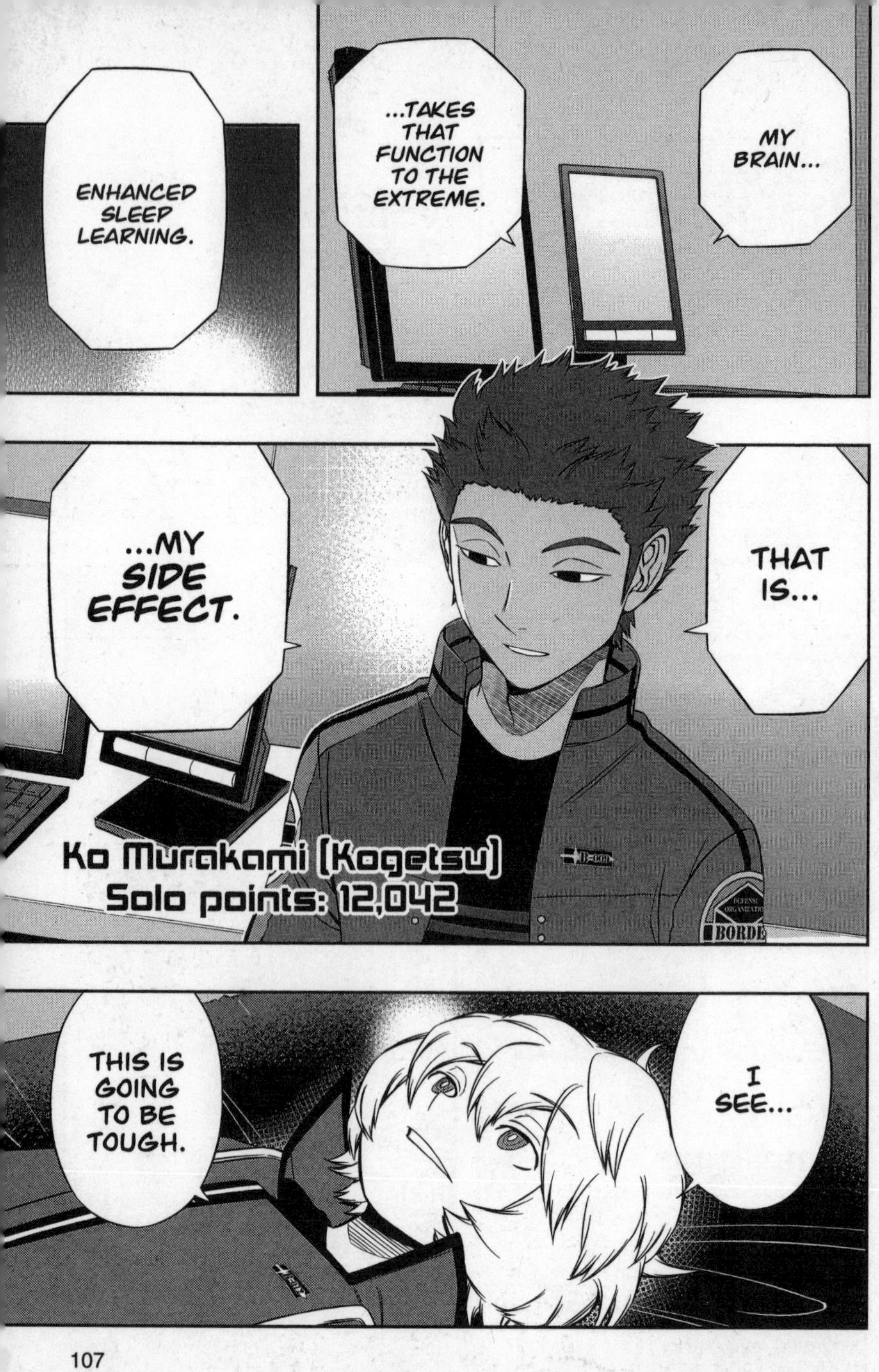
MY BRAIN...
...TAKES THAT FUNCTION TO THE EXTREME.
ENHANCED SLEEP LEARNING.
THAT IS...
...MY SIDE EFFECT.
Ko Murakami (Kogetsu)
Solo points: 12,042
I SEE...
THIS IS GOING TO BE TOUGH.

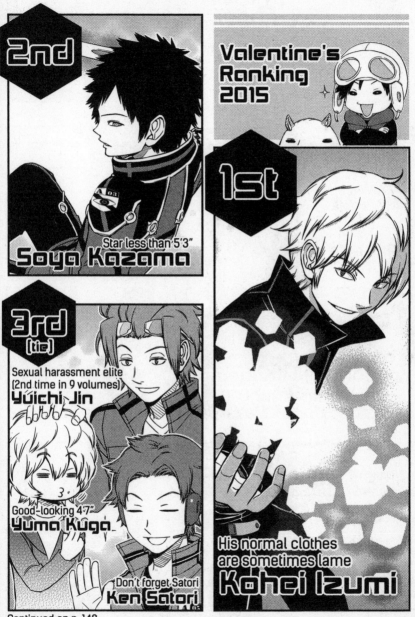

Valentine's Ranking 2015
1st
His normal clothes are sometimes lame
Kohei Izumi
2nd
Star less than 5'3"
Soya Kazama
3rd
(tie)
Sexual harassment elite
(2nd time in 9 volumes)
Yúichi Jin
Good-looking 4'7"
Yuma Kuga
Don't forget Satori
Ken Satori

Continued on p. 148

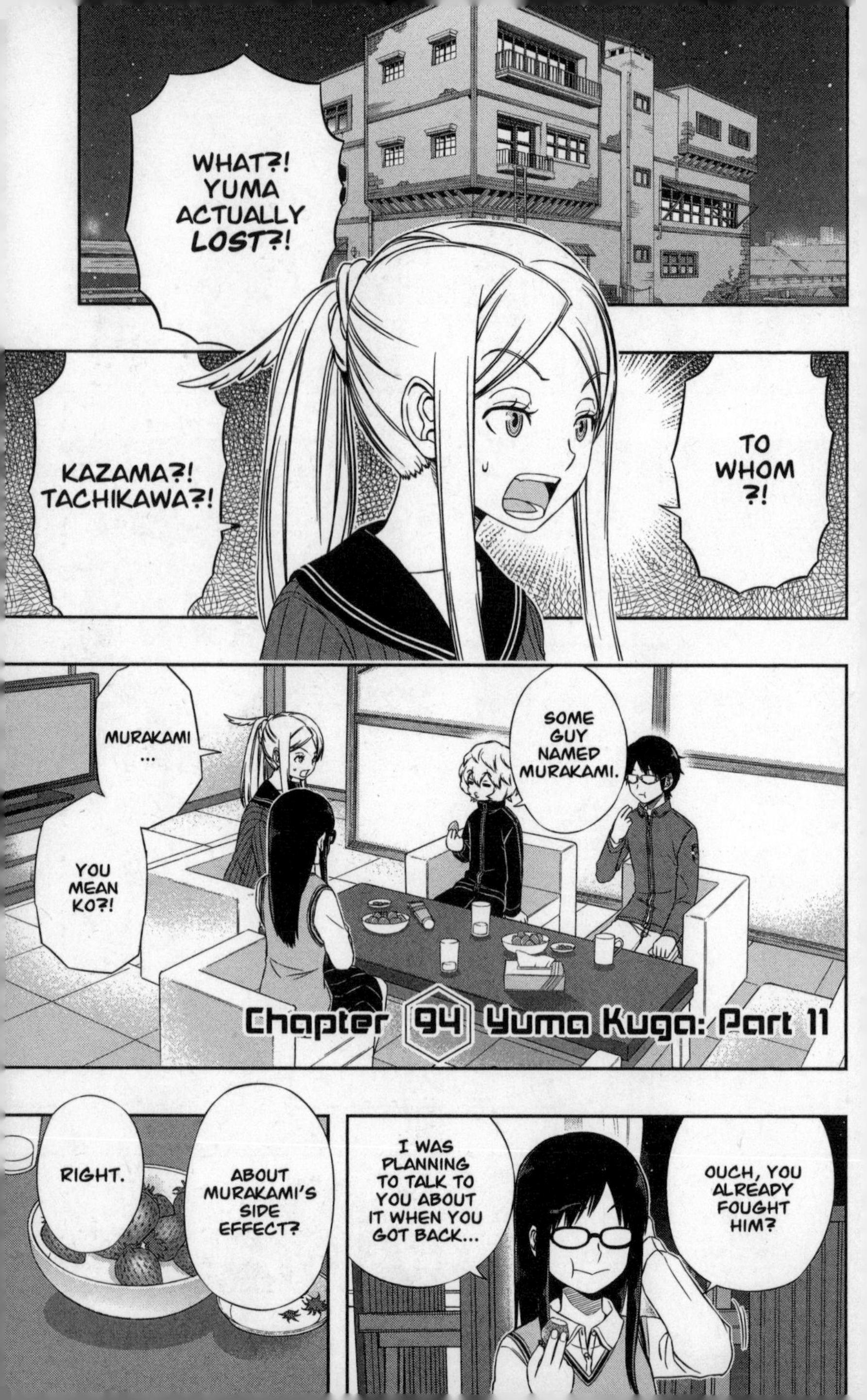
WHAT?! YUMA ACTUALLY LOST?!
TO WHOM?!
KAZAMA?! TACHIKAWA?!
SOME GUY NAMED MURAKAMI.
MURAKAMI ...
YOU MEAN KO?!
Chapter 94 Yuma Kuga: Part 11
OUCH, YOU ALREADY FOUGHT HIM?
I WAS PLANNING TO TALK TO YOU ABOUT IT WHEN YOU GOT BACK...
ABOUT MURAKAMI'S SIDE EFFECT?
RIGHT.

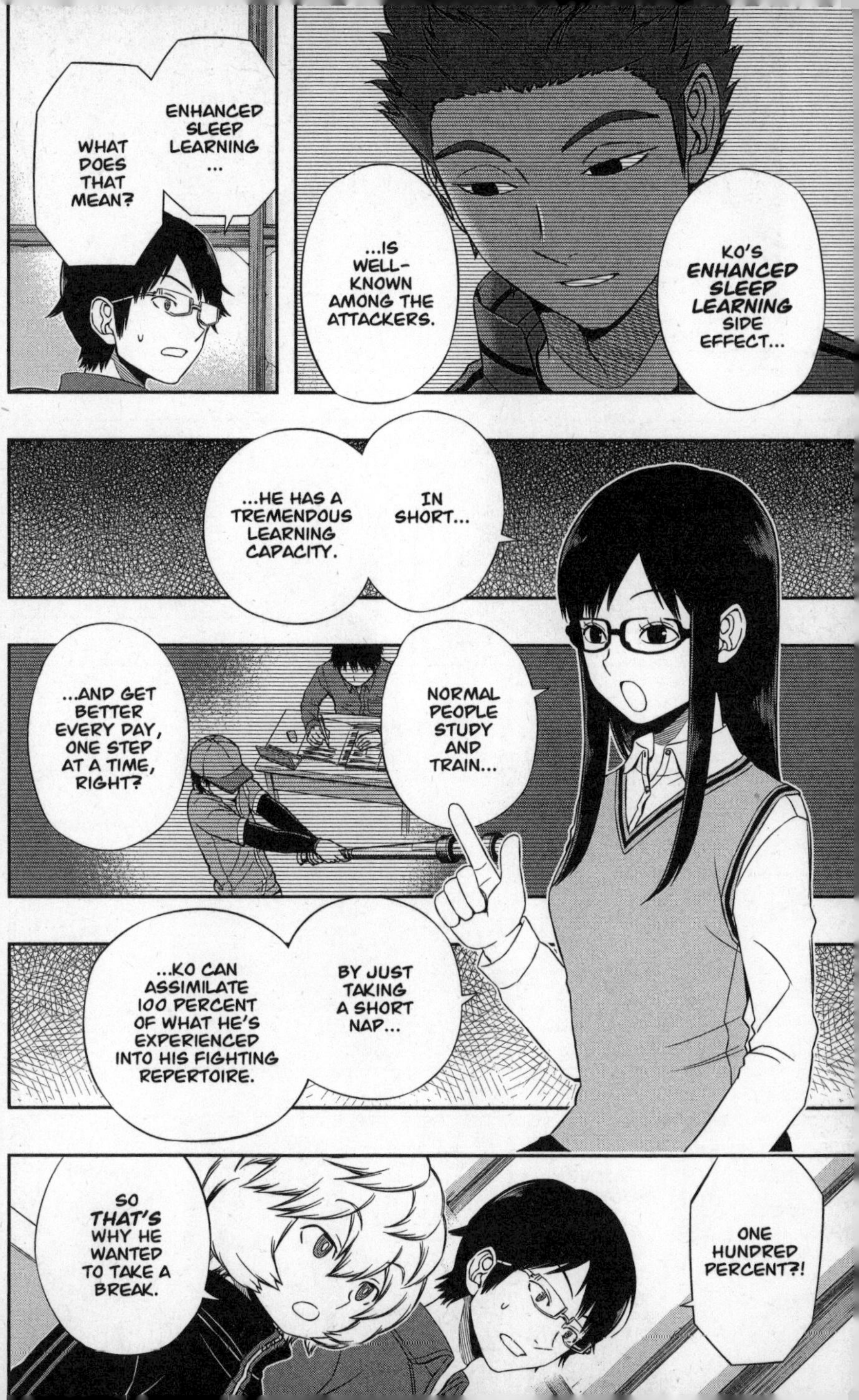
KO'S ENHANCED SLEEP LEARNING SIDE EFFECT...
...IS WELL-KNOWN AMONG THE ATTACKERS.
ENHANCED SLEEP LEARNING ...
WHAT DOES THAT MEAN?
IN SHORT...
...HE HAS A TREMENDOUS LEARNING CAPACITY.
NORMAL PEOPLE STUDY AND TRAIN...
...AND GET BETTER EVERY DAY, ONE STEP AT A TIME, RIGHT?
BY JUST TAKING A SHORT NAP...
...KO CAN ASSIMILATE 100 PERCENT OF WHAT HE'S EXPERIENCED INTO HIS FIGHTING REPERTOIRE.
ONE HUNDRED PERCENT?!
SO THAT'S WHY HE WANTED TO TAKE A BREAK.

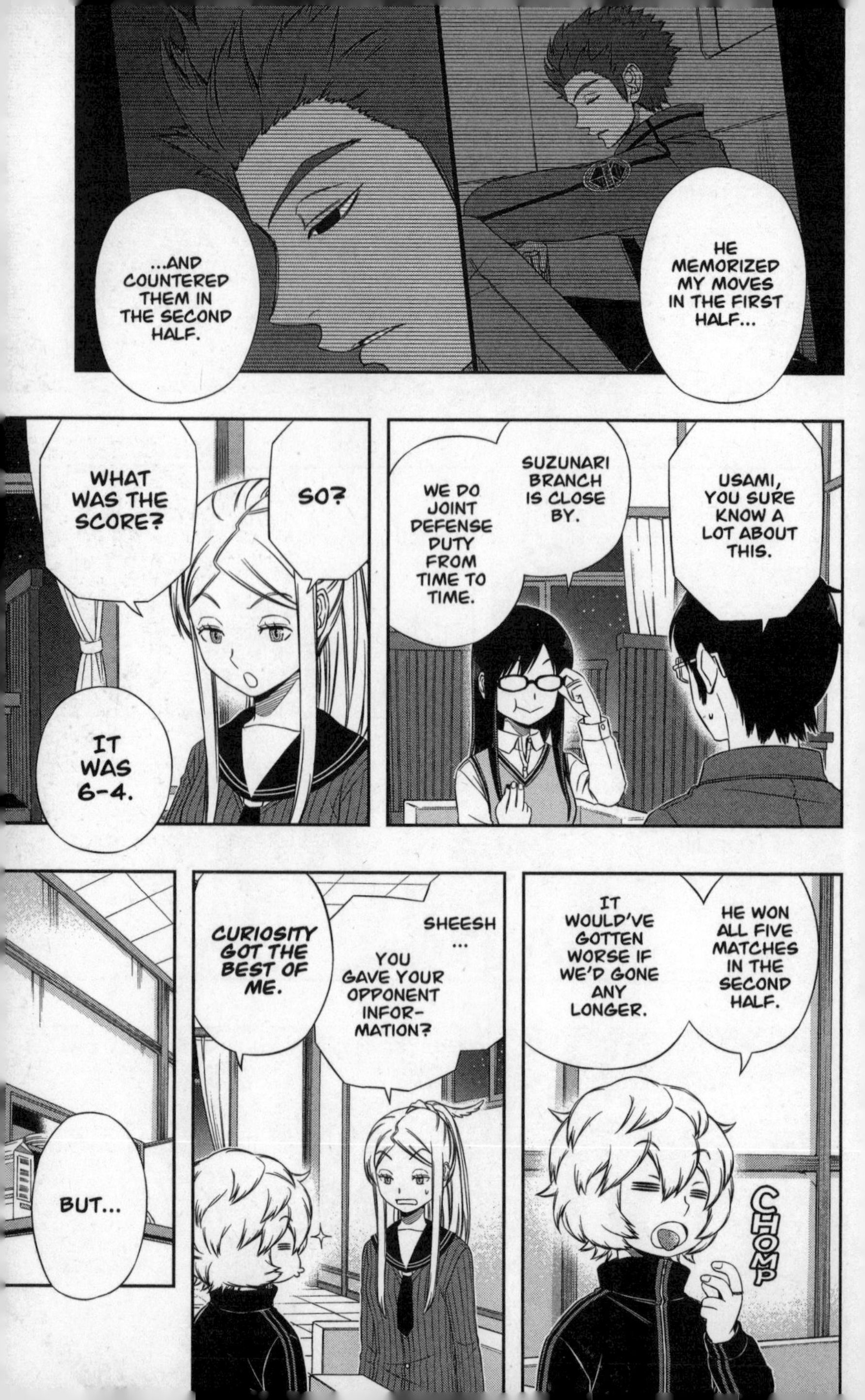
HE MEMORIZED MY MOVES IN THE FIRST HALF...
...AND COUNTERED THEM IN THE SECOND HALF.
USAMI, YOU SURE KNOW A LOT ABOUT THIS.
SUZUNARI BRANCH IS CLOSE BY.
WE DO JOINT DEFENSE DUTY FROM TIME TO TIME.
SO?
WHAT WAS THE SCORE?
IT WAS 6-4.
HE WON ALL FIVE MATCHES IN THE SECOND HALF.
IT WOULD'VE GOTTEN WORSE IF WE'D GONE ANY LONGER.
CHOMP
SHEESH...
YOU GAVE YOUR OPPONENT INFOR-MATION?
CURIOSITY GOT THE BEST OF ME.
BUT...

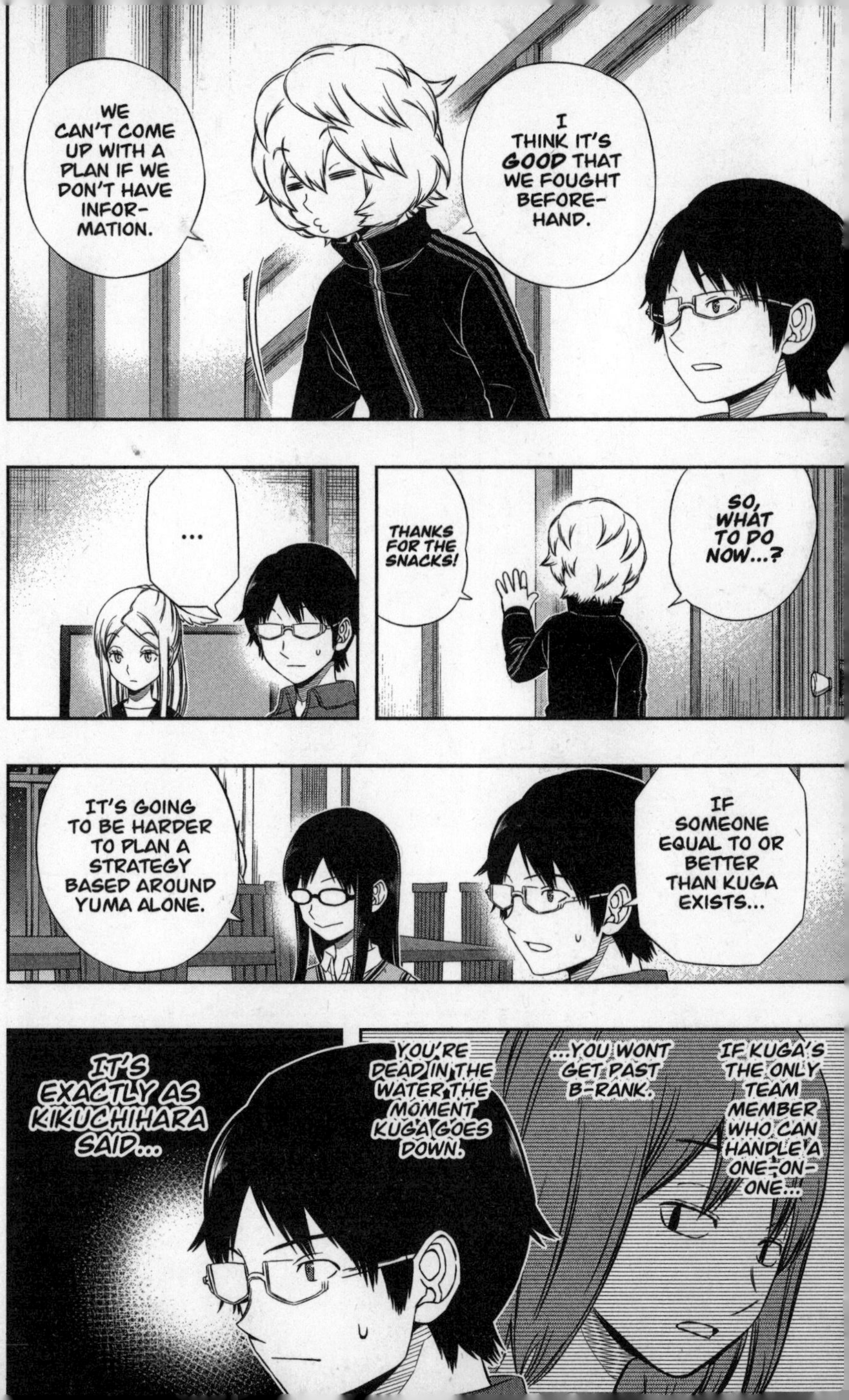
I THINK IT'S GOOD THAT WE FOUGHT BEFORE-HAND.
WE CAN'T COME UP WITH A PLAN IF WE DON'T HAVE INFOR-MATION.
SO, WHAT TO DO NOW...?
THANKS FOR THE SNACKS!
...
IF SOMEONE EQUAL TO OR BETTER THAN KUGA EXISTS...
IT'S GOING TO BE HARDER TO PLAN A STRATEGY BASED AROUND YUMA ALONE.
IF KUGA'S THE ONLY TEAM MEMBER WHO CAN HANDLE A ONE-ON-ONE...
...YOU WONT GET PAST B-RANK.
YOU'RE DEAD IN THE WATER THE MOMENT KUGA GOES DOWN.
IT'S EXACTLY AS KIKUCHIHARA SAID...

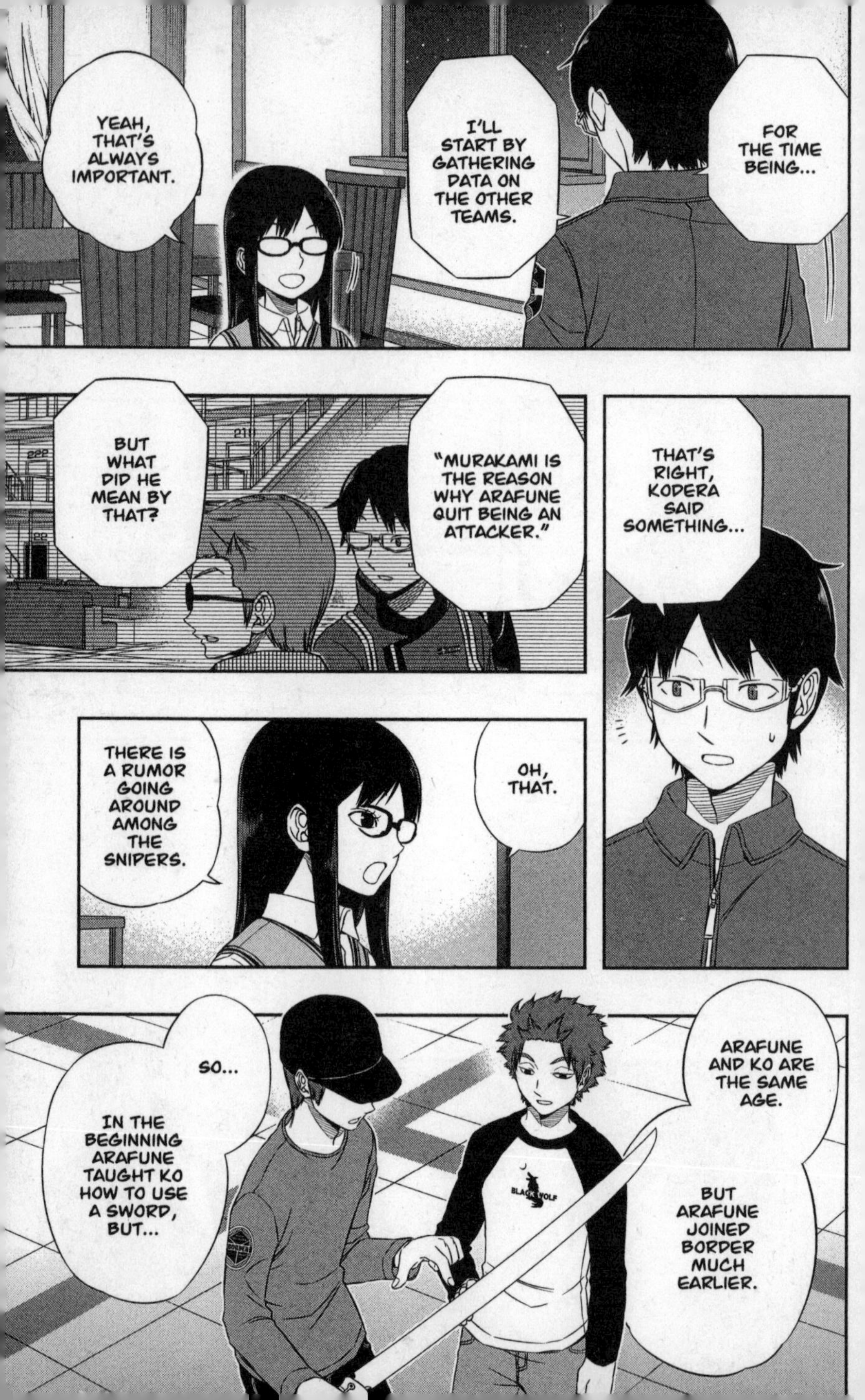
FOR THE TIME BEING...
I'LL START BY GATHERING DATA ON THE OTHER TEAMS.
YEAH, THAT'S ALWAYS IMPORTANT.
THAT'S RIGHT, KODERA SAID SOMETHING...
"MURAKAMI IS THE REASON WHY ARAFUNE QUIT BEING AN ATTACKER."
BUT WHAT DID HE MEAN BY THAT?
OH, THAT.
THERE IS A RUMOR GOING AROUND AMONG THE SNIPERS.
ARAFUNE AND KO ARE THE SAME AGE.
BUT ARAFUNE JOINED BORDER MUCH EARLIER.
SO...
IN THE BEGINNING ARAFUNE TAUGHT KO HOW TO USE A SWORD, BUT...

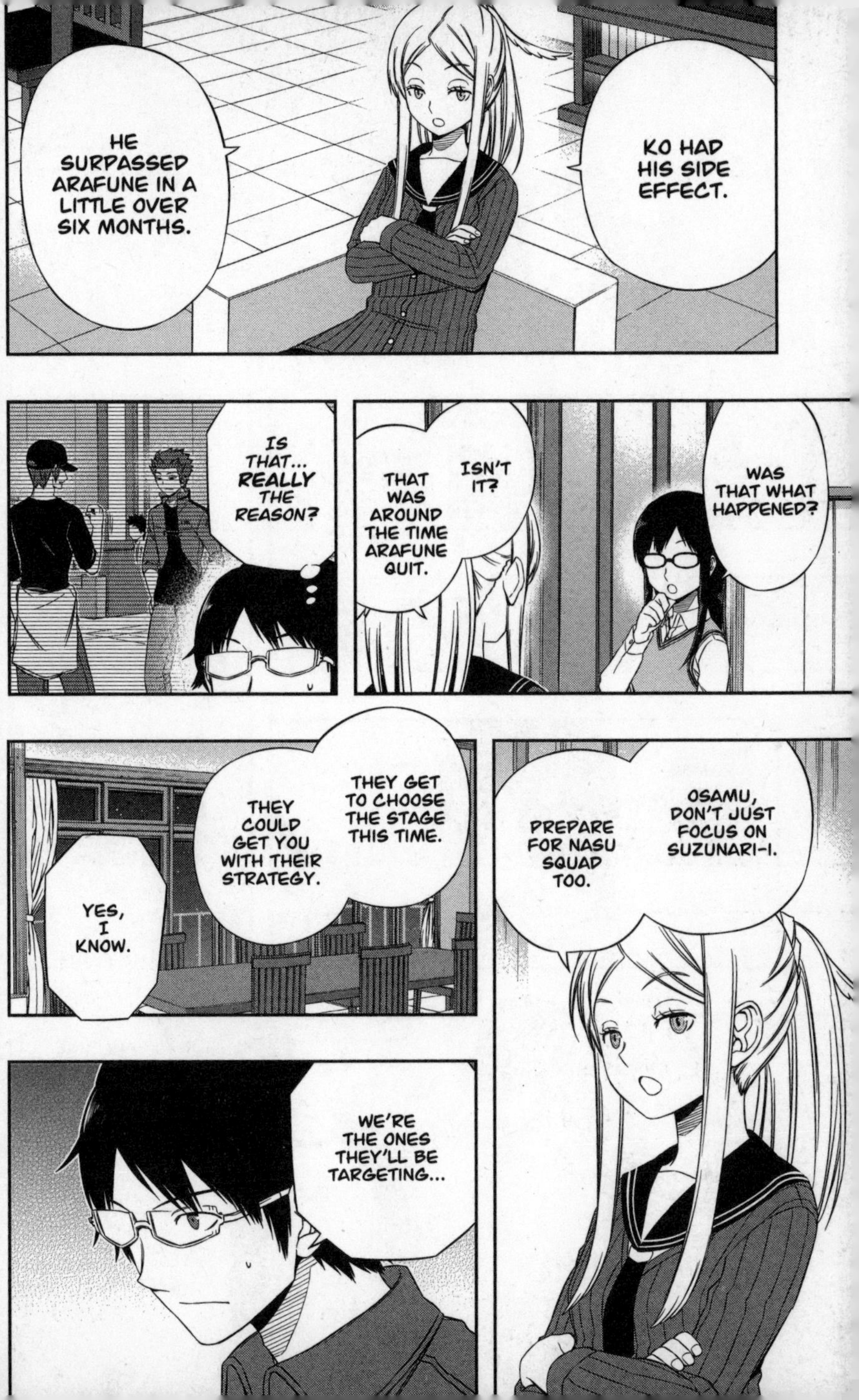
KO HAD HIS SIDE EFFECT.
HE SURPASSED ARAFUNE IN A LITTLE OVER SIX MONTHS.
WAS THAT WHAT HAPPENED?
THAT WAS AROUND THE TIME ARAFUNE QUIT.
ISN'T IT?
IS THAT... REALLY THE REASON?
OSAMU, DON'T JUST FOCUS ON SUZUNARI-1.
PREPARE FOR NASU SQUAD TOO.
THEY GET TO CHOOSE THE STAGE THIS TIME.
THEY COULD GET YOU WITH THEIR STRATEGY.
YES, I KNOW.
WE'RE THE ONES THEY'LL BE TARGETING...

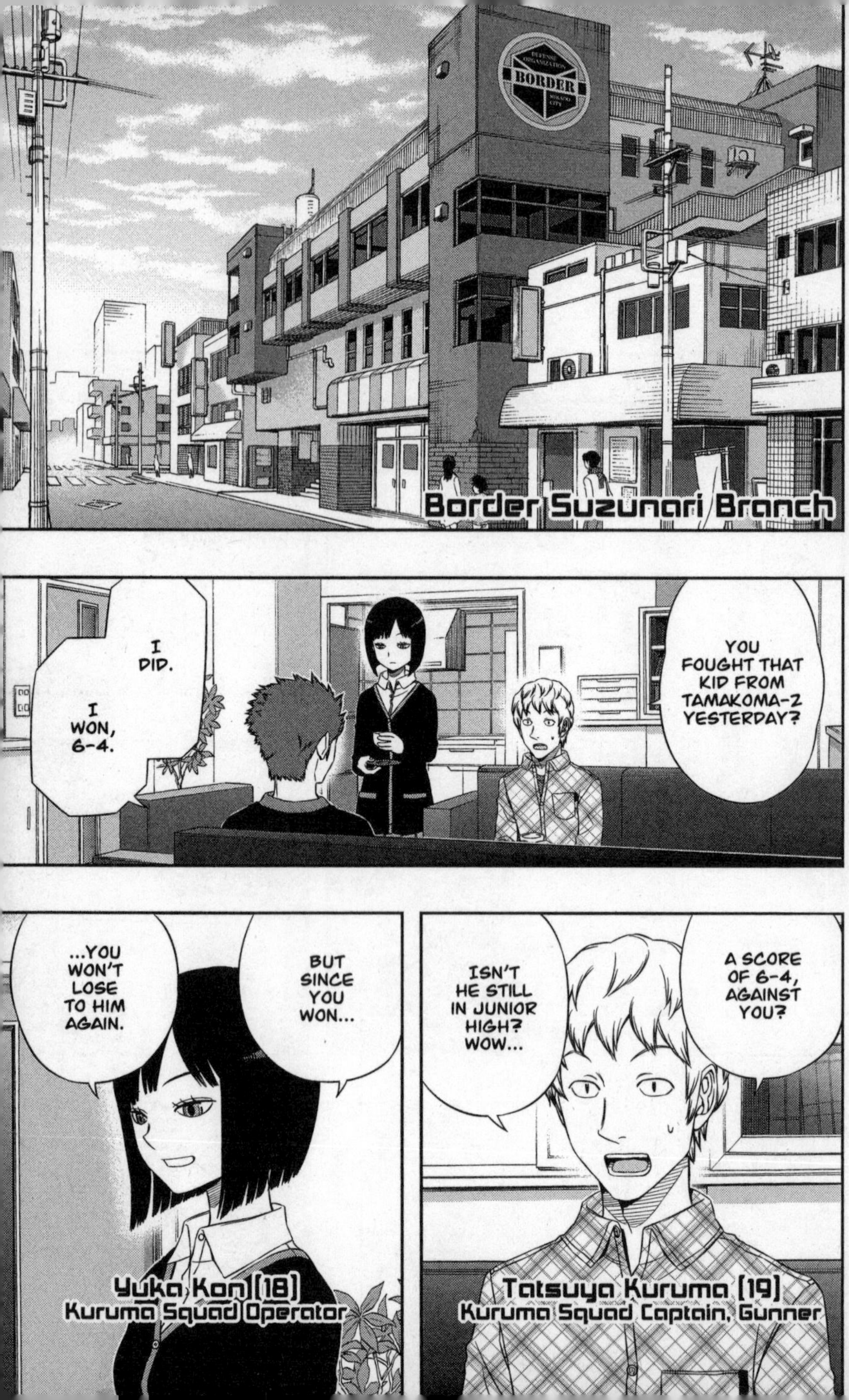
BORDER
Border Suzunari Branch
YOU FOUGHT THAT KID FROM TAMAKOMA-2 YESTERDAY?
I DID.
I WON, 6-4.
A SCORE OF 6-4, AGAINST YOU?
ISN'T HE STILL IN JUNIOR HIGH? WOW...
Tatsuya Kuruma (19)
Kuruma Squad Captain, Gunner
BUT SINCE YOU WON...
...YOU WON'T LOSE TO HIM AGAIN.
Yuka Kon (18)
Kuruma Squad Operator

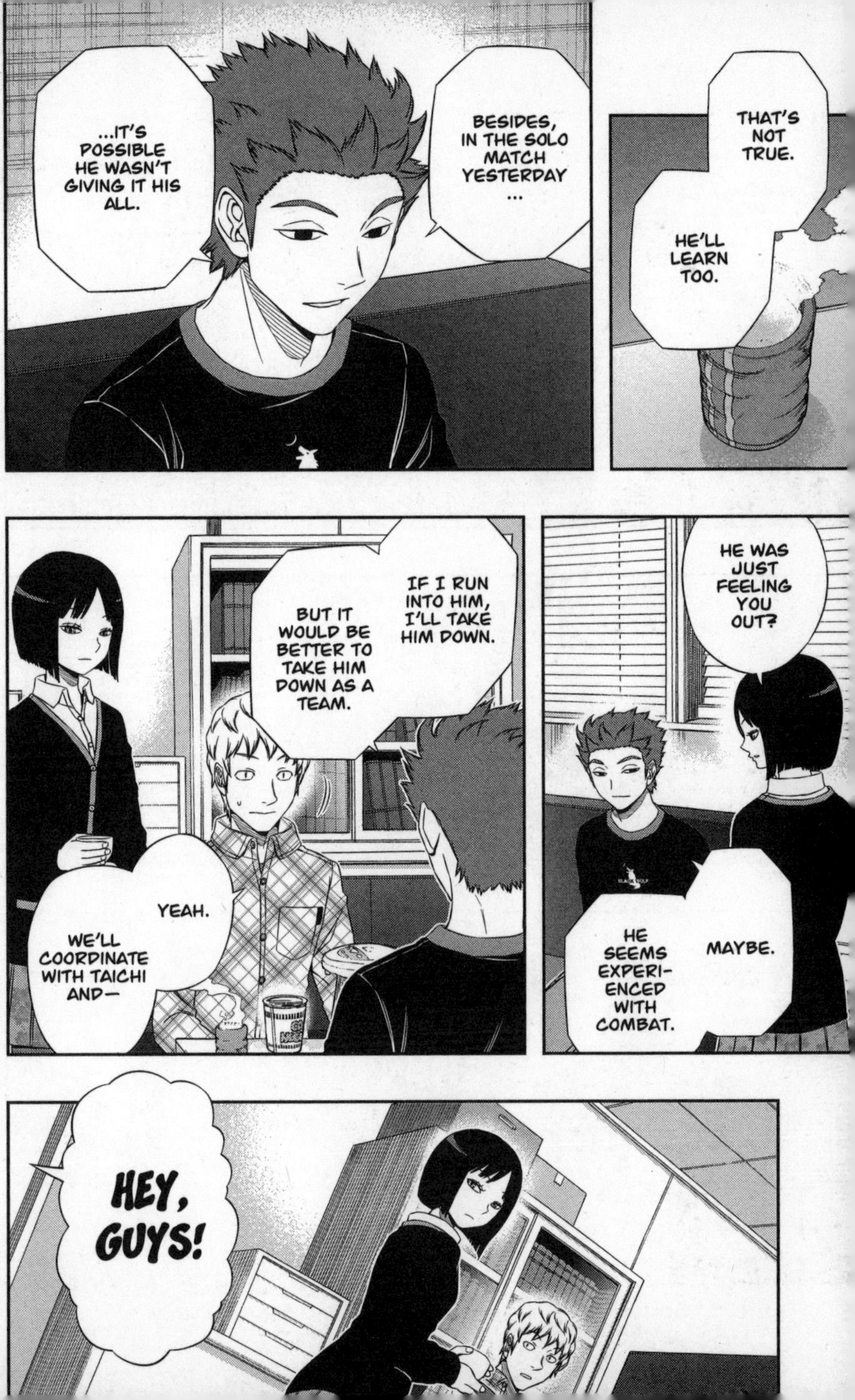
THAT'S NOT TRUE.
HE'LL LEARN TOO.
BESIDES, IN THE SOLO MATCH YESTERDAY...
...IT'S POSSIBLE HE WASN'T GIVING IT HIS ALL.
HE WAS JUST FEELING YOU OUT?
MAYBE.
HE SEEMS EXPERIENCED WITH COMBAT.
IF I RUN INTO HIM, I'LL TAKE HIM DOWN.
BUT IT WOULD BE BETTER TO TAKE HIM DOWN AS A TEAM.
YEAH.
WE'LL COORDINATE WITH TAICHI AND—
HEY, GUYS!

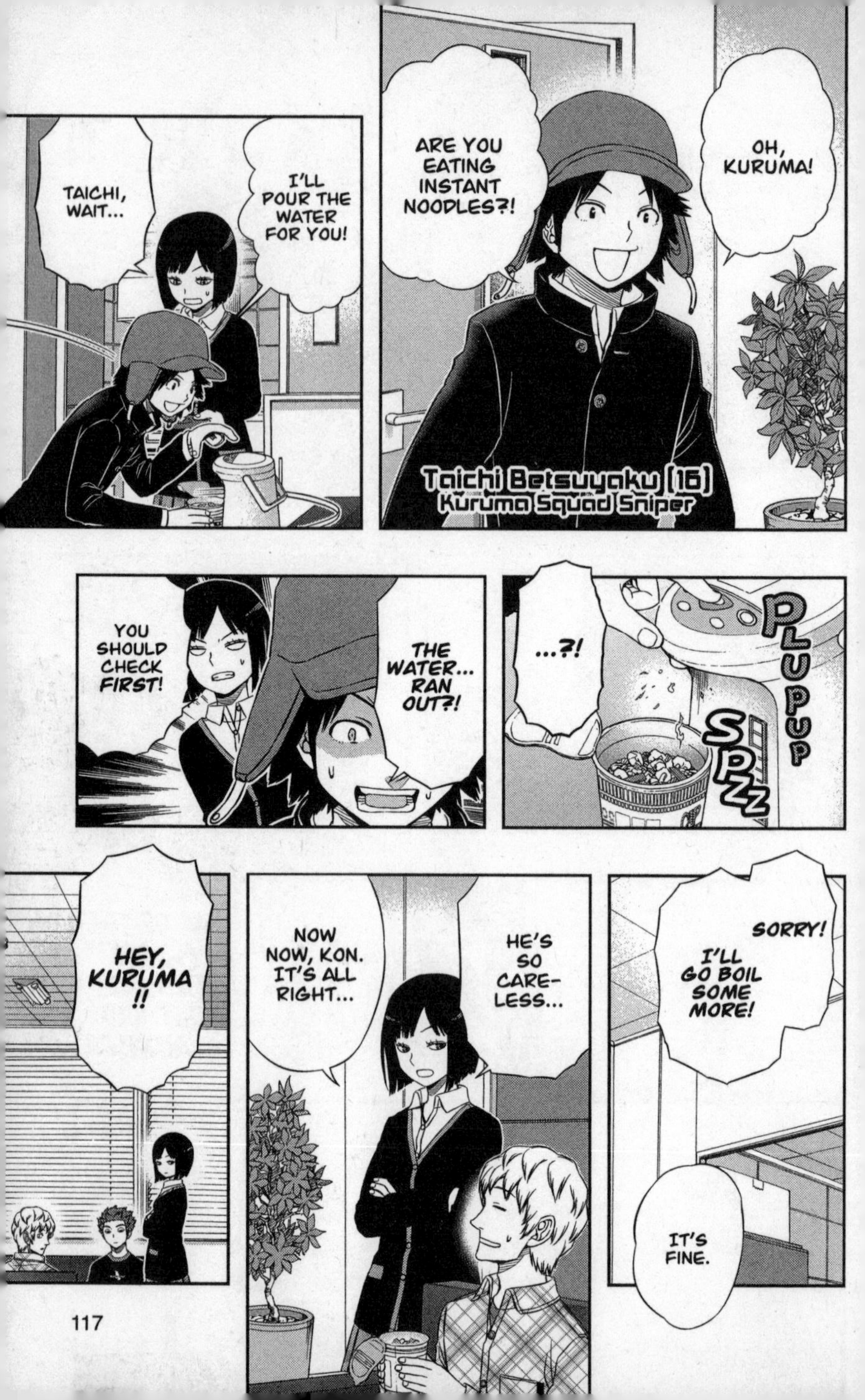

OH, KURUMA!
ARE YOU EATING INSTANT NOODLES?!
Taichi Betsuyaku (16)
Kuruma Squad Sniper
I'LL POUR THE WATER FOR YOU!
TAICHI, WAIT...
...?!
PLUPUP
SPZZ
THE WATER... RAN OUT?!
YOU SHOULD CHECK FIRST!
SORRY! I'LL GO BOIL SOME MORE!
IT'S FINE.
HE'S SO CARE-LESS...
NOW NOW, KON. IT'S ALL RIGHT...
HEY, KURUMA!!

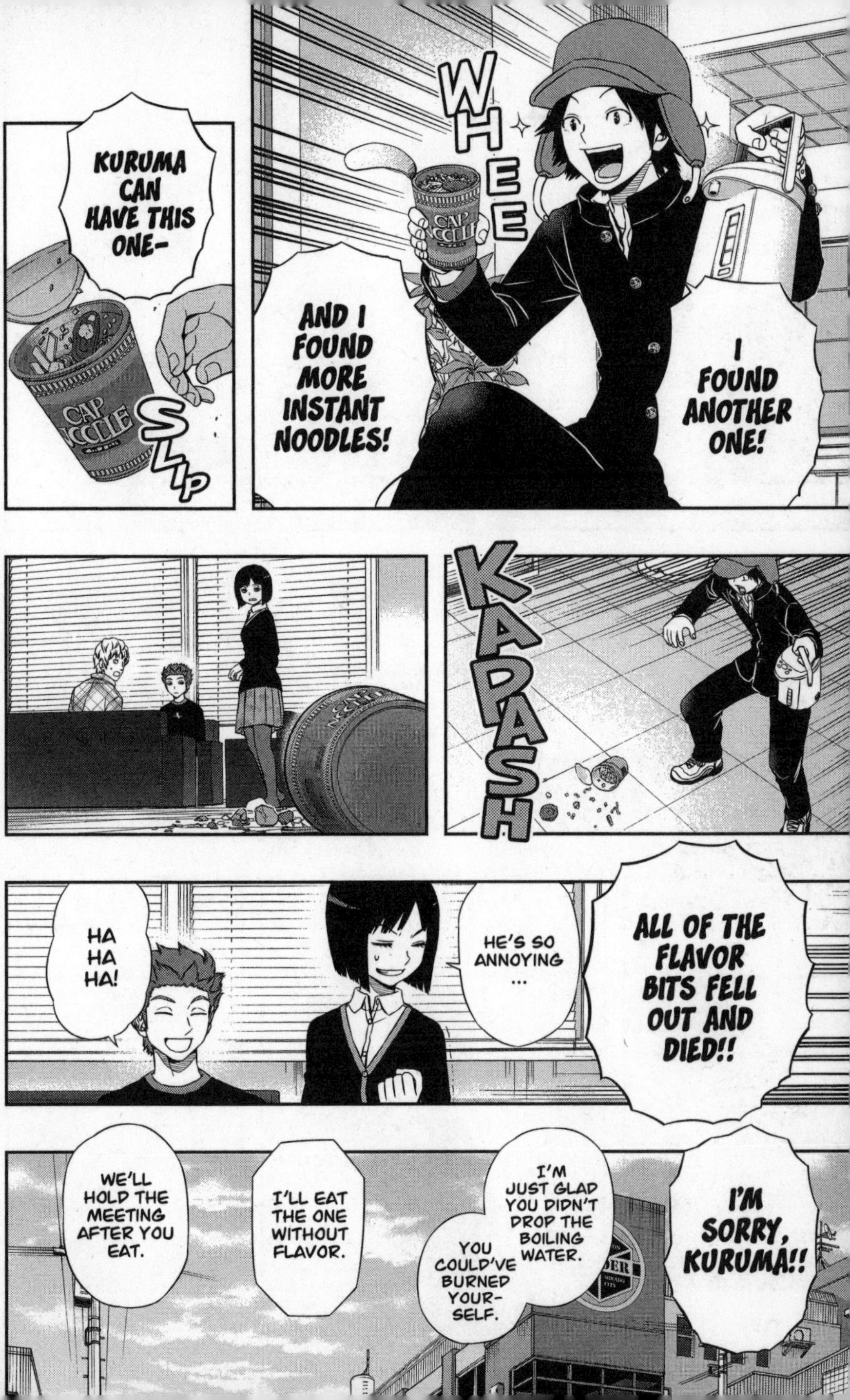
WHEE
I FOUND ANOTHER ONE!
AND I FOUND MORE INSTANT NOODLES!
KURUMA CAN HAVE THIS ONE-
SLIP
KAPASH
ALL OF THE FLAVOR BITS FELL OUT AND DIED!!
HE'S SO ANNOYING ...
HA HA HA!
I'M SORRY, KURUMA!!
I'M JUST GLAD YOU DIDN'T DROP THE BOILING WATER.
YOU COULD'VE BURNED YOURSELF.
I'LL EAT THE ONE WITHOUT FLAVOR.
WE'LL HOLD THE MEETING AFTER YOU EAT.

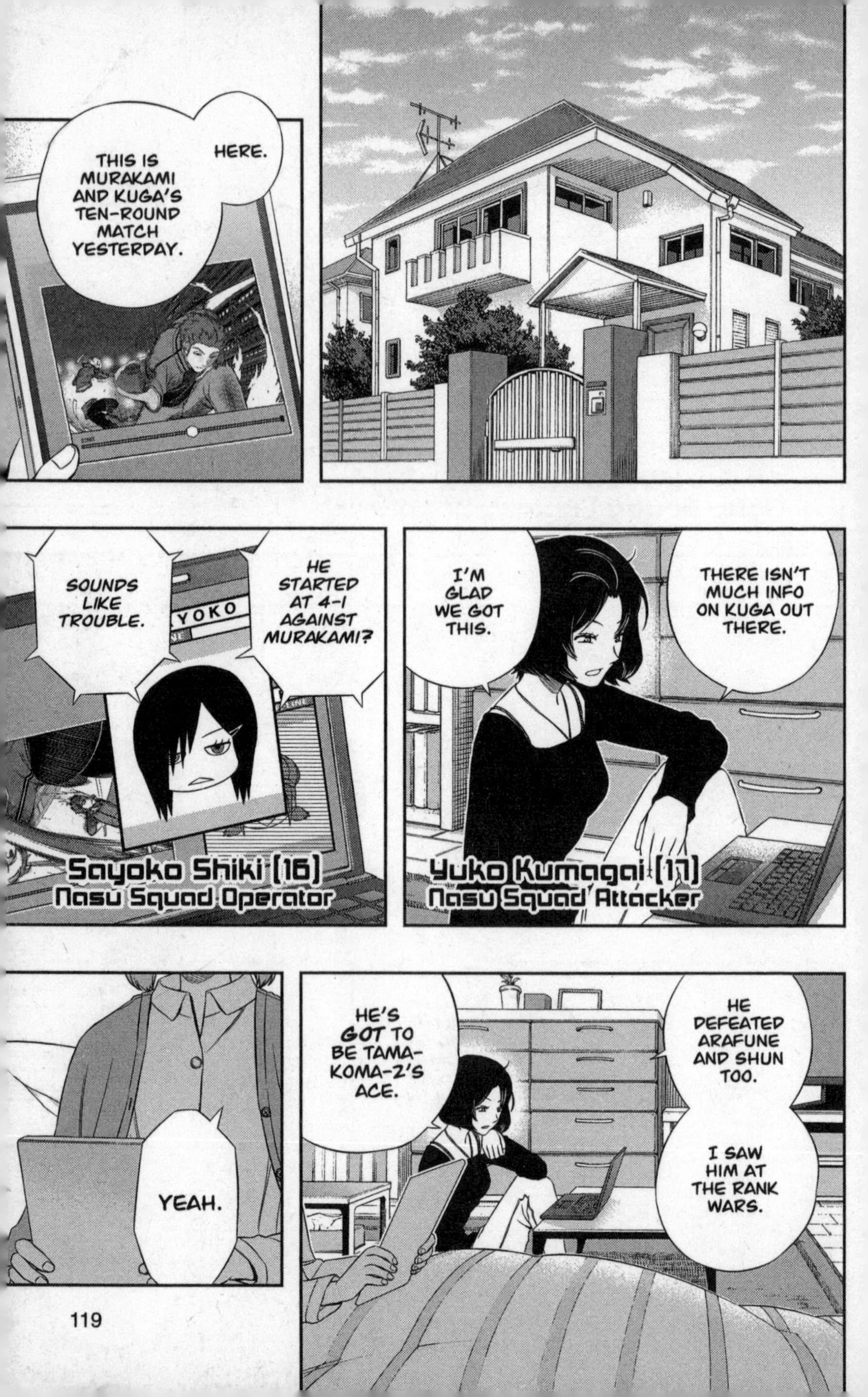
HERE.
THIS IS MURAKAMI AND KUGA'S TEN-ROUND MATCH YESTERDAY.
THERE ISN'T MUCH INFO ON KUGA OUT THERE.
I'M GLAD WE GOT THIS.
Yuko Kumagai (17) Nasu Squad Attacker
HE STARTED AT 4-1 AGAINST MURAKAMI?
SOUNDS LIKE TROUBLE.
Sayoko Shiki (16) Nasu Squad Operator
HE DEFEATED ARAFUNE AND SHUN TOO.
I SAW HIM AT THE RANK WARS.
HE'S **GOT** TO BE TAMA-KOMA-2'S ACE.
YEAH.

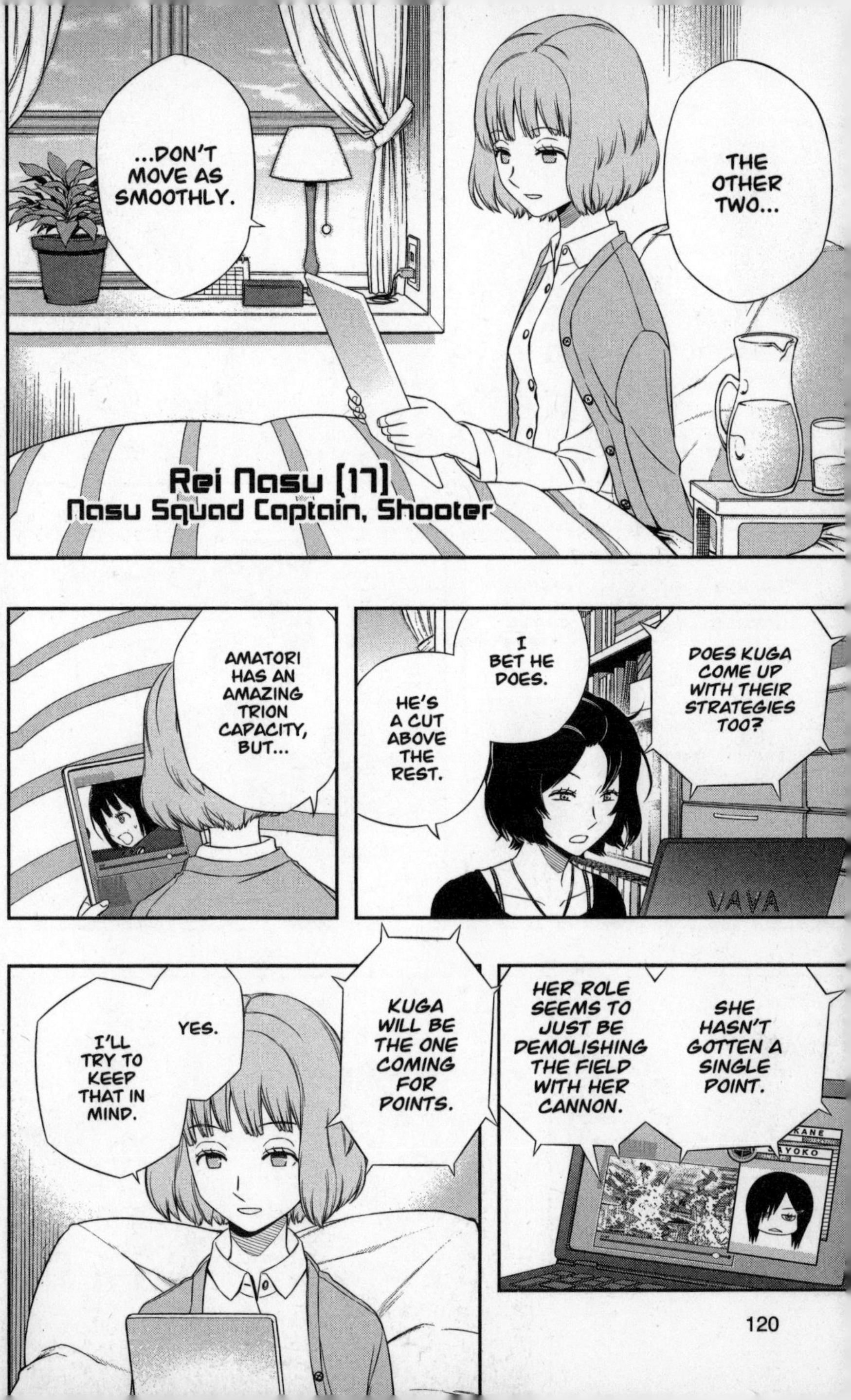
THE OTHER TWO...
...DON'T MOVE AS SMOOTHLY.
Rei Nasu (17)
Nasu Squad Captain, Shooter
DOES KUGA COME UP WITH THEIR STRATEGIES TOO?
I BET HE DOES.
HE'S A CUT ABOVE THE REST.
VAVA
AMATORI HAS AN AMAZING TRION CAPACITY, BUT...
SHE HASN'T GOTTEN A SINGLE POINT.
HER ROLE SEEMS TO JUST BE DEMOLISHING THE FIELD WITH HER CANNON.
KUGA WILL BE THE ONE COMING FOR POINTS.
YES.
I'LL TRY TO KEEP THAT IN MIND.

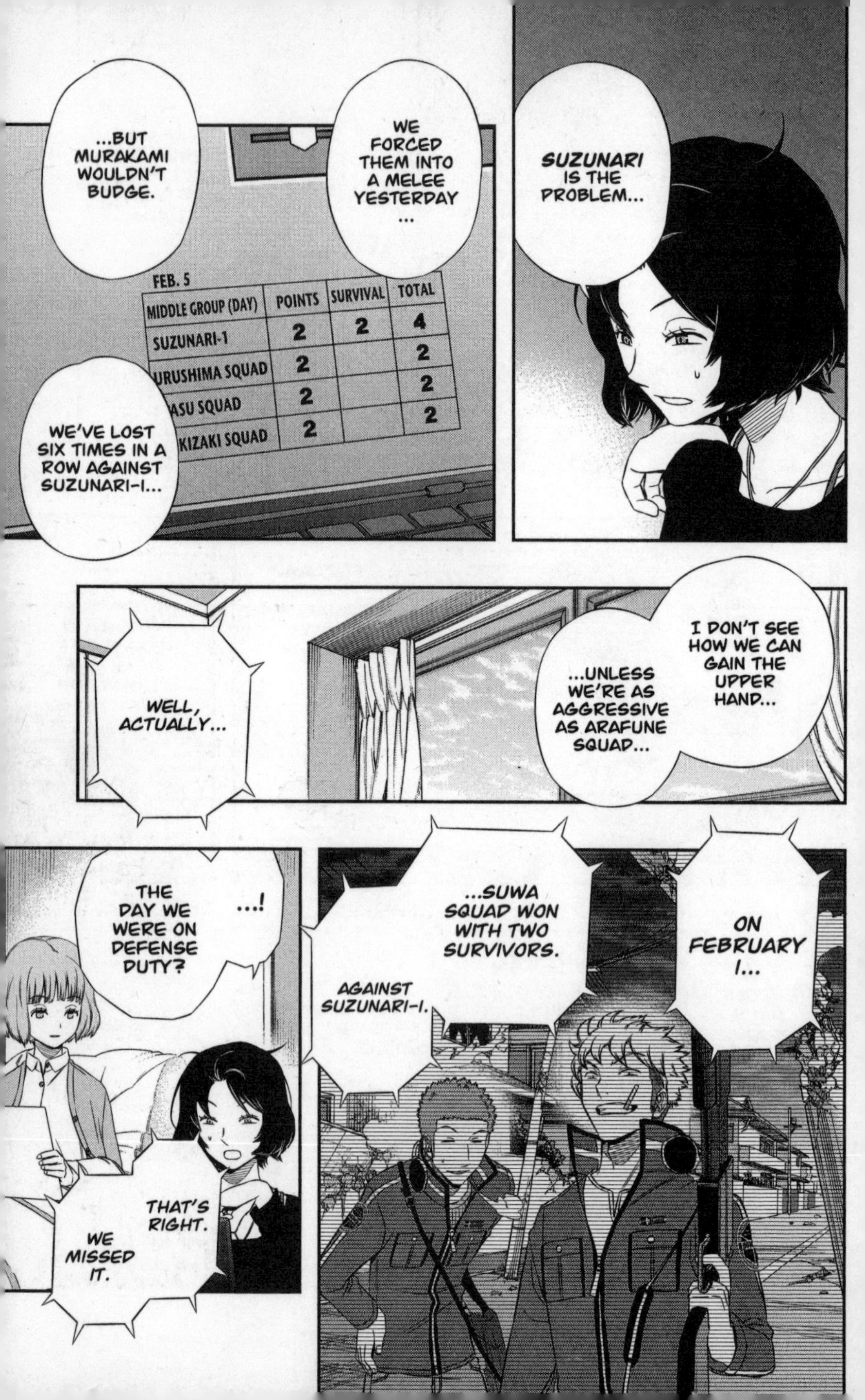
SUZUNARI IS THE PROBLEM...
WE FORCED THEM INTO A MELEE YESTERDAY ...
...BUT MURAKAMI WOULDN'T BUDGE.
FEB. 5
MIDDLE GROUP (DAY) POINTS SURVIVAL TOTAL
SUZUNARI-1 2 2 4
URUSHIMA SQUAD 2 2
ASU SQUAD 2 2
KIZAKI SQUAD 2 2
WE'VE LOST SIX TIMES IN A ROW AGAINST SUZUNARI-1...
I DON'T SEE HOW WE CAN GAIN THE UPPER HAND...
...UNLESS WE'RE AS AGGRESSIVE AS ARAFUNE SQUAD...
WELL, ACTUALLY...
ON FEBRUARY 1...
...SUWA SQUAD WON WITH TWO SURVIVORS.
AGAINST SUZUNARI-1.
...!
THE DAY WE WERE ON DEFENSE DUTY?
THAT'S RIGHT.
WE MISSED IT.

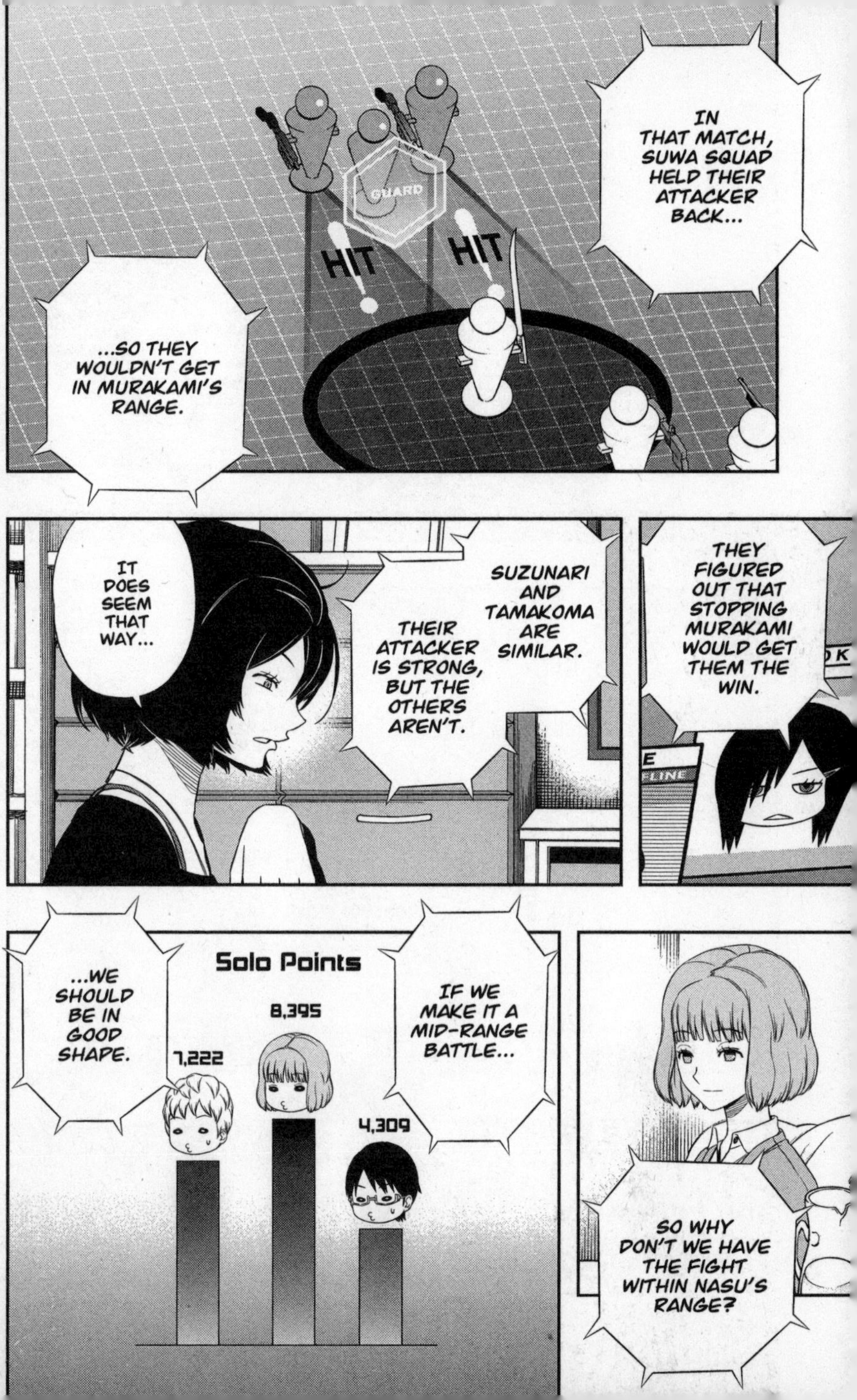
IN THAT MATCH, SUWA SQUAD HELD THEIR ATTACKER BACK...
GUARD
HIT
HIT
...SO THEY WOULDN'T GET IN MURAKAMI'S RANGE.
THEY FIGURED OUT THAT STOPPING MURAKAMI WOULD GET THEM THE WIN.
SUZUNARI AND TAMAKOMA ARE SIMILAR.
THEIR ATTACKER IS STRONG, BUT THE OTHERS AREN'T.
IT DOES SEEM THAT WAY...
SO WHY DON'T WE HAVE THE FIGHT WITHIN NASU'S RANGE?
IF WE MAKE IT A MID-RANGE BATTLE...
Solo Points
8,395
7,222
4,309
...WE SHOULD BE IN GOOD SHAPE.

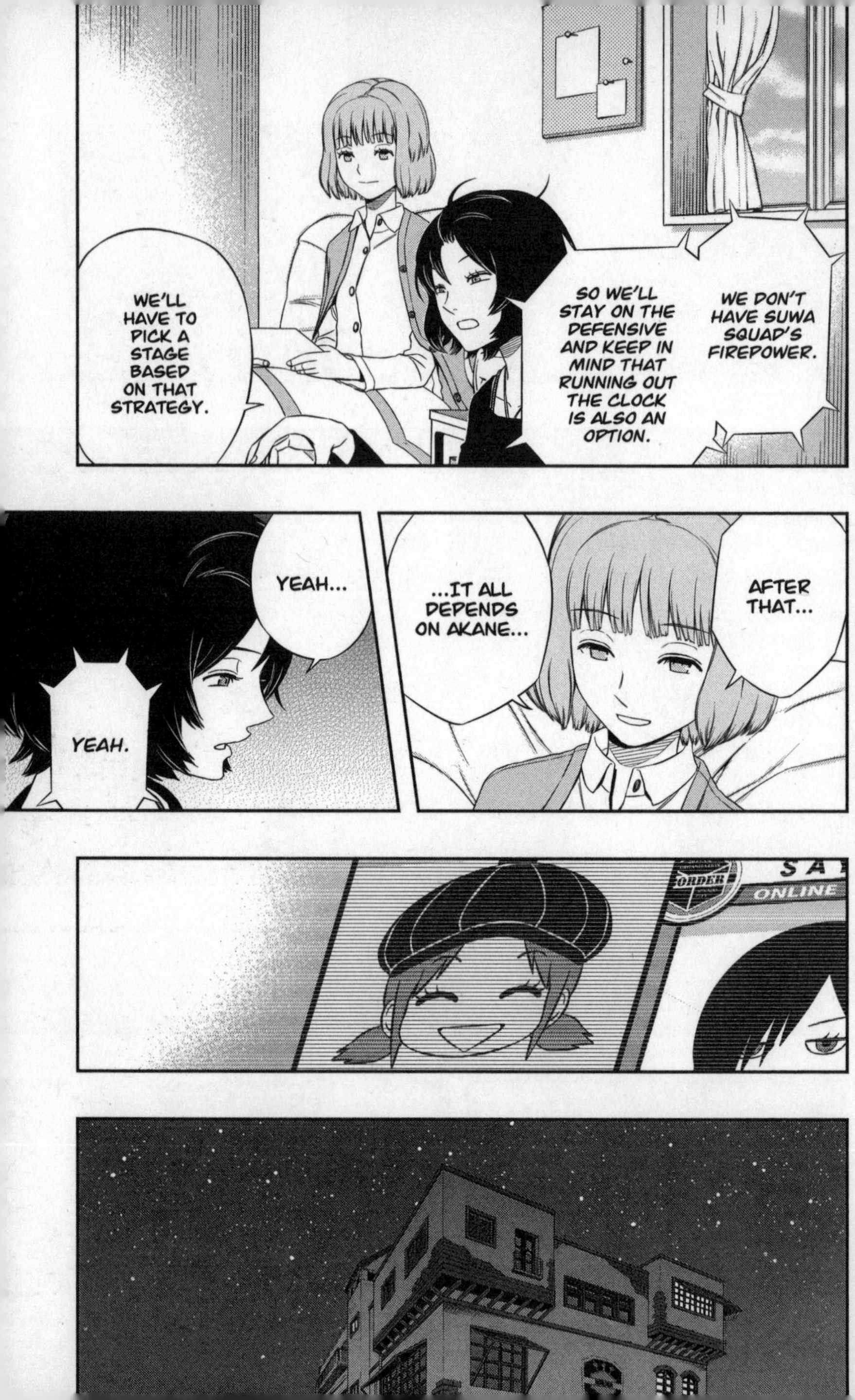
WE DON'T HAVE SUWA SQUAD'S FIREPOWER.
SO WE'LL STAY ON THE DEFENSIVE AND KEEP IN MIND THAT RUNNING OUT THE CLOCK IS ALSO AN OPTION.
WE'LL HAVE TO PICK A STAGE BASED ON THAT STRATEGY.
AFTER THAT...
...IT ALL DEPENDS ON AKANE...
YEAH...
YEAH.
ONLINE

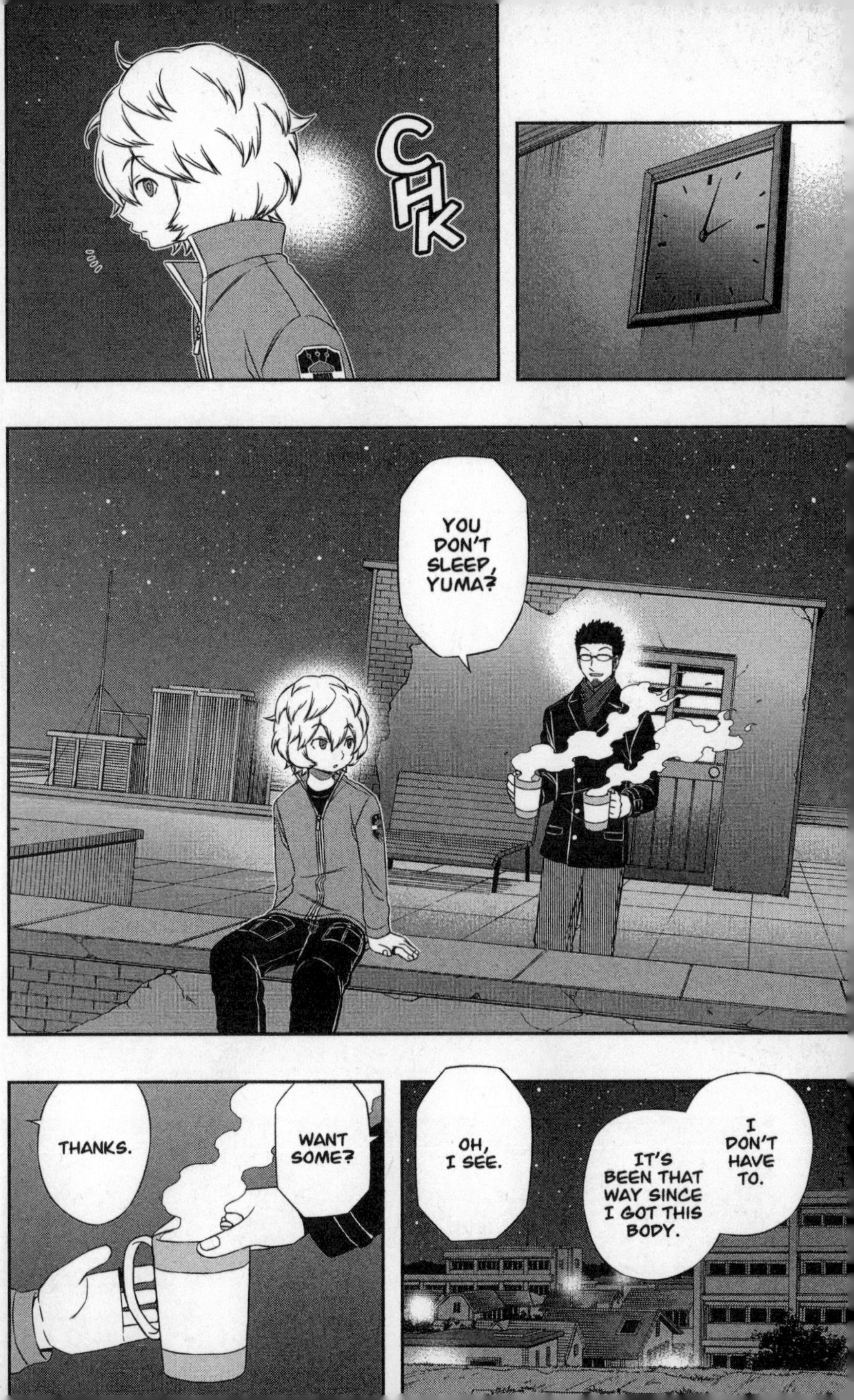
CHK
YOU DON'T SLEEP, YUMA?
I DON'T HAVE TO.
IT'S BEEN THAT WAY SINCE I GOT THIS BODY.
OH, I SEE.
WANT SOME?
THANKS.

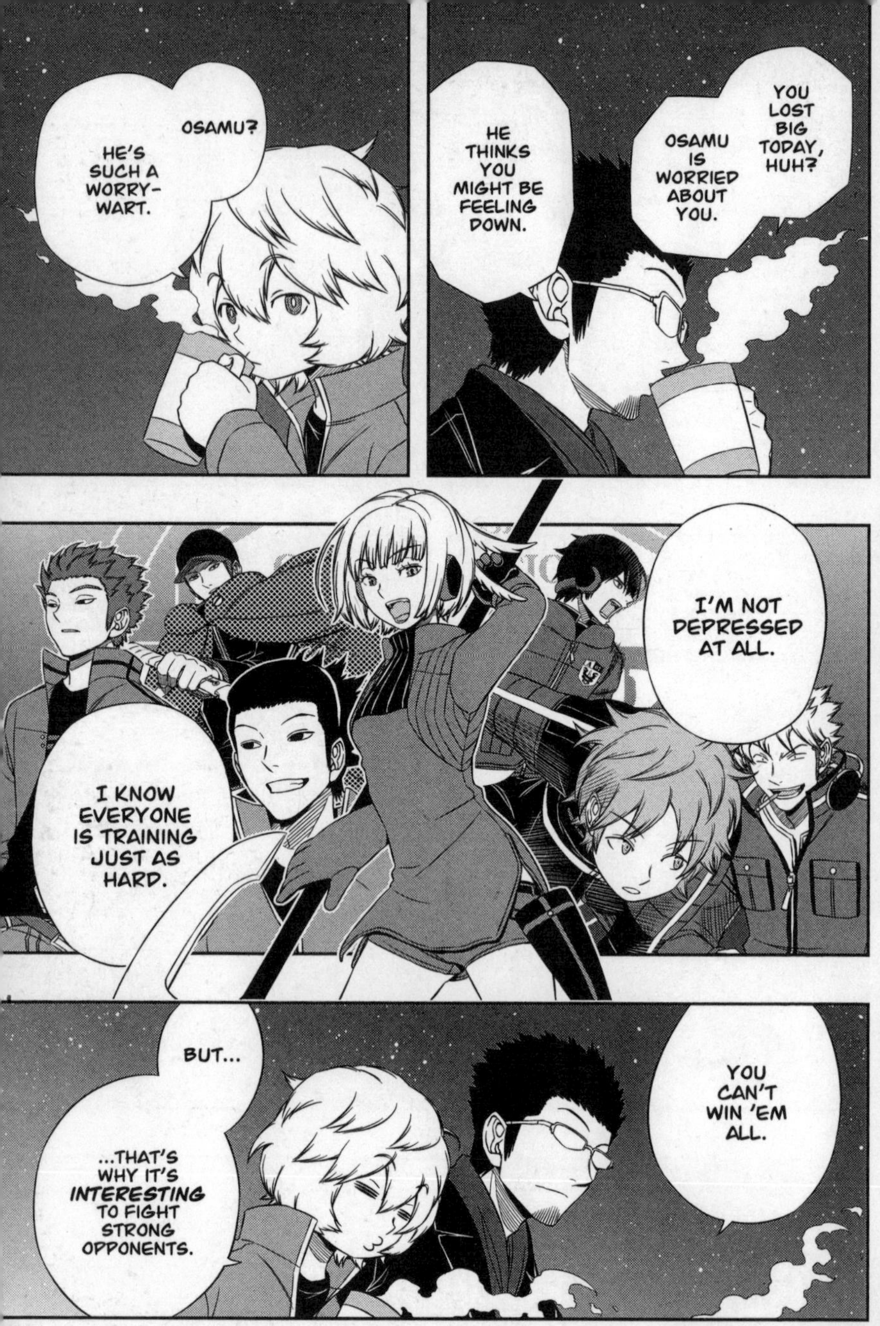
YOU LOST BIG TODAY, HUH?
OSAMU IS WORRIED ABOUT YOU.
HE THINKS YOU MIGHT BE FEELING DOWN.
OSAMU?
HE'S SUCH A WORRY-WART.
I'M NOT DEPRESSED AT ALL.
I KNOW EVERYONE IS TRAINING JUST AS HARD.
YOU CAN'T WIN 'EM ALL.
BUT...
...THAT'S WHY IT'S INTERESTING TO FIGHT STRONG OPPONENTS.

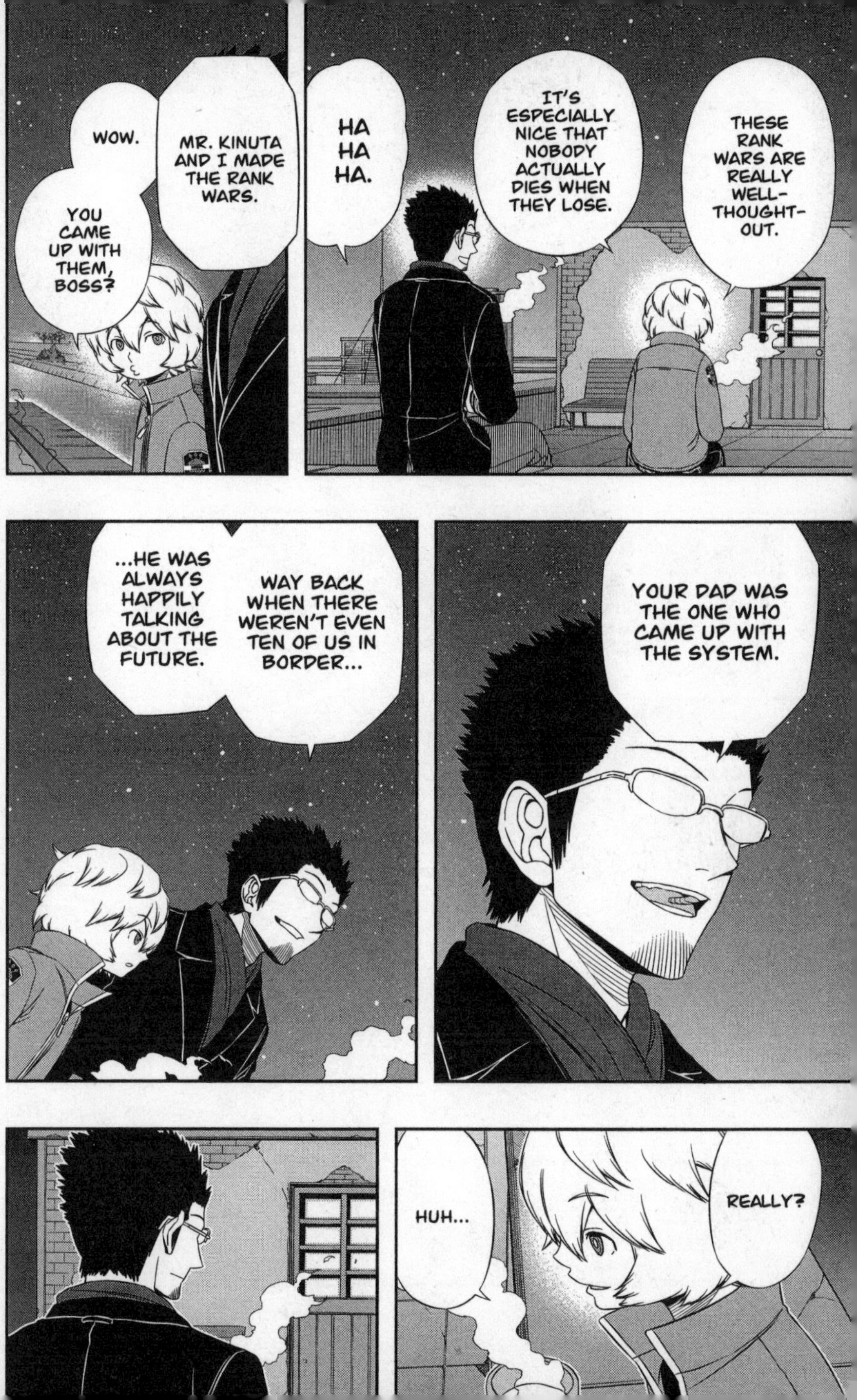

THESE RANK WARS ARE REALLY WELL-THOUGHT-OUT.
IT'S ESPECIALLY NICE THAT NOBODY ACTUALLY DIES WHEN THEY LOSE.
HA HA HA.
MR. KINUTA AND I MADE THE RANK WARS.
WOW.
YOU CAME UP WITH THEM, BOSS?
YOUR DAD WAS THE ONE WHO CAME UP WITH THE SYSTEM.
WAY BACK WHEN THERE WEREN'T EVEN TEN OF US IN BORDER...
...HE WAS ALWAYS HAPPILY TALKING ABOUT THE FUTURE.
REALLY?
HUH...

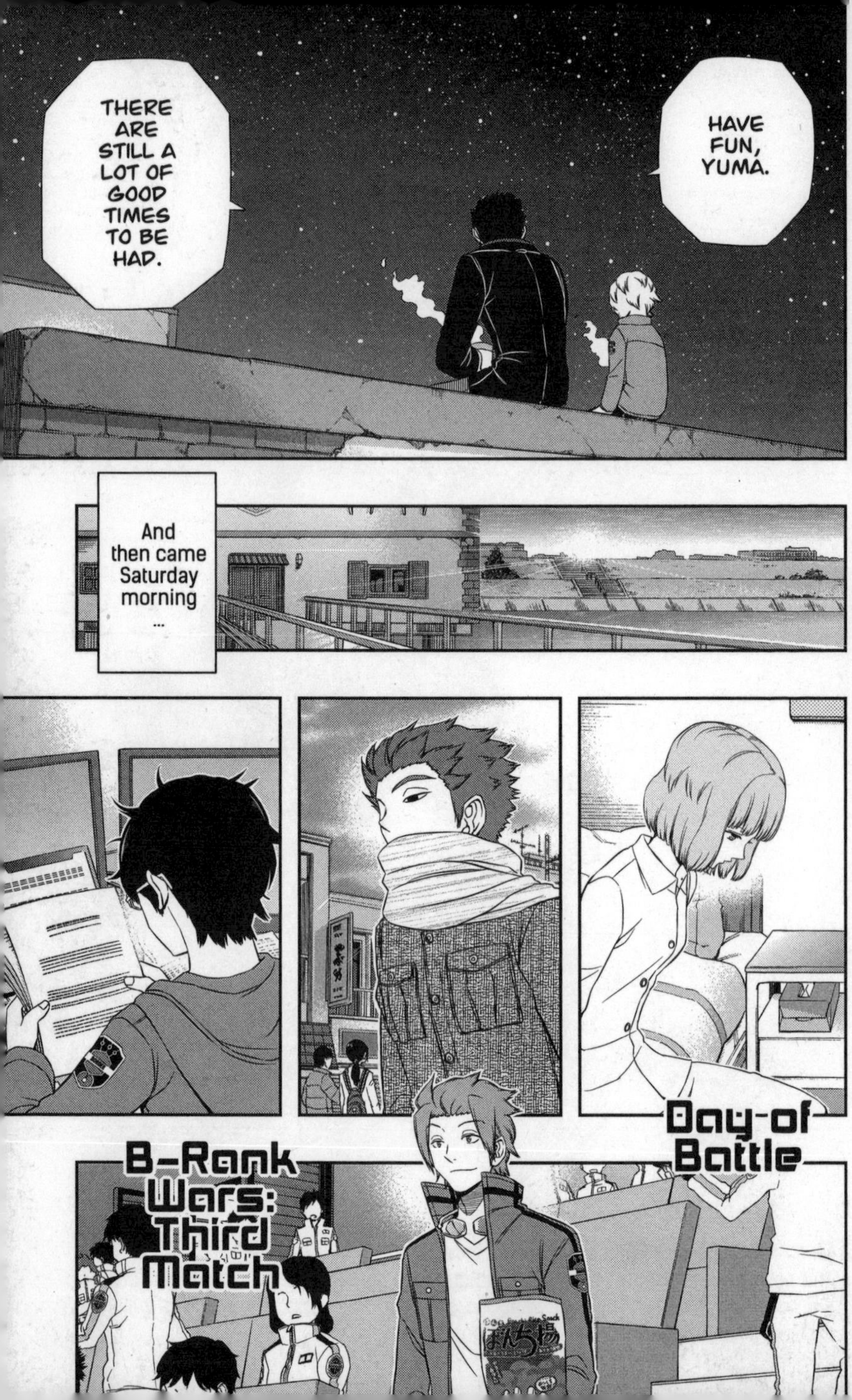
HAVE FUN, YUMA.
THERE ARE STILL A LOT OF GOOD TIMES TO BE HAD.
And then came Saturday morning ...
Day of Battle
B-Rank Wars: Third Match

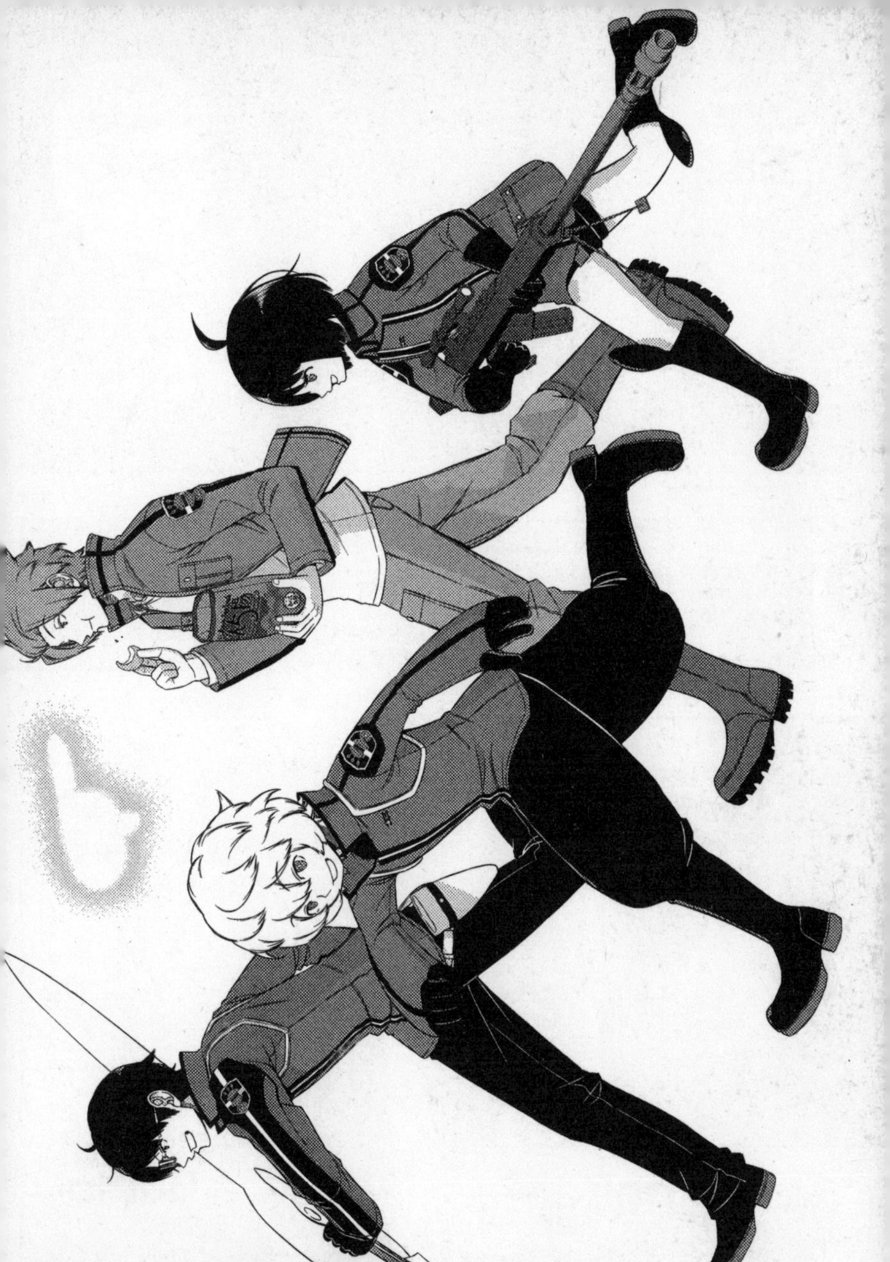

■ **2015 *Weekly Shonen Jump* Issue 27 issue cover**
The designer wanted the four main characters running toward the future. They also wanted them to be holding their weapons, so maybe it should've been more valiant. Osamu, it's dangerous to run with a Raygust!

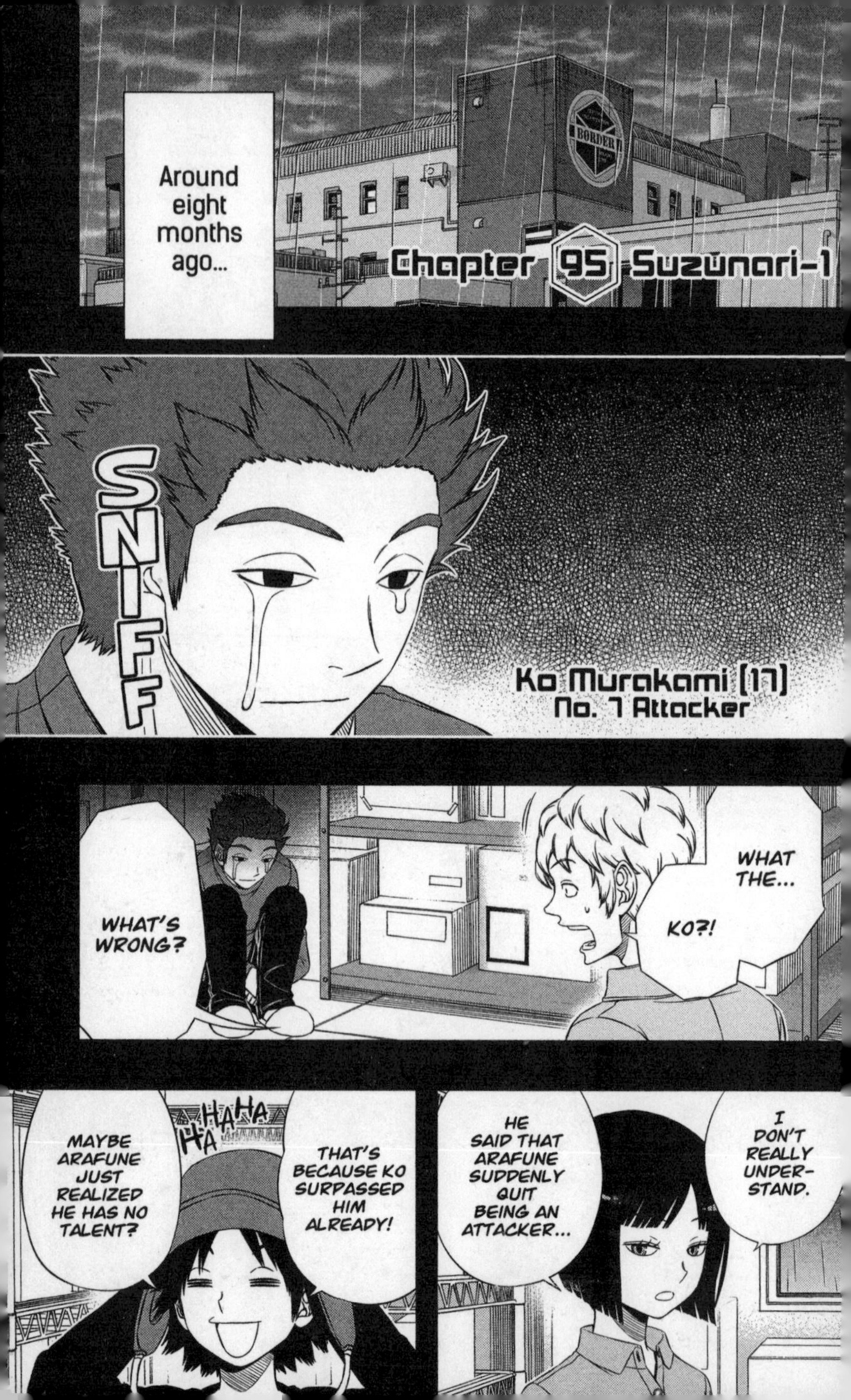
Chapter 95 Suzūnari-1
Around eight months ago...
Ko Murakami (17)
No. 1 Attacker
SNIFF
WHAT THE...
KO?!
WHAT'S WRONG?
I DON'T REALLY UNDER-STAND.
HE SAID THAT ARAFUNE SUDDENLY QUIT BEING AN ATTACKER...
THAT'S BECAUSE KO SURPASSED HIM ALREADY!
HAHAHA
MAYBE ARAFUNE JUST REALIZED HE HAS NO TALENT?

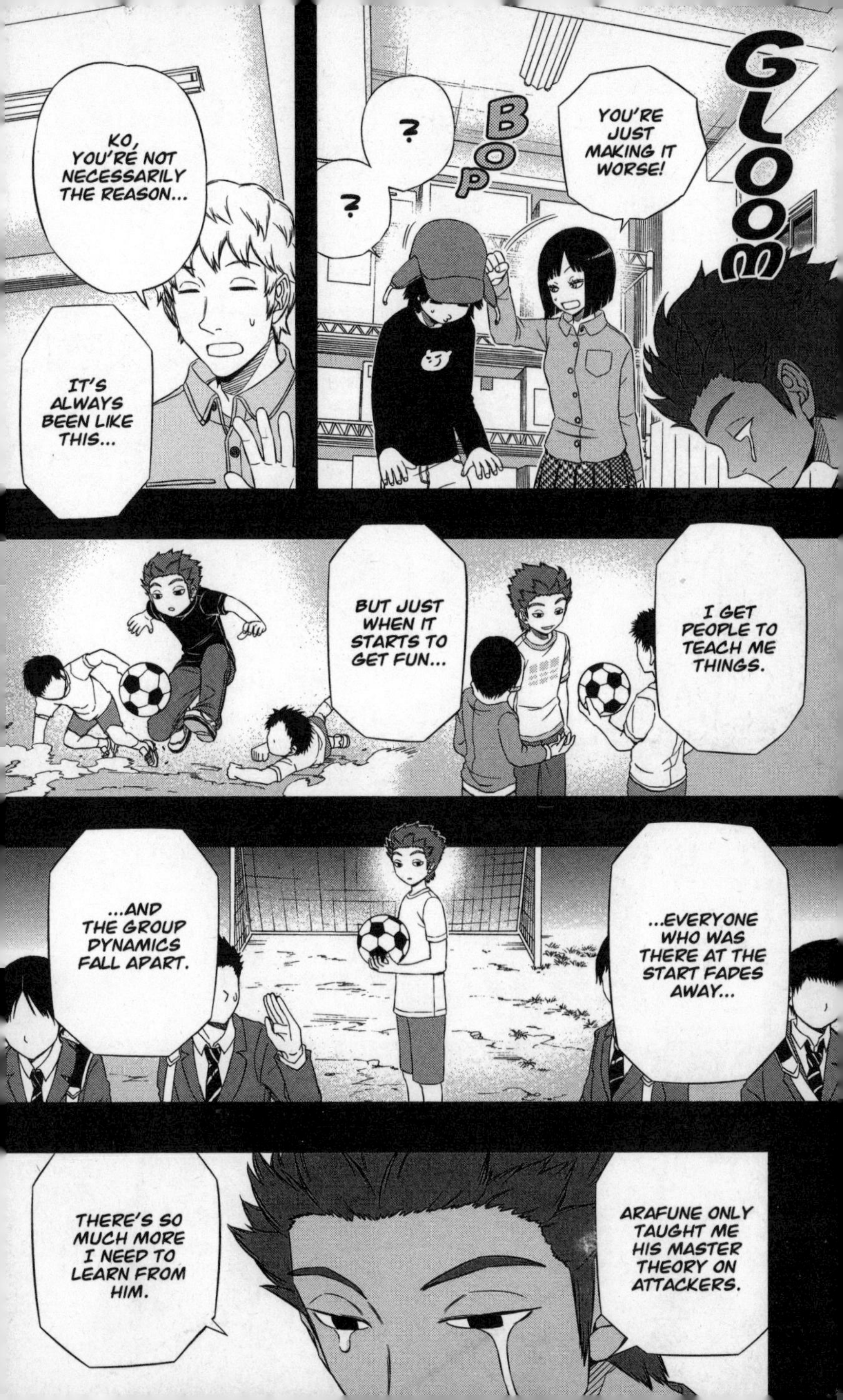
GLOOM
YOU'RE JUST MAKING IT WORSE!
BOP
?
?
KO, YOU'RE NOT NECESSARILY THE REASON...
IT'S ALWAYS BEEN LIKE THIS...
I GET PEOPLE TO TEACH ME THINGS.
BUT JUST WHEN IT STARTS TO GET FUN...
...EVERYONE WHO WAS THERE AT THE START FADES AWAY...
...AND THE GROUP DYNAMICS FALL APART.
ARAFUNE ONLY TAUGHT ME HIS MASTER THEORY ON ATTACKERS.
THERE'S SO MUCH MORE I NEED TO LEARN FROM HIM.

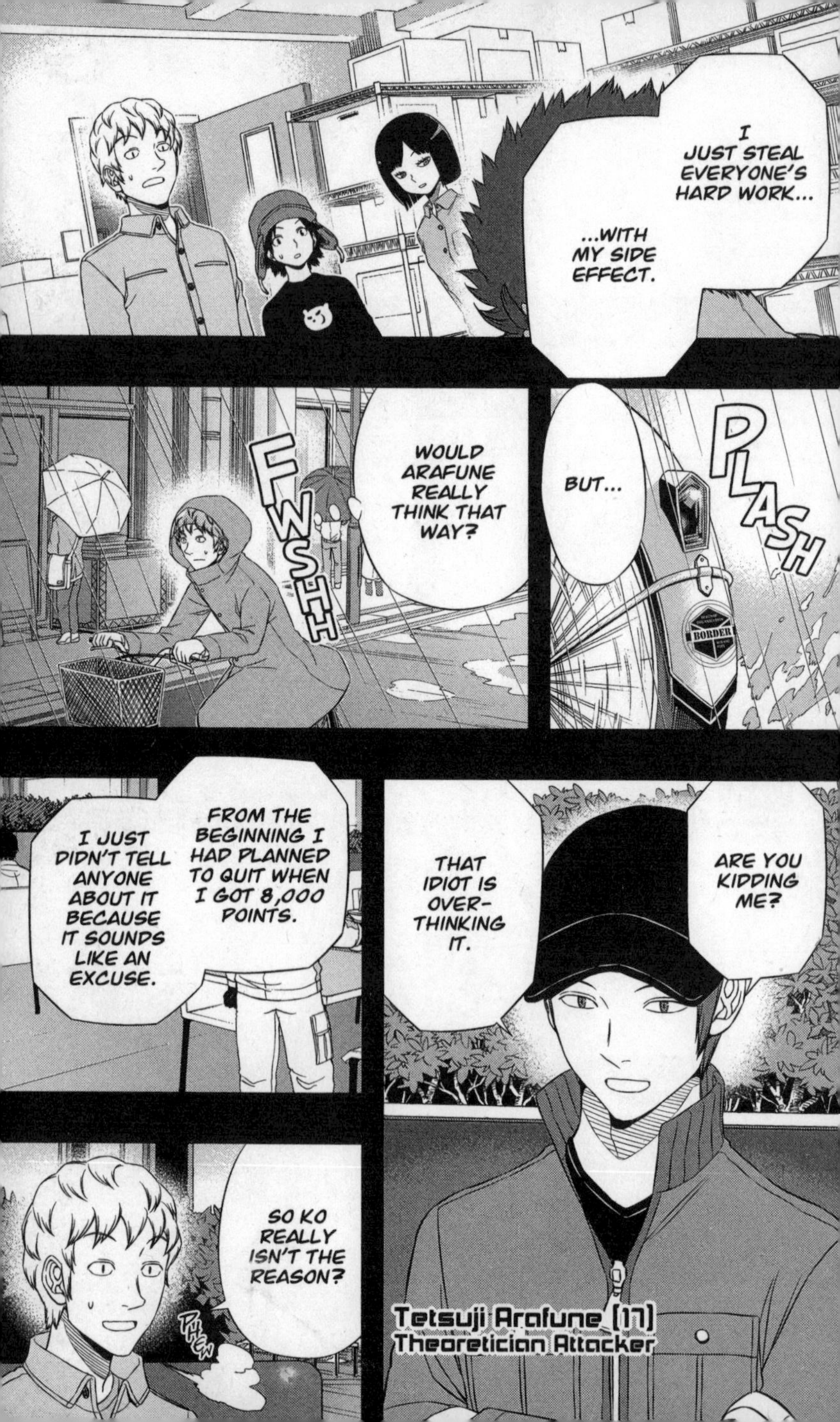
I JUST STEAL EVERYONE'S HARD WORK...
...WITH MY SIDE EFFECT.
BUT...
PLASH
WOULD ARAFUNE REALLY THINK THAT WAY?
FWSHH
ARE YOU KIDDING ME?
THAT IDIOT IS OVER-THINKING IT.
Tetsuji Arafune (17) Theoretician Attacker
FROM THE BEGINNING I HAD PLANNED TO QUIT WHEN I GOT 8,000 POINTS.
I JUST DIDN'T TELL ANYONE ABOUT IT BECAUSE IT SOUNDS LIKE AN EXCUSE.
SO KO REALLY ISN'T THE REASON?
PHEW

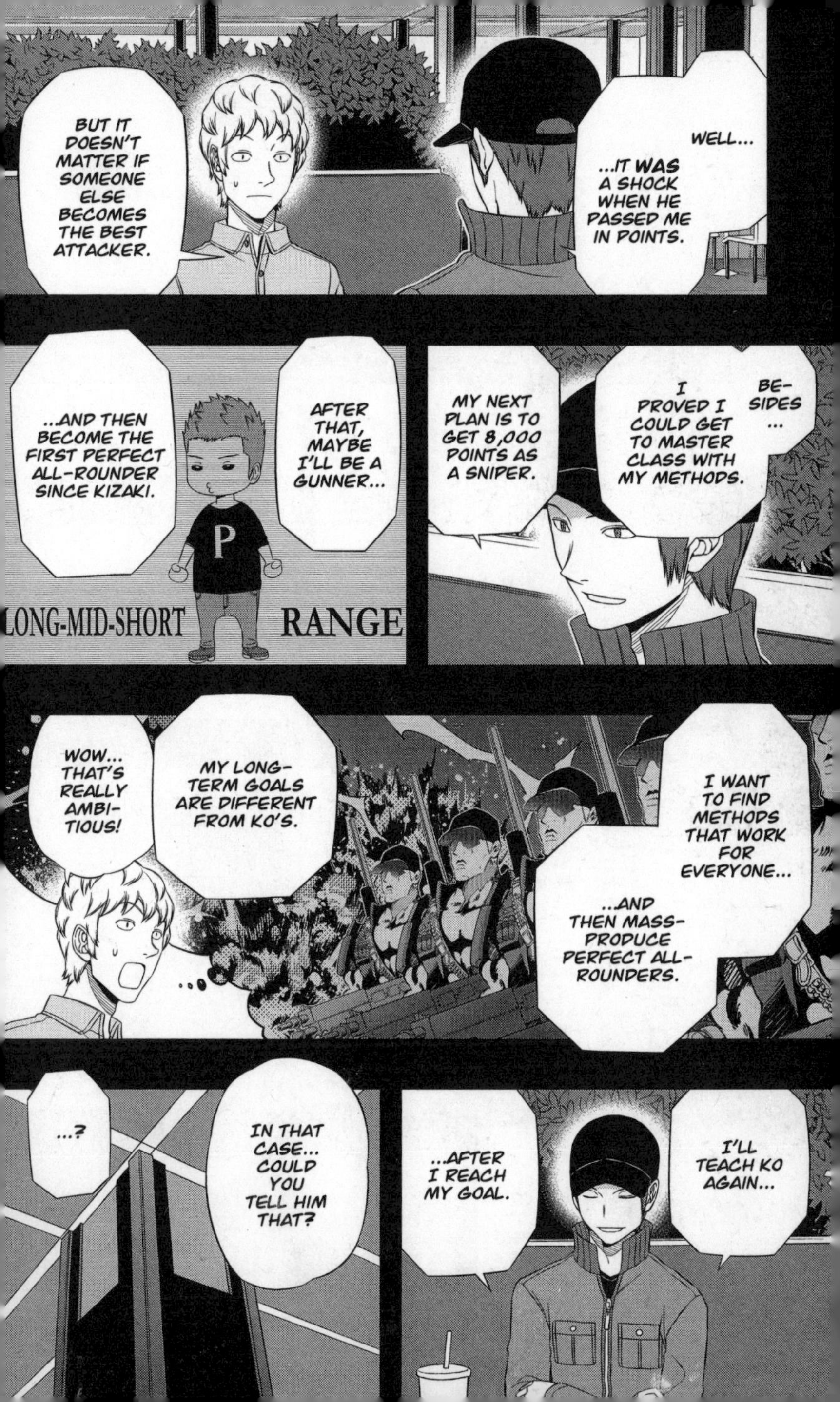
WELL...
...IT WAS A SHOCK WHEN HE PASSED ME IN POINTS.
BUT IT DOESN'T MATTER IF SOMEONE ELSE BECOMES THE BEST ATTACKER.
BESIDES...
I PROVED I COULD GET TO MASTER CLASS WITH MY METHODS.
MY NEXT PLAN IS TO GET 8,000 POINTS AS A SNIPER.
AFTER THAT, MAYBE I'LL BE A GUNNER...
...AND THEN BECOME THE FIRST PERFECT ALL-ROUNDER SINCE KIZAKI.
LONG-MID-SHORT
RANGE
I WANT TO FIND METHODS THAT WORK FOR EVERYONE...
...AND THEN MASS-PRODUCE PERFECT ALL-ROUNDERS.
MY LONG-TERM GOALS ARE DIFFERENT FROM KO'S.
WOW... THAT'S REALLY AMBITIOUS!
I'LL TEACH KO AGAIN...
...AFTER I REACH MY GOAL.
IN THAT CASE... COULD YOU TELL HIM THAT?
...?

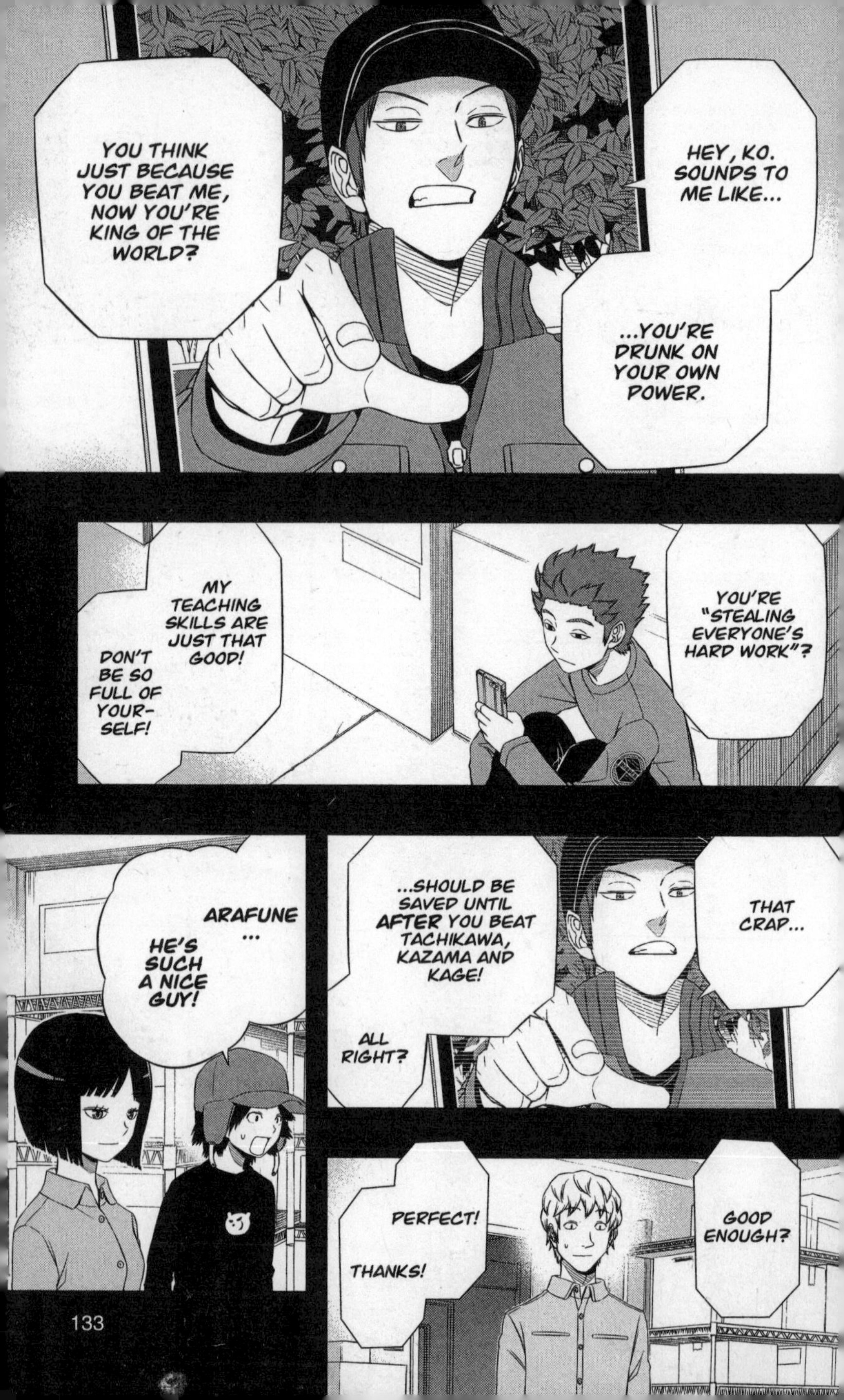

HEY, KO. SOUNDS TO ME LIKE...
...YOU'RE DRUNK ON YOUR OWN POWER.
YOU THINK JUST BECAUSE YOU BEAT ME, NOW YOU'RE KING OF THE WORLD?
YOU'RE "STEALING EVERYONE'S HARD WORK"?
MY TEACHING SKILLS ARE JUST THAT GOOD!
DON'T BE SO FULL OF YOUR-SELF!
THAT CRAP...
...SHOULD BE SAVED UNTIL AFTER YOU BEAT TACHIKAWA, KAZAMA AND KAGE!
ALL RIGHT?
GOOD ENOUGH?
PERFECT!
THANKS!
ARAFUNE ...
HE'S SUCH A NICE GUY!

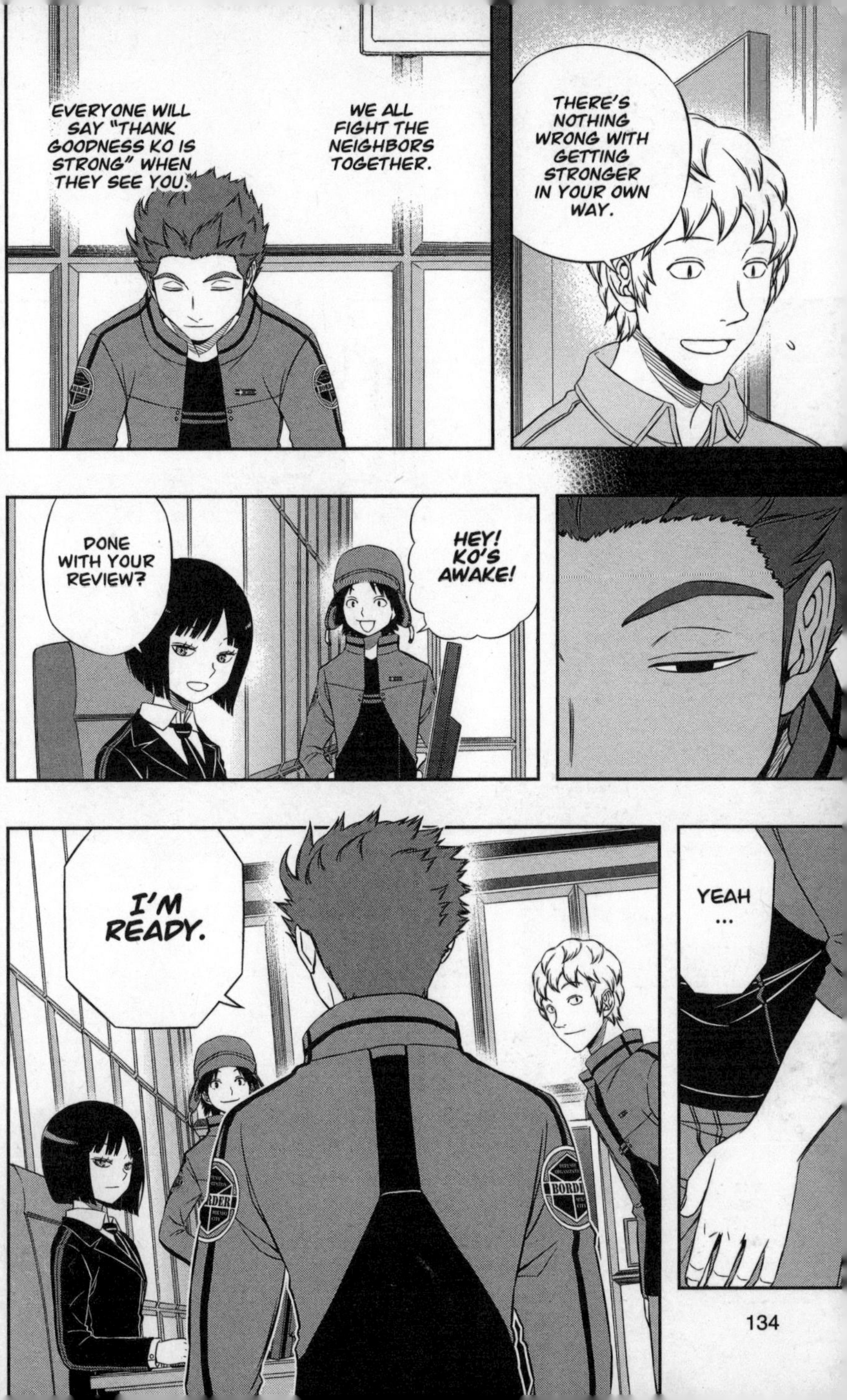
THERE'S NOTHING WRONG WITH GETTING STRONGER IN YOUR OWN WAY.
WE ALL FIGHT THE NEIGHBORS TOGETHER.
EVERYONE WILL SAY "THANK GOODNESS KO IS STRONG" WHEN THEY SEE YOU.
HEY! KO'S AWAKE!
DONE WITH YOUR REVIEW?
YEAH ...
I'M READY.

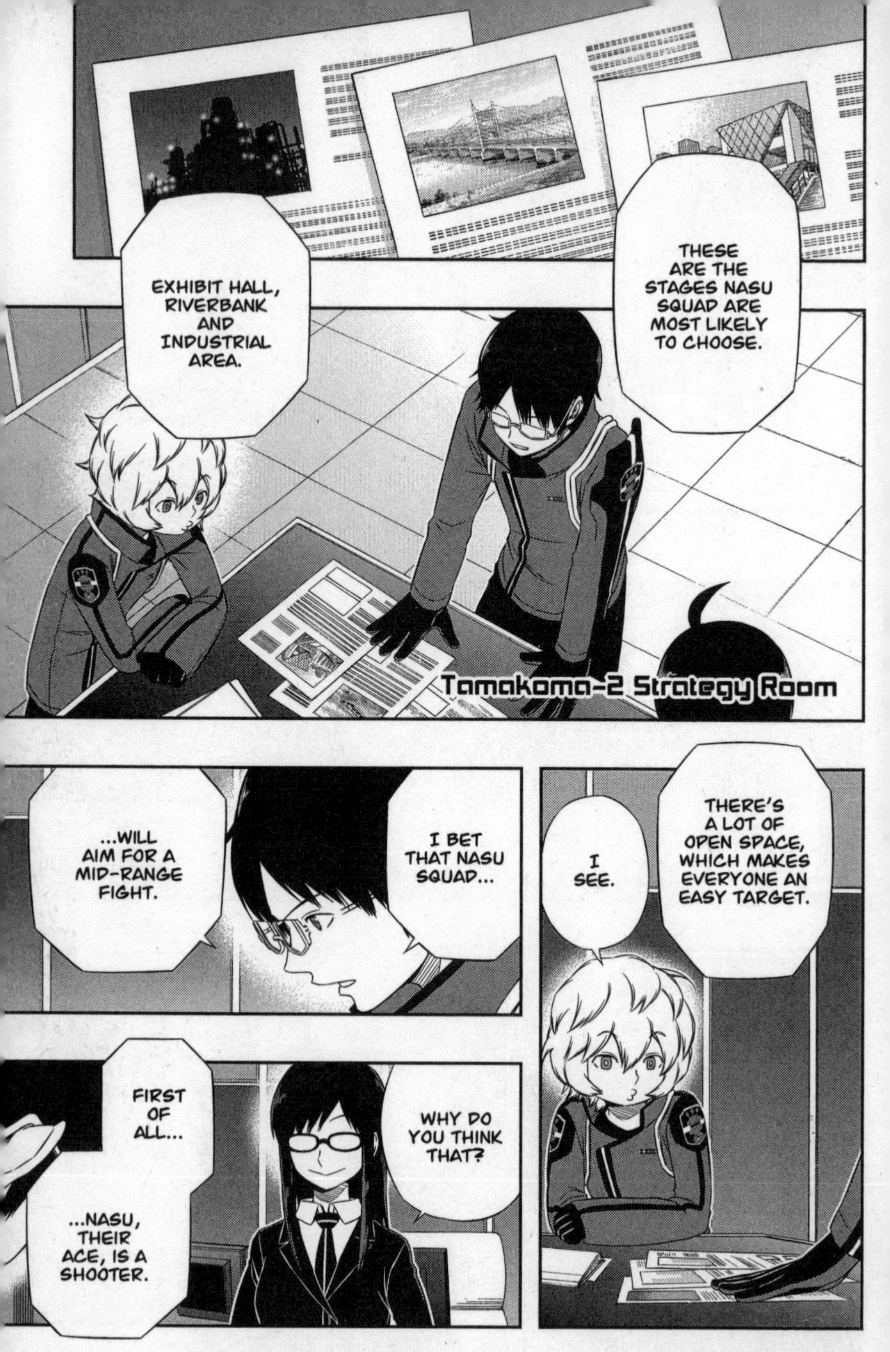
THESE ARE THE STAGES NASU SQUAD ARE MOST LIKELY TO CHOOSE.
EXHIBIT HALL, RIVERBANK AND INDUSTRIAL AREA.
Tamakoma-2 Strategy Room
THERE'S A LOT OF OPEN SPACE, WHICH MAKES EVERYONE AN EASY TARGET.
I SEE.
I BET THAT NASU SQUAD...
...WILL AIM FOR A MID-RANGE FIGHT.
WHY DO YOU THINK THAT?
FIRST OF ALL...
...NASU, THEIR ACE, IS A SHOOTER.

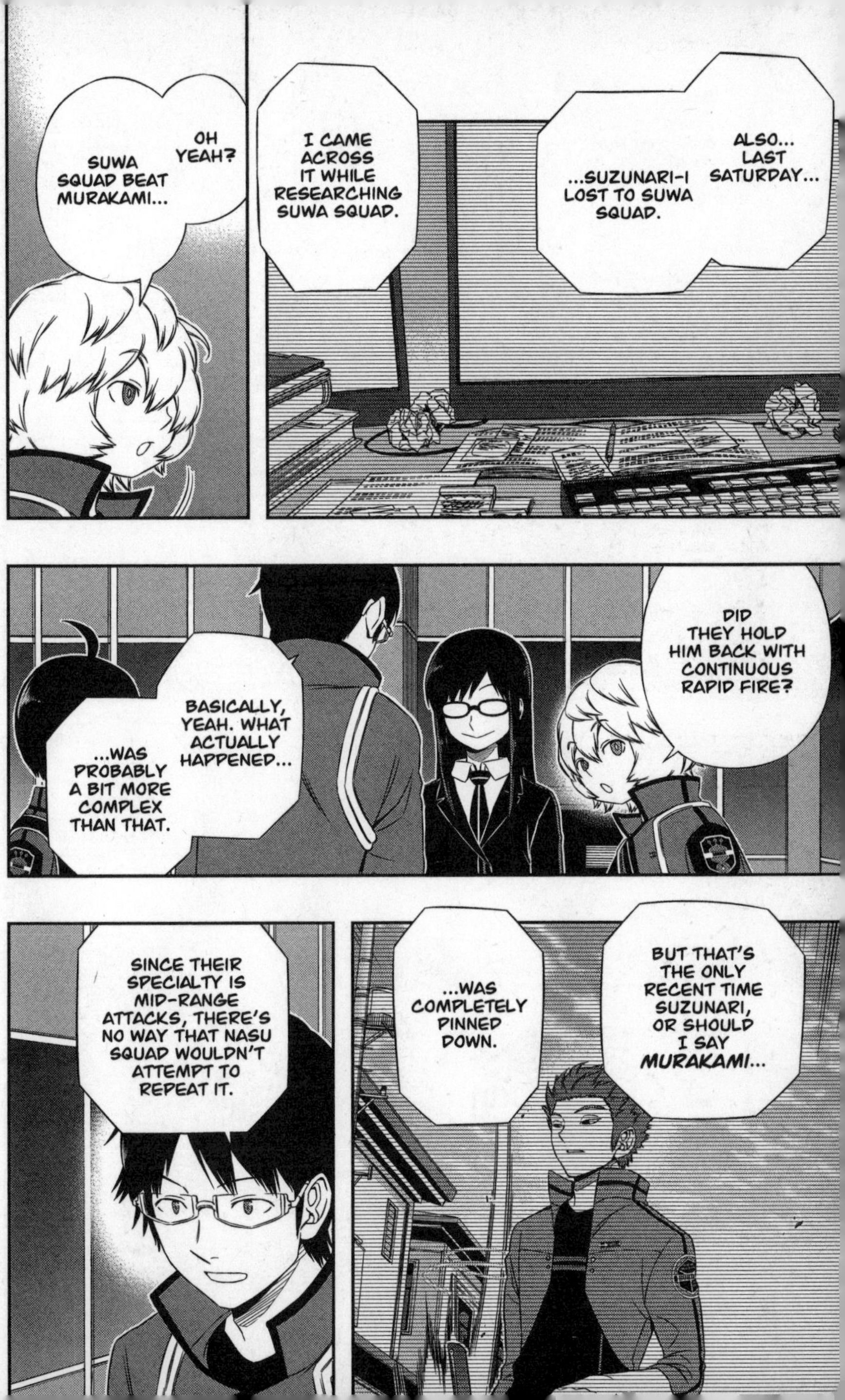
ALSO... LAST SATURDAY...
...SUZUNARI-I LOST TO SUWA SQUAD.
I CAME ACROSS IT WHILE RESEARCHING SUWA SQUAD.
OH YEAH?
SUWA SQUAD BEAT MURAKAMI...
DID THEY HOLD HIM BACK WITH CONTINUOUS RAPID FIRE?
BASICALLY, YEAH. WHAT ACTUALLY HAPPENED...
...WAS PROBABLY A BIT MORE COMPLEX THAN THAT.
BUT THAT'S THE ONLY RECENT TIME SUZUNARI, OR SHOULD I SAY *MURAKAMI*...
...WAS COMPLETELY PINNED DOWN.
SINCE THEIR SPECIALTY IS MID-RANGE ATTACKS, THERE'S NO WAY THAT NASU SQUAD WOULDN'T ATTEMPT TO REPEAT IT.

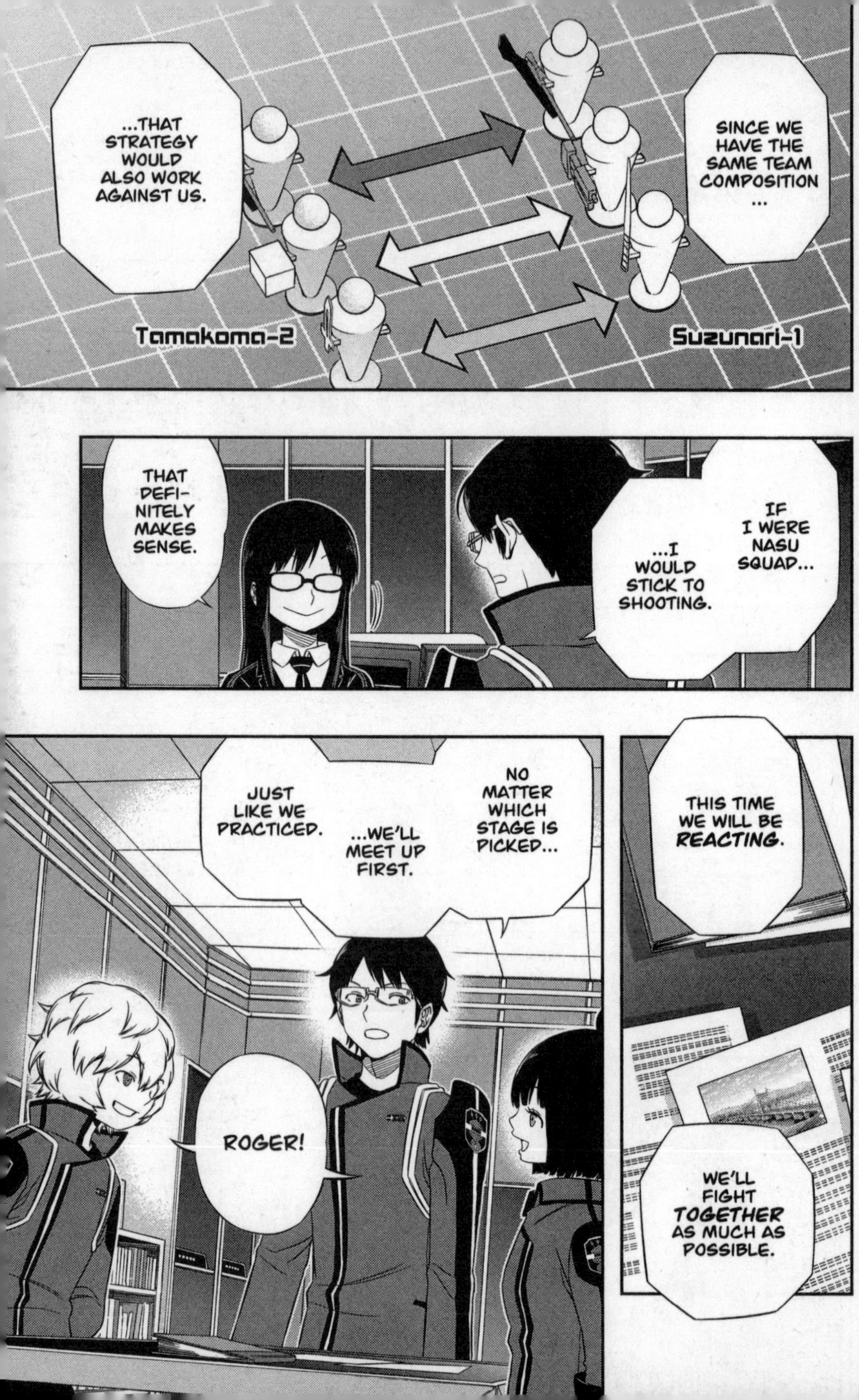
SINCE WE HAVE THE SAME TEAM COMPOSITION...
...THAT STRATEGY WOULD ALSO WORK AGAINST US.
Suzunari-1
Tamakoma-2
IF I WERE NASU SQUAD...
...I WOULD STICK TO SHOOTING.
THAT DEFINITELY MAKES SENSE.
THIS TIME WE WILL BE REACTING.
WE'LL FIGHT TOGETHER AS MUCH AS POSSIBLE.
NO MATTER WHICH STAGE IS PICKED...
...WE'LL MEET UP FIRST.
JUST LIKE WE PRACTICED.
ROGER!

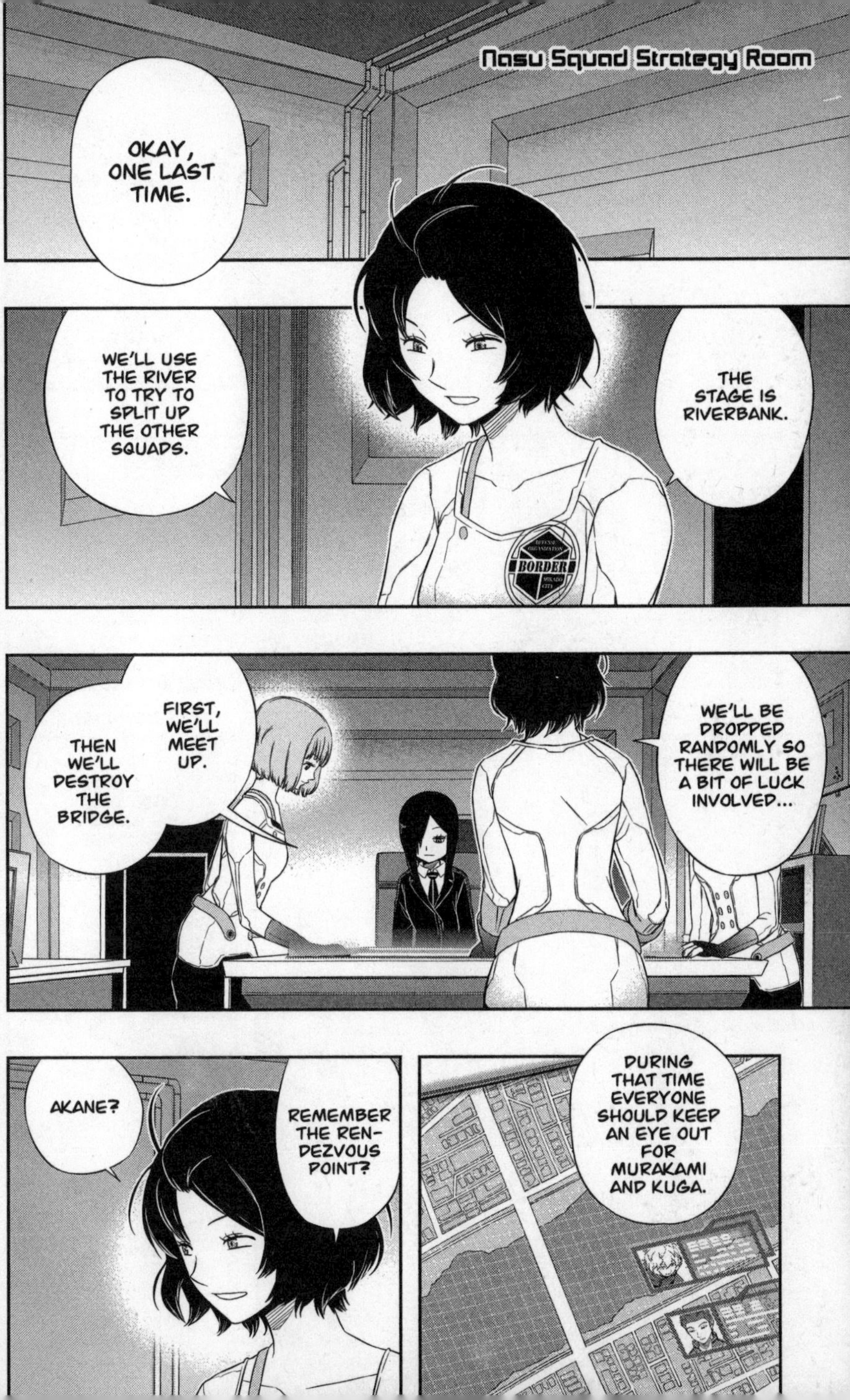
Nasu Squad Strategy Room
OKAY, ONE LAST TIME.
THE STAGE IS RIVERBANK.
WE'LL USE THE RIVER TO TRY TO SPLIT UP THE OTHER SQUADS.
WE'LL BE DROPPED RANDOMLY SO THERE WILL BE A BIT OF LUCK INVOLVED...
FIRST, WE'LL MEET UP.
THEN WE'LL DESTROY THE BRIDGE.
DURING THAT TIME EVERYONE SHOULD KEEP AN EYE OUT FOR MURAKAMI AND KUGA.
REMEMBER THE REN-DEZVOUS POINT?
AKANE?

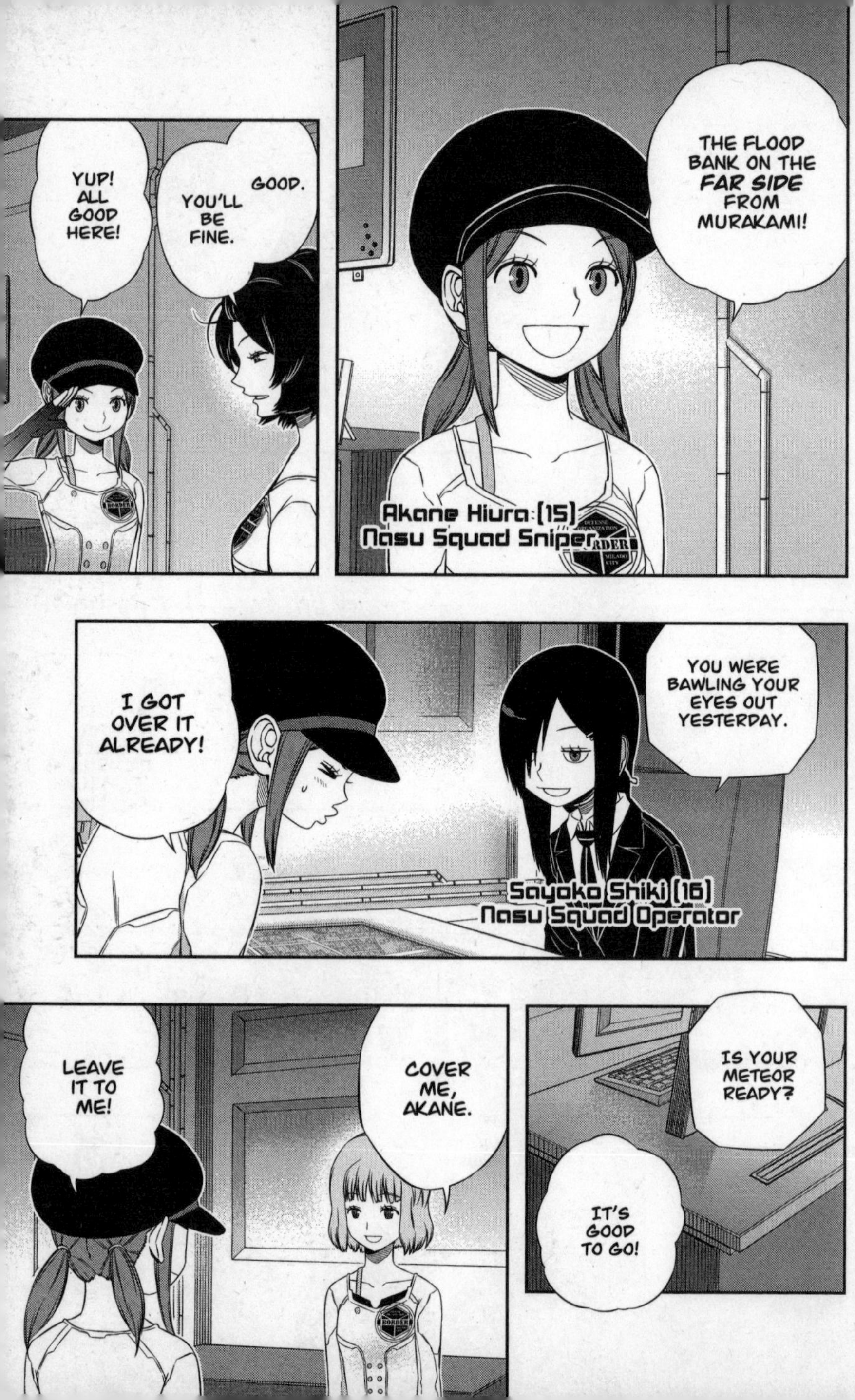
THE FLOOD BANK ON THE FAR SIDE FROM MURAKAMI!
Akane Hiura (15) Nasu Squad Sniper
GOOD. YOU'LL BE FINE.
YUP! ALL GOOD HERE!
YOU WERE BAWLING YOUR EYES OUT YESTERDAY.
Sayoko Shiki (16) Nasu Squad Operator
I GOT OVER IT ALREADY!
IS YOUR METEOR READY?
IT'S GOOD TO GO!
COVER ME, AKANE.
LEAVE IT TO ME!

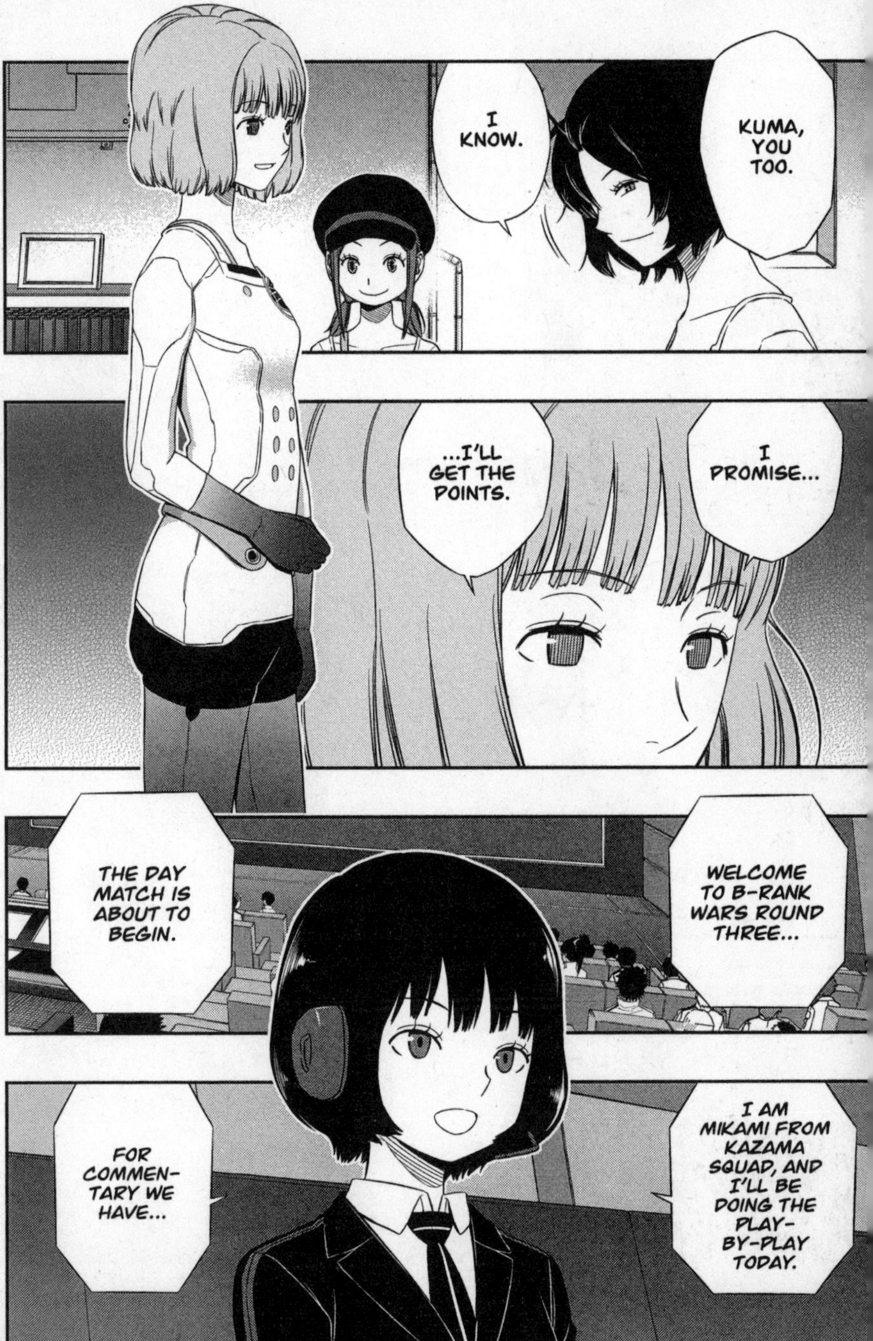
KUMA, YOU TOO.
I KNOW.
I PROMISE...
...I'LL GET THE POINTS.
WELCOME TO B-RANK WARS ROUND THREE...
THE DAY MATCH IS ABOUT TO BEGIN.
I AM MIKAMI FROM KAZAMA SQUAD, AND I'LL BE DOING THE PLAY-BY-PLAY TODAY.
FOR COMMENTARY WE HAVE...

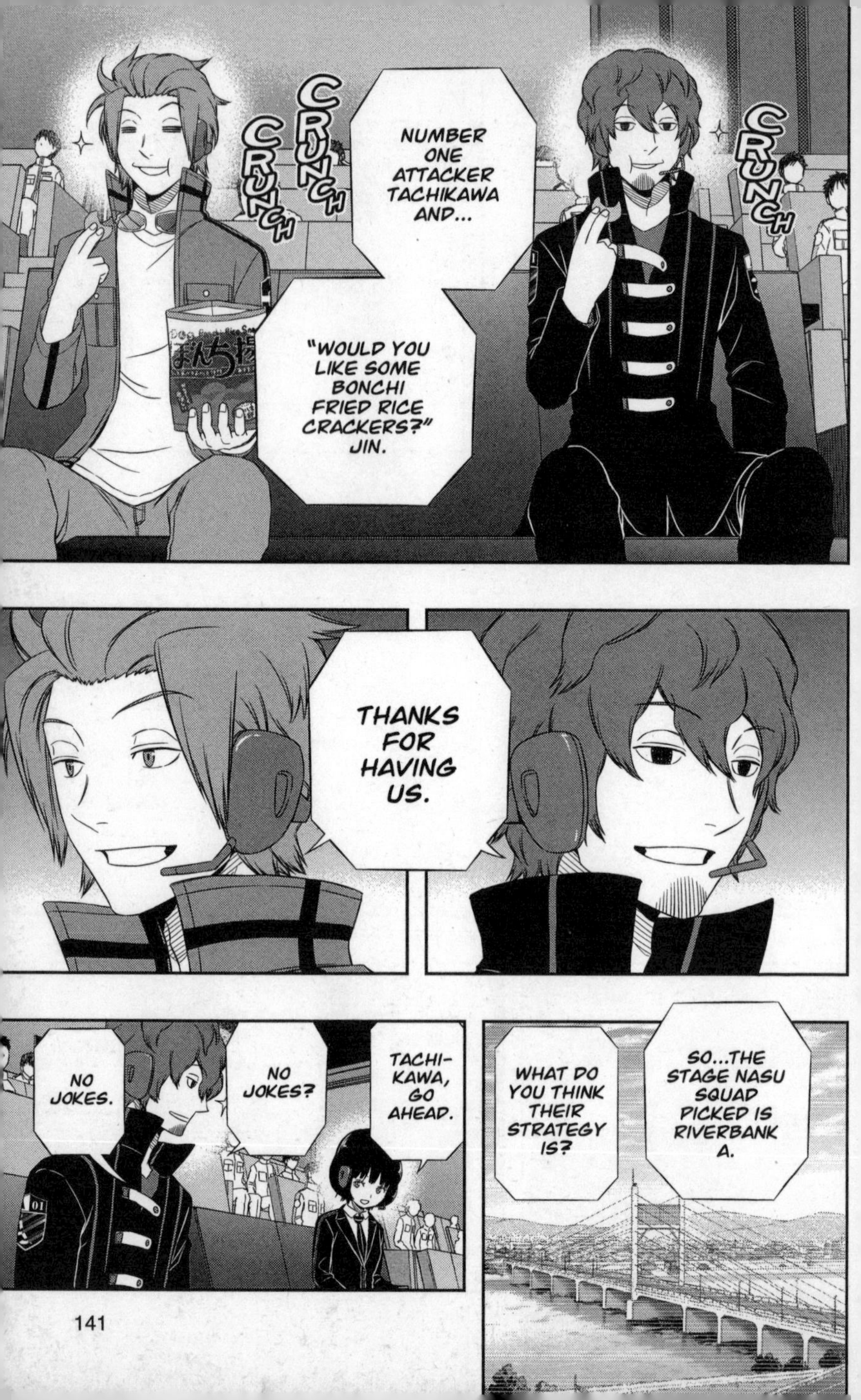
CRUNCH
NUMBER ONE ATTACKER TACHIKAWA AND...
"WOULD YOU LIKE SOME BONCHI FRIED RICE CRACKERS?" JIN.
CRUNCH
CRUNCH
THANKS FOR HAVING US.
SO...THE STAGE NASU SQUAD PICKED IS RIVERBANK A.
WHAT DO YOU THINK THEIR STRATEGY IS?
TACHI-KAWA, GO AHEAD.
NO JOKES?
NO JOKES.

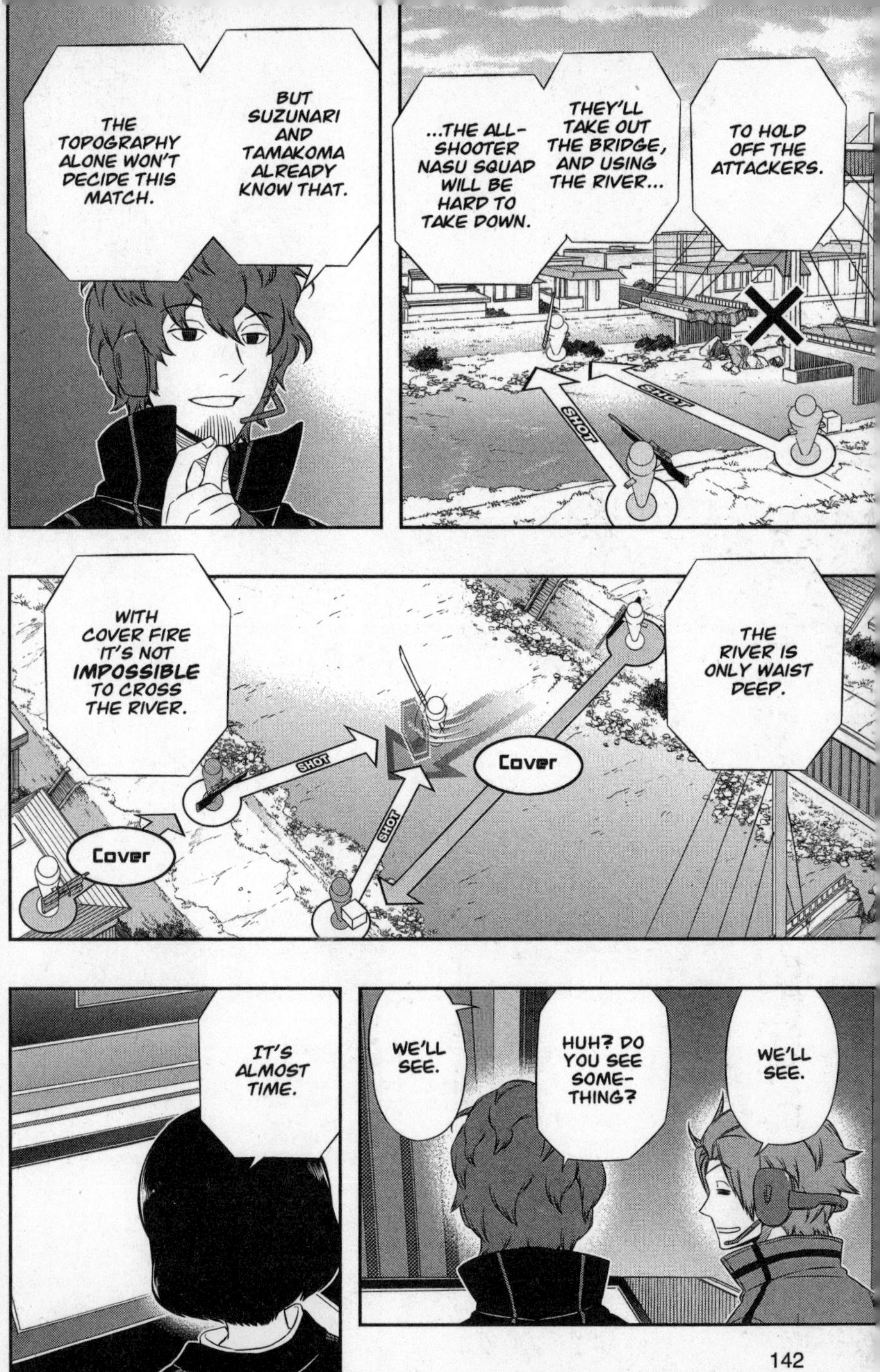
THE TOPOGRAPHY ALONE WON'T DECIDE THIS MATCH.
BUT SUZUNARI AND TAMAKOMA ALREADY KNOW THAT.
...THE ALL-SHOOTER NASU SQUAD WILL BE HARD TO TAKE DOWN.
THEY'LL TAKE OUT THE BRIDGE, AND USING THE RIVER...
TO HOLD OFF THE ATTACKERS.
SHOT
SHOT
WITH COVER FIRE IT'S NOT IMPOSSIBLE TO CROSS THE RIVER.
THE RIVER IS ONLY WAIST DEEP.
SHOT
SHOT
Cover
Cover
IT'S ALMOST TIME.
WE'LL SEE.
HUH? DO YOU SEE SOMETHING?
WE'LL SEE.

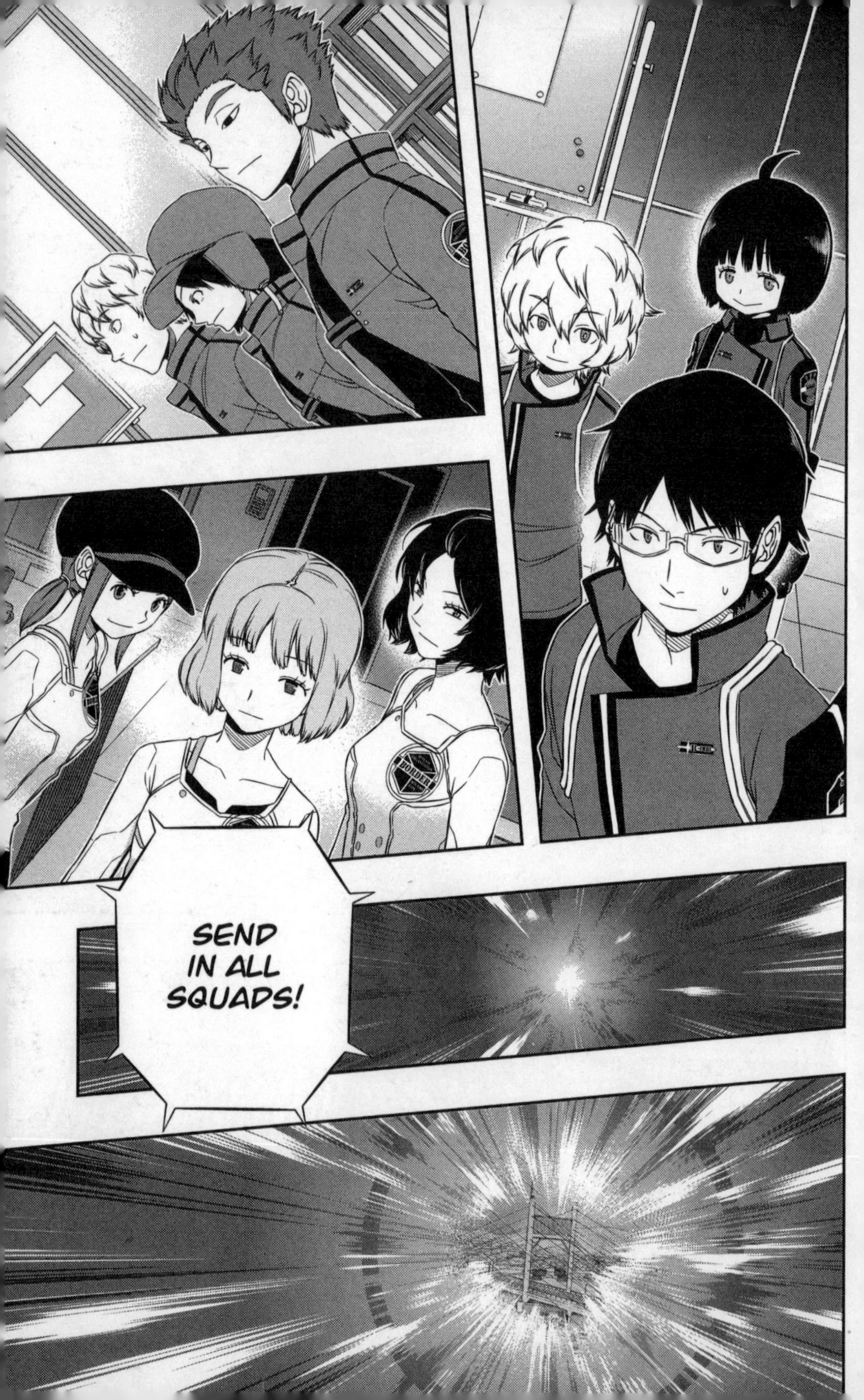
SEND IN ALL SQUADS!

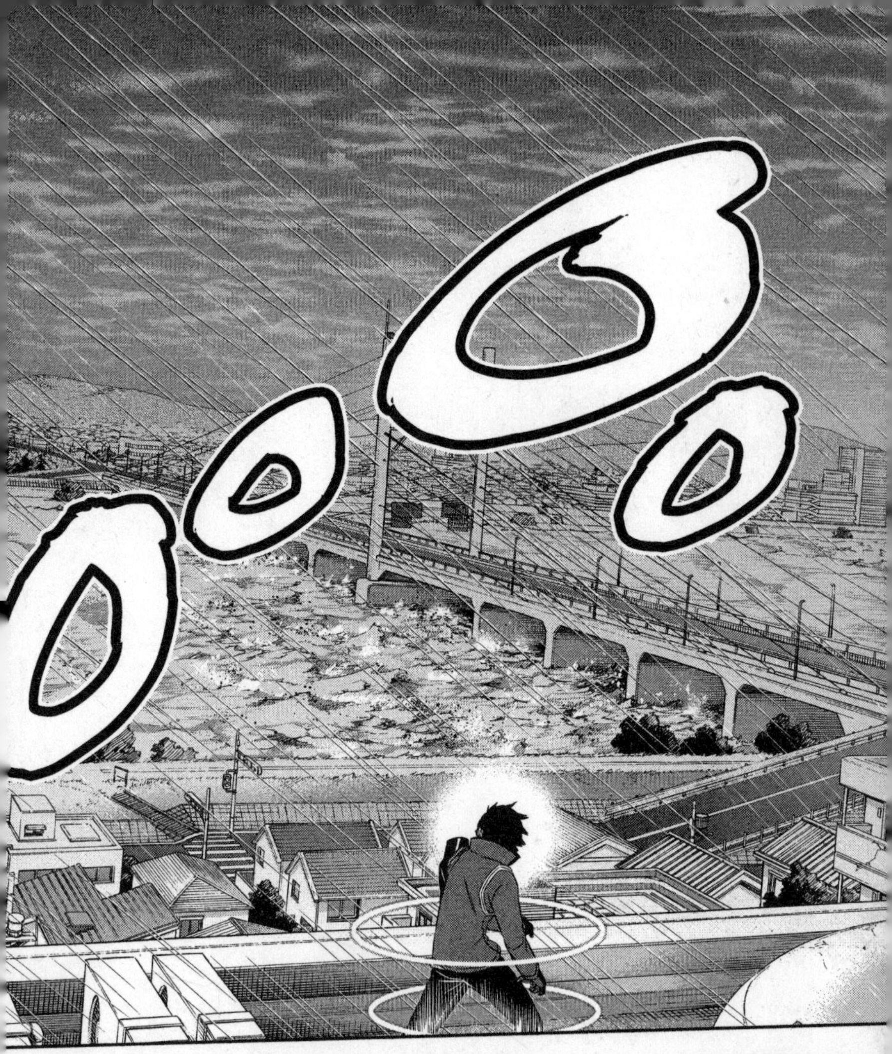
DOOOO
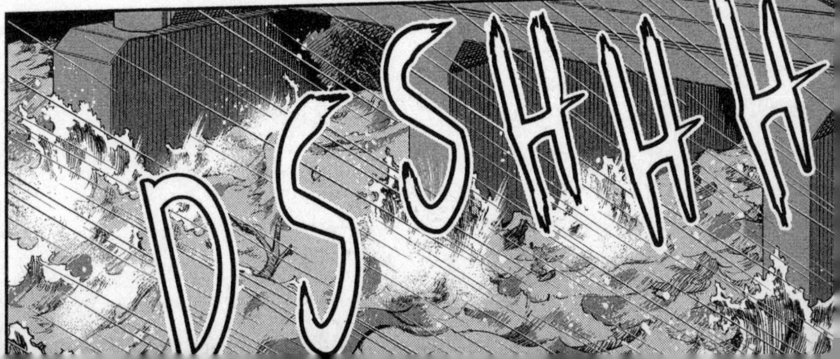
DSSHHH

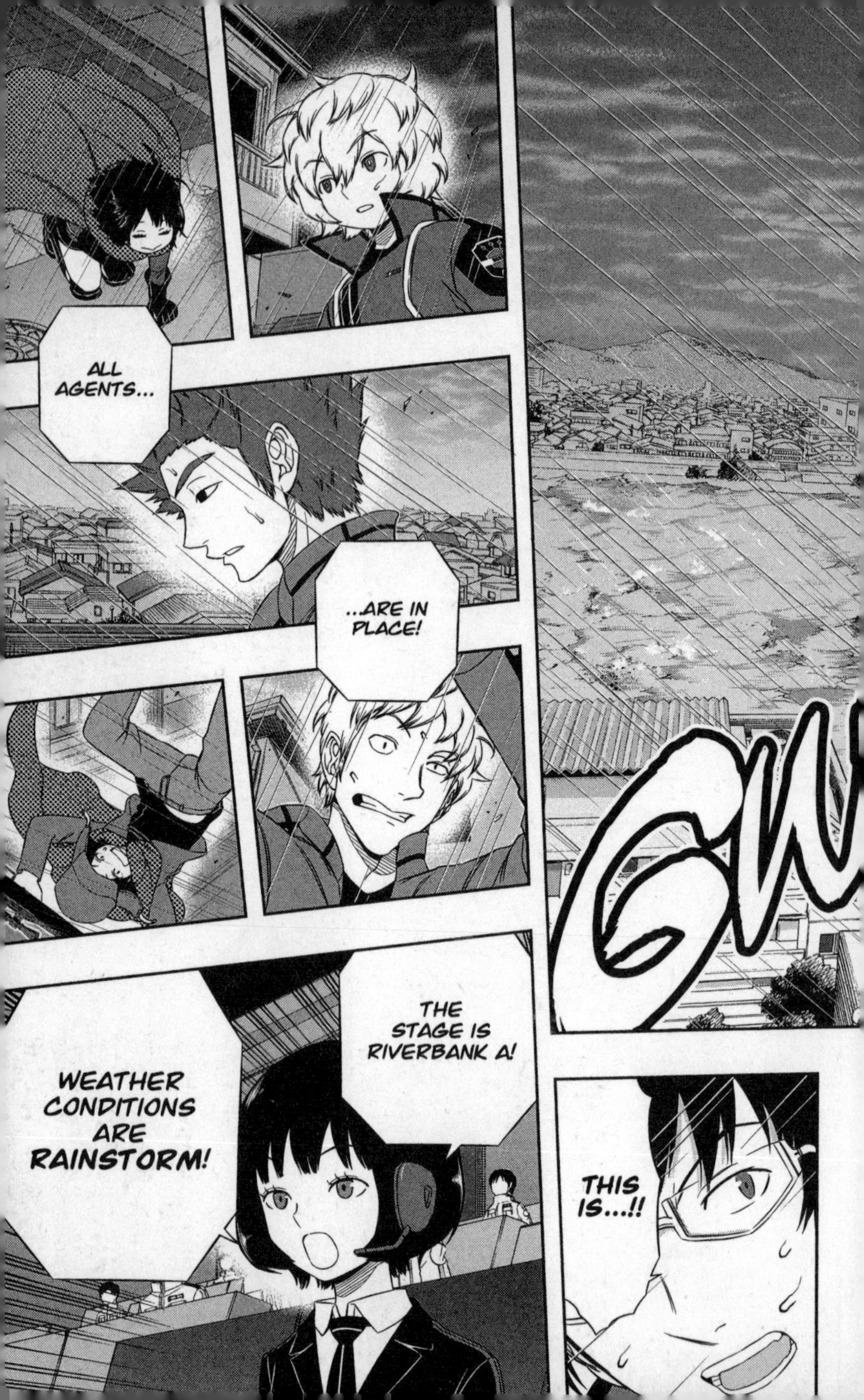
ALL AGENTS...
...ARE IN PLACE!
THIS IS...!!
THE STAGE IS RIVERBANK A!
WEATHER CONDITIONS ARE RAINSTORM!

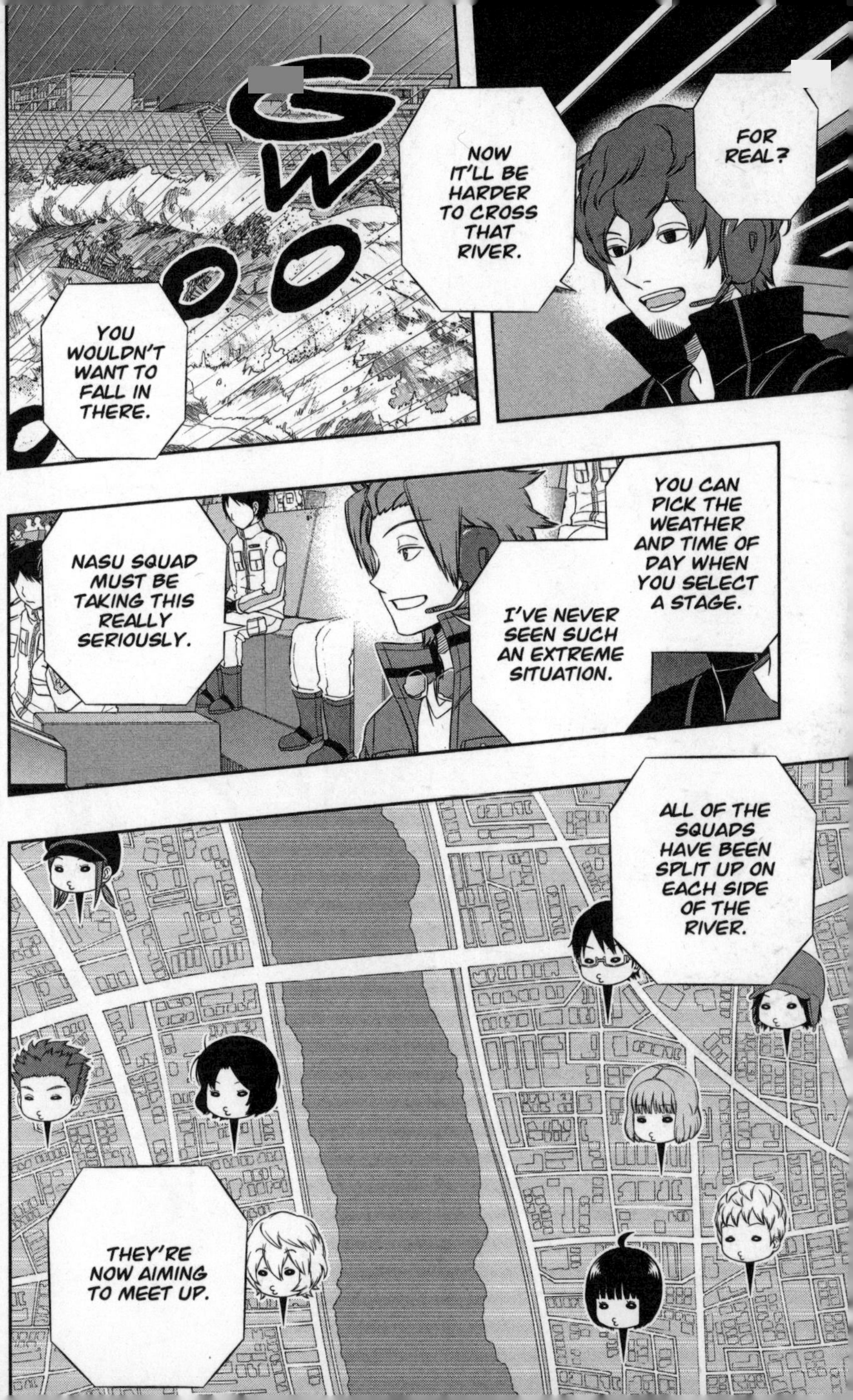
FOR REAL?
NOW IT'LL BE HARDER TO CROSS THAT RIVER.
GWOOOO
YOU WOULDN'T WANT TO FALL IN THERE.
YOU CAN PICK THE WEATHER AND TIME OF DAY WHEN YOU SELECT A STAGE.
I'VE NEVER SEEN SUCH AN EXTREME SITUATION.
NASU SQUAD MUST BE TAKING THIS REALLY SERIOUSLY.
ALL OF THE SQUADS HAVE BEEN SPLIT UP ON EACH SIDE OF THE RIVER.
THEY'RE NOW AIMING TO MEET UP.

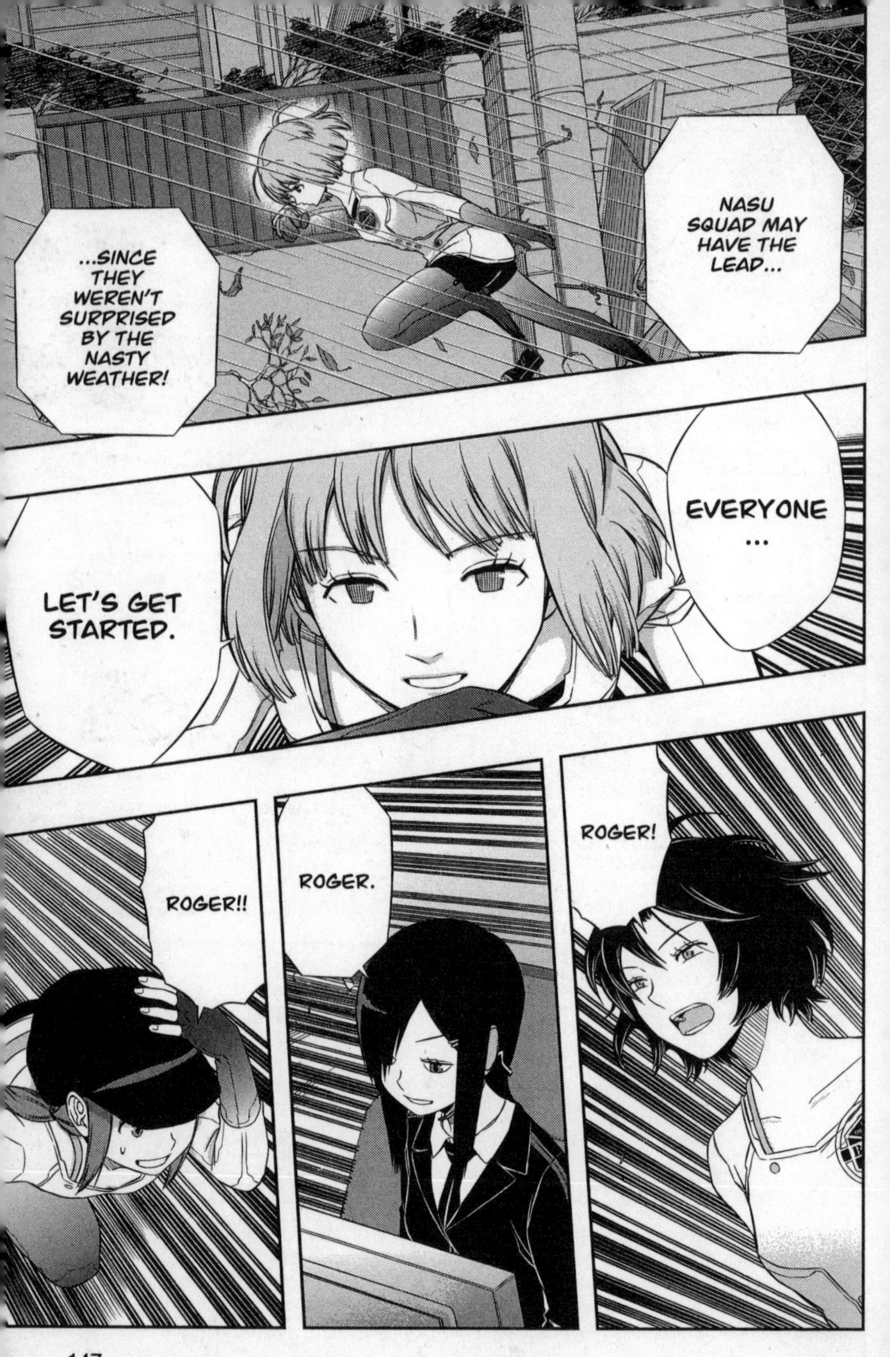
NASU SQUAD MAY HAVE THE LEAD...
...SINCE THEY WEREN'T SURPRISED BY THE NASTY WEATHER!
EVERYONE...
LET'S GET STARTED.
ROGER!
ROGER.
ROGER!!

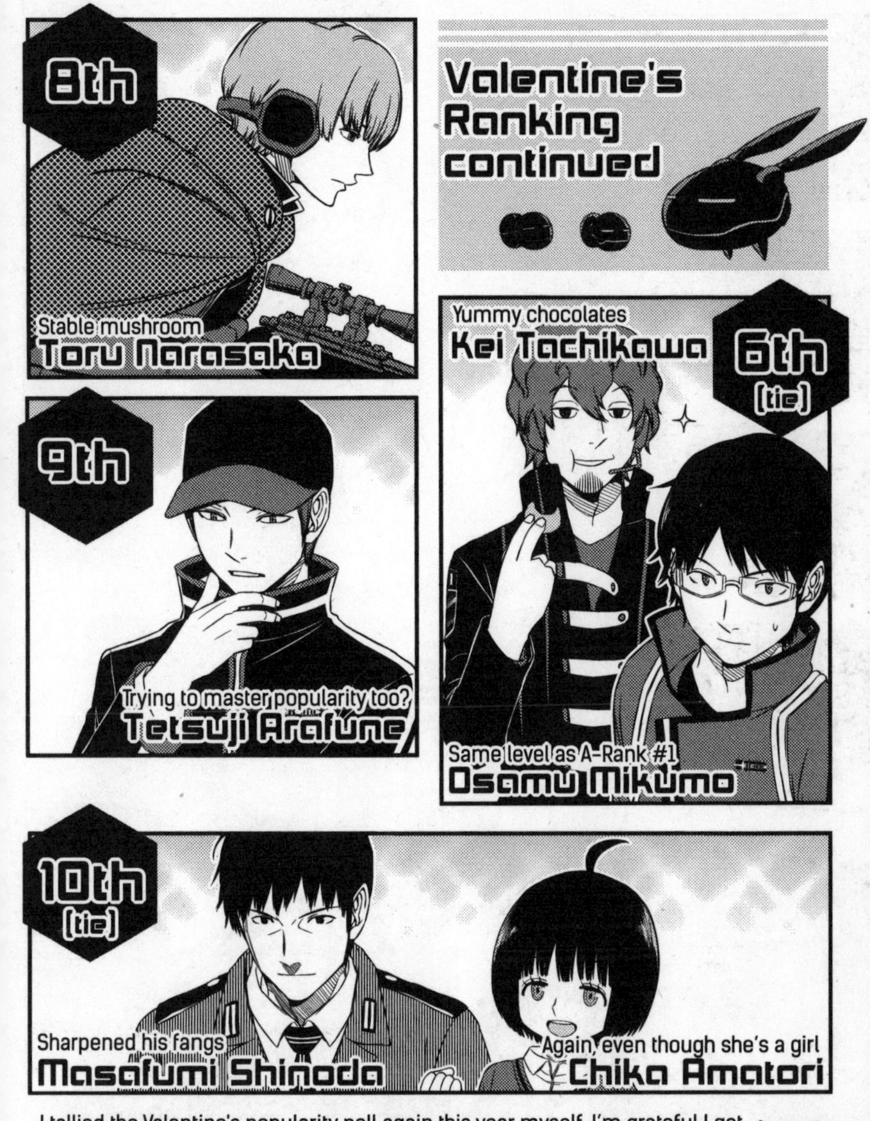
Valentine's Ranking continued
Yummy chocolates
Kei Tachikawa
6th (tie)
Same level as A-Rank #1
Osamu Mikumo
8th
Stable mushroom
Toru Narasaka
9th
Trying to master popularity too?
Tetsuji Arafune
10th (tie)
Again, even though she's a girl
Chika Amatori
Sharpened his fangs
Masafumi Shinoda

I tallied the Valentine's popularity poll again this year myself. I'm grateful I get to fill up these bonus pages. I received about five times as many chocolates, sweets and goodies as last year, which made walking through the hallway difficult for some time. I'm so thankful for your support. I gained even more weight! I might need a sign that says "Please do not feed."

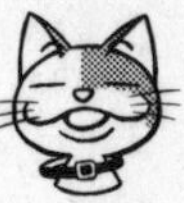

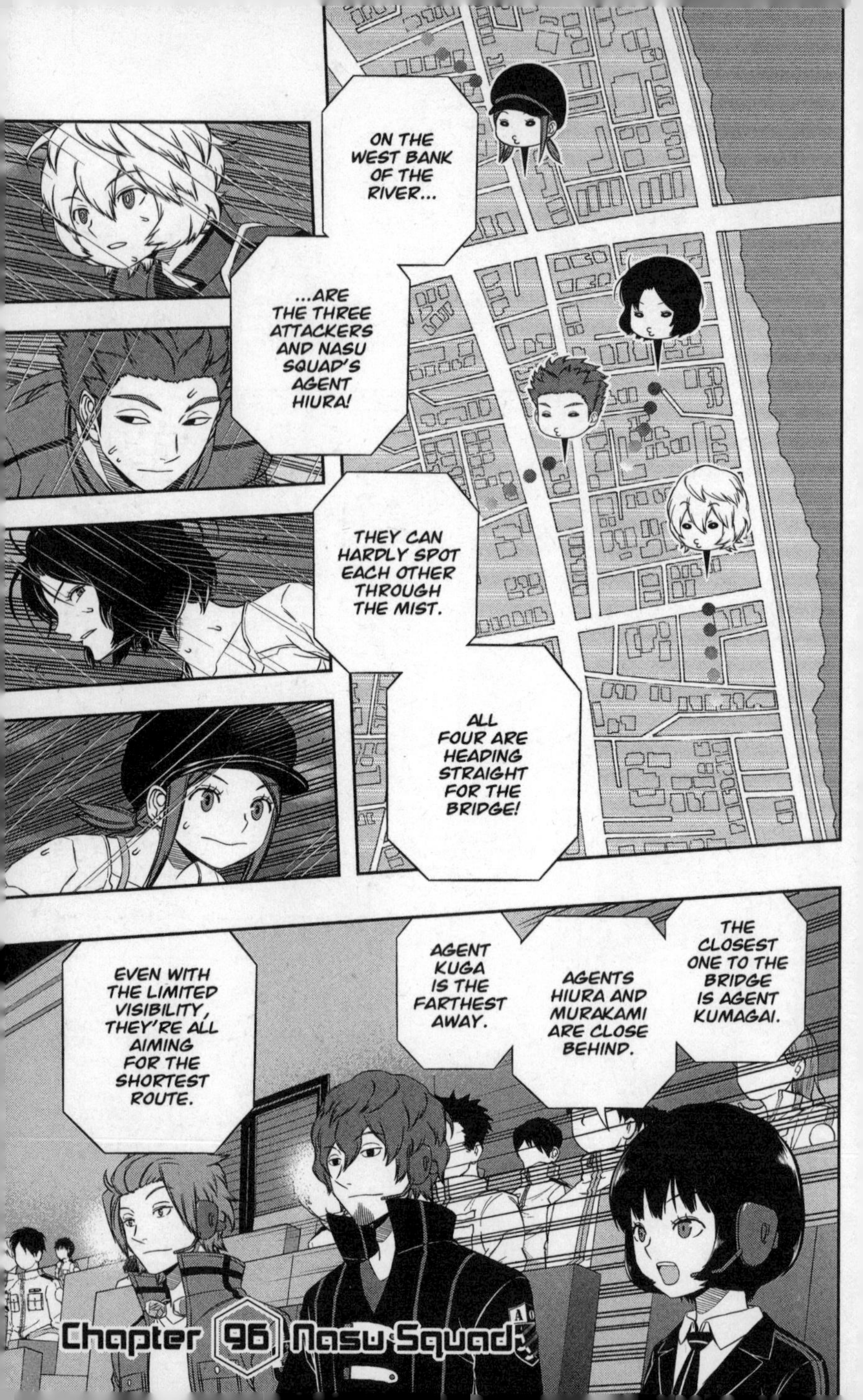
ON THE WEST BANK OF THE RIVER...
...ARE THE THREE ATTACKERS AND NASU SQUAD'S AGENT HIURA!
THEY CAN HARDLY SPOT EACH OTHER THROUGH THE MIST.
ALL FOUR ARE HEADING STRAIGHT FOR THE BRIDGE!
THE CLOSEST ONE TO THE BRIDGE IS AGENT KUMAGAI.
AGENTS HIURA AND MURAKAMI ARE CLOSE BEHIND.
AGENT KUGA IS THE FARTHEST AWAY.
EVEN WITH THE LIMITED VISIBILITY, THEY'RE ALL AIMING FOR THE SHORTEST ROUTE.
Chapter 96 Nasu Squad

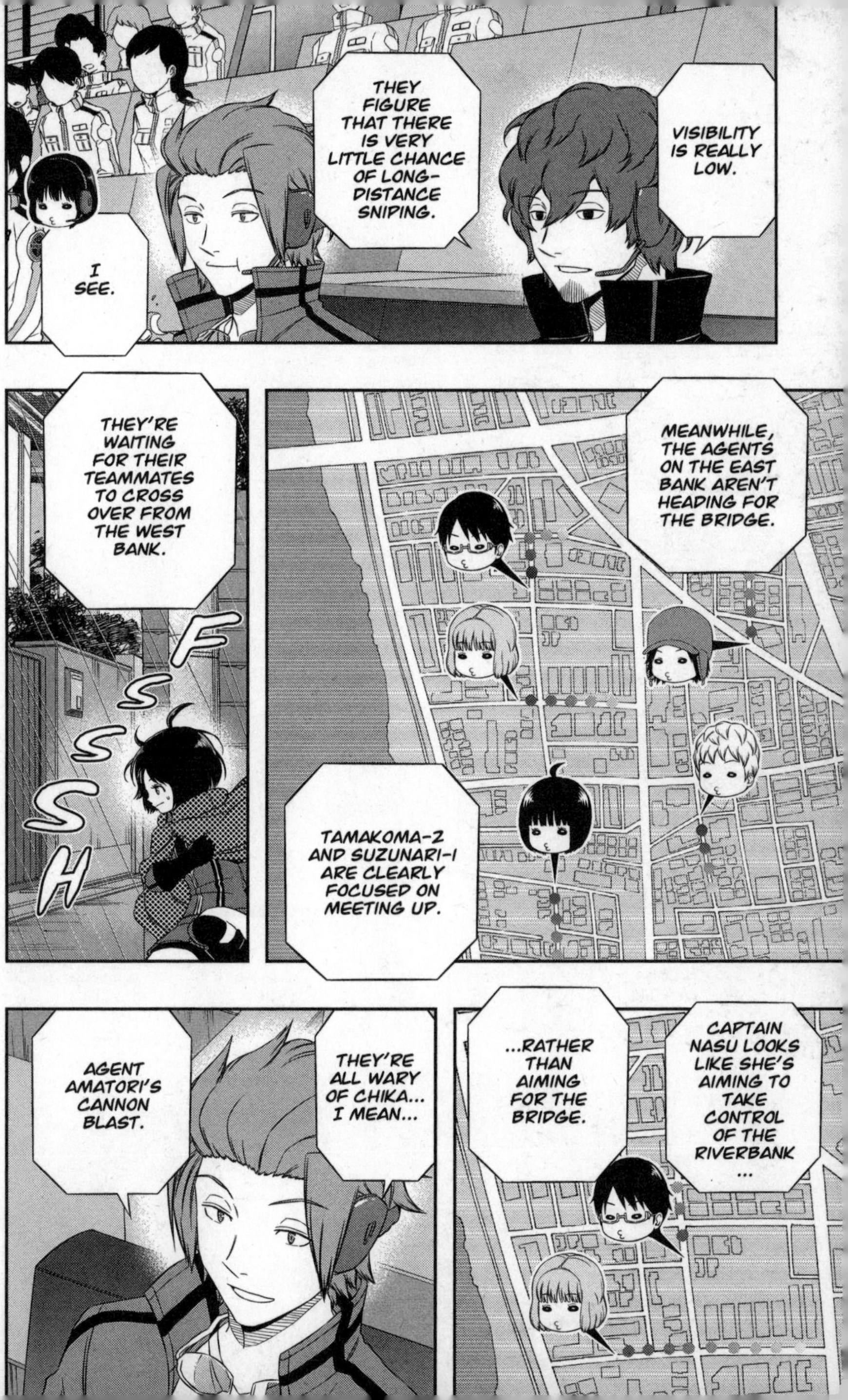
VISIBILITY IS REALLY LOW.
THEY FIGURE THAT THERE IS VERY LITTLE CHANCE OF LONG-DISTANCE SNIPING.
I SEE.
MEANWHILE, THE AGENTS ON THE EAST BANK AREN'T HEADING FOR THE BRIDGE.
TAMAKOMA-2 AND SUZUNARI-1 ARE CLEARLY FOCUSED ON MEETING UP.
THEY'RE WAITING FOR THEIR TEAMMATES TO CROSS OVER FROM THE WEST BANK.
FSSSSH
CAPTAIN NASU LOOKS LIKE SHE'S AIMING TO TAKE CONTROL OF THE RIVERBANK ...
...RATHER THAN AIMING FOR THE BRIDGE.
THEY'RE ALL WARY OF CHIKA... I MEAN...
AGENT AMATORI'S CANNON BLAST.

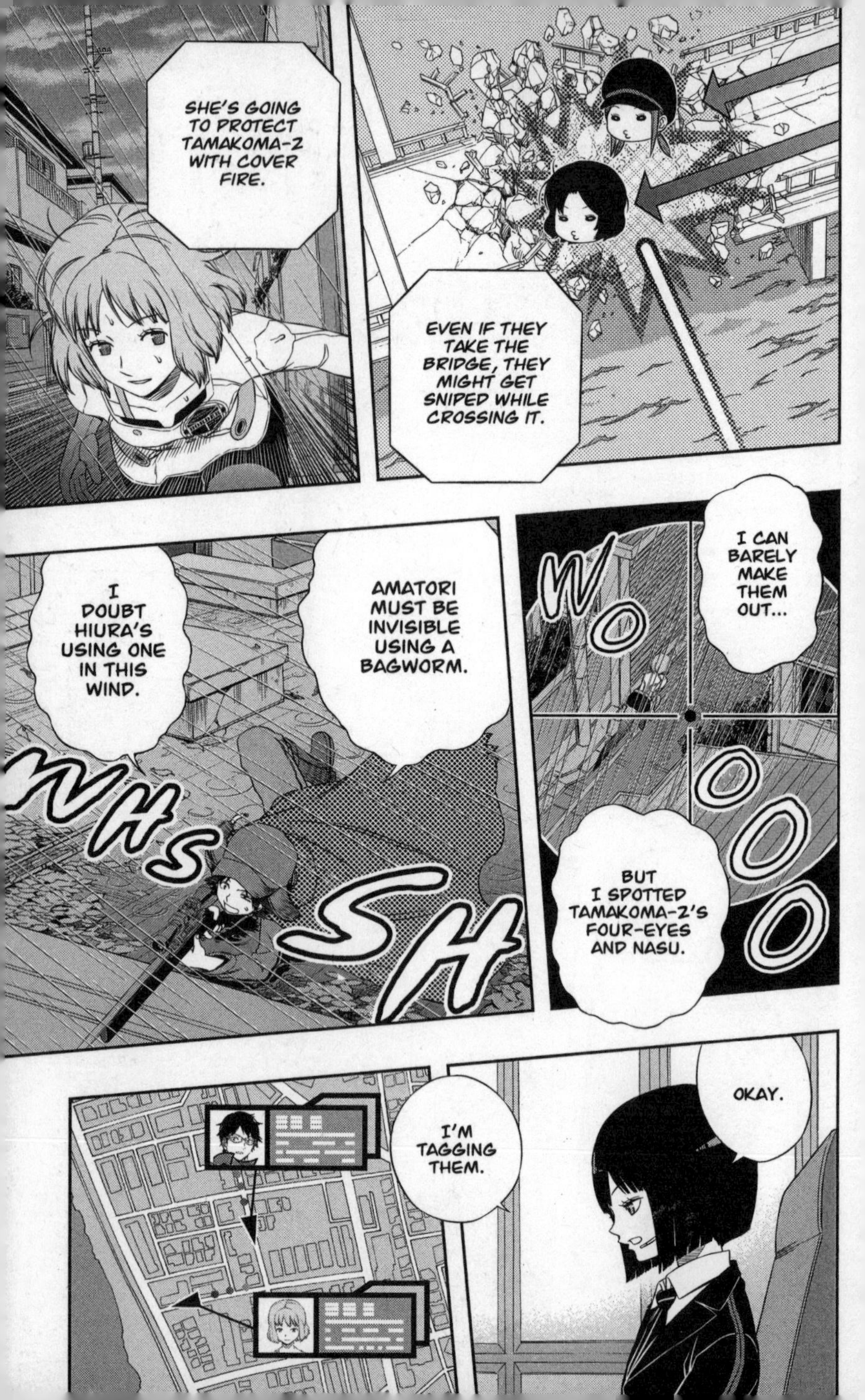
EVEN IF THEY TAKE THE BRIDGE, THEY MIGHT GET SNIPED WHILE CROSSING IT.
SHE'S GOING TO PROTECT TAMAKOMA-2 WITH COVER FIRE.
I CAN BARELY MAKE THEM OUT...
WOOOOO
BUT I SPOTTED TAMAKOMA-2'S FOUR-EYES AND NASU.
AMATORI MUST BE INVISIBLE USING A BAGWORM.
I DOUBT HIURA'S USING ONE IN THIS WIND.
OKAY.
I'M TAGGING THEM.

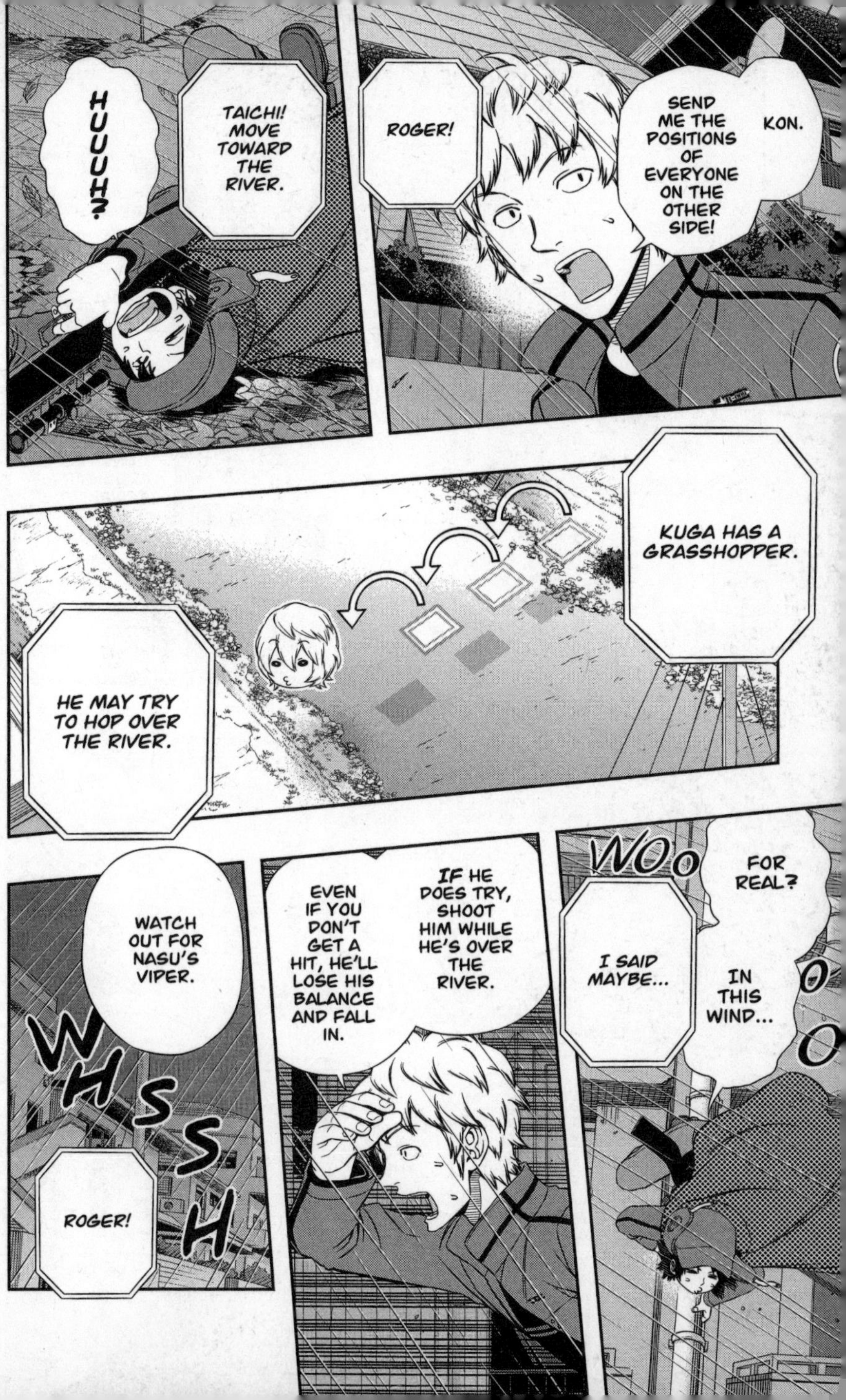
KON.
SEND ME THE POSITIONS OF EVERYONE ON THE OTHER SIDE!
ROGER!
TAICHI! MOVE TOWARD THE RIVER.
HUUUH?
KUGA HAS A GRASSHOPPER.
HE MAY TRY TO HOP OVER THE RIVER.
FOR REAL?
IN THIS WIND...
I SAID MAYBE...
WOOOO
IF HE DOES TRY, SHOOT HIM WHILE HE'S OVER THE RIVER.
EVEN IF YOU DON'T GET A HIT, HE'LL LOSE HIS BALANCE AND FALL IN.
WATCH OUT FOR NASU'S VIPER.
ROGER!
WHSSSH

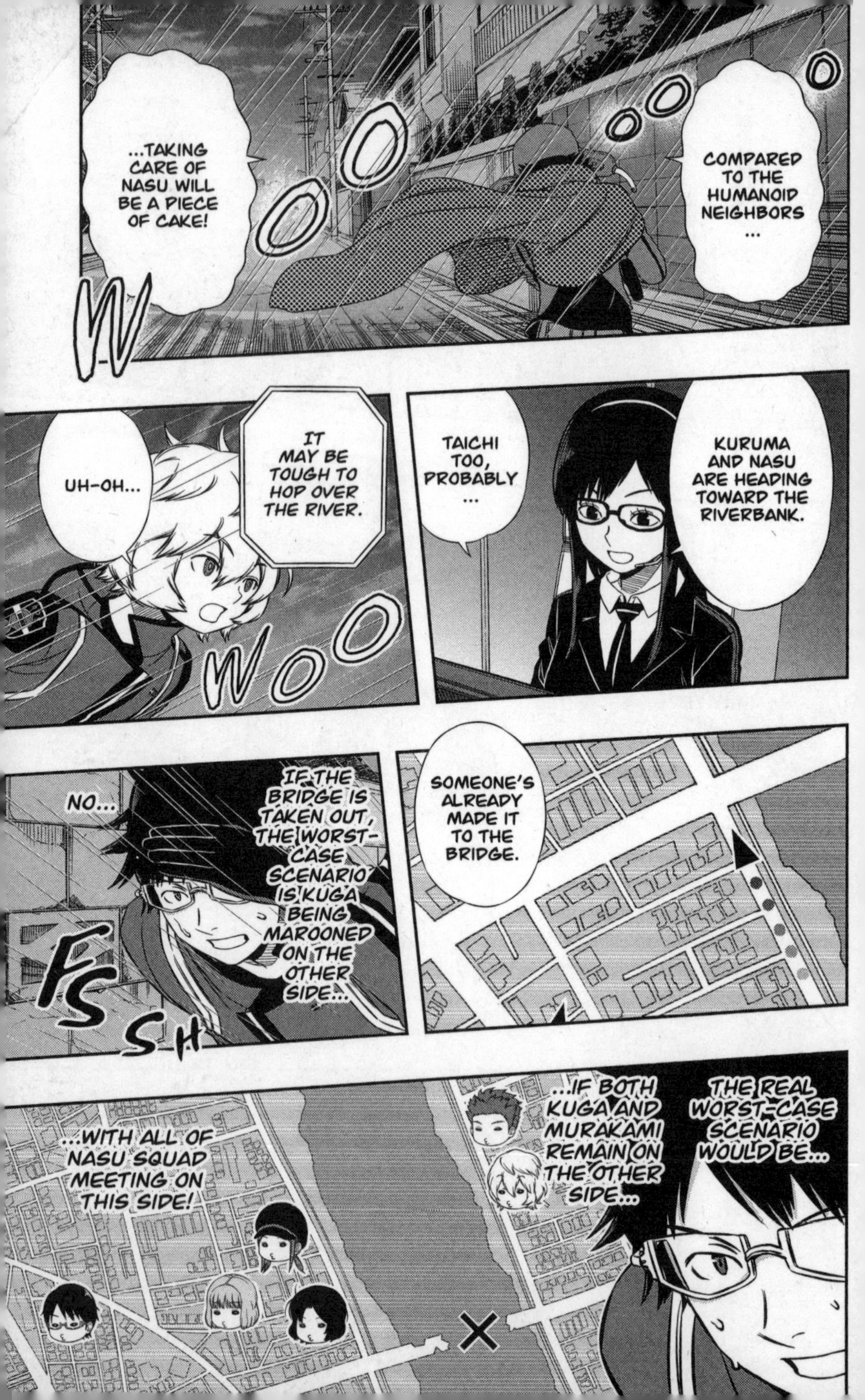
COMPARED TO THE HUMANOID NEIGHBORS ...
...TAKING CARE OF NASU WILL BE A PIECE OF CAKE!
WOOOOOO
KURUMA AND NASU ARE HEADING TOWARD THE RIVERBANK.
TAICHI TOO, PROBABLY ...
IT MAY BE TOUGH TO HOP OVER THE RIVER.
UH-OH...
WOOO
SOMEONE'S ALREADY MADE IT TO THE BRIDGE.
IF THE BRIDGE IS TAKEN OUT, THE WORST-CASE SCENARIO IS KUGA BEING MAROONED ON THE OTHER SIDE...
NO...
FSSH
THE REAL WORST-CASE SCENARIO WOULD BE...
...IF BOTH KUGA AND MURAKAMI REMAIN ON THE OTHER SIDE...
...WITH ALL OF NASU SQUAD MEETING ON THIS SIDE!

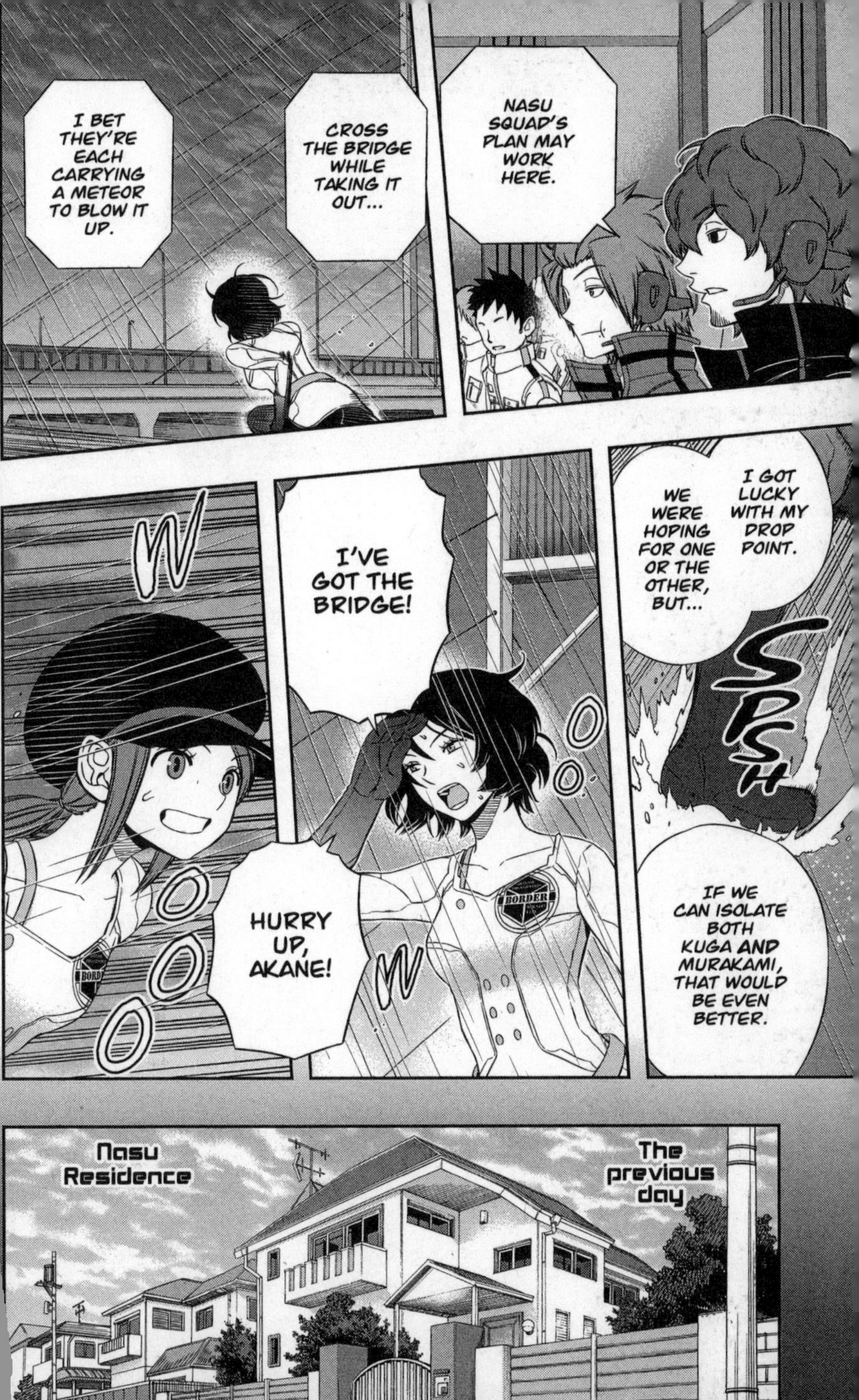
NASU SQUAD'S PLAN MAY WORK HERE.
CROSS THE BRIDGE WHILE TAKING IT OUT...
I BET THEY'RE EACH CARRYING A METEOR TO BLOW IT UP.
I GOT LUCKY WITH MY DROP POINT.
WE WERE HOPING FOR ONE OR THE OTHER, BUT...
SPSH
IF WE CAN ISOLATE BOTH KUGA AND MURAKAMI, THAT WOULD BE EVEN BETTER.
I'VE GOT THE BRIDGE!
HURRY UP, AKANE!
W
W
The previous day
Nasu Residence

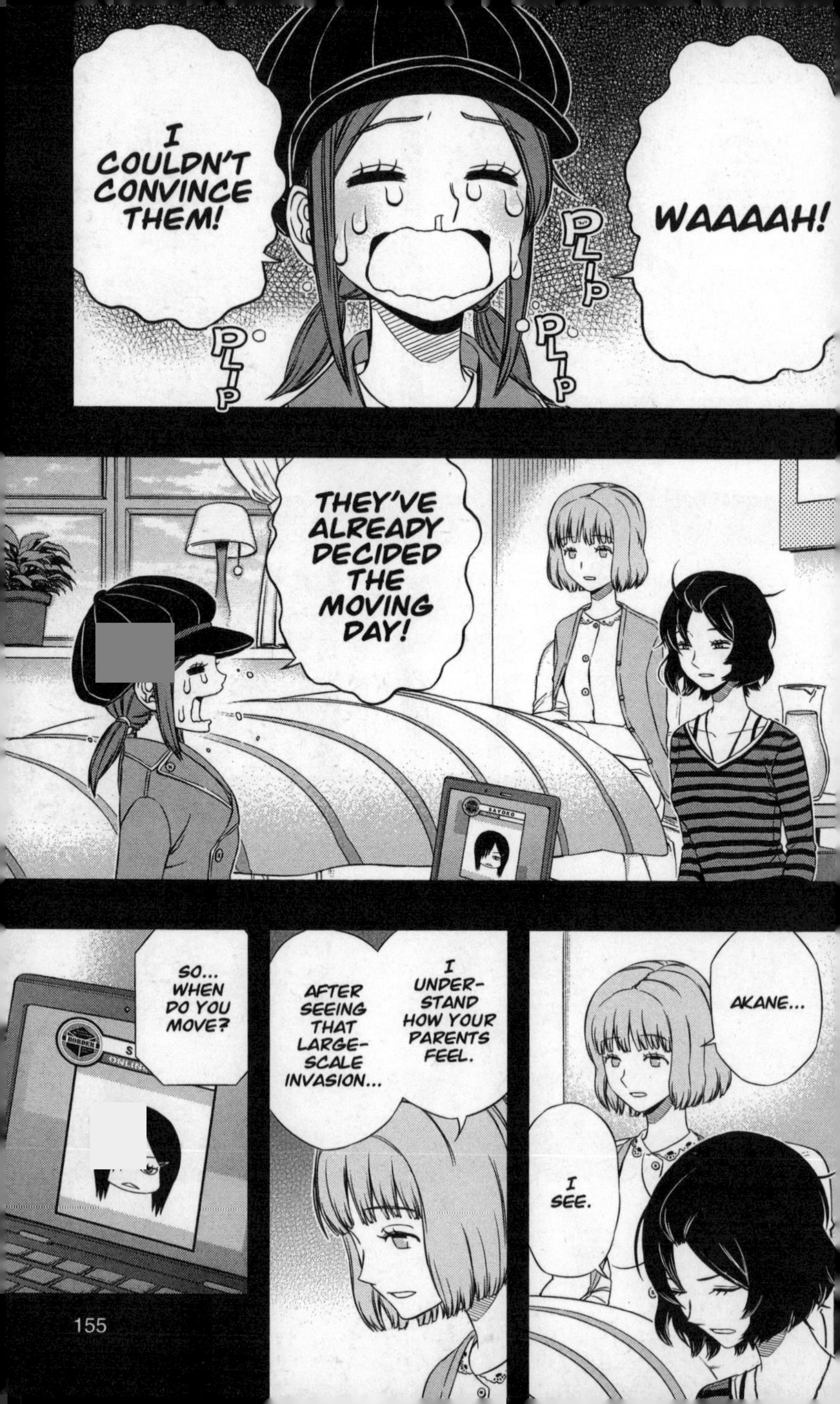
WAAAAH!
I COULDN'T CONVINCE THEM!
PLIP PLIP
PLIP
THEY'VE ALREADY DECIDED THE MOVING DAY!
SAYOKO
AKANE...
I SEE.
I UNDER-STAND HOW YOUR PARENTS FEEL.
AFTER SEEING THAT LARGE-SCALE INVASION...
SO... WHEN DO YOU MOVE?
BORDER

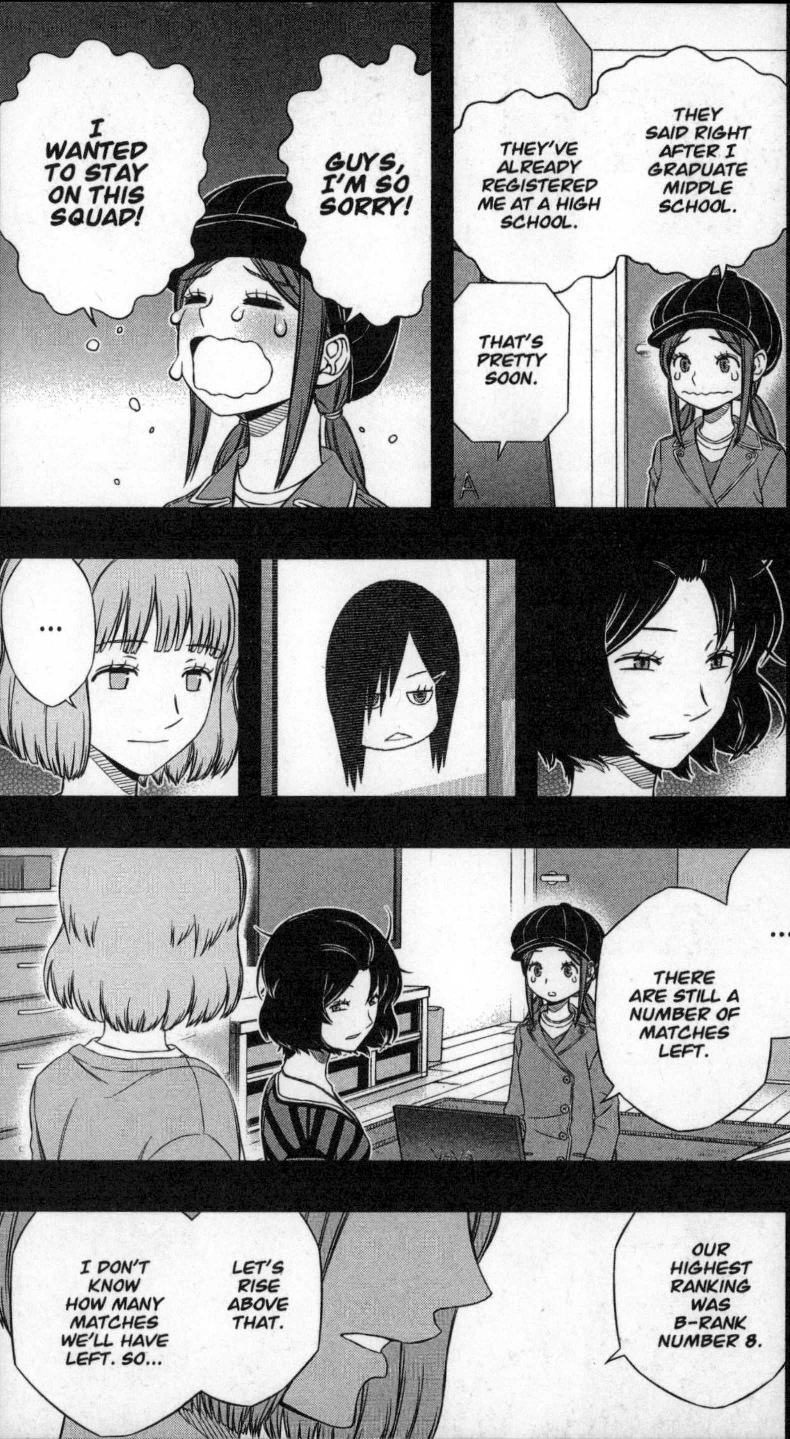
THEY SAID RIGHT AFTER I GRADUATE MIDDLE SCHOOL.
THEY'VE ALREADY REGISTERED ME AT A HIGH SCHOOL.
THAT'S PRETTY SOON.
GUYS, I'M SO SORRY!
I WANTED TO STAY ON THIS SQUAD!
...
...
THERE ARE STILL A NUMBER OF MATCHES LEFT.
OUR HIGHEST RANKING WAS B-RANK NUMBER 8.
LET'S RISE ABOVE THAT.
I DON'T KNOW HOW MANY MATCHES WE'LL HAVE LEFT. SO...

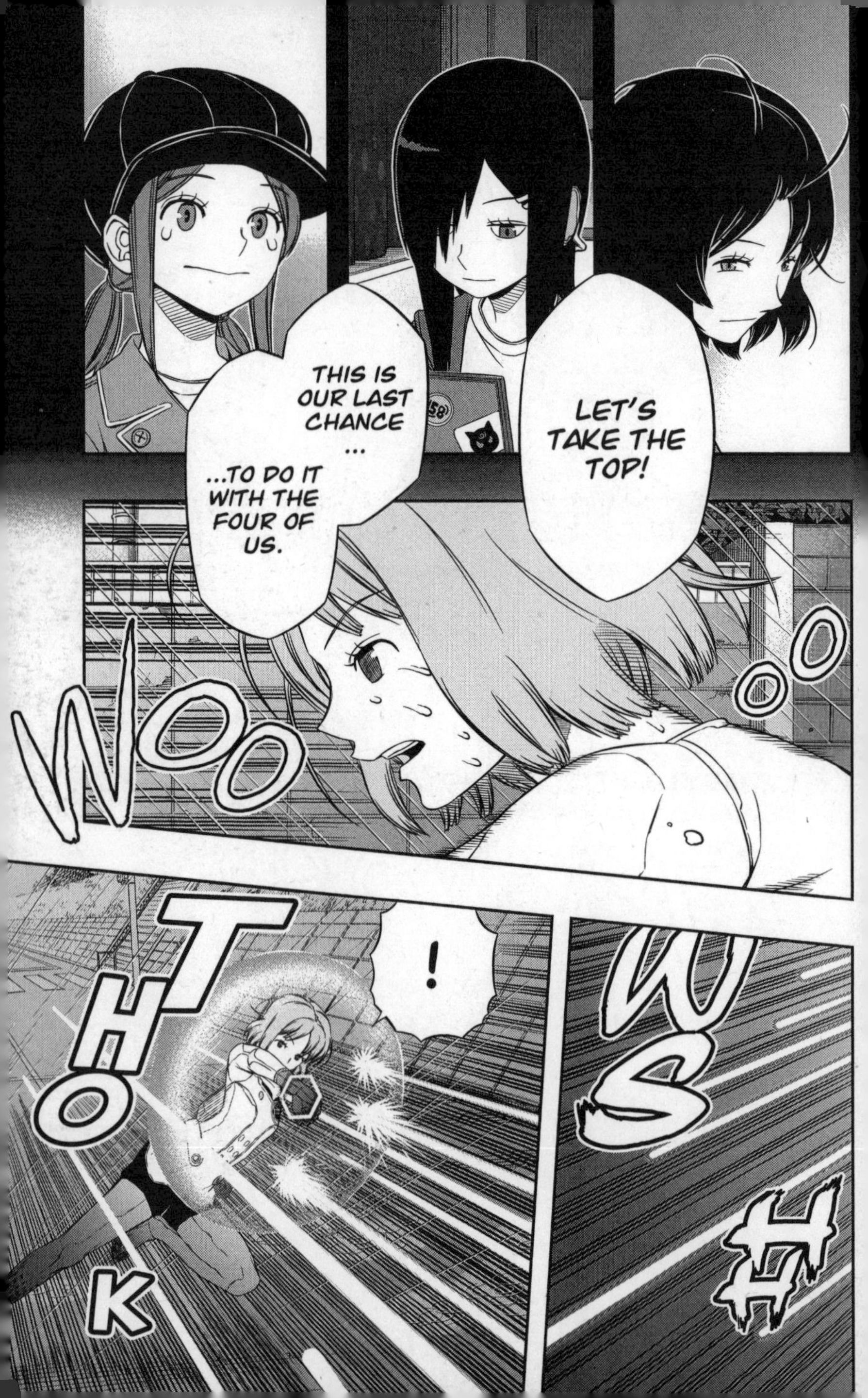
LET'S TAKE THE TOP!
THIS IS OUR LAST CHANCE ...
...TO DO IT WITH THE FOUR OF US.
WOOOOOO
WSHH
!
THOK

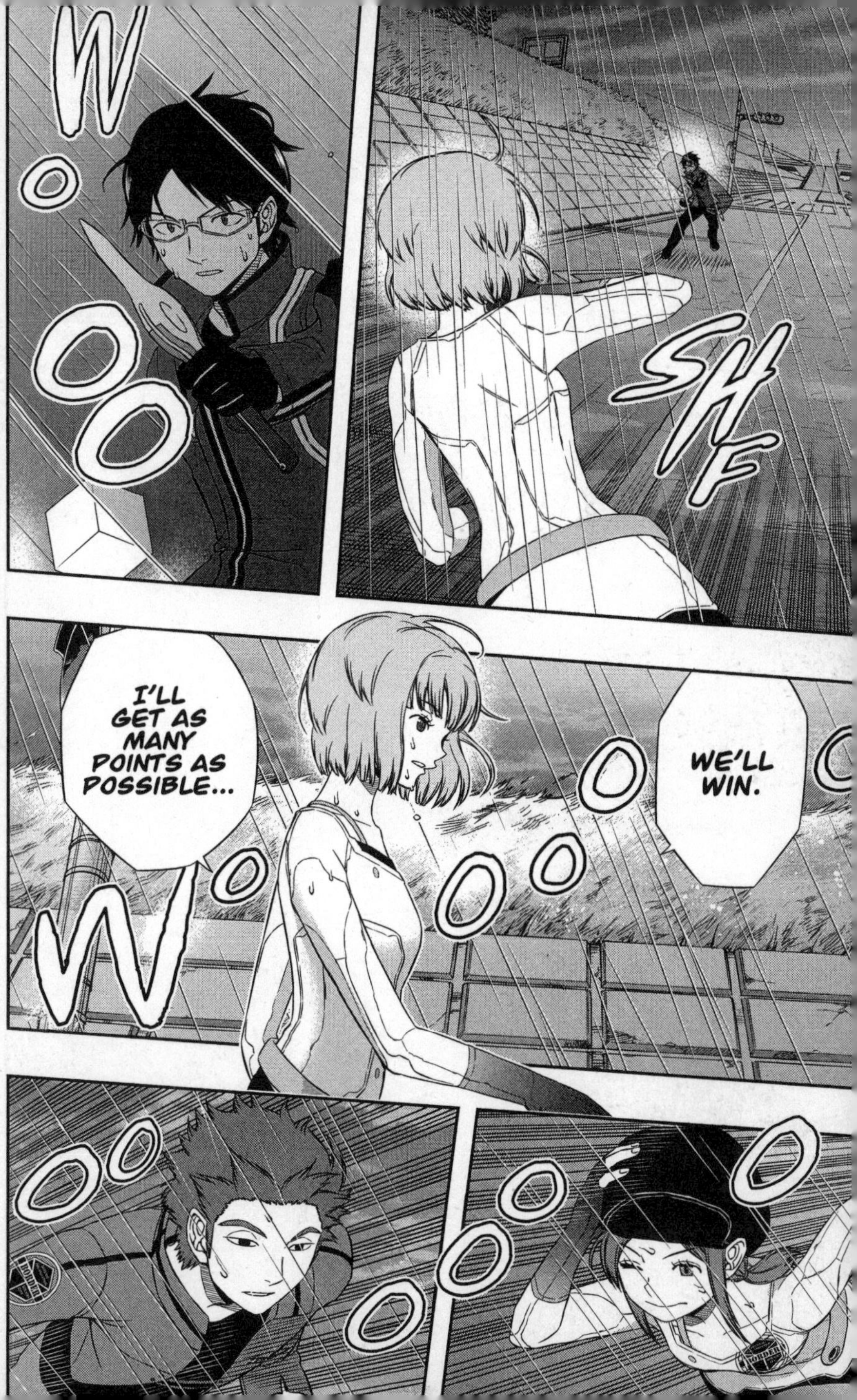
SHF
WOOO
WE'LL WIN.
I'LL GET AS MANY POINTS AS POSSIBLE...
WOOOOO

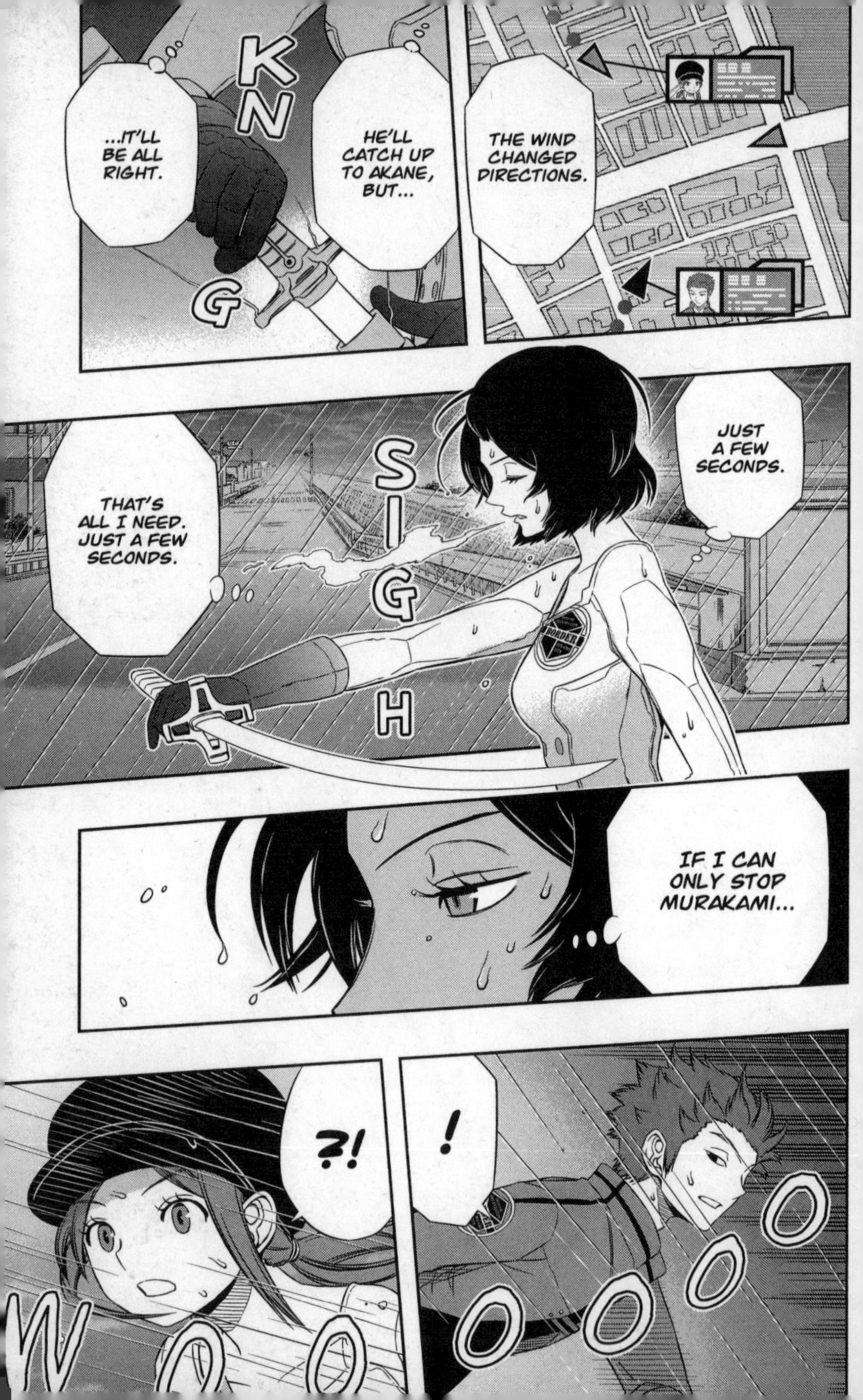
THE WIND CHANGED DIRECTIONS.
HE'LL CATCH UP TO AKANE, BUT...
KNG
...IT'LL BE ALL RIGHT.
JUST A FEW SECONDS.
SIGH
THAT'S ALL I NEED. JUST A FEW SECONDS.
BORDER
IF I CAN ONLY STOP MURAKAMI...
!
?!
WOOOOOOOO

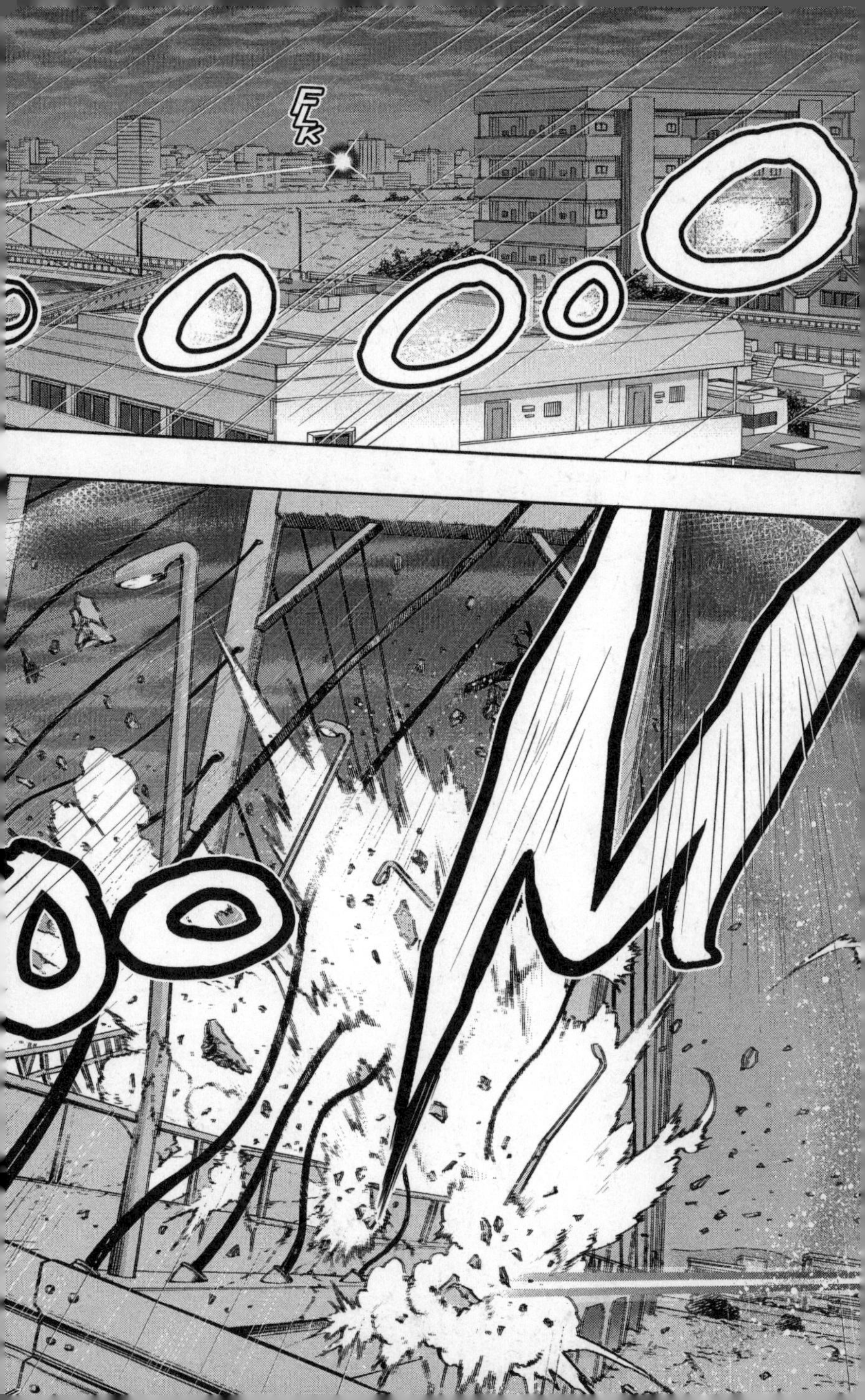
FLK
OOOOO
OOM

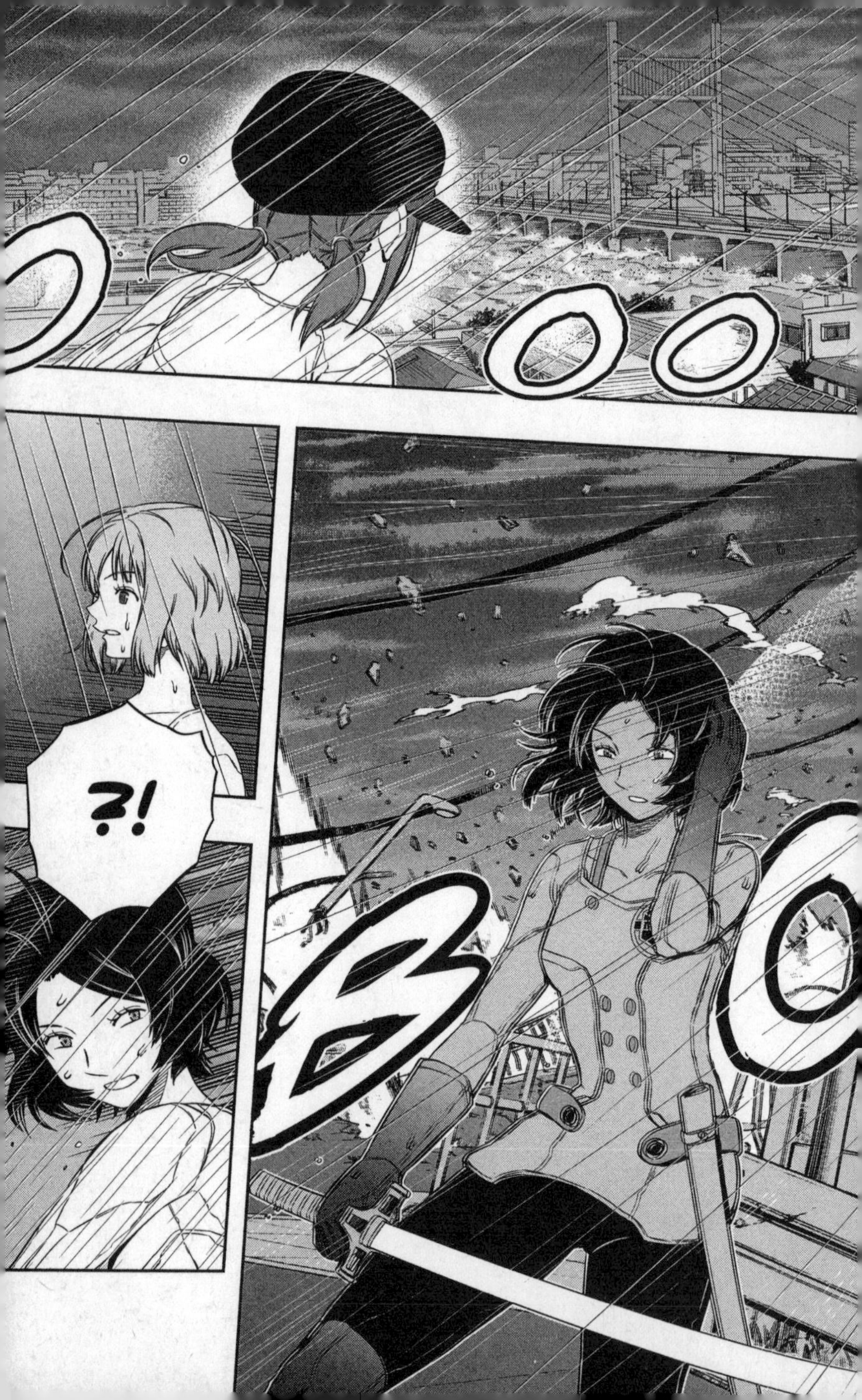
?!

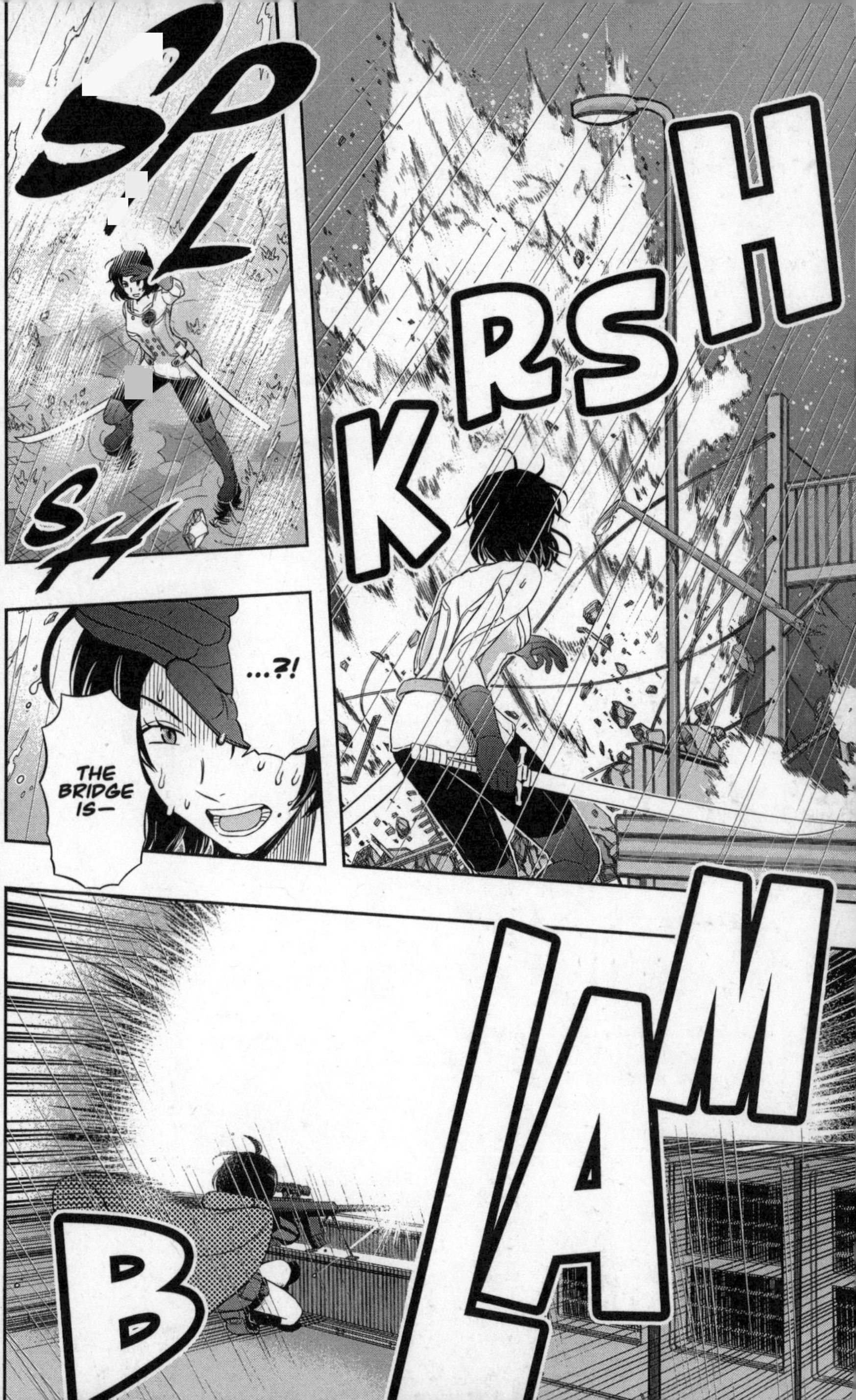
KRSHH
SPL
SHH
...?!
THE BRIDGE IS—
BLAM

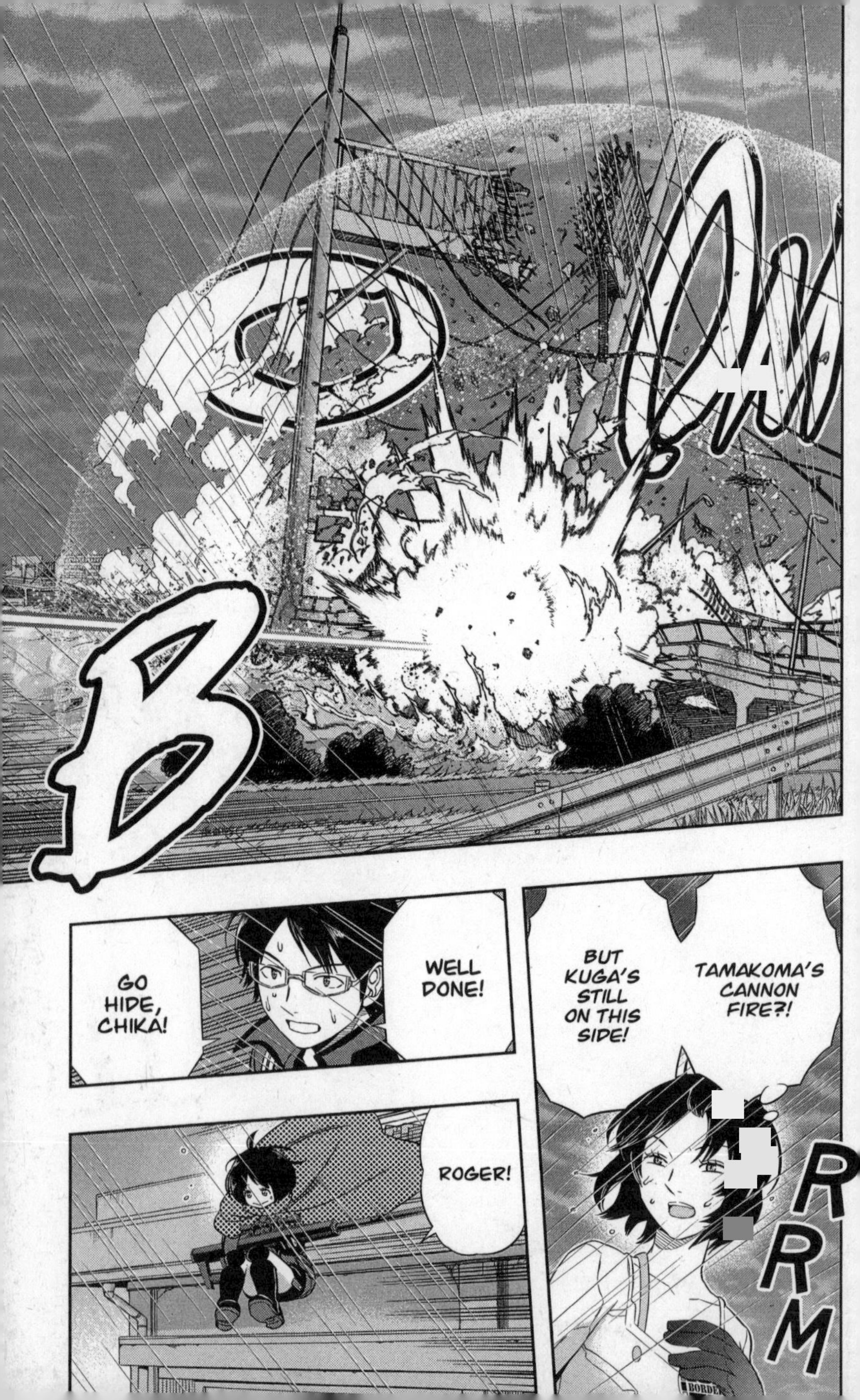
B
TAMAKOMA'S CANNON FIRE?!
BUT KUGA'S STILL ON THIS SIDE!
RRRM
WELL DONE!
GO HIDE, CHIKA!
ROGER!

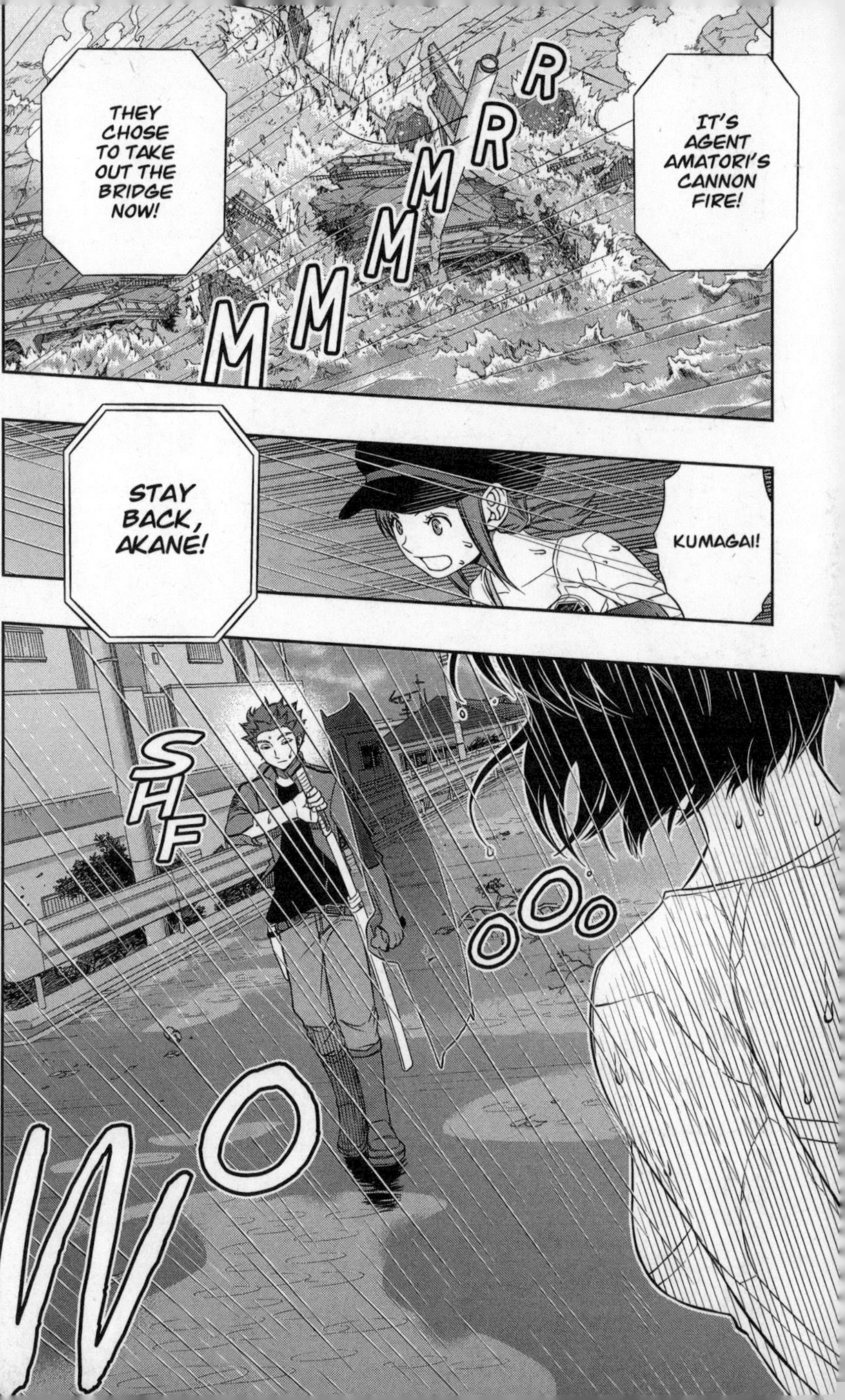
IT'S AGENT AMATORI'S CANNON FIRE!
MMMMMRR
THEY CHOSE TO TAKE OUT THE BRIDGE NOW!
KUMAGAI!
STAY BACK, AKANE!
SHF
OOOO
WO

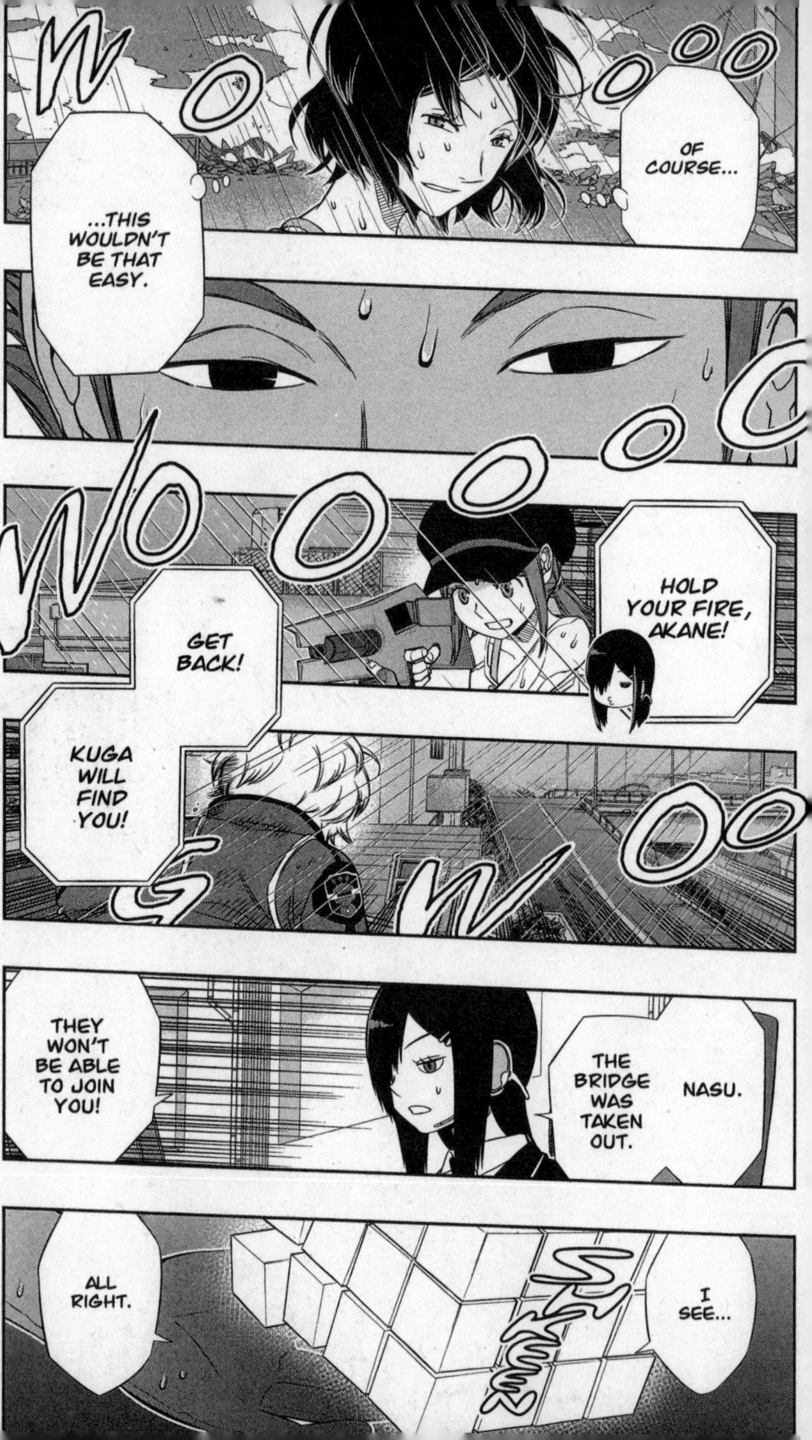
OF COURSE...
...THIS WOULDN'T BE THAT EASY.
HOLD YOUR FIRE, AKANE!
GET BACK!
KUGA WILL FIND YOU!
NASU.
THE BRIDGE WAS TAKEN OUT.
THEY WON'T BE ABLE TO JOIN YOU!
I SEE...
ALL RIGHT.

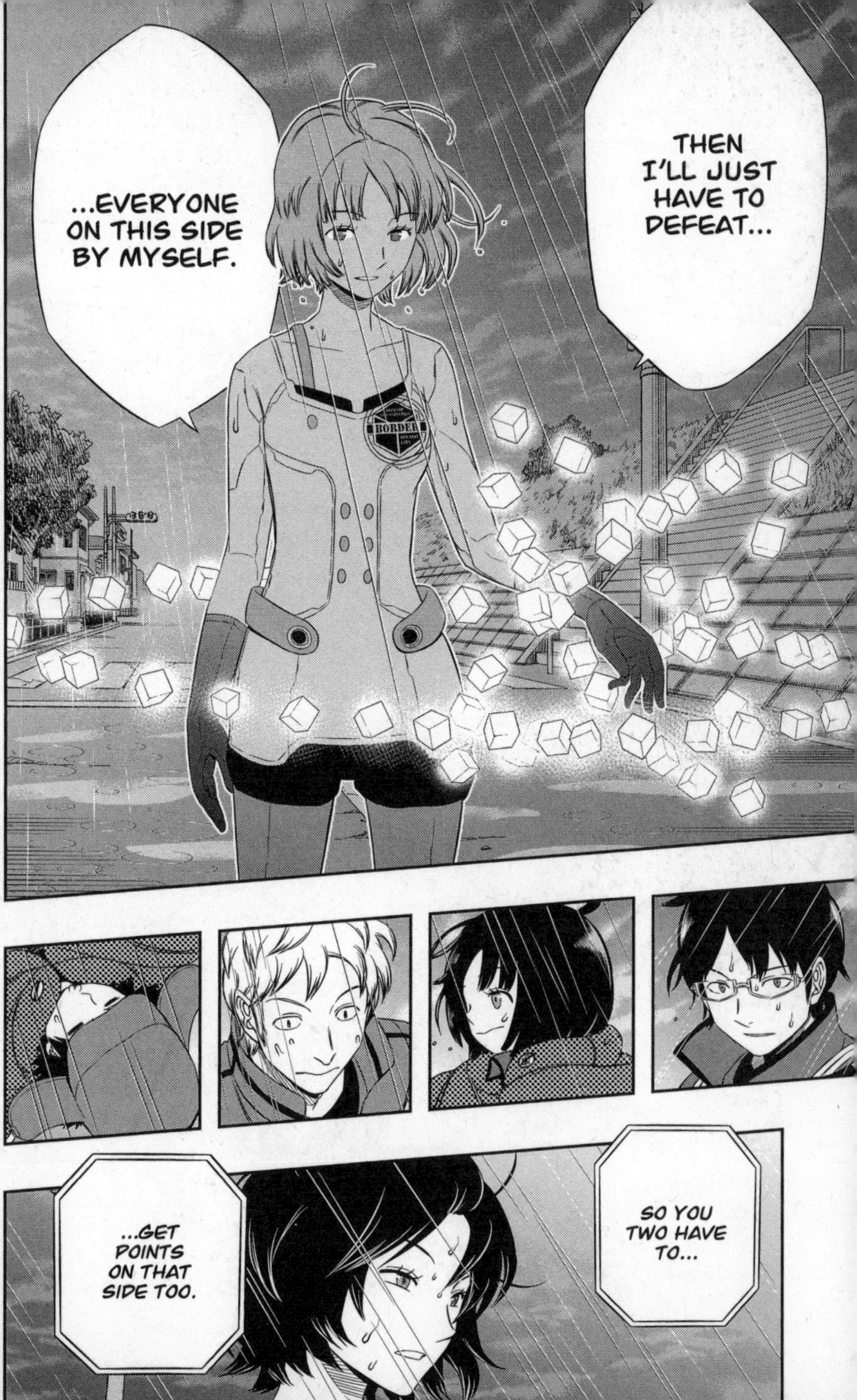
THEN I'LL JUST HAVE TO DEFEAT...
...EVERYONE ON THIS SIDE BY MYSELF.
SO YOU TWO HAVE TO...
...GET POINTS ON THAT SIDE TOO.

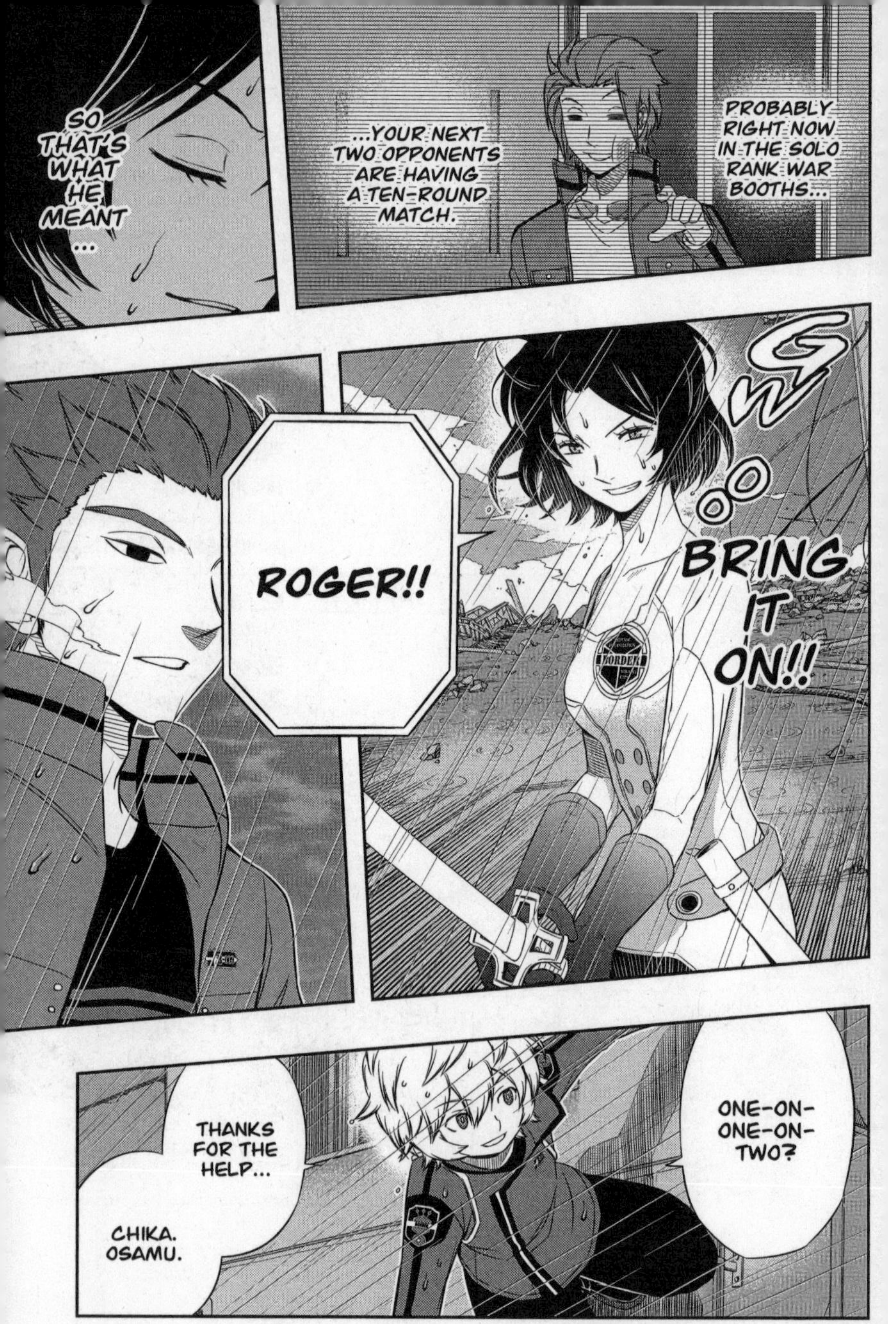
PROBABLY RIGHT NOW IN THE SOLO RANK WAR BOOTHS...
...YOUR NEXT TWO OPPONENTS ARE HAVING A TEN-ROUND MATCH.
SO THAT'S WHAT HE MEANT...
BRING IT ON!!
ROGER!!
ONE-ON-ONE-ON-TWO?
THANKS FOR THE HELP...
CHIKA. OSAMU.

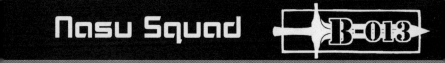

Nasu Squad

B-013

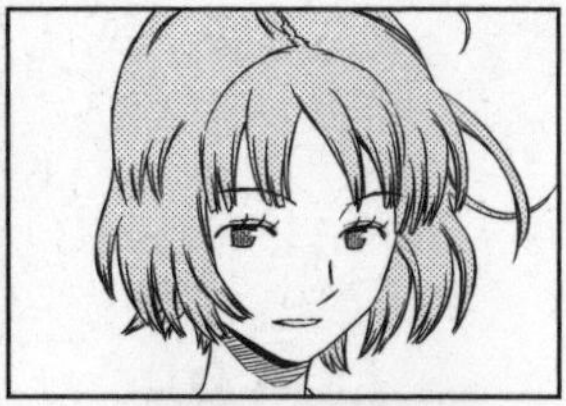

Rei Nasu
Captain, Shooter

■17 years old (High school student)
■Born June 16

■Lepus, Blood type O
■Height: 5'3"
■Likes: Canned peaches, movies, teammates, exercise in her Trion body

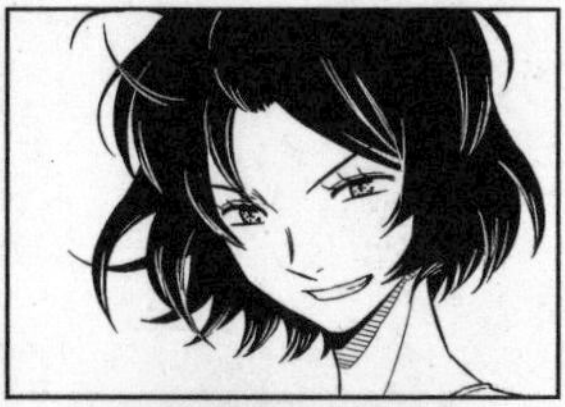

Yuko Kumagai
Attacker

■17 years old (High school student)
■Born April 14

■ Falco, Blood type O
■Height: 5'7"
■Likes: Apples, noodles with beef, all sports

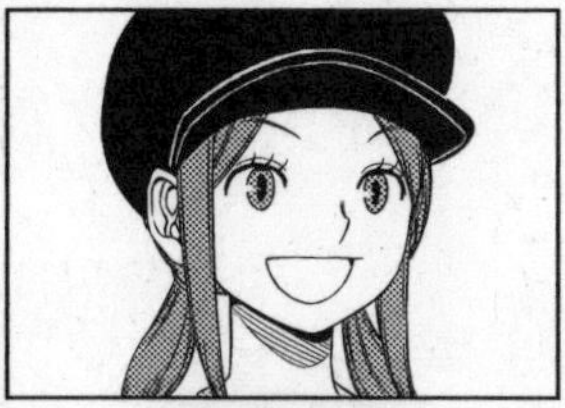

Akane Hiura
Sniper

■15 years old (Middle school student)
■Born July 7

■ Gladius, Blood type O
■Height: 5'1"
■Likes: Collecting hats, cats, soft serve ice cream

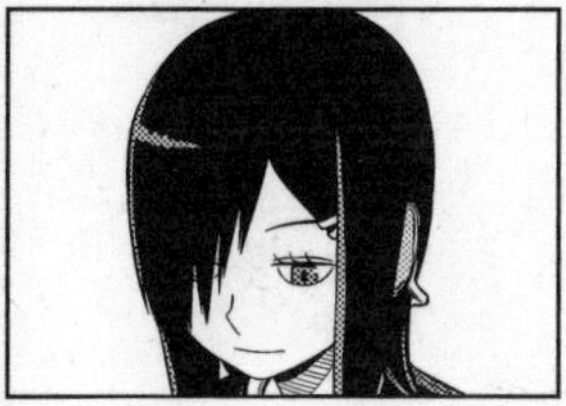

Sayoko Shiki
Operator

■16 years old (High school student)
■Born Aug. 9

■ Aptenodytes, Blood type A
■Height: 5'1"
■Likes: Games, water, reading, shopping online

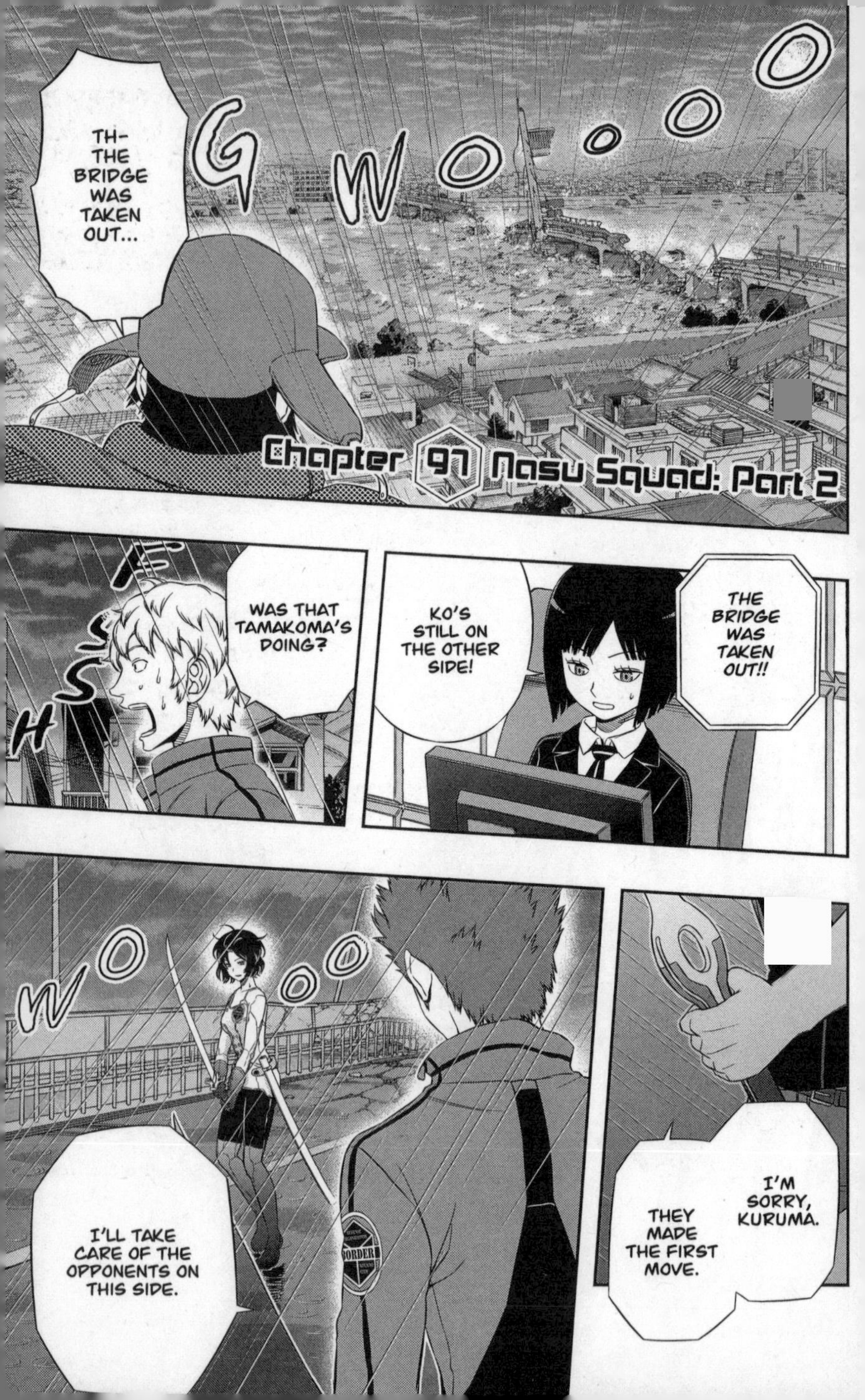
GWOOOO
TH- THE BRIDGE WAS TAKEN OUT...
Chapter 97 Nasu Squad: Part 2
THE BRIDGE WAS TAKEN OUT!!
KO'S STILL ON THE OTHER SIDE!
WAS THAT TAMAKOMA'S DOING?
HSSS
I'M SORRY, KURUMA.
THEY MADE THE FIRST MOVE.
WOOO
I'LL TAKE CARE OF THE OPPONENTS ON THIS SIDE.
BORDER

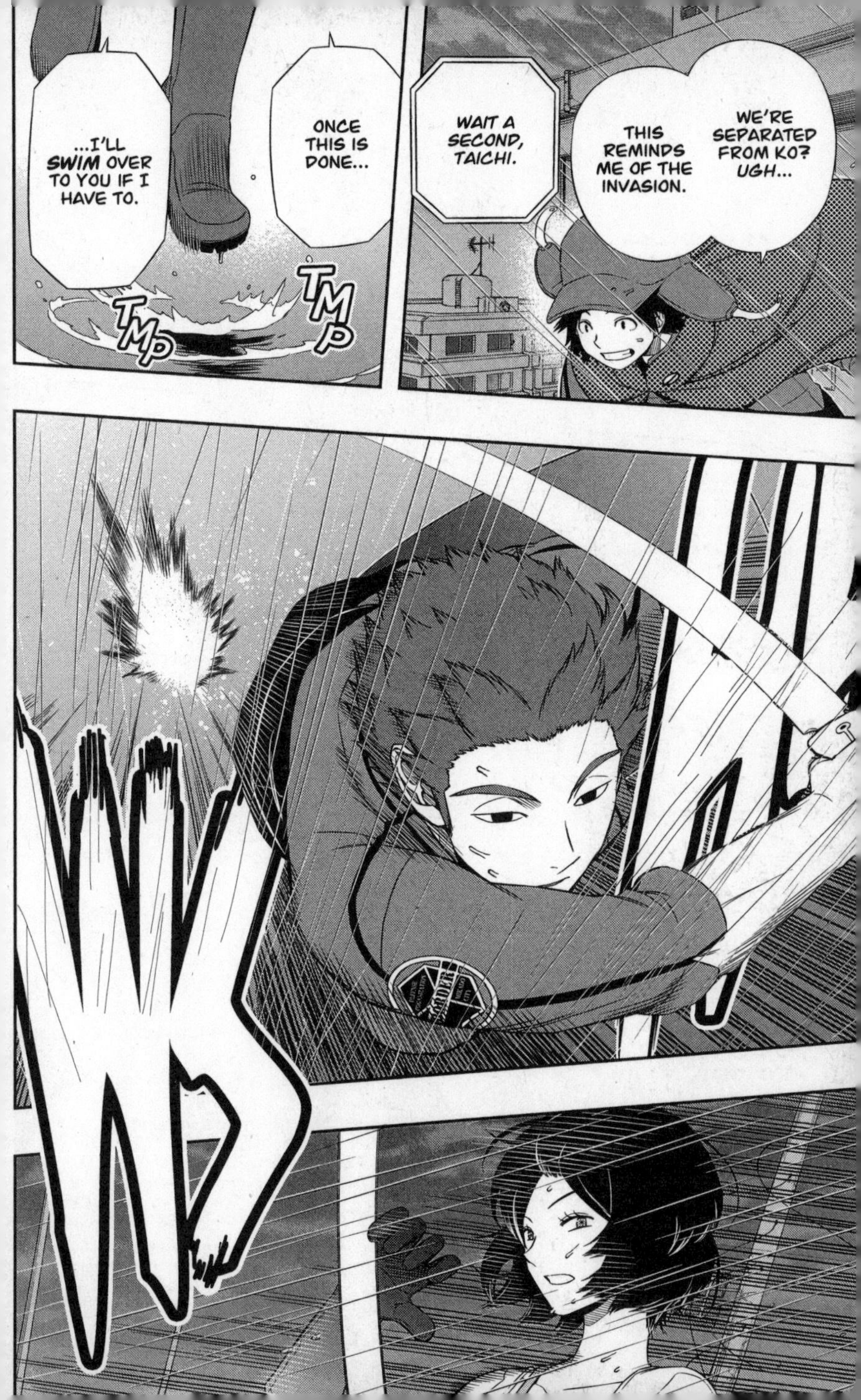
WE'RE SEPARATED FROM KO? UGH...
THIS REMINDS ME OF THE INVASION.
WAIT A SECOND, TAICHI.
ONCE THIS IS DONE...
...I'LL SWIM OVER TO YOU IF I HAVE TO.
TMP
TMP

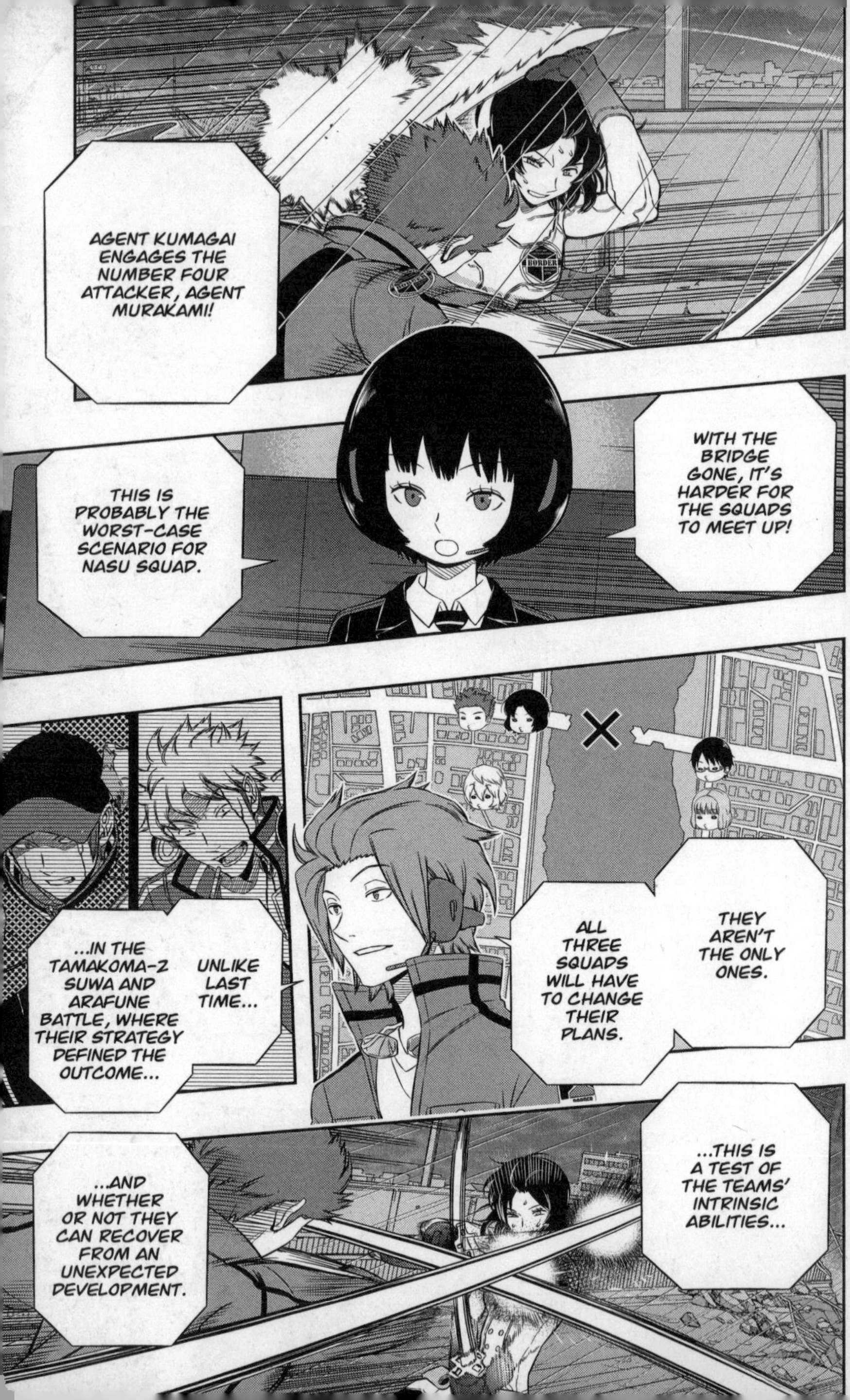
AGENT KUMAGAI ENGAGES THE NUMBER FOUR ATTACKER, AGENT MURAKAMI!
WITH THE BRIDGE GONE, IT'S HARDER FOR THE SQUADS TO MEET UP!
THIS IS PROBABLY THE WORST-CASE SCENARIO FOR NASU SQUAD.
THEY AREN'T THE ONLY ONES.
ALL THREE SQUADS WILL HAVE TO CHANGE THEIR PLANS.
UNLIKE LAST TIME...
...IN THE TAMAKOMA-2 SUWA AND ARAFUNE BATTLE, WHERE THEIR STRATEGY DEFINED THE OUTCOME...
...THIS IS A TEST OF THE TEAMS' INTRINSIC ABILITIES...
...AND WHETHER OR NOT THEY CAN RECOVER FROM AN UNEXPECTED DEVELOPMENT.

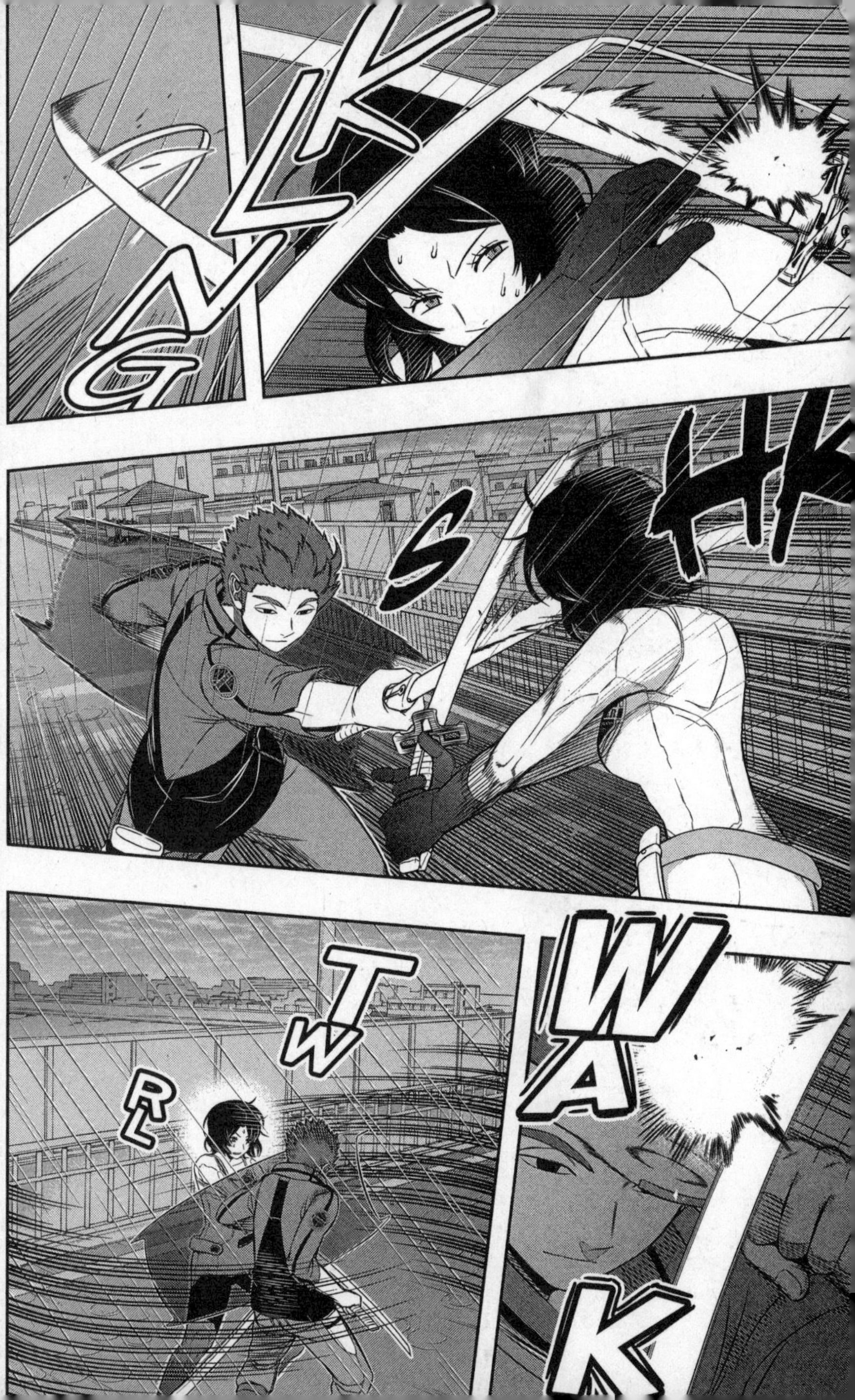
KLANG
SHK
WAK
TWRL

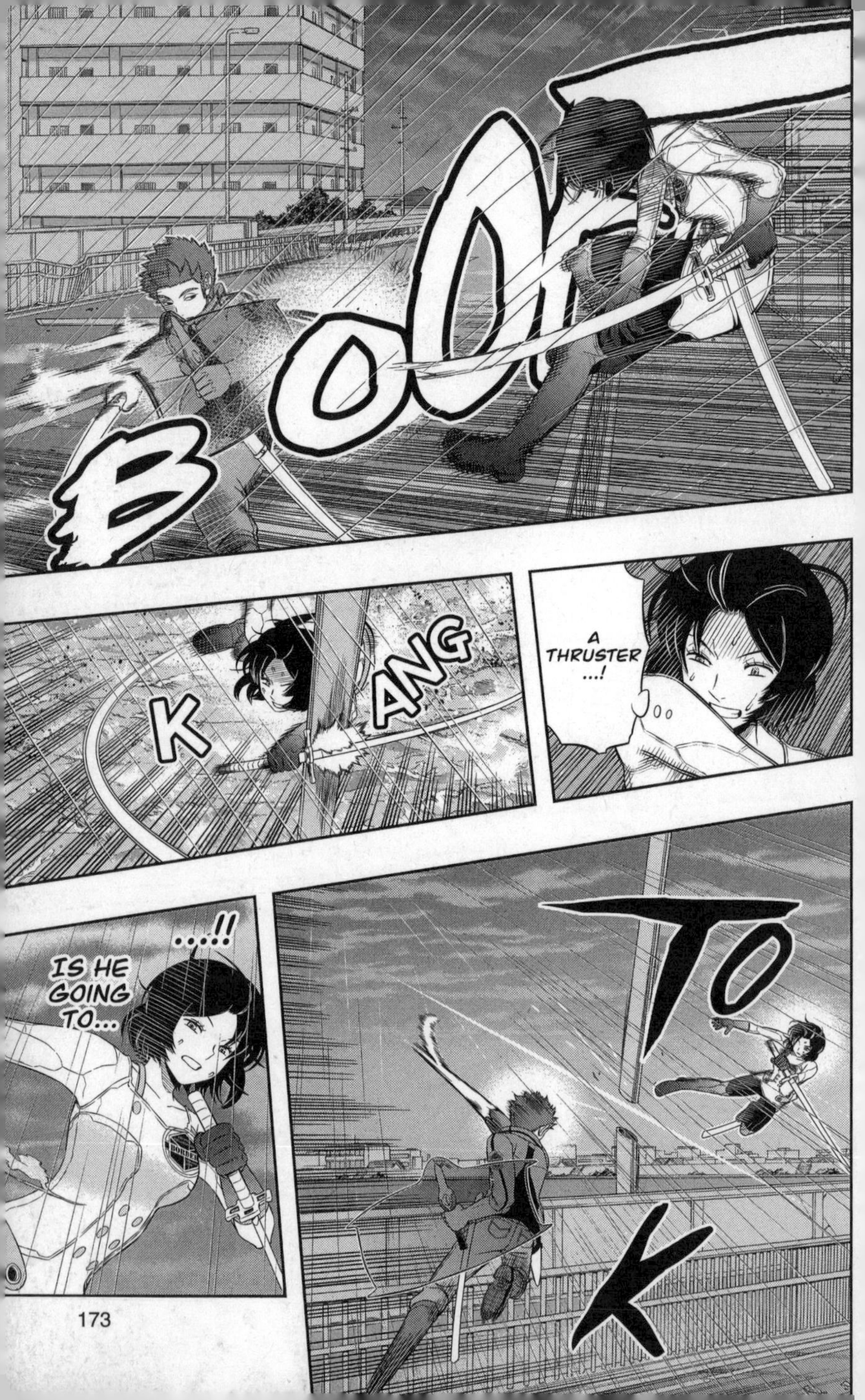
A THRUSTER ...!
KANG
TOK
...!!
IS HE GOING TO...

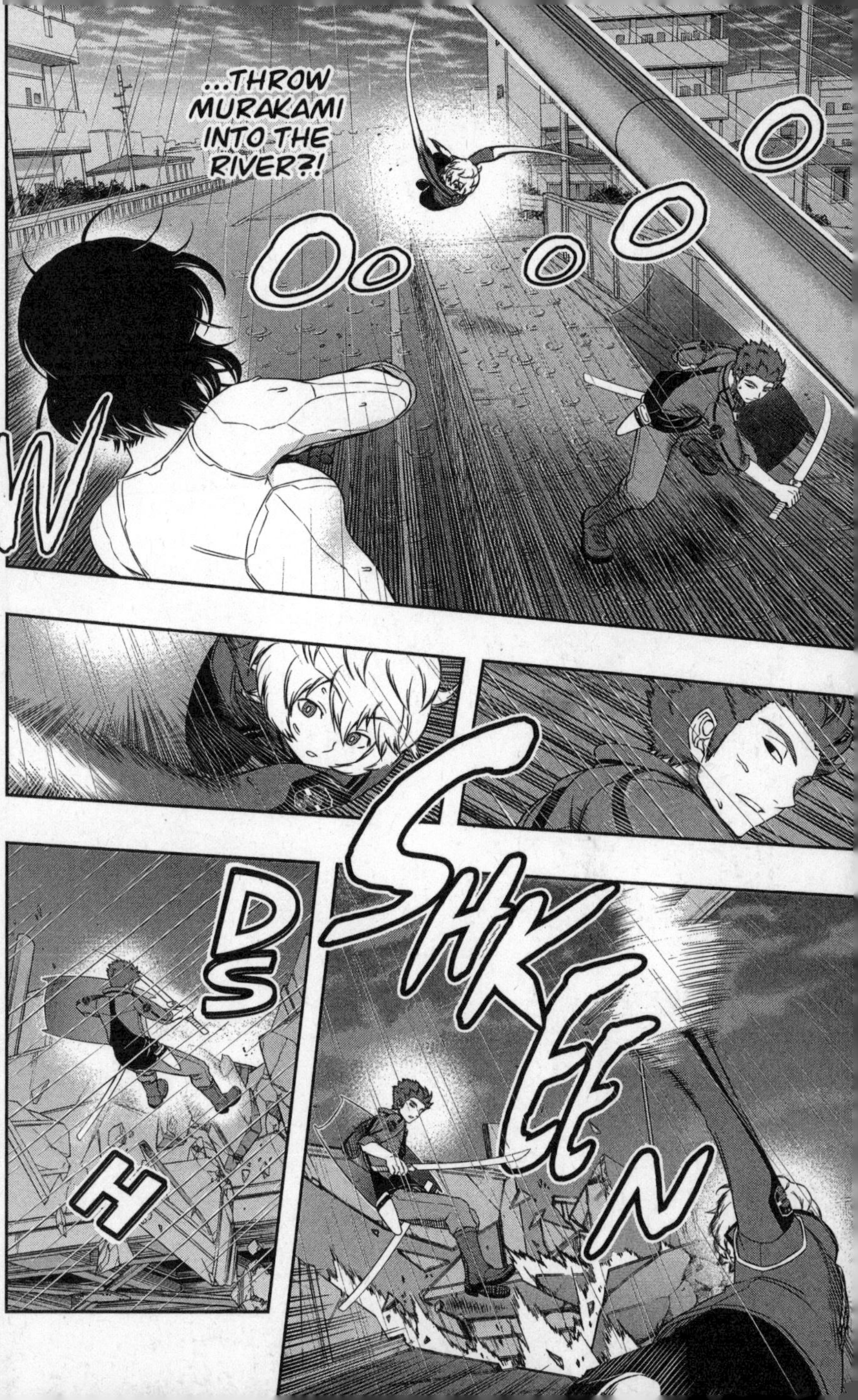
...THROW MURAKAMI INTO THE RIVER?!
WOOOOO
SHKEEN
DSH

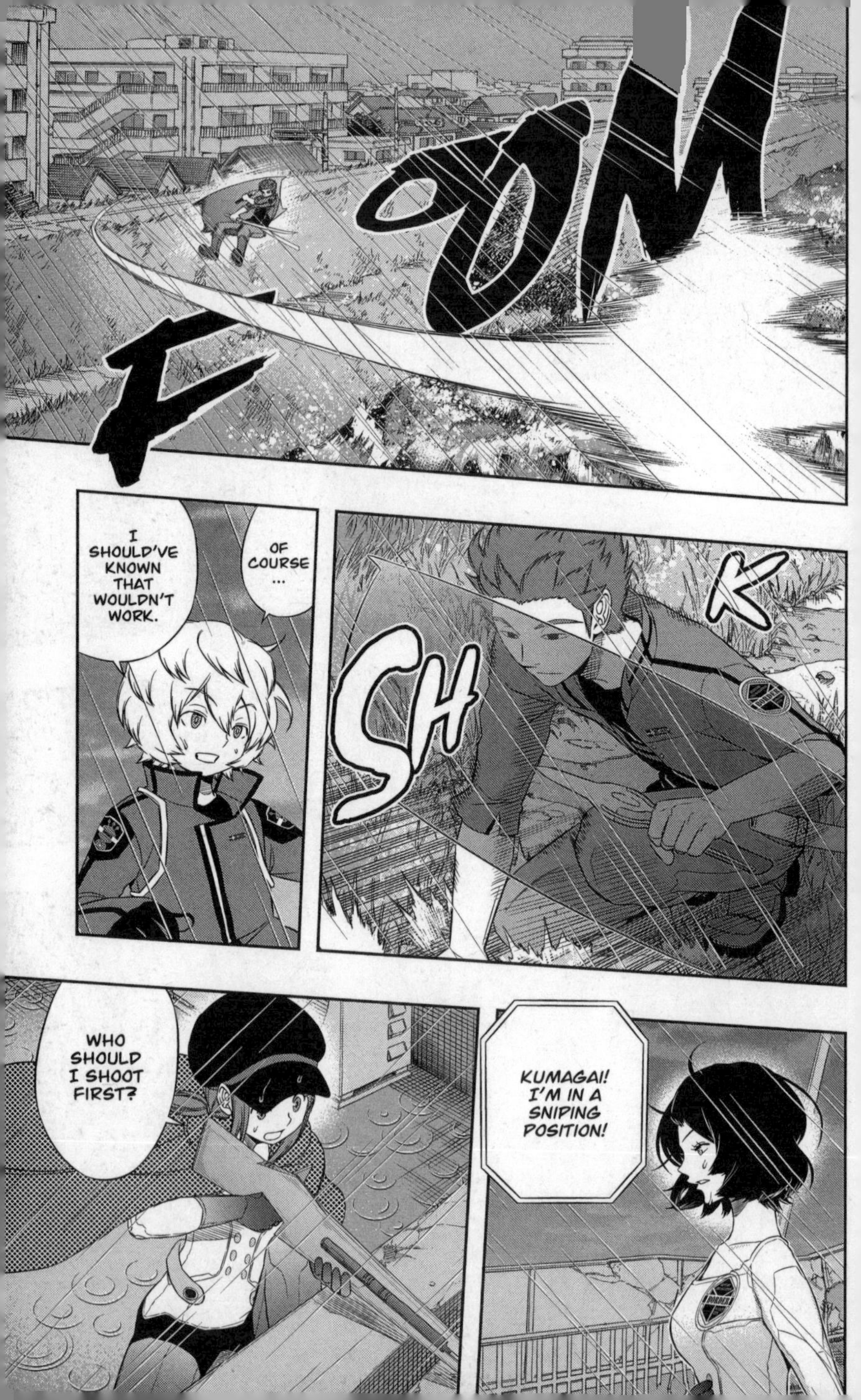
SHK
OF COURSE...
I SHOULD'VE KNOWN THAT WOULDN'T WORK.
KUMAGAI! I'M IN A SNIPING POSITION!
WHO SHOULD I SHOOT FIRST?

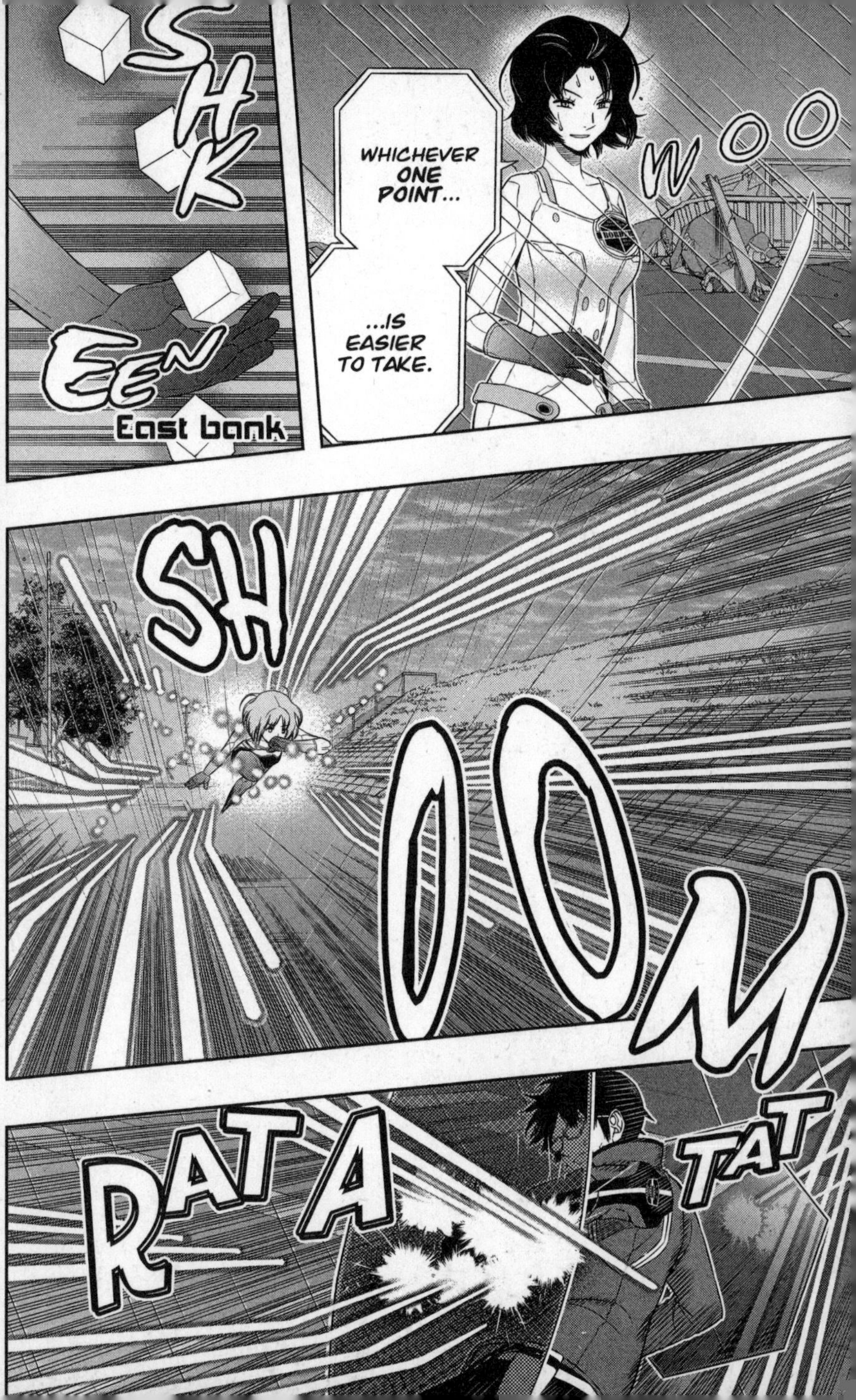
WHICHEVER ONE POINT...
...IS EASIER TO TAKE.
WOOO
SHK
EEN
East bank
SHOOM
RATATAT

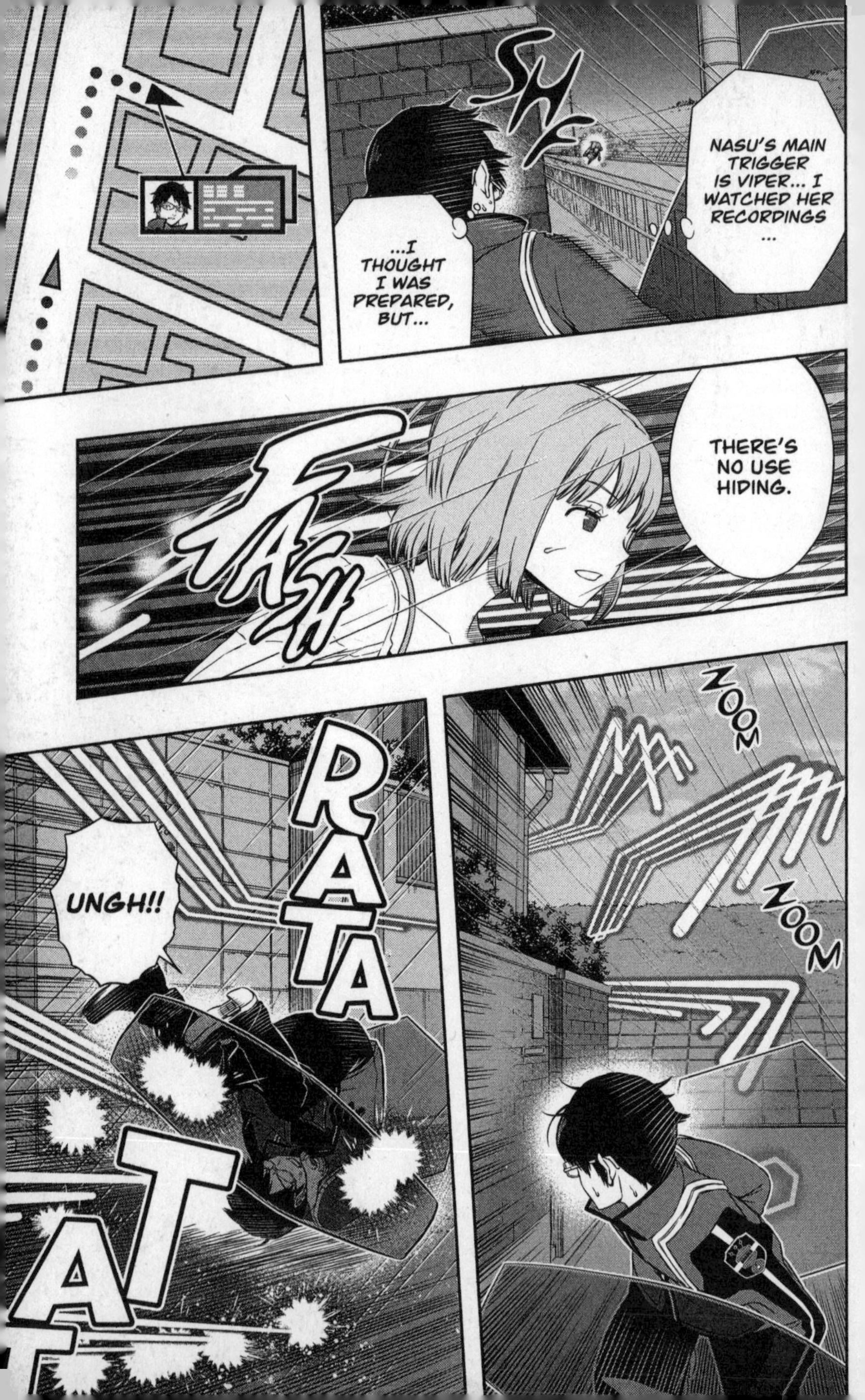

NASU'S MAIN TRIGGER IS VIPER... I WATCHED HER RECORDINGS ...
SHH
...I THOUGHT I WAS PREPARED, BUT...
THERE'S NO USE HIDING.
FASH
ZOOM
ZOOM
RATA
UNGH!!
TAT

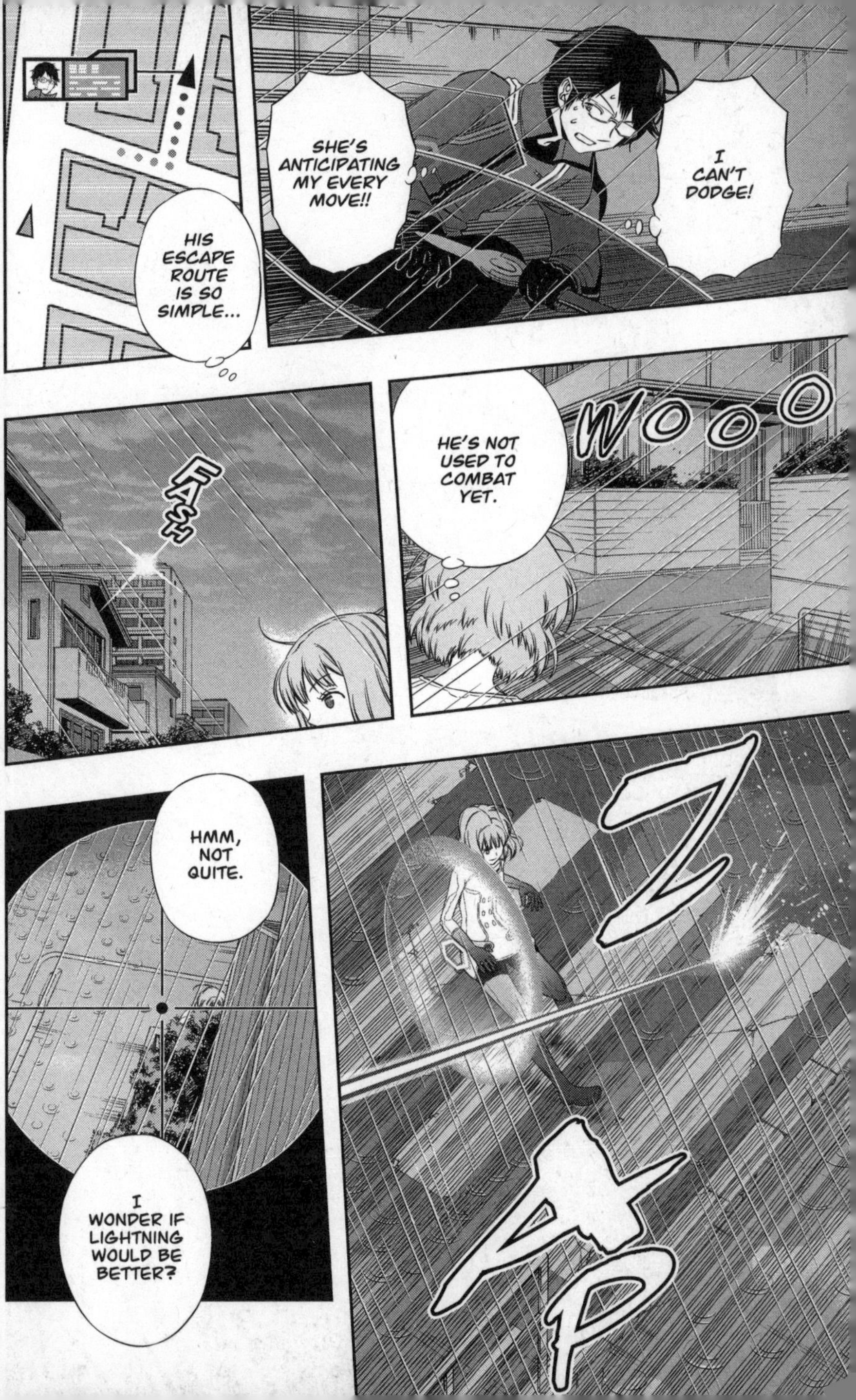
I CAN'T DODGE!
SHE'S ANTICIPATING MY EVERY MOVE!!
HIS ESCAPE ROUTE IS SO SIMPLE...
WOOO
HE'S NOT USED TO COMBAT YET.
FASH
ZZAP
HMM, NOT QUITE.
I WONDER IF LIGHTNING WOULD BE BETTER?

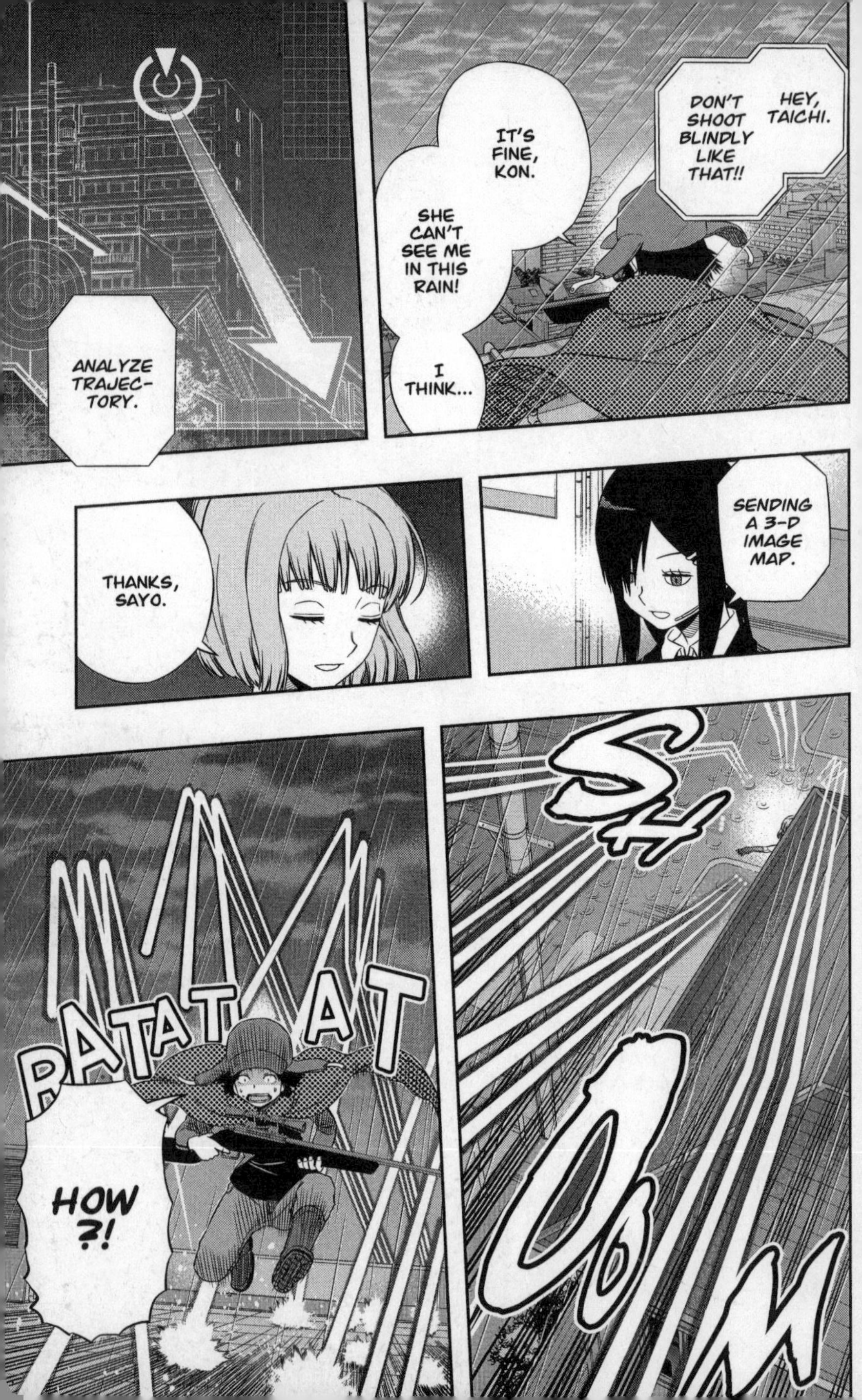
HEY, TAICHI.
DON'T SHOOT BLINDLY LIKE THAT!!
IT'S FINE, KON.
SHE CAN'T SEE ME IN THIS RAIN!
I THINK...
ANALYZE TRAJECTORY.
SENDING A 3-D IMAGE MAP.
THANKS, SAYO.
HOW?!

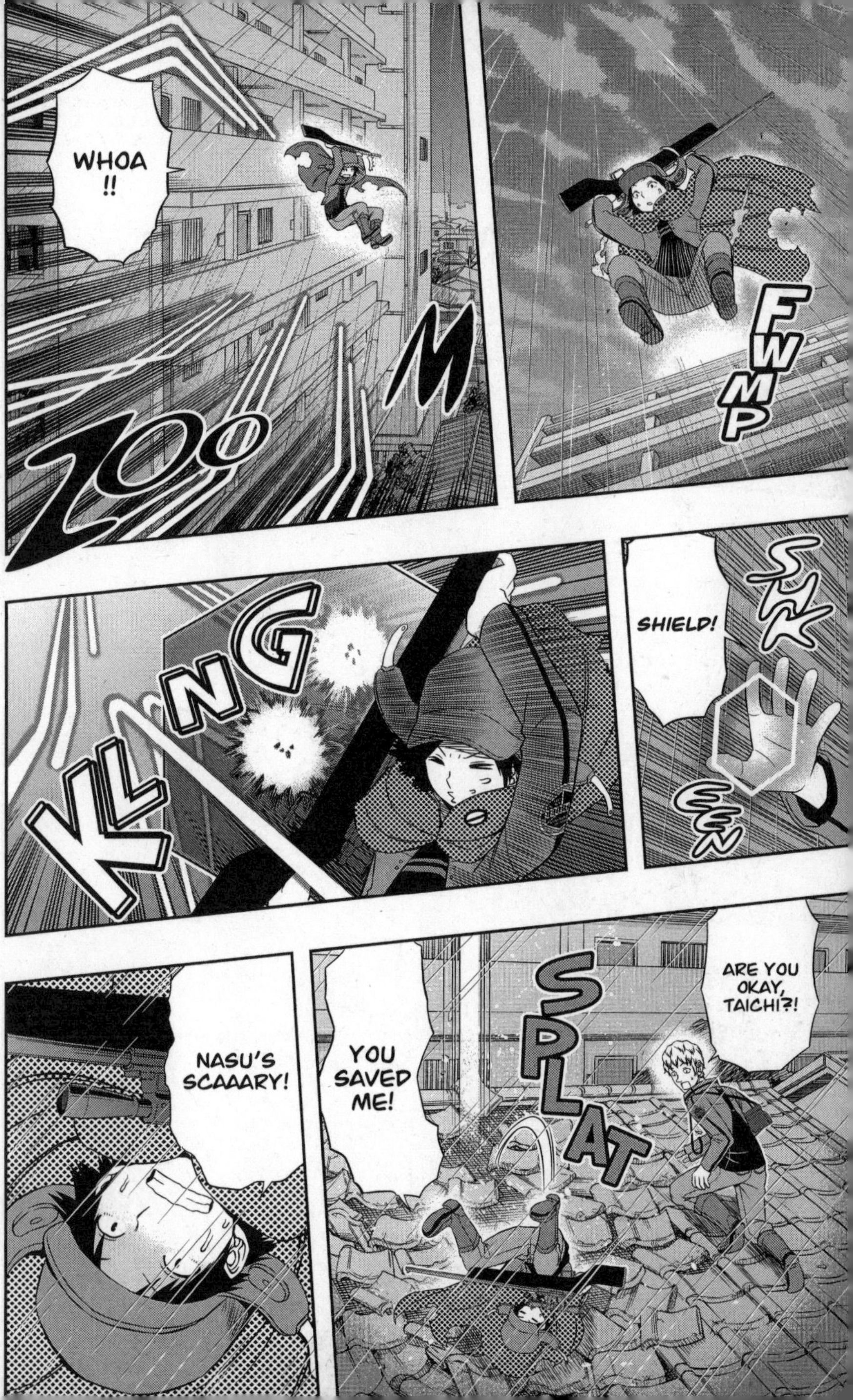
FWMP
WHOA !!
ZOOOM
SHIELD!
SHK
EEN
KLANG
ARE YOU OKAY, TAICHI?!
SPLAT
YOU SAVED ME!
NASU'S SCAAARY!

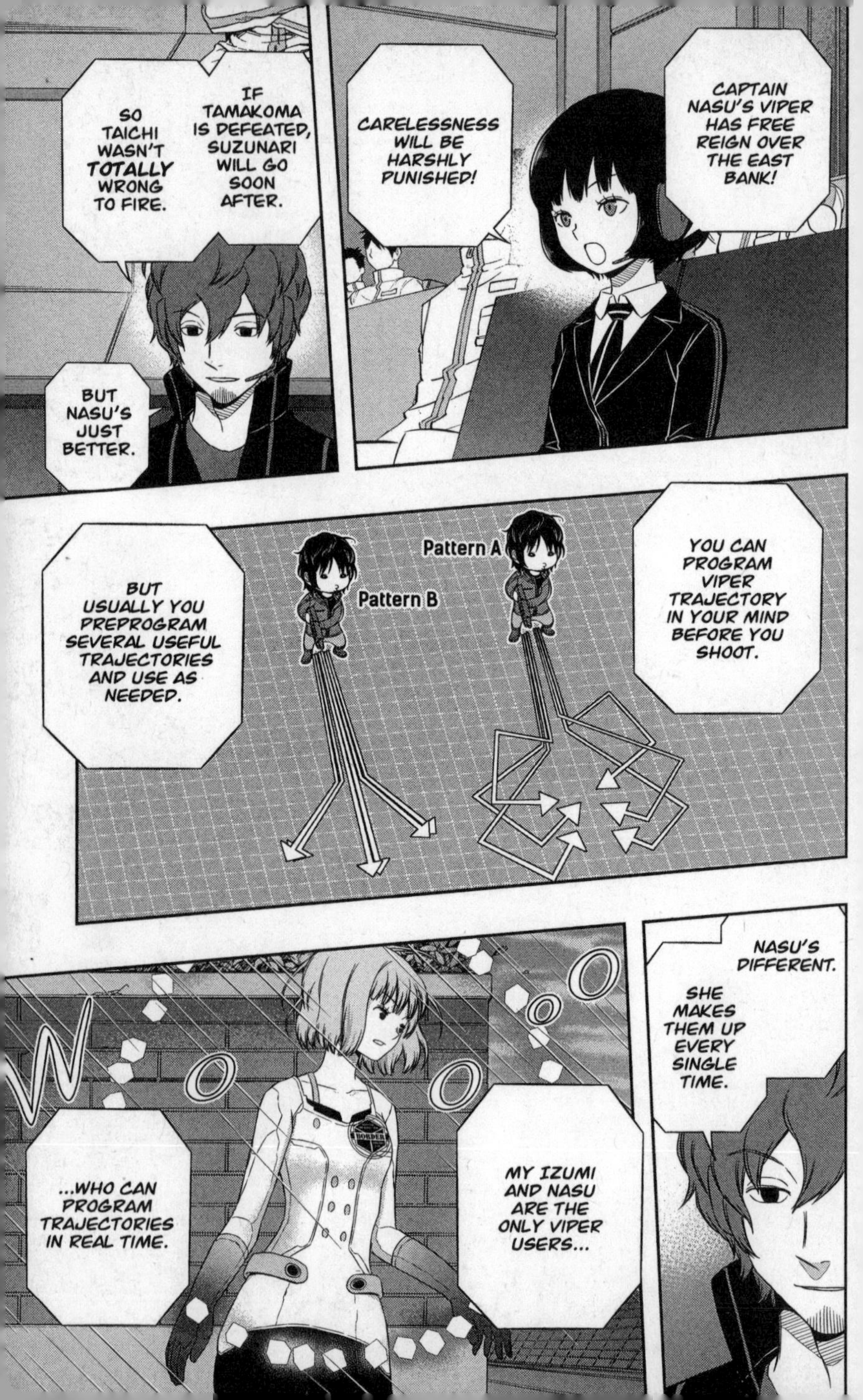
CAPTAIN NASU'S VIPER HAS FREE REIGN OVER THE EAST BANK!
CARELESSNESS WILL BE HARSHLY PUNISHED!
IF TAMAKOMA IS DEFEATED, SUZUNARI WILL GO SOON AFTER.
SO TAICHI WASN'T **TOTALLY** WRONG TO FIRE.
BUT NASU'S JUST BETTER.
YOU CAN PROGRAM VIPER TRAJECTORY IN YOUR MIND BEFORE YOU SHOOT.
Pattern A
Pattern B
BUT USUALLY YOU PREPROGRAM SEVERAL USEFUL TRAJECTORIES AND USE AS NEEDED.
NASU'S DIFFERENT.
SHE MAKES THEM UP EVERY SINGLE TIME.
MY IZUMI AND NASU ARE THE ONLY VIPER USERS...
...WHO CAN PROGRAM TRAJECTORIES IN REAL TIME.

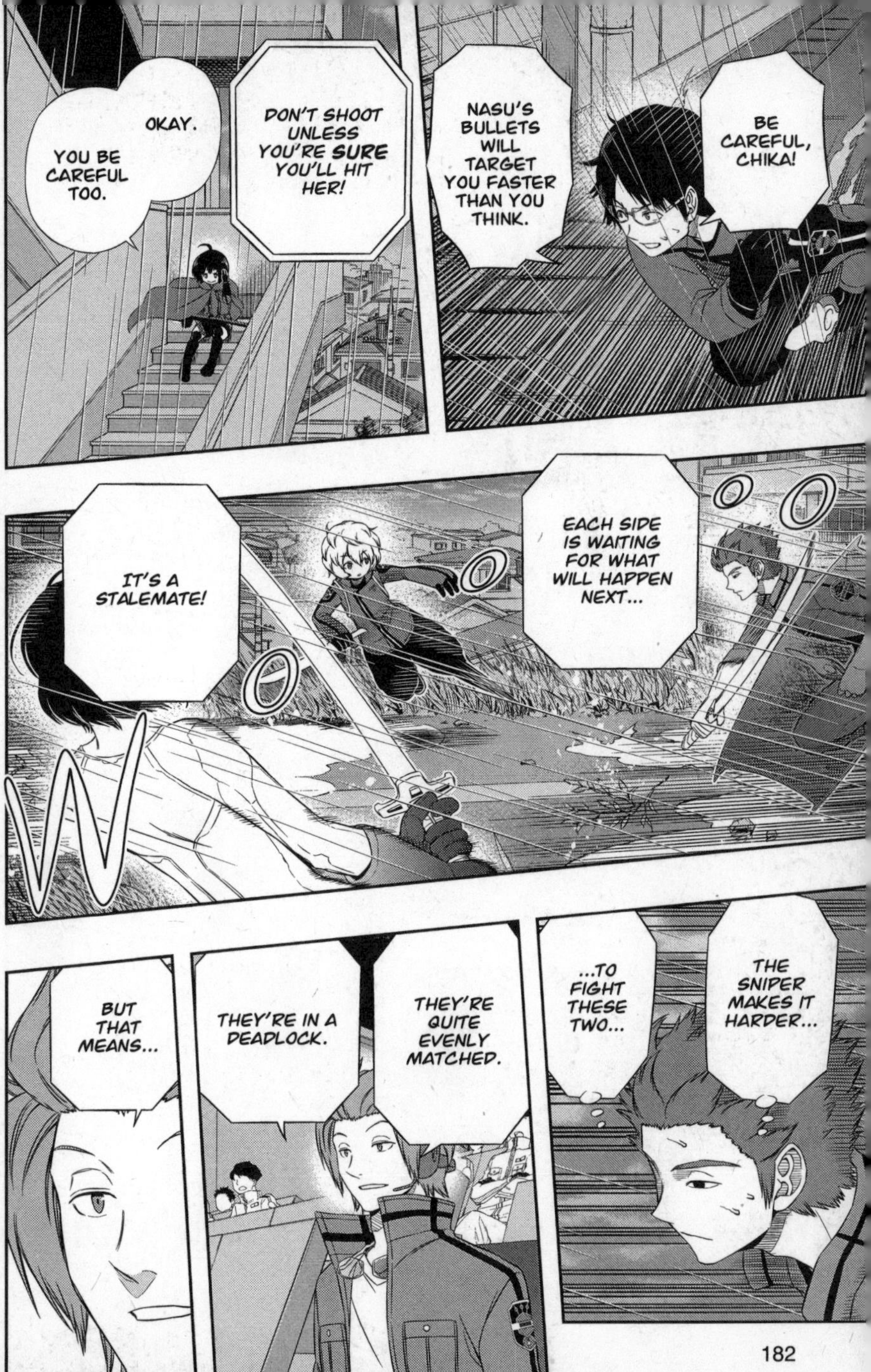
BE CAREFUL, CHIKA!
NASU'S BULLETS WILL TARGET YOU FASTER THAN YOU THINK.
DON'T SHOOT UNLESS YOU'RE SURE YOU'LL HIT HER!
OKAY.
YOU BE CAREFUL TOO.
EACH SIDE IS WAITING FOR WHAT WILL HAPPEN NEXT...
IT'S A STALEMATE!
THE SNIPER MAKES IT HARDER...
...TO FIGHT THESE TWO...
THEY'RE QUITE EVENLY MATCHED.
THEY'RE IN A DEADLOCK.
BUT THAT MEANS...

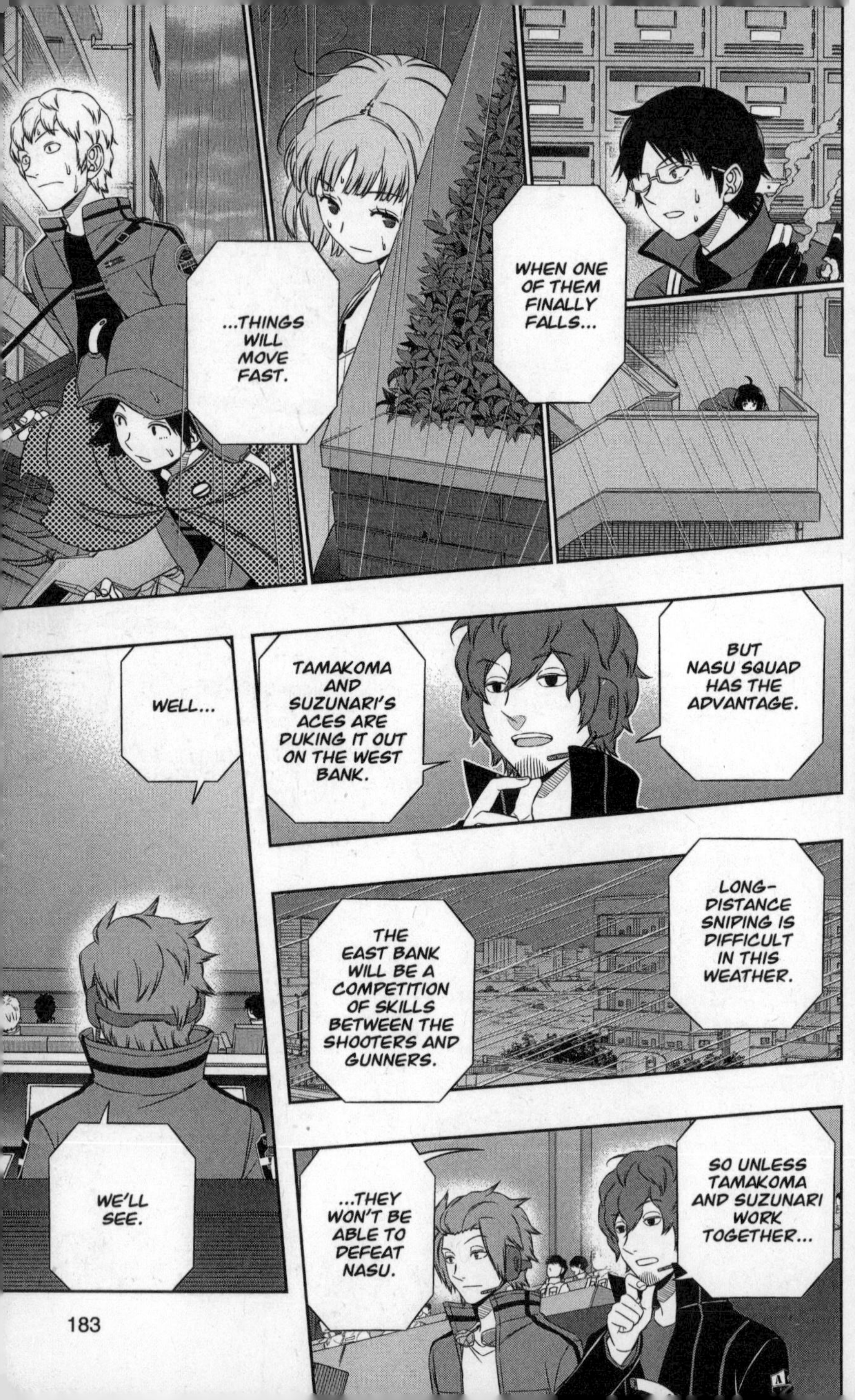
WHEN ONE OF THEM FINALLY FALLS...
...THINGS WILL MOVE FAST.
BUT NASU SQUAD HAS THE ADVANTAGE.
TAMAKOMA AND SUZUNARI'S ACES ARE DUKING IT OUT ON THE WEST BANK.
LONG-DISTANCE SNIPING IS DIFFICULT IN THIS WEATHER.
THE EAST BANK WILL BE A COMPETITION OF SKILLS BETWEEN THE SHOOTERS AND GUNNERS.
SO UNLESS TAMAKOMA AND SUZUNARI WORK TOGETHER...
...THEY WON'T BE ABLE TO DEFEAT NASU.
WELL...
WE'LL SEE.

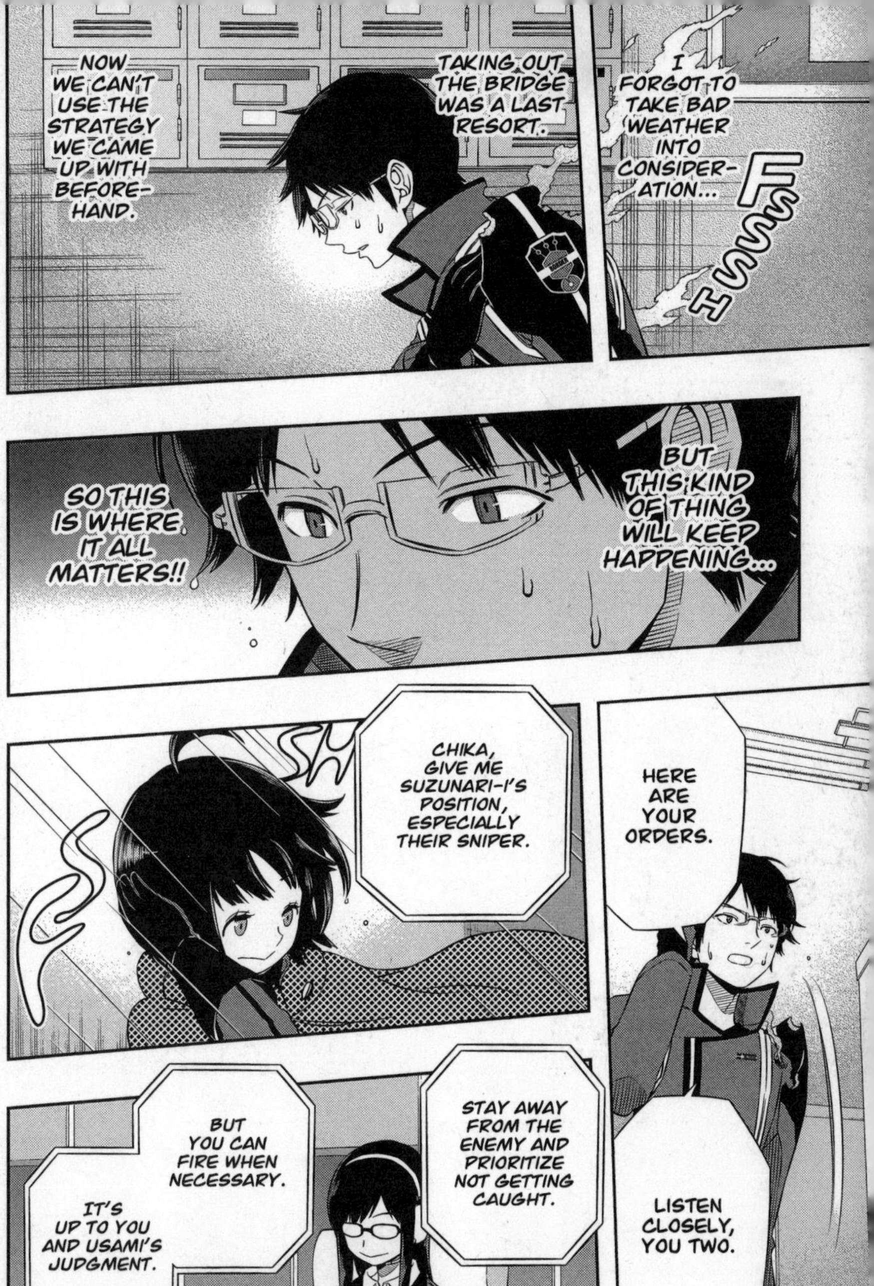
I FORGOT TO TAKE BAD WEATHER INTO CONSIDER-ATION...
FSSSH
TAKING OUT THE BRIDGE WAS A LAST RESORT.
NOW WE CAN'T USE THE STRATEGY WE CAME UP WITH BEFORE-HAND.
BUT THIS KIND OF THING WILL KEEP HAPPENING...
SO THIS IS WHERE IT ALL MATTERS!!
HERE ARE YOUR ORDERS.
LISTEN CLOSELY, YOU TWO.
CHIKA, GIVE ME SUZUNARI-I'S POSITION, ESPECIALLY THEIR SNIPER.
SH
STAY AWAY FROM THE ENEMY AND PRIORITIZE NOT GETTING CAUGHT.
BUT YOU CAN FIRE WHEN NECESSARY.
IT'S UP TO YOU AND USAMI'S JUDGMENT.

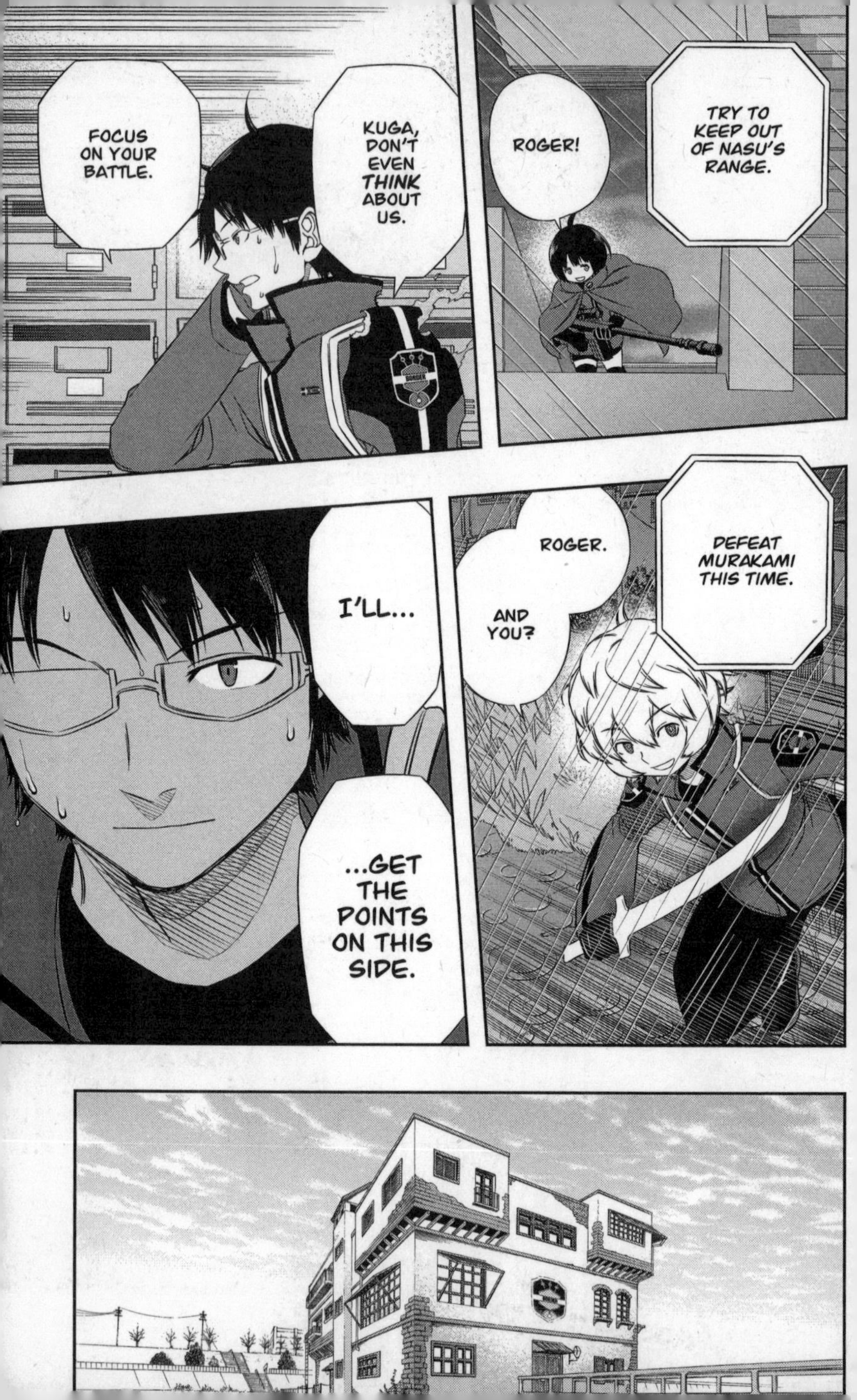
TRY TO KEEP OUT OF NASU'S RANGE.
ROGER!
KUGA, DON'T EVEN THINK ABOUT US.
FOCUS ON YOUR BATTLE.
DEFEAT MURAKAMI THIS TIME.
ROGER.
AND YOU?
I'LL...
...GET THE POINTS ON THIS SIDE.

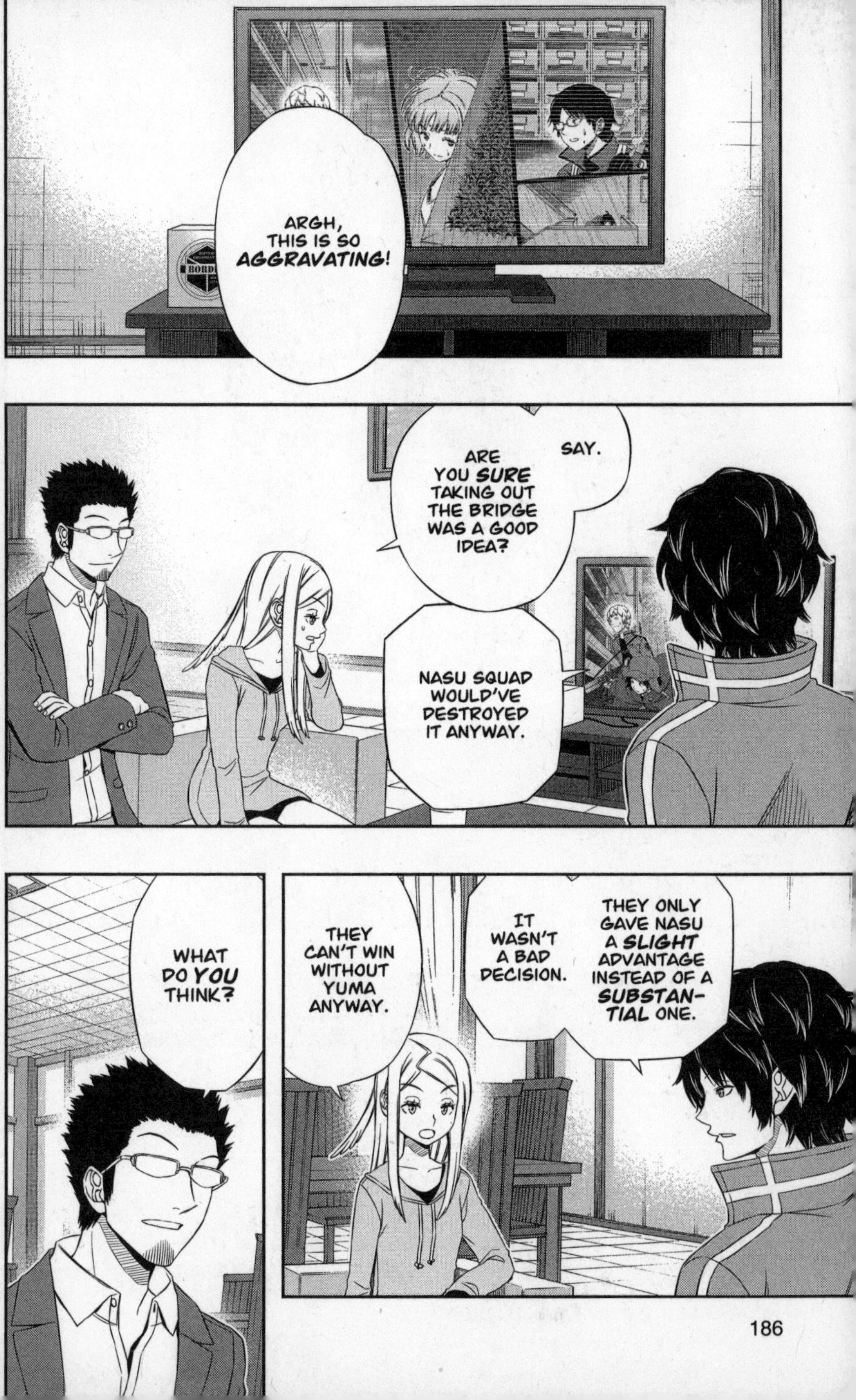

ARGH, THIS IS SO AGGRAVATING!
SAY.
ARE YOU SURE TAKING OUT THE BRIDGE WAS A GOOD IDEA?
NASU SQUAD WOULD'VE DESTROYED IT ANYWAY.
THEY ONLY GAVE NASU A SLIGHT ADVANTAGE INSTEAD OF A SUBSTAN-TIAL ONE.
IT WASN'T A BAD DECISION.
THEY CAN'T WIN WITHOUT YUMA ANYWAY.
WHAT DO YOU THINK?

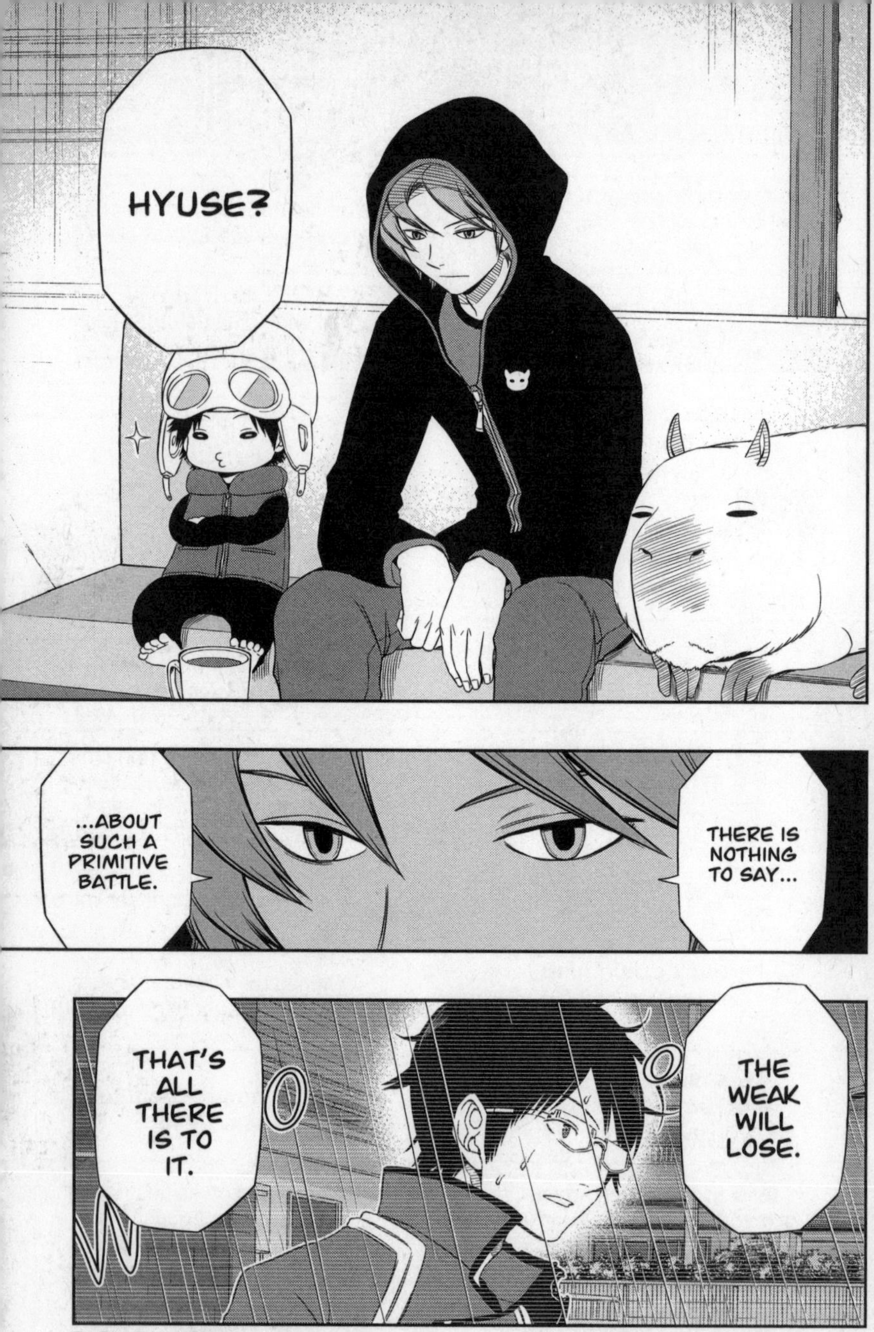
HYUSE?
THERE IS NOTHING TO SAY...
...ABOUT SUCH A PRIMITIVE BATTLE.
THE WEAK WILL LOSE.
THAT'S ALL THERE IS TO IT.

To Be Continued In ***World Trigger*** 12!

World Trigger Tagline Awards

Honorable Mentions

Tagline	Comment
The machine prayed for this boy to have the will to live. (by Coda)	The notion of a machine praying is very Replica. I got choked up.
Weakness and helplessness aren't the same thing. (by Servo)	This should be Osamu's motto. Poster for vol. 2.
Run through the battlefield! (by Asagi)	Spot-on for the developments in vol. 8. Poster for vol. 8.
Daily life turns into a battlefield. (by Waka)	It's cool how it doesn't lay it on too thick. Poster for vol. 6.
The other side of the story. (by Hikari)	Objectifying the reader's point of view. Poster and paper band for vol. 4.
These glasses aren't for show. (by cube)	The most stylish among the glasses submissions. Jean-Baptiste also put in a vote.
Show me your strength. (by GZGZ)	It reflects Kazama's character. Poster and paper band for vol. 5.
Throw it down with all you've got. (by Hyoya)	Slogan for all Border agents. Poster and paper band for vol. 8.
This is the fun part of team combat!! (by Yokayo)	I also recommend team combat. Poster for vol. 7.
One fought. Two met. Three began their journey. (by Pagupani)	A beautiful expression brimming with love. My manager put in a vote for this one. Poster for vol. 3.
Pride is a catalyst for character development. (by B*S)	Perfect for Kitora. Poster for vol. 6.

Those tears will one day become a blade. (by SCRTS)	This is for vol. 9, but it could be used for various characters and not just Miwa.
Power of the individual vs. the power of numbers. (by Bail-outer)	The theme of the battle against Aftokrator. Poster and paper band for vol. 7.
There are as many reasons to fight as there are people. (by Miyabi)	One of the themes throughout the manga from now into the future.
A world you can see from a position of weakness. (by Rin)	This is the reason I tell the story from Osamu's point of view. Poster for vol. 5.
Four-Eyes fights gallantly. (by Silver Osamu)	Sounds very Osamu. Poster for vol. 2.
Toward a future to protect. (by Taka'aki Uemura)	It shows more resolve than "want to protect." Poster for vol. 8.
953 seconds of turmoil. (by Jen)	I like this. It's cool and interesting. Poster for vol. 9.
Across the Border. (by Cobalt)	Multiple meanings. Poster for vol. 1.
All battles converge here. (by Niru)	It makes me want to reread the arc. Poster for vol. 9.
This encounter was a crossroads for the future. (by Bamsuke)	I wish I could've used this for chapter 1. Poster for vol. 1.

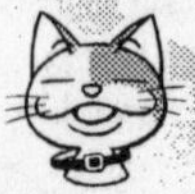

We used the honorable mentions on posters in train stations. There were entries we couldn't use because of certain combinations of phrases, but I would've used them all if I could. I think about this a lot, but *World Trigger* is blessed with the best reader participation projects. Thank you to everyone who entered!

WORLD TRIGGER

Bonus Character Pages

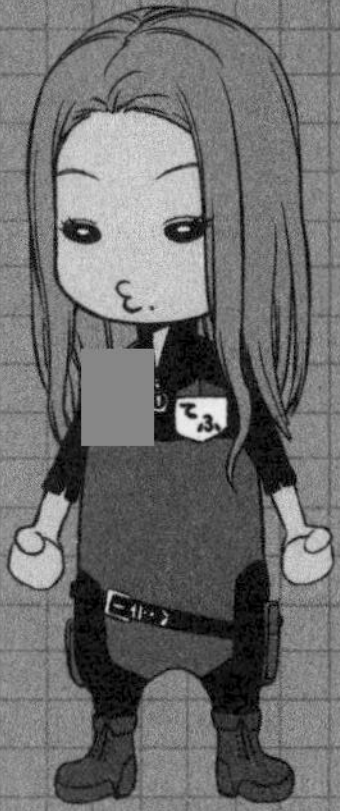

KAKO

Flying Diva Lady

She's got the runway walk and is a my-way-or-the-highway kind of gal. Shooter with a beauty mark. A free spirit with a celebrity aura even though her family is normal, so she must be a mutant. Her hobby has been cooking weird fried rice since she was six, leaving a ton of victims in her wake. Mint chocolate fried rice killed Tsutsumi. Salmon roe custard fried rice killed Tachikawa. Tsutsumi fell victim to honey-smelt fried rice. Daichi Tsutsumi died twice!

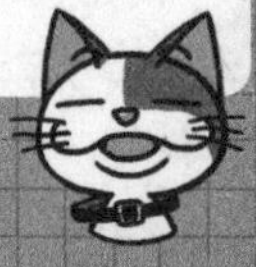

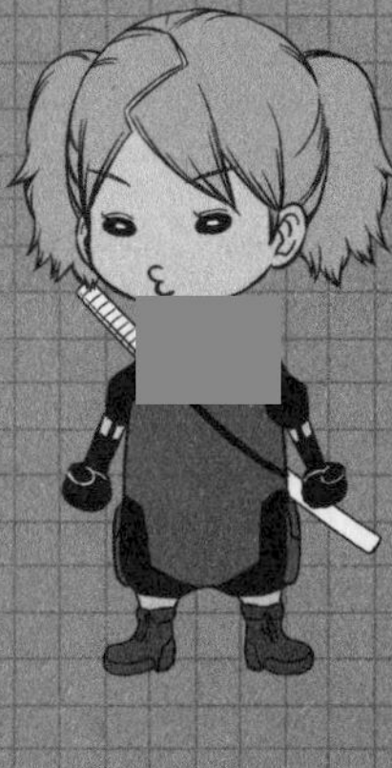

KUROE

Blossoming Ninja Girl

She looks like she's the same age as Chika, but she is one year younger, making her the youngest A-Rank agent. She went to elementary school in the mountains with Midorikawa and used to fish and forage for mushrooms. It only took her a few months to evolve into a city girl after attending middle school there. Since she was trained in the mountains, she can't die eating Kako's horrible fried rice. Daichi Tsutsumi dies a lot though.

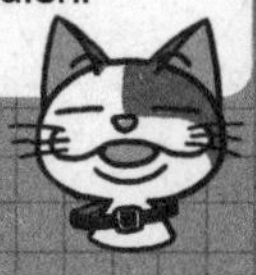

*Badge: Butterfly

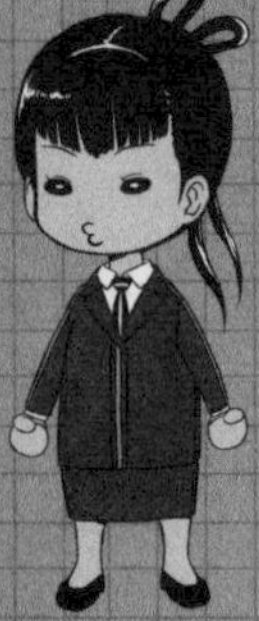

KAGAMI

One-hour Train Commute to College

Creative Operator who is slated to go to a fine arts university. She always keeps colored clay in her desk drawers, and creates weird little dolls to express her joy when her Squad wins, or regret when they lose. I thought of having Arafune send one of those dolls to Osamu after their battle and leaving him speechless, but with regret, it was omitted. An A-cup with unlimited creativity.

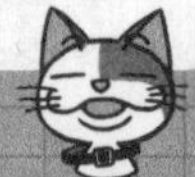

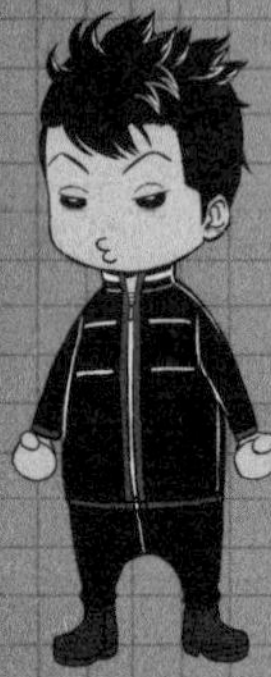

POCARI

Even the Voice in His Head Is Quiet

Keeps up with the happenings in tthe world of Snipers, something most people are unfamiliar with. He's chattier and more normal via text. I had an idea to have him send a text to Hisato, "Sorry I egged you on☆ I feel like you're growing to where you don't need me anymore (T∀T)" but there weren't enough pages. Hisato would've replied, "Thanks for the point (^-^)"

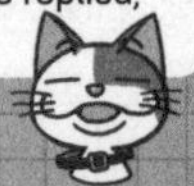

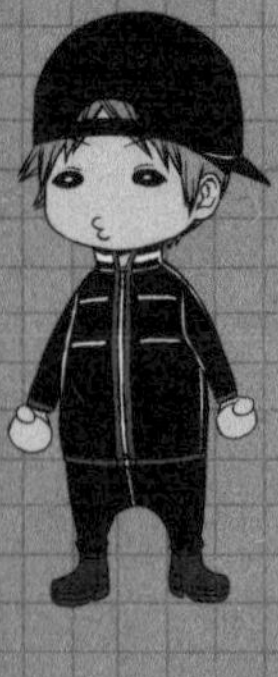

YOSHITO

Explosive Bedhead

The author is always getting this lackadaisical Sniper's age wrong. He was among the 17-year-olds for a while, but he de-aged to 16 years old. Like Pocari above, I had an idea for him to send a text, "Don't be mean to the Snipers (ΦдΦ)," but that was cut for no reason. I feel sorry for him, so even though he whines and complains, I'll say that he's a precise Sniper who practices diligently.

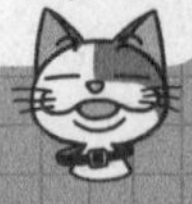

YOU'RE READING THE WRONG WAY!

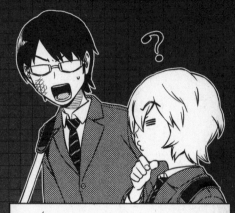

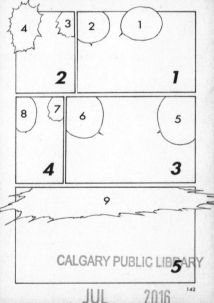

World Trigger reads from right to left, starting in the upper-right corner. Japanese is read from right to left, meaning that action, sound effects, and word-balloon order are completely reversed from the English order.

142